Columbia College

Columbia College

150 Years of Courage, Commitment, and Change

Paulina A. Batterson

UNIVERSITY OF MISSOURI PRESS
COLUMBIA AND LONDON

University of Missouri Press, Columbia, Missouri 65201
Printed and bound in the United States of America

5 4 3 2 1   05 04 03 02 01

Library of Congress Cataloging-in-Publication Data

Batterson, Paulina A. (Paulina Ann), 1930–
  Columbia College : 150 years of courage, commitment, and change / Paulina A. Batterson.
    p. cm.
  Includes bibliographical references and index.
  ISBN 0-8262-1324-3 (alk. paper)
  1. Columbia College (Mo.)—History. I. Title.

LD3489.5.C65 B38 2001
378.778'29—dc21   00-067670

∞ This paper meets the requirements of the
American National Standard for Permanence of Paper
for Printed Library Materials, Z39.48, 1984.

Designer: Stephanie Foley
Typesetter: BOOKCOMP
Printer and Binder: Thomson-Shore, Inc.
Typeface: Galliard

To the Guardian Angels

Contents

Acknowledgments

THE COMPLETION OF THIS STUDY owes much to the whole "Columbia College family." First, Gerald Brouder had the confidence in me to request that I undertake the project. Then Bonnie Brouder provided invaluable assistance in gathering materials and photographs, and Lori Ewing, the president's executive assistant, saw me through many needs, large and small. The genuine enthusiasm of all who eased my task reminded me regularly of why the college should be remembered in a history. These individuals include the information systems staff, who tended my computer needs; maintenance personnel, who shouldered the burden of moving seemingly countless very heavy boxes of materials; the cheerful and cooperative mail room and duplication staff; and the always helpful Stafford Library staff. The highly professional services of the Western Historical Manuscripts staff at Ellis Library eased the rather daunting prospect of researching 1,352 folders of materials relating to the college.

No words of gratitude could be sufficient to thank adequately Allean Lemmon Hale, whose generosity in sharing materials merely added to my indebtedness to her for her role as the author of the college's first history, *Petticoat Pioneer.*

The need to present accurate and objective depictions led me to prevail upon the services of some individuals whose wisdom and memory of recent administrations would keep me on target. Those who gave their time to read and react to some portions of the first draft and who encouraged me greatly with their support include trustees Tom Atkins, Don Landers, Marvin Owens, Don Schubert, Dan Scotten, B. D. Simon, and Marty Toler; Academic Dean Terry Smith; President Gerald Brouder; and faculty members Dennis Grev and Sidney Larson. A very special thank-you goes to Christine Cotton for her editorial expertise applied to all chapters of the first draft. I also appreciate the thoughtful and insightful guidance of Mel George, former president of the University of Missouri Systems, who served as a reader for the University of Missouri Press. I owe a deep debt of gratitude to my copyeditor, Annette Wenda, for her patience and skill. My thanks to those, nearly fifty in all, whom I interviewed, especially former academic dean Mary Miller, former presidents Merle Hill and Donald Ruthenberg, and Desmond Lee, son of former president Edgar Lee. Above all, my son, Jack, and his wife, Mary, have given me the kind of moral support any author would appreciate in addition to technical help.

Writing a college history may seem a simple enough undertaking compared with weightier subjects, but Columbia College was and is no simple little college, nor is its history. Its pioneering role has received scant notice beyond the Midwest, in eastern educational circles. The quality of its teaching, strong throughout its history, has perhaps been lost in the glare of its university friend and neighbor. The college's history has much to teach, and I have learned much from its many examples of loyalty and dedication.

Columbia College

1

Where Others Fear to Tread

As for training young ladies through a long intellectual course, as we do young men, it can never be done. They will die in the process.

—the Reverend John Todd, quoted in
In the Company of Educated Women, by Barbara Solomon

FEW IN THE NINETEENTH CENTURY doubted that grave dangers lurked behind the foolish hopes of some that young women could achieve success in higher education. As late as 1873, Edward Clarke, writing in *Sex in Education*, stated that higher education would destroy the ability of women to bear children by overtaxing the female body at a critical stage of its development. Clarke, a retired Harvard Medical School professor, studied the cases of seven Vassar students and concluded that if they used up their "limited energy" on studying, they would surely endanger their "female apparatus." The female student could not "do all this, and retain unimpaired health and a future secure from neuralgia, uterine disease, hysteria, and other derangements of the nervous system."[1]

Sex in Education was merely one of many expressions of opposition to higher education for women, opposition originating largely in the well-established eastern men's colleges. The Reverend John Todd saw danger in "forcing the intellect of women beyond what her physical organism will possibly bear" as it would cause them to be "puny, nervous, and their whole earthly existence a struggle between life and death." The presidents of Amherst, Harvard, Williams, and Yale managed to dissuade Sophia Smith from founding Smith College for fourteen years before she finally prevailed in opening the women's college in 1875. President Charles W. Eliot of Harvard remained a particularly ardent foe of admitting women to his institution more than two hundred years after Harvard had opened its doors to men in 1636. The popular magazine *Littell's Living Age* quoted an 1860 article from the *Saturday Review,* magnanimously granting that "any plausible view on the subject is worth examining," but concluding that "[t]he greatest argument against the existence of this equality of intellect in women is, that it does not exist." Particularly revealing testimony to the public attitude came from Martha Carey, president of Bryn Mawr: "Before I myself went to college I had never seen but one college woman. I had heard that such a woman was staying at the house of an acquaintance. I went to see her with fear." President Carey further recalled that when she went to Germany for a doctorate in 1879, her family and friends politely refrained from reference to her, as she had disgraced her parents.[2]

In view of such negative attitudes toward women's ability to survive, much less benefit from, higher education, the founding of Christian Female College, now Columbia College, clearly defied contemporary mores. Founded in Columbia, Missouri, in 1851 to supplement the male-only University of Missouri, it became the first college for women west of the Mississippi River.

Christian College, as it was generally called, had the audacity to open almost a generation before the obstructionism in the East gave way and decades before the founding of such prestigious eastern women's colleges as Vassar (1865), Wellesley (1875), Smith (1875), Bryn Mawr (1884), Barnard (1889), and Radcliffe (1894). Just as incredible for the time, Christian College opened not as a finishing school but at a truly collegiate level, sharing some texts, faculty, and board members with the University of Missouri, with which some of its founders were associated. The fledgling college survived, grew, and eventually flourished against all odds to become the present Columbia College.

Not just any pioneer community would support such a bold and improbable undertaking, but Columbia's distinguishing characteristics provided an unusually supportive environment for education. Its population, predominantly Kentuckian and Virginian in origin, proved progressive in economic policy, forward looking in educational matters, conservative in politics, and largely Southern in leanings. Its prosperity resulted partly from its advantageous location near Boon's Lick Trail's crossing of the Missouri River as well as from the large number of professional people among its settlers. The flourishing commerce included slave trade. On the eve of the Civil War, there were 5,034 slaves in Boone County and 14,399 whites. Slave sales were common, and as late as 1864 twenty-two slaves belonging to John W. Rollins sold for prices of $25 to $208. Politically, Boone County was the banner Whig county of the state. Major James S. Rollins, a founder of the University of Missouri in 1839, was the Whig candidate for governor in 1848 and again in 1857, losing the second time by a mere 329 votes in an election still clouded by the possibility of collusion. Rollins and local newspaper editor

William F. Switzler together made Columbia a Whig stronghold right up to the collapse of the Whig state organization in the mid-1850s.

A description of Columbia showed a well-established community:

> On the eve of the Civil War, Columbia was a bustling town with seven general stores, a tobacco shop, five clothing stores, two hotels, a bank, a jeweler, four shoe stores, two furniture makers, two saddlers, two hardware stores, three drug stores, a book store, six wagon and carriage makers, five blacksmiths, seven doctors, six lawyers, three colleges, five churches, and a newspaper. From a population of 130 in 1823, Columbia had grown to 1,541 in 1860 and enjoyed a political and cultural influence far in excess of its numbers.[3]

From its very origin, Columbia displayed extraordinary educational foresight. Even before the county was fully organized in 1820, the Smithton Associates, a land company, gave the Boone County commissioners ten acres of land at the southwest edge of town on the condition that the state university be placed there. After the Columbia Company replaced the Smithton group on December 24, 1824, the county court and the Columbia Company instead transferred twenty-four lots on the southeastern corner of town to the newly organized Columbia College for men as a possible seat for a university.[4]

Other educational ventures prior to the 1850s featured early academies. Baptists had founded the Bonne Femme Academy for boys in 1829 at a location six miles south of Columbia. By 1833, primary schools included one for girls and two for boys. Although the earliest schools were private or "subscription" schools, "district" or "common" schools existed as early as 1834 as forerunners to the public school system, but even they required fees of $2.50 to $5.00 per term based on the number of courses taken.[5]

Of more direct interest to the present Columbia College, the opening in 1833 of the Columbia Female Academy expanded immediate opportunities for women's education and proved of lasting importance. Before its closure in 1855, the academy offered primary and high school levels of study. Opening in the fall of 1833 in the Presbyterian church, the academy purchased a lot on the southwest corner of Tenth and Cherry Streets and occupied its new building on that site in 1837. That same year, the state legislature incorporated the academy, giving trustees the power "to purchase or receive by donation" and to "grant, bargain, sell or convey, or otherwise dispose of" property.[6]

The academy, frequently referred to as the "Lucy Wales Academy" after its best-known teacher and principal, never offered any college-level courses. However, it did create an environment favorable to women's education. By preparing high school students for college, it may well have been a factor in encouraging the incorporation of the two women's colleges in Columbia:

Christian Female College in 1851, which would become Columbia College, and Baptist Female College in 1857, which would become Stephens College.

The 1830s also saw the first steps leading to the establishment of the University of Missouri in Columbia in 1839, thus encouraging the founding in 1851 of Christian Female College as a female counterpart. The legislature expressed its intent to found a state university in a centrally located town that had demonstrated its seriousness by establishing its own local men's college. Therefore, a Boone County committee, activated in 1831, created a seminary to be offered to the state legislature as a site for the state university. The committee succeeded in the chartering on February 11, 1833, of Columbia College, and this men's college, located on south Sixth Street in Columbia, became the immediate predecessor of the University of Missouri. Although the first academic session opened on November 3, 1834, supporters failed to move a university bill through the state legislature in the 1834, 1836, and 1838 sessions. When a "memorial" was finally introduced on December 7, 1838, it proposed the establishment of a university in Fayette in Howard County, just to the west of Boone County. The memorial, referred to the committee of the whole, failed by only one vote, thirty-six to thirty-seven, nearly depriving Boone County of its goal. Four days later, James S. Rollins of Columbia introduced a bill to offer the Columbia College property as a university site. Both propositions then went before the education committee, which deadlocked in its debate between the Fayette and Columbia sites.[7]

Benjamin Emmons, who chaired the education committee, managed to break the deadlock by reporting out a bill that would remove the choice of a university site from the legislature. This bill, actually drafted by James Rollins, "Father of the University," authorized six central Missouri counties to bid for the university site, but the real contest eventually narrowed to Howard, Boone, and Callaway Counties. Each contending county held mass meetings, choosing a central committee responsible for soliciting funds, and enthusiasm sometimes overcame ethics in the race to put in the highest bid. The Howard County committee bought 200 acres near Fayette for $30 per acre, entering the bid at $80 per acre. When the Boone County committee heard of this tactic, Columbia bought 220 acres of the James S. Rollins farm for $25 per acre, reporting the price as $75. Once the bids were opened in Jefferson City, Boone County prevailed with $82,300 in cash and land supposedly valued at $36,000. The land later sold for only $5,965.75, providing the university with a total of roughly $88,000. Columbia College for men finally became the site for the beginning of university classes on April 14, 1841, and was used until the new academic hall was first occupied in the spring of 1843. Because legislation to organize the university was still incomplete, university faculty technically acted as faculty of Columbia College.[8]

Politics, which would later also complicate the founding of a women's college, influenced university affairs almost from the start. When the first president, John Hiram Lathrop of New York, became the subject of attack for his antislavery views, he was pressured into leaving the university in 1849, going on to become chancellor of the University of Wisconsin. The incoming president, James Shannon of Bacon College in Kentucky, proved a staunch supporter of higher education for women. He had reportedly stated that he "would not consent to locate anywhere without having a female school of the highest grade."[9]

A major leader in the founding of Christian Female College, Shannon became one of Columbia's most controversial figures, winning both enemies and worshipers. An elder in the Christian Church (the Disciples of Christ), he accepted the presidency of the university with the understanding that he would continue preaching, and his personal evolution from Presbyterian to Baptist to Christian Church reflected the movement of the Christian Church itself in seeking a more flexible, democratic form of religion better suited to the frontier environment. Shannon took office at commencement exercises on July 4, 1850, and remained as president until his resignation in 1856 when the Missouri legislature prohibited the practice of any profession, which would include preaching, by any professor or president of the university.[10]

Shannon, at the age of fifty, had already become a power in education and in the church by the time he came to Columbia in 1848. A professor of ancient languages at the University of Georgia, he had helped found the Baptist coeducational Mercer College nearby, and he then served as president of the State College in Jackson, Louisiana, in 1836. He left that more lucrative role in 1840 to take up the presidency of Bacon College in Harrodsburg, Kentucky, a training school for Christian Church ministers. By the time Shannon became president of the University of Missouri, the founding of a college for women had been a subject of correspondence among Christian Church leaders in Missouri and Kentucky. Shannon himself, with thirteen children, six of whom were daughters, had a distinct interest in such a school.[11]

Thomas M. Allen, a Christian Church leader and another major figure in the founding of both the university and Christian College, had been on the committee to select a site for the University of Missouri and had personally contributed six hundred dollars to the subscription fund. As early as 1844, he wrote John Gano in Kentucky, "Do you know of any good Brother well qualified to take charge of a female school . . . ? if so, I wish he would come to Columbia. . . . A competent person of the right *grit* would soon overcome all opposition."[12]

A prominent advocate of education, Allen proved the most active of the three founders in his determination to establish a college for women. He had been a trustee of the Columbia College for men in 1833 and of the Columbia Female Academy that same year. He acted as trustee for a total of six schools and as a member of the Board of Visitors of West Point. The first president of the University of Missouri Board of Curators, he became in 1851 the first president of the Board of Trustees of Christian Female College. Called by his contemporaries "an ornament to the community," he was also a member of the county fair board, a founder of Columbia's first fire insurance company, and a member of the state railroad commission. He socialized with the Whig-Presbyterian faction and was a close friend of Maj. James Rollins and of Col. William Switzler, despite their political differences and denominational disputes. Politically, he called himself a "union Democrat" during the Civil War and a "liberal Republican" during Reconstruction.[13]

Allen's greatest achievements, however, may have come in his role as a religious reformer. The early 1800s experienced a rash of church quarrels in the United States, and Allen fit into the role of those who chose the name "Christian" or "Disciples of Christ," wanting to return to the simple Christianity of Jesus. Allen had attempted to reform the Presbyterian rigidity in Kentucky and Virginia and later moved to Missouri on a personal crusade, giving up his law practice to preach. His reform church stressed the need for all denominations of Christians to unite, relying on the use of the New Testament to replace separate creeds. He had come under the influence of Christian Church reformers Barton W. Stone and Alexander Campbell and chose to dedicate his life to their causes in what he called a "race for men's souls." When Allen came to Boone County in 1836, there were three Christian churches, each with a dozen or so members. Fourteen years later, in 1850, there were thirty thousand members in Missouri, owing largely to Allen's zeal. When he died in October 1871, his obituary described his role in religion:

> He went everywhere—by steamboat, by stagecoach, on horseback. He preached tirelessly—in schoolhouses, in log cabins, in town halls. He baptized in cold pasture streams. Once he hit quicksand but pronounced the benediction before climbing out. He took no money. He used no notes. A backwoods audience did not 'hold' with a preacher who read sermons. He had as large an acquaintance as any man in Missouri and a half-a-dozen towns named a street for him.[14]

The third founder of Christian College, also a church leader, David Patterson Henderson visited Columbia in the summer of 1848. He had recently helped establish a female school in Eureka, Illinois, and shared Allen's vision. When Henderson's success in speaking before a meeting in Columbia led to an offer that he stay as minister, he accepted on the condition that local Christian Church leaders help him establish a "collegiate institution for women."[15]

Henderson, who had joined the Disciples of Christ in Columbia in 1848, had toured Missouri with Allen, entertaining visions of "raising thousands of dollars" and "swaying multitudes." Henderson, like Allen, had been a protégé of Barton Stone and had turned to preaching after practicing law. Both were aggressive crusaders, with Henderson the more magnetic speaker, dabbling in both journalism and evangelism. Henderson had served as the associate editor of Stone's *Christian Messenger* at the age of thirty-one. His powers of persuasion had led a New Orleans editor to help him raise money and a Louisville matron to lend him her thirty-room mansion. He returned to Columbia in February 1849, just a few months before Shannon became president of the University of Missouri.[16] These three—Allen, Shannon, and Henderson—became the founders of Christian Female College.

Events leading to the establishment of a women's college in Columbia accelerated with Shannon's arrival and his involvement in university and church politics. Although his support on the university Board of Curators came partially from Baptist members, indicating that his election as university president was not strictly denominational, some curators had clearly been looking for a Christian Church leader as president. Thomas Allen had written his friend John Gano, "Who will make a good President . . . ? Any of our Brethren . . . ?" With Shannon, the future of both the university and a prospective women's college seemed to lie in the same hands. He may have been responsible for the arrival in Columbia of Samuel Hatch, an elder of the Christian Church and a professor at Bacon College, along with a colleague, H. H. White. Financial troubles at Bacon could also have enticed Hatch and White to look for other opportunities. Henderson stimulated public interest in Hatch's visit, while Henderson and Allen together arranged a meeting of a small group in the sheriff's office on November 16, 1849. After an exchange of views with Hatch, the group proceeded to plan a citizen mass meeting. With Shannon's Baptist support on the university board and his record of helping to found a Baptist college in Georgia, his leadership had the potential for bringing unity between the Baptist and Christian Church forces.[17]

With this auspicious beginning, advocates of a female college held a public meeting at the Boone County Courthouse on November 21, 1849. Columbia's *Missouri Statesman* of November 23, 1849, reported the desire for a women's college to be a community effort, reflecting remarkable interest and unanimity of feeling of "our citizens of all parties and denominations." Names of attendees included many who had previously been involved in all manner of progressive projects in Columbia.[18]

Hatch's earlier meeting with selected town leaders had produced a plan for consideration at the mass meeting on November 21. That plan assigned Hatch and White the leadership role in establishing the college but denied them any denominational controls. According to the plan, at least thirty acres of land would be purchased through subscriptions. Hatch and White would each receive ten acres in return for committing eight to ten thousand dollars and providing scientific equipment and a residence hall. The remaining ten acres would go to William Jewell, Warren Woodson, and Moss Prewitt as trustees representing the subscribers. Hatch and White would have rent-free control of an academic building provided by the trustees and would have the option to buy the college buildings during the first ten years. To discourage rival denominational suspicions that the Disciples intended to impose church control on the college, the plan provided that under no circumstances could the school become, either by "its course of instruction or rules of government, sectarian."[19]

Opposition to the proposed plan grew in the days following the November 21 meeting. The opposing denominations (Baptist, Presbyterian, and Methodist) activated their members, dominating a second meeting at the courthouse on November 24. Still suspicious of the Christian Church leaders' motivations, they put forth their own plan aimed at placing control of the school with the subscribers and trustees rather than with Hatch and White. In this second plan, the two promoters would be under the supervision of the trustees and of a seven-member board of visitors appointed annually by the trustees. It would be the duty of the board to "inquire into the course of instruction pursued by the pupils and their progress—the general order enjoined and observed—the degree of attention paid to moral character, and especially whether any of the fundamental provisions of this article . . . have been either evaded or disregarded."[20]

The alternate plan expanded the Board of Trustees to include James S. Rollins, T. M. Allen, William F. Switzler, and James R. Boyce, in addition to the original group of Jewell, Woodson, and Prewitt. It also demanded more of Hatch and White. Under its terms, they were to spend eight thousand dollars toward construction of a residence hall and purchase two thousand dollars' worth of scientific equipment before receiving the ten acres of land. The trustees were not to begin construction of the academic hall until six thousand dollars in subscriptions had been raised. Only the ban on sectarianism carried over from the first plan. As final protection against Christian Church influence, board members would be selected from the leading religious denominations and would be equally divided, "as near as may be, between the different denominations of Boone County." Of the trustees specified in the second plan, Jewell, Woodson, Prewitt, and Boyce were Baptists, whereas Rollins and Switzler were Presbyterians. This left the Christian Church faction (dominant in the first plan) with only the better-liked Allen as a trustee in the second plan.

The original intent that citizens join to found a women's college in Columbia had floundered upon denominational and political differences so pronounced that on December 1 a third meeting was held in an attempt to repair the split. The issues were clearly drawn between the two opposing plans. The willingness in the first plan to give unfettered freedom to Hatch and White, and thus to Christian Church influence, was blocked in the second plan by placing stringent limits on Hatch and White and increasing the role of the trustees. The second plan also overwhelmed Disciples' influence on the board of trustees by adding a strong Presbyterian contingent to the Baptist members already present. Switzler and Rollins, Presbyterian lawyers, led the debate in the December 1 meeting, while Allen, Henderson, and Christian Church layman Samuel A. Young argued for the original plan. Sectarian sides had already been chosen, and personal and political differences hardened the lines of denominational factionalism. Switzler and Rollins, longtime personal friends, already distrusted Shannon's leadership of the University of Missouri as well as his opposition to the Whig faction that they represented. With neither group inclined to compromise, the December 1 meeting failed to reconcile the differences. A motion to refer the two plans to a joint committee of "five ladies and five gentlemen" passed, and yet another meeting was set for December 6. When a compromise proposed by the committee at that meeting failed, the Christian Church faction, whose supporters dominated the meeting, carried the day with a motion to approve the first plan. Opposition forces withdrew to emerge another day.[21]

Difficulties surrounding the creation of Christian College reflected strains already present in the nation as a whole. Tensions born of the fundamentalist movement, the Great Awakening, led to the creation of splinter groups that formed their own churches and struggled to build new congregations. Meanwhile, the reliance on Bible reading gave rise to increased emphasis on education, and included in new schools at all levels were more denominational colleges. In Missouri, they included Central College (Methodist), William Jewell (Baptist), Culver-Stockton (Disciples), and Westminster (Presbyterian). Disciples reflected this trend but refrained from exercising direct control over Christian College. Nevertheless, opposition forces, which later organized the Baptist Female College (the future Stephens College), remained apprehensive. Their worst fear was that Shannon might attempt to inject religious influence into the University of Missouri. Alexander Campbell's regret at the "lack of religious zeal" at the university, expressed during his 1845 visit to Columbia, and his definition of education as "handmaiden to religion and morality" had been widely reported.[22]

The founding of Christian College was, indeed, affected by Shannon's double role as the president of the University of Missouri and a founder and trustee of the women's college. Other denominations heartily disliked the role of the Christian Church in luring converts away from the older congregations. This dislike was exacerbated by the personal feud between Shannon, who had replaced Lathrop as president, and Switzler, a personal friend of Lathrop. Also, factionalism among the university curators tended to be both political and sectarian. Christian Church curators Caleb Stone and Turner R. Haden Smith, Democrats, led the opposition to Whig influence on the board and had fought to remove Lathrop, a Whig, in 1849.

Stone then became president of the Board of Curators and helped proslave Democrats obtain Shannon's election as president of the university. The Whig faction, led by Switzler and Rollins, tended to be Presbyterians, whereas the Democrats tended to be Baptists, Methodists, or Disciples. Thus, the first plan for the college left out the Presbyterians but showed a willingness to compromise with the Baptists, whereas the alternate plan by Switzler and Rollins added three Presbyterians and created a majority of Whigs in what came to be called the Whig-Presbyterian faction. Switzler had already become suspicious that Shannon was injecting too much Bacon College influence into the University of Missouri and moved in his alternate plan to check Christian Church influence in the proposed college by placing restraints on the role of Hatch and White. Consistent with this split, Allen, a champion of the Christian Church group, successfully moved rejection of the plan created by Switzler and Rollins.[23]

Switzler proved a formidable adversary. He had close ties to Rollins and to Thomas Miller, who edited the openly Whig *Columbia Patriot* until 1841. Switzler then took over the *Patriot,* changing the name in 1843 to the *Missouri Statesman.* Called the "dean of Missouri journalists," Switzler edited the paper for forty-six years and helped make Columbia a Whig stronghold. His massive *History of Boone County* remains a major source for early history, and he also excelled as an authority on constitutional law. He served in the state legislature in the 1840s and 1850s, was president of the Columbia Lyceum, and helped establish one of the first circulating libraries in central Missouri.[24]

A dynamic, tempestuous Irishman, Shannon remained the center of controversy in the early 1850s, constantly writing letters relating to feuds and rumors. The Whig-Presbyterian faction refused to relinquish the charge that Shannon hoped to convert the University of Missouri into a training school for Christian Church ministers, as Bacon College had been, despite the lack of supporting evidence. Shannon strove vigorously to root out the perpetrators of insults and rumors, while denying all charges. A letter of February 18, 1851, described a "consultation" held in Columbia among several Disciples to discuss how to handle the reputation of the Christian Church in light of a charge against Shannon in a letter to the editor appearing in the *Statesman.* The writer had accused Shannon of slandering the Presbyterians by stating that "the Presbyterians if let alone, will go to the D__l."[25] The exchange of this charge and others finally led Shannon in 1851 to write to Switzler in the *Statesman:*

> It is with unfeigned regret that I feel compelled to correct, or even notice a single one of the many vile slanders, that have been industriously circulated about me in this community, and throughout the state, during the last twelve months. . . . It is well known, that, from the time of my arrival in Columbia

> down to the present hour, a systematic course of opposition, misrepresentation, and slander, in the private circle, and in the public press has industriously prosecuted to keep an *excitement* that would cripple, if not destroy the university.[26]

Another rumor spread about Shannon was that he had sixteen children and seven stepchildren. Actually, in 1849, Shannon had eight children living, and one had died. Only one daughter, fourteen, was close to college age. The oldest, at twenty, was soon to be married, whereas the rest of the children ranged in age from one to eleven. Four more children were born to the Shannon family in Missouri for a total of thirteen children, six of whom were daughters. Shannon had no stepchildren, but he did educate his deceased brother's two daughters who came to Columbia in 1851.[27]

When Shannon finally declined his next reelection in 1862 for another six-year term as president of the university, the Board of Curators conferred an honorary LL.D. on him. The accompanying resolution referred to his "powerful intellect and exalted genius, as well as his rare moral worth and sterling integrity."[28] Despite university politics, Shannon's dual role as president of the university and dominant figure on the Christian College Board of Trustees initiated a close bond between the two institutions that would work to the advantage of the women's college in future years.

The final stage of the founding of Christian College began at a dinner party at Ellerslie, the country home of T. M. Allen. The dinner honored John Augustus Williams of Kentucky, a former student of Shannon who had once lived in Shannon's home and who had been chosen as the prospective president of the college. Attending the dinner, in addition to Allen, Henderson, and Shannon, were physicians Turner R. Haden Smith and Walter Lenoir; university faculty members George Matthews, William W. Hudson, and Robert Grant; and merchant Alexander Douglass. With the divisiveness of past meetings behind them, the group agreed upon a plan for a "chartered institution under the control of a board of trustees composed solely of our brethren and friends." Henderson and Shannon later worked out the details of a charter, which had been discussed with Williams before he returned to Kentucky. An experienced educator, Shannon wrote much of the charter in the library of his home on the university campus, borrowing heavily from the wording of the university charter. Allen gave his approval to the document, and the three founders laid plans for the necessary legislative action. Henderson and Allen successfully obtained the passage of an act of the General Assembly of Missouri on January 18, 1851, "to incorporate a Female College." Board members a month later named it Christian Female College.[29]

Half of the twenty incorporators of Christian College came from Boone County and half from nine other counties in the state. A highly distinguished group, the incorporators included twelve members with college educations, three college presidents, five legislators, five doctors, and five lawyers, confirming that the college was a statewide effort, not just a community venture. Non–Boone Countians in the group were: Rep. John A. Phelps of Springfield, who later became governor of Missouri; merchant James Cephas Fox, the first white settler of Monroe County, who had founded the town of Palmyra and its Christian Church; Elijah Patterson, a state representative from Lewis County; John Jameson, a Christian Church lay preacher, who had been Speaker of the United States House of Representatives; state senator Wayman Crow, a St. Louis merchant and philanthropist and a prominent Unitarian and Whig, who later cofounded Washington University in St. Louis; Lewis Bryan, a prosperous Christian Church member and early settler of Palmyra in Marion County, who was related to Daniel Boone; Huntsville community leader J. J. Allen; Fayette merchant Weston Favel Burch, a wealthy investor and a director of the Missouri State Bank, a newspaper publisher, superintendent of a road company, and supporter of Howard High School; Moses Lard of Liberty, a prominent Christian Church leader; and Samuel S. Church of St. Louis.

Most crucial to the college's future, the ten local incorporators, in addition to Allen, Henderson, and Shannon, were: leading Democrat and physician Turner R. Haden Smith, secretary of the university Board of Curators and treasurer of Christian College; William Wilson Hudson, twice acting president of the university, who was a Whig and a nonchurch member; physician William McClure; Gen. Thomas S. Grant; and Robert S. Barr, a wealthy merchant. Two others, Flavil Vivian and Levi T. Smith, lived only a short time after the incorporation and were replaced by Christian College president John Augustus Williams and Judge Alexander Persinger.

Although most incorporators were members of the Christian Church, they never intended that the college be denominational in its teaching. Christian Church members, rather than regarding themselves as a sect, saw the name "Christian" as a unifying term for all believers. The charter reflected this intent with the specific statement that "into this institution no sectarian feature has been incorporated, and in it no sectarian influence whatever will be exerted."[30]

The founding of a women's college put Christian College well ahead of its time, even when compared with the state of education in the East. The most prevalent schools for women, nationwide, were academies, numbering more than six thousand at the height of their influence in 1850. They offered no more than a high school education, and few had college preparatory courses. They generally served middle-class families before the public school systems existed. Many were coeducational, admitting women largely as a convenience to families but not opening all courses to them. After about 1815, female seminaries concentrated on raising the instructional level of academies to approach that of men's colleges. Thus, the word *seminary* usually implied an improvement over academies. Some seminaries promised to prepare women for college, and a few actually evolved into true colleges, such as Mary Lyon's Mount Holyoke. Originating as a female seminary in 1836, Mount Holyoke officially became a college in 1888. Although seminaries did much to call attention to the need for improved opportunities for women, their courses usually fell short of the college level. For example, Emma Willard, who opened a school in Middlebury, Vermont, in 1814, offered instruction in only four major areas: religion and moral training; sciences of the mind and natural philosophy; domestic instruction; and "ornamental" education, meaning drawing, music, and writing.[31]

Another major leader in women's education, Catherine Beecher, founded the Hartford Female Seminary in Connecticut, later establishing a school in Cincinnati, and eventually moving on to found the Milwaukee Female College. An active advocate of the need to upgrade women's education, Beecher created the American Women's Education Association in 1852 to encourage funding for women's colleges. Her emphasis, influencing many later leaders, called for liberal arts courses, endowments, and coequal teachers for women.[32]

A few brave pioneers in women's education founded actual colleges in the period from the 1830s to the 1850s. Georgia Female College opened at Macon, Georgia, in 1838 as a true college, the first chartered in the United States to award a college degree to women. Oberlin College in Ohio admitted women in 1833 but did not allow them to be college degree candidates until 1837. Ohio proved fertile ground for women's education, with the Wesleyan Female College at Cincinnati in 1843, the Oxford Female College in 1852, and the Ohio Wesleyan Female College at Delaware in 1853, which became part of Ohio Wesleyan University in 1877. Antioch College in Ohio, founded in 1852, was the first college in the United States to open its doors as a coeducational institution. In Illinois, the Illinois Conference Female Academy of 1847 became a college in 1851, and Mary Sharp College was founded in Winchester, Tennessee, in 1853. Another early college, Auburn Female University, was chartered in 1852 but moved to Elmira, New York, to gain more financial support, receiving a new charter in 1855 as Elmira Female College. Founded considerably later, from 1865 to 1894, came the well-known eastern women's colleges, Vassar, Wellesley, Smith, Bryn Mawr, Barnard, and Radcliffe.[33]

The drive for coeducation lagged behind the founding of women's colleges, but some educators saw coeducation as the only way to ensure true equality of education for women. The Midwest, with institutional patterns less rigidly set, pioneered in opening the doors of state universities to women; the University of Iowa became coeducational in 1855, followed by the University of Wisconsin in 1867. In 1869 and 1870, Kansas, Indiana, Minnesota, Missouri, Michigan, and California joined the list.

Just as Christian College rivaled most eastern women's colleges with its early founding date, its pioneering role also prevailed in the West. Not only was it the first women's college chartered west of the Mississippi, but its creation also stimulated the organization five years later of a second women's college in Columbia, Baptist Female College. The chartering of Lindenwood College in 1853 made Missouri the home of yet another early women's college.

The role of Christian College as the first women's college in Columbia and the first west of the Mississippi was challenged in 1915 when Stephens College, the former Baptist Female College, began to claim 1833 as its founding date. However, an abundance of evidence supports the 1856–1857 founding date for Baptist Female College. That evidence is set forth in the Appendix of this work.

E. C. Davis, a local newspaper editor, celebrated the historic role of Christian College in the first "Anniversary Address" to Christian Female College on July 2, 1852: "[T]hus have we planted in our midst the first FEMALE COLLEGE in Missouri. I do not mean to say the first female institution empowered to confer honors on Literature, by virtue of chapters. By no means. I mean a COLLEGE as defined and understood by SCHOLARS."[34]

2

Setting the Tone

JOHN AUGUSTUS WILLIAMS: 1851–1856

No education can be regarded as useful or philosophical unless it be adapted to the nature of the individual.

—John Augustus Williams, "Inaugural Address"

WITH ITS VERY FOUNDING, Christian College clearly accepted the challenge of granting opportunities to those previously denied access to higher education—a challenge that would become a major tenet of the institution. It made the assumption that women, equal to men in intellectual capacity, could benefit from a collegiate experience as challenging as that offered to men. John Augustus Williams, first president of the Christian Female College, from 1851 to 1856, gave life to both the tradition and the assumption, setting the academic tone for the new institution at a distinctly collegiate level from its inception.

Williams's inaugural address stood as an important statement of his philosophy of education, touching upon timeless issues with surprisingly modern overtones. He was adamantly opposed to the "rote system" of learning: "The erudite book-worm can never . . . become better educated than his shelves: he has no higher title to the honor of the name than a circulating *library*." Particularly obnoxious to Williams was the "pencil system" of marking and memorizing a text. He would use thoughtful lectures, not texts, to stimulate minds and saw knowledge as merely a tool, convinced that development of critical thinking skills marked the truly educated person. Nor did he accept any one teaching method as applicable to all: "No education can be regarded as useful or philosophical, unless it be adapted to the nature of the individual."[1] His devotion to individual attention for each student placed him well ahead of his time, establishing the concept as a tradition at Christian College.

In another timeless theme, Williams condemned the mercenary nature of a society in which all is measured by "pecuniary advantages," making "reason, taste, and fancy subservient to the petty schemes of selfish aggrandizement." He whimsically adopted the language of capitalism to argue for respecting education for its "pecuniary advantages." He presented education as a good investment, a form of capital that, through use, enriches rather than impoverishes one's stock. He described knowledge as "a productive capital, an immaterial stock, capable of yielding a certain amount of profits, when combined with the requisite labor." Education, the best legacy a parent could leave a child, remained above the reach of floods, pestilence, fire, and bankruptcy and was "a capital into which time, health, and energy are always easily convertible."[2] Thus Williams dealt with the educator's perennial dilemma of making peace between the practical and the intellectual worlds.

Not only did Williams need to "sell" education, but he also faced the far more difficult task of selling "female education." Recognizing the dependent role of a woman, he concluded that she was necessarily incapacitated by the lack of education. He argued that men had a monopoly on attainment because of their superior education: "The avarice of man has claimed and appropriated all the avenues to wealth, as well as fame; and she who was made to share his glory as a companion through life, often finds, when too late, that even her subsistence is the result of her dependence, and that, as an isolated being, she must claim from humanity as a boon, that support which she would gladly have earned as a recompense." According to Williams, woman should lean on man not of necessity but "from a gracious and tender affection."[3]

Early Christian College publications, for which Williams was responsible, also set a high academic tone. The first circular, dated June 28, 1851, described the nature of the student who should seek admission:

> It is desirable that no young lady will seek admission into this school, who is not determined to devote her whole energy and attention to her moral and mental improvement. Those who cannot, for the time being, abstract their minds from the fascinations of society, or who aspire *merely* to a *superficial* or fashionable Education, are earnestly advised to seek elsewhere. . . . This institution has been established with the view of affording YOUNG LADIES the opportunity of acquiring a thorough *Collegiate Education,* by introducing a more extensive course of study, and a more rigid discipline of the mind than is usual in the ordinary school for girls.[4]

Early catalogs were excellent. The 1852 catalog, much more than the term implies, reprinted the first anniversary address by Edwin Curtis Davis. Davis, editor of the *Columbia Sentinel*, a rival newspaper of Switzler's *Statesman*, allied himself with James Shannon, who used the *Sentinel* for university printing. The catalog won first prize over Switzler's entry at the Boone County Fair and was a great success, and the first thousand copies proved so popular that more had to be printed. The quality of this and other publications owed much to Williams's earlier role as a journalist and to contributions by Allen and Henderson, both of whom wrote for periodicals.[5]

Later catalogs reiterated the seriousness of purpose expected of Christian College students and included essays on proper teaching methods as well as justifications of women's education. According to the 1854 catalog:

> We are, in fact, trammeled with no particular system; nor are we biased by the old customs and educational prejudices of the age. We repudiate as utterly useless, or injurious, many of the popular notions about the education of girls: yet, we endeavor to retain and apply all that is excellent in the modern "Female School." The branches of learning which we prescribe, are useful, either as practical or as disciplinary studies. . . . We endeavor to avoid that *mockery* of the girl [finishing schools], which consists in carrying her hastily and superficially over the course of study. We do not seek to *accomplish* her *at the sacrifice of education*.[6]

The 1855 catalog described Christian College teaching, stressing the need to educate students to "*think for themselves* on all subjects. . . . The rote-system, with all its labor-saving appliances, is repudiated. We regard it as a certain cause of mental paralysis." With the intent that "Ladies should receive as thorough an intellectual training as is given young Men in our Universities," Williams matched the Christian College calendar to that of the University of Missouri. The 1854 catalog implied a high degree of selectivity: "The number of . . . members of the Collegiate Family will be limited. . . . Fifty pupils only will be admitted." Even though the program drew increasing enrollments, financial inability to provide sufficient facilities kept numbers down. By 1854, catalog terms demanded that the tuition of $150 be paid in advance, with no refund except for illness.[7]

With no building of its own, the college opened its first session on April 7, 1851, in the one-room Christian church on Seventh Street across from the courthouse. The student body consisted of seven girls: Anna Hitt, Emma Gordon, Ann Thomas Harris, Amanda Ellis, Mary E. Carter, Matilda Stone, and Sallie Bedford. By the beginning of the first regular session in September, however, thirty-six students had enrolled for classes, comparing well with the seventy-five men attending the University of Missouri. The number swelled to seventy by midyear, with thirty-one from other Missouri towns and five from Illinois, Virginia, and Louisiana.[8]

During the summer of 1851, as the building committee of the Board of Trustees considered specifications for a structure to accommodate both classrooms and living quarters, an opportunity arose to purchase the unfinished home of James Bennett. Bennett, a local physician and large landowner, had died in Hangtown, California, on his way to the gold rush. In addition to being one of Columbia's best-trained doctors, he had been involved in the town's affairs from its beginning. He had served as a court-appointed member of the Columbia Board of Trustees to govern the newly established town. A member of the building committee for the men's Columbia College in 1832, he was a large subscriber in the drive to make Columbia the site of the University of Missouri. He served also on the Board of Trustees to found the Columbia Female Academy in 1833.[9]

The *First Circular of the Christian Female College* announced in the summer of 1851 that "a commodious new building, with five large rooms, in a retired and beautiful part of the village, has been obtained for the accommodation of the College the ensuing session." Bennett's estate included a twenty-nine-acre plot north of town where his home remained under construction at the time of his death. The executor of the estate was James Rollins, Bennett's brother-in-law and a member of the Whig faction in Columbia. Negotiations for the purchase of the property fell to Allen, who had remained a friend of both Rollins and Switzler. The terms of the purchase were favorable. The Christian College Board of Trustees would pay $5,500 at 5 percent interest over a four-year period, but payments were not to begin until after the first year. The college also gained a forty-foot strip of land to the downtown area of Columbia at Tenth Street and Broadway. Trustees immediately approved a forty-by-fifty-foot extension at the rear of the Bennett house but cautiously specified that they would suspend operations anytime funds proved inadequate.[10]

The tone of the 1851 circular was overly optimistic, as the college did not occupy the building until later in the 1851–1852 session. The college began its fall session by boarding out-of-town students "with the most respectable families" in town at two dollars per week, "including washing." As some of the same families boarded university men, the college lost several girls to marriage during its first session. William Y. Hitt provided classroom space, allowing the use of a two-room storehouse at the front of his property on the northwest corner of Hitt and Cherry Streets. The building stood just a block east of the Columbia Female Academy and across the street from the original site intended for a male college but never used for that purpose. President Williams and his family boarded at Hitt's home, one of the finest houses in Columbia, where Alexander Campbell had once visited.[11]

A faculty of three for the April session grew to five by the second semester of the regular session. By comparison, many girls' schools of the 1850s had only "The President and the Lady," and even the University of Missouri boasted a regular faculty of only seven members. Williams himself taught literature, Bible, education, Latin, and Greek. An able musician and composer, he invested heavily in the first budget to acquire four pianos for student use and introduced bass, tenor, alto, and soprano parts into the town choir. Prominent among the other Christian College faculty, Susan E. Jones of Jacksonville, Illinois, a graduate of "one of the best colleges for women in the land," had taught in Illinois at Walnut Grove Academy, now Eureka College. At Walnut Grove, she and her evangelist father, John T. Jones, had known David Patterson Henderson. Jones acted as principal of natural science at Christian College and later helped to establish preparatory academies for the college. Rebecca Jane Galbraith, who had also taught at Walnut Grove, became the principal of natural science and mathematics, and Ella Van Allen, who taught instrumental music, had probably been a student of Williams. Professor William Alexander, of "the polite arts," taught drawing and painting. A professor at the University of Missouri, he became the first of several shared faculty in the early years.[12]

In addition to the "Collegiate Faculty," the college maintained a three-member "Domestic Faculty." The chief of these, Dr. C. E. Williams of Kentucky, President Williams's father, served as a father figure or "patron" and financial officer while acting as a resident physician and teaching anatomy and physiology. Dr. Williams's wife served as chief matron, and President Williams's wife, Louisa Hathaway Williams, was assistant matron. Together, the domestic faculty and Williams took "absolute control over every such Pupil, as far as it regards health, manners, habits, finances, and morals." In addition to academic studies, each student devoted a "reasonable portion" of her time to "Domestic Science," the "theory and practice of Good House Keeping." Williams firmly believed that practical knowledge must accompany the liberal arts for a well-rounded education. A text by Catherine Beecher, *A Treatise on Domestic Science,* covered every aspect of housekeeping.[13]

A comparison of Christian College and Mount Holyoke catalogs illustrates Williams's knowledge of contemporary practices in the East. Whereas Mount Holyoke offered more botany and natural history, Christian College included more English, mathematics, and Bible study. Languages were optional in both programs. The sophomore, junior, and senior courses outlined in the early Christian College catalogs were a close match to those of Mount Holyoke, using many of the same textbooks.[14]

The 1854 catalog's listing of required courses and texts indicated a significant level of difficulty:

> *Freshman*—Arithmetic, Ancient History, Grammar, Ancient Geography, Natural Philosophy, Five Books of Moses, Composition, Mental Arithmetic.
> *Sophomore*—Ray's Algebra, Natural History of Animals, Plants, Minerals, Modern History, Rhetoric, Jewish Scripture, Modern Geography.
> *Junior*—Ray's Algebra, Geometry, Chemistry, Practical Botany, Physiology, Geology, Criticism, the Four Gospels.

Senior—Trigonometry, Analytical Geometry, Mental Science, Logic, Ethics, Constitutional Law, Astronomy, English and Sacred Literature, Acts of Apostles.

Textbooks accompanying these courses included Wayland's *Political Economy,* Mrs. Lincoln's *Botany,* Whately's *Logic,* Alexander's or Paley's *Evidences of Christianity,* Parker's *Natural Philosophy,* and Goodrich's histories. Students studied Hume, Bacon, Swift, Milton, Shakespeare, and Irving, among others. Optional studies included languages, drawing, painting, embroidery, vocal music, piano, guitar, and choir. However, these studies were allowed only if time remained after completion of the more serious academic courses.[15]

To John Augustus Williams, the Bible served as the indispensable text. He noted in his inaugural address that it should "be incorporated as common law, for the regulation of behavior, the formation of manners, and the discipline of the heart. . . . It comprehends all that is known, while on the true nature and destiny of man, it contains all that we can know, because it is all that God has chosen to reveal." In later catalogs, Williams demoted the Bible from *the* prominent text to *a* prominent text. He also relaxed his rigid controls somewhat, referring to domestic chores as "encouraged" rather than "expected." At no point, however, was there any relaxation in the demand for excellence in teaching. As early as May 1852, a Board of Trustees committee, created to investigate the state of the teaching, reported that all went well and that the students were, indeed, being taught to think.[16]

Also in May 1852, the board embarked on a creative venture of founding preparatory schools in other Missouri towns. The charter had authorized trustees to establish departments "whenever the interests of education should require it." Williams and Henderson proposed "subordinate, auxiliary and homogeneous academies in different sections of the State . . . to qualify young ladies for entrance into Christian College." The college would be "a nucleus around which a beautiful and substantial system of Female education is being built up in the state. . . . [A]uxiliary schools will soon be planted, all centering their energies to this point with a view of . . . placing female instruction at a higher standard in Missouri."[17]

The board charged Williams with founding preparatory academies during his summer "vacation" and created an "Academic Department" to supervise the project. In addition to administering the college's inaugural year, teaching, fund-raising, and overseeing construction, Williams did manage to establish two schools in the summer of 1852. One was created as part of Christian College itself and endured for seventy-five years. The other, the Christian Academy at Palmyra, Missouri, opened under the leadership of Winthrop H. Hopson, a local physician. Hopson, a graduate of the University of Missouri and St. Louis Medical College, later abandoned medicine to preach and became the state evangelist of the Christian Church. He opened the Palmyra academy in June 1852 in a three-story building with eight faculty members. Incorporated by the legislature on February 5, 1855, it flourished, serving 110 pupils by 1856. Events of 1857, however, brought the demise of the academy when Palmyra underwent the multiple crises of a smallpox epidemic, a severe drought, and financial panic.[18]

An incredibly energetic first academic year for the college reached its peak with a week of final examinations and an official celebration of the occupation of the Bennett home. A packed house attended the public oral exams each day, and the college held its dedication on July 2, 1852, with the choir singing a special ode composed by students just that afternoon. E. C. Davis made the principal address, speaking of the college in the most laudatory terms. Davis compared Christian College favorably with other women's colleges, especially with the Ohio Female College (Wesleyan Female College of Cincinnati) and the Wesleyan College of Georgia (Georgia Female College). The *Sentinel,* Davis's newspaper, described the exam week and the "large and intelligent audience in attendance throughout." A July 8 editorial complimented the

> rigid discipline of mind which governs this institution. We have met with few teachers who understand so thoroughly the philosophy of education as has President Williams. He acts upon the Greek plan of *drawing out the mind,* rather than putting into the mind. . . . We were astonished at the proficiency of the class in Logic. Its most abstruse principles were discussed—not *repeated*—and nice distinctions drawn which would have reflected honor on many Seniors in our male colleges and universities. . . . We have never seen young ladies put to severer tests, and yet stand their ground so *manfully.*[19]

Still acclaiming the end-of-year events in the next weekly issue, Davis ran a long laudatory letter submitted by "A Stranger," who observed the examinations as he visited Columbia:

> The young ladies are taught to *think*. They are *compelled* to think. They take nothing for granted, no matter by whom affirmed . . . and they never yielded the point until they were convinced by arguments. . . . [T]his was the most satisfactory examination that I have witnessed. . . . They will compare favorably with the same number of young ladies I have ever known examined in any school. . . . How different such young ladies are from the pale, sickly, hot-house plants of the old States. Already, some of the sensible young gentlemen of the old states are seeking wives in Missouri.[20]

Even Shannon's nemesis, William Switzler, applauded the successful first year: "This institution, we are happy to learn, is in a most flourishing and prosperous condition, and takes the lead in the way of Female Education in the State." In like vein, the *Statesman* the next year praised the second year's exams: "Suffice it to say, a more brilliant commencement has never graced the close of any institution."[21]

Christian College ranked students in the initial class according to previous education, resulting in the designation of a junior class the first year. Although several of the 1855 graduates had entered the college in 1851, three of the first graduates had attended only one year before the first commencement on July 1, 1853. Ages of the students varied from thirteen to thirty, reflecting a typical practice of colleges of that era. Of the first six graduates, five immediately became teachers or principals.[22]

Academic attainment went hand in hand with a sheltered environment, and early circulars described regulations governing a Christian College student:

> All profuse use of ornament is strictly prohibited.
> No pupil shall appear upon the street, or visit any public place whatever, except by permission.
> Pupils are not allowed to attend night meetings, without permission.
> No pupil shall receive directly or indirectly the attentions of gallants.
> No young lady shall contract any debts, or make any purchases without express permission from parent or teacher.
> Early rising and early morning walks are enjoyed.
> Attendance at night meetings, prohibited.
> Pupils allowed to attend public worship on Sundays.
> Ornamental studies cannot be pursued to the neglect of regular courses.
> Bible lectures every evening, and Chapel exercises every morning, at which all pupils are required to attend.
> Each pupil must keep a correct account of incidental expenses, and transmit a copy of the same from time to time, to her Parents.[23]

The rules of the 1854 catalog caused indignation among trustees, who ordered the catalog withdrawn and reprinted to read that "Pupils are *required* to attend public worship on Sundays." Trustees also imposed their will on Williams when a motion by Shannon demanded that the president and a majority of his assistants be Christian Church members. The motion passed unanimously despite Williams's objections.[24]

Conformity of dress for all "except those in black" was intended "to prevent the formation of extravagant habits and tastes, and to remove all distinctions but those of merit." Winter uniforms required "plain worsted dresses, maroon or green" with "green hoods trimmed and lined with scarlet. White aprons." Summer dresses were of "pink calico or lawn" with "white sunbonnets trimmed with scarlet ribbon. Aprons."[25]

A fast-paced day developed student physical endurance as well as intellectual toughness. Students rose at six, engaged in the morning walk, attended chapel, and practiced until time for classes. Classes continued until late afternoon and included a daily composition. After class came more practice, bookkeeping, chores, and a Bible lecture each evening. Students seldom left campus, but rules permitted callers and a trip downtown every sixth Saturday. They marched "in their rows of green bonnets all the way from college to town, carefully flanked by the President and members of the faculty." On rare occasions, students attended meetings of the literary society at the University of Missouri. This led to the founding of Christian College's own literary society, the Mary Phelps Institute, which met each Friday, giving students a chance to read their own compositions and discuss literary matters. Their role model, Mary Phelps, was the wife of trustee John Phelps, who later became governor of Missouri.[26]

Although the academic program went well, unexpected problems resulted from the college's close identification with the Christian Church faction in sectarian and political controversies between Shannon and Switzler. The bitterness between the factions, seen as early as 1849, intensified throughout Shannon's tenure as university president. Switzler regularly used the *Statesman* to attack the Christian Church group, labeled "Campbellites." Shannon infuriated Switzler by denying him access to report on university board meetings and by shifting the lucrative university printing contract from the *Statesman* to Davis's *Sentinel*.[27]

The precedent for excluding Switzler from board meetings actually predated Shannon's presidency. A rule going back to the early days of the university provided that, on request of any board member, the meeting would be cleared of visitors until completion of the question before the board. As no such request had ever been made, the rule seemed a dead letter. However, the meeting of September 3, 1849, at which Lathrop resigned as president, took place under particularly acrimonious conditions. Switzler, a strong Lathrop supporter, had just printed some especially disparaging remarks against individual curators who, after lengthy debate, barred Switzler from the meeting. Switzler took on the board with full fury and, for a time, boycotted university news. Because the question of whether to elect Shannon was imminent, Switzler blamed Shannon's influence for the curators' action, particularly after the board proceeded to elect Shannon at the next day's meeting.[28]

With the *Statesman* representing the Whig-Presbyterian views, Shannon fought back through the pages of the *Sentinel*. Switzler charged that the *Sentinel* was created merely as a Shannon platform with Shannon actually writing some of the editorials. After the *Sentinel* changed hands in 1853 and became the *Missouri Dollar Journal*, Shannon's letters and articles became even more openly aggressive.

Shannon played into the hands of his enemies by becoming increasingly indiscreet. He participated in mass meetings supporting the Missouri invasions of Kansas and engaged in a spectacular quarrel with Sen. Thomas Hart

Benton, becoming a leader of the anti-Benton faction within the Democratic Party. As Shannon's speeches took a more extremist proslavery turn, Benton Democrats in the state legislature combined with Whig members to move against him, overpowering the anti-Benton, pro-Shannon group in the legislature. Shannon's downfall with the legislature stemmed especially from a speech he developed for use throughout the state. The speech began with a denunciation of Rollins, Switzler, and Shannon's other opponents, proceeding to justify slavery on the basis of the Bible and natural law and denying the power of the national government to exclude slavery in the territories. Shannon drew critical press coverage, becoming too extreme for even the proslave group. His old colleague Thomas Allen wrote to John D. Gano on August 10, 1855: "Oh, how his friends are grieving over his course. It must inevitably lead to his removal from his present position."[29]

The legislature reacted to Shannon's role with a statute inducing his resignation but not ending his influence. Although the faculty and the president had originally enjoyed tenure, the statute of 1855 limited their term of office to six years. It further forbade the practice of any profession other than teaching, including preaching. Finally, it terminated the appointments of the faculty, the president, and the board. The outgoing board defiantly elected Shannon to a six-year term, which he declined, resigning at the July 1856 meeting.[30]

Ironically, the legislature failed to elect a new Board of Curators, leaving it to Gov. Sterling Price, an anti-Benton, proslavery Democrat, to appoint the new group. As a result, all but three curators were new appointees, and all supported the Shannon position. Caleb Stone, one of the three members reappointed, became secretary. Stone, president of the board when Lathrop resigned, had been instrumental in hiring Shannon and was also an influential trustee of Christian College. Another of the three curators reappointed, Shannon's son-in-law, became treasurer. Professor William Hudson, the new president of the board, remained carefully nonpolitical and held no church affiliation. However, Hudson and Shannon retained a close friendship, naming sons for each other, and both served as trustees of Christian College. After his resignation, Shannon left almost immediately to become the first president of Christian University (later Culver-Stockton) in Canton, Missouri. He died in 1859 at the age of sixty.[31]

Although overtones of the heated controversy between Shannon and his enemies had no direct impact on Christian College, Shannon's high-profile role clearly caused tension. An event of March 4, 1852, a tragic shooting, illustrated the severity of the sectarian and political divisiveness surrounding both the university and the college. The shooting involved Robert A. Grant, a tutor assisting university professor William Hudson. Grant, the fiancé of Sue Jones of the Christian College faculty, was also a friend of Christian College trustee D. P. Henderson and had three relatives who attended the college. By implication, Shannon's enemies at the university associated Grant with the Christian or "Campbellite" group in Columbia. The instigator of the quarrel and ultimate victim of the shooting, George Clarkson, a university student and son of a Columbia doctor, represented the Whig-Presbyterian faction.[32]

Clarkson, sixteen years old and hotheaded, came before the university faculty for causing a fight with a fellow student and was fined fifty of his one hundred credit points. Leaving Academic Hall, Clarkson happened upon Grant. According to testimony at the trial, as quoted in the *Statesman,* Grant asked, "What did they do with you?" Clarkson replied, "I am satisfied, but I will flog him yet." Shannon, observing the exchange, demanded, with Clarkson still present, that Grant repeat the conversation. Considering this a new offense, Shannon then ordered the faculty to reassemble immediately and instructed Clarkson to reappear for further disciplinary action. Clarkson, blaming Grant for informing on him, caned Grant and at first refused to reappear. Witnesses testified that Clarkson called Grant "a damned Campbellite Democrat" and threatened to get a pistol and shoot him. Grant reportedly made no retaliation. After the faculty reconvened and expeditiously expelled Clarkson from the university, Clarkson obtained a pistol and laid in wait for Grant to emerge from a drawing lesson. Meanwhile, he composed a letter to Grant, referring to him as a "devilish Campbellite Shannonite" and a "degraded Democratic Campbellite."[33]

Anticipating danger, Hudson warned Grant to arm himself, whereupon Grant sent out for a Colt revolver. Hudson, his art professor, loaded it for him. When Grant entered the area where Clarkson waited, Clarkson attacked first with a cane, breaking it over Grant and repeating the slurs. Before Clarkson could aim the pistol, however, Grant fired, intending only to ward off Clarkson but instead wounding him fatally. Grant immediately turned himself in. Clarkson died nine days later. With the outcome of the trial never in doubt, Grant was acquitted on a plea of self-defense, but his career at the university ended. Although he received a vote of support from students and was allowed to finish the semester, the university dismissed him with a letter of appreciation for his services. Frank Stevens, historian of the University of Missouri, concluded: "It was tragic how religious bigotry and political hatred were involved in this case."[34]

The tragedy indirectly benefited Christian College. His association with the university no longer possible, Grant and his bride, Sue Jones Grant, contributed greatly to the completion of the college's development of preparatory academies in other Missouri towns. In 1852 the couple founded the Northeast Academy in Canton, where Grant became a faculty member of Christian University. The Grants also headed the Paris Female Seminary in 1854, and Sue Grant went on to found the De Soto Female Institute. The last of the preparatory schools, the St. Joseph Academy, was founded in 1855, the work of the former *Sentinel* editor, E. C. Davis, and of J. K. Rogers, a former recruiting agent and future president of Christian College.[35]

On the Christian College campus, Williams faced both personal and professional problems. Severe illness struck soon after the opening of the 1852 regular session. Unable to walk across the road, Williams went to class by horseback and taught from a couch. He began to regain his strength only to be devastated by the death of his two-year-old daughter, Mary Belle. In addition, the name "Christian College" became a symbol of the quarrels pitting Shannon against his enemies. Meant to define values in a broad sense, without sectarian connotation, the name nonetheless carried denominational overtones that possibly inhibited contributions from opposition groups. The need for greater funding kept the college in the cramped quarters of the original buildings, and facilities failed to keep pace with the needs of a swelling enrollment, forestalling the ideal of 150 resident students. Board action of August 1851 had approved the forty-by-fifty-foot extension to the Bennett house, but trustees almost immediately countermanded the action with an order to suspend building for lack of funds. The foundation remained unfinished when Williams left the presidency in 1856.[36]

The five-room Bennett house, one hundred feet in length and fifty feet wide, consisted of a basement and three stories. The college partitioned each level, including the basement, into four rooms. On the main floor, President Williams and his family lived in one room at the back and shared the front parlor with those seniors who had "drawing room privileges." The other back room housed the patron, Dr. Williams, and his family. The remaining front room became the president's study, the school library, and a classroom. There were four large rooms upstairs and four in the attic, where sloping walls led to tiny windows almost down to the floor. Students utilized trundle beds, sleeping eight to a room. Partitions in the basement created a kitchen, dining room, storeroom, and servants' quarters.[37]

When the college enrollment reached 101 in the second year and 130 in the third, the number of boarders grew to 50 and then to 70. Students were being turned away, and the primary school had to be discontinued for lack of space. In desperation, Williams built two frame cottages, each flanking the main building, and added an ell to the eastern one consisting of three twenty-foot-square rooms. He even converted the smokehouse into a classroom.

A committee of the Board of Trustees examined the property and reported at the May 2, 1856, meeting that 114 people were living in the house and two cottages. Of 150 students, 85 were residents. In addition, 8 faculty, 8 family members of the president and the patron, and 13 of the 18 servants lived on the premises. The same room might be used as a study hall, piano practice hall, and a sleeping room. Some 60 nonresident students also used the campus.[38]

Trustees continued to stress the need for completion of the two-story addition on the still-empty foundation on the north side of the main building. Plans envisioned a dining room and one classroom on the bottom floor with a chapel upstairs. The chapel would be divided into two classrooms by sliding doors. The board also recommended the addition of two-story wings on each side of the main hall, each housing two classrooms and four lodging rooms. In addition, the college needed a large icehouse, one or more cisterns, the necessary outhouses, and a plank fence around the grounds. These needs remained in the planning stage at the time of Williams's resignation in 1856.[39]

The lack of funding for the new women's college did not necessarily indicate a lack of support for the concept of female education. The heavy expenses borne by Columbia's population of one thousand in the 1850s included the building of the Plank Road to Providence on the Missouri River, fund-raising to lure a railroad to town, and the need to support the university entirely by private subscriptions. Efforts to bolster the Columbia Female Academy further drained resources from Christian College. Although Christian Church followers tried to support Christian College, they also felt compelled to give financial support to Bethany College in West Virginia, Christian University in Canton, and the Kentucky Orphan School.[40]

Board discussions focused overwhelmingly on financial matters, with repeated vows to do better in soliciting subscriptions, while increasingly blaming Williams for the college's financial plight. When the board had originally authorized the president to take possession of the house and land, it had specifically stated that the president would make improvements at his own expense. Therefore, when Williams submitted a bill for eleven stoves, a rail fence, a latched gate on the west, and a plank fence, the board ignored it. Trustees did agree to pay for desks and a "privy of suitable dimensions." Trustees also relinquished a four-dollar-per-student fee owed by Williams to the board in order to help him furnish the new building, "*provided* that the resolution shall not be understood as to relinquish the right on the part of the Board . . . to charge a modest rent." After paying $569.97 for carpentry, $33.55 for insurance, and $71.00 for lumber and writing tables, trustees showed a balance of $26.00.[41]

Among the trustees, only David Patterson Henderson made genuinely strenuous efforts at fund-raising. At the May 4, 1852, meeting, Henderson reported raising $1,284.50 in the "foreign field" in two short tours of remote Missouri counties. Stating that trustees should take pleasure "as Masters of the first and only Female College in the State," he noted that "we are surrounded by difficulties and embarrassments." He then made an offer. He would raise a sum equal to that raised by any other board member toward liquidation of the debt on the Bennett home and necessary improvements. Henderson pledged to "traverse this State, and, if necessary, other states" to raise half the "liabilities" if any other board member would agree to do the same by accepting his offer before July 4. The response proved disappointing. Trustees merely gave Henderson the title of "Early and Steadfast Friend of Christian College" and passed a resolution "To request Elder D. P. Henderson to continue his important services in behalf of the Institution in the foreign as well as domestic fields." Discouraged, Henderson soon turned his efforts toward raising an endowment of fifty thousand dollars for the founding in 1853 of Christian University in Canton, the first coeducational institution west of the Mississippi. Shannon and Robert and Sue Grant later joined Henderson in this effort.[42]

Trustees made repeated vows to campaign for new subscriptions. The May 2, 1853, meeting included a pledge to raise at least double the amount of former subscriptions but concluded with a resolution that Williams was expected to keep the building, fencing, and grounds in good condition at his own expense. Henderson continued to prod the board by introducing a resolution on July 5, 1853, "to make a more vigorous effort in behalf of Christian College than has heretofore been made in Boone County, and . . . make this effort at some early day not later than May 1, 1854, . . . by canvassing the whole county."[43]

Hoping to arouse community support, the *Sentinel* issued an editorial challenge: "Let our citizens then put their shoulders to the wheel and complete Christian College. *Double* her accommodations—make her capacious enough to admit one hundred and fifty young ladies." By the July 5, 1854, board meeting, the treasurers' report showed receipts of $4,987.80 and disbursements of $4,987.20 for a balance of $0.60.[44]

The unclear relationship between the president and the board in financial matters exacerbated the situation. Early presidents leased the college from the board rather than being paid a salary, a practice that blurred lines of authority in policy making and in determining responsibility for the college's financial functioning. The president made a payment to the board for each tuition collected in return for the lease. Trustees, theoretically, would use these payments and any funds raised from contributions to pay for improvements or additions to the physical plant. Thus, the remaining tuition belonged to the president, who had the obligation of providing for all expenses of running the college. The president's personal income came from funds remaining after expenses. The larger the student body, the greater the profit to the president, and limitations in housing limited that profit, serving as a constant irritant in early administrations. Presidents and trustees struggled to define mutual financial obligations until 1920 when Edgar Lee became the first president to receive a salary.

As financial problems intensified, relations between Williams and the board deteriorated, especially between Shannon and Williams. Although Allen headed the board as president, Shannon was its undisputed leader, making or seconding virtually every resolution during the college's first administration. It was Shannon who moved the name "Christian Female College" on February 3, 1851, although Williams later claimed credit for the name. Once mentor and student, Shannon and Williams increasingly clashed in a conflict that would last even beyond Williams's resignation in July 1856. Partially a clash of strong personalities, their differences intensified with the increase of financial problems and with Williams's abolitionist stance and Shannon's strong proslave position.[45]

Board action at the April 7, 1851, meeting had set the president's fee to the board at four dollars per student tuition. This fee, temporarily relinquished by the board in 1852, became a major source of dissension between trustees and Williams when Shannon took the lead in October 1854 in reinstating the fee. Meanwhile, Williams's claim against the board for his 1852 expenditures remained unpaid and a source of friction. The board repeatedly demanded that Williams present the proper papers for the expenses and consistently declared any papers presented not to be in proper order. Finally, the board created a committee of three to settle the claim by compromise, but exchanges merely escalated the bitterness until the committee, in May 1856, asked to be released from further attempts.[46]

Realizing that completion of the addition to the main building and other improvements could wait no longer, the board resorted to an attempt to get a loan from Williams. Trustees proposed to Williams that he advance funds, not to exceed $7,500, secured by a second mortgage on the college property. The agreement would require that there be no foreclosure on the property for six years. Also, the board would receive a twelve-month notice of any foreclosure after that time. Williams's response of May 3 went to the May 9 board meeting:

> The entertainment of a proposition to do anything more for this institution in a pecuniary way, than what I have already done, must assume that a satisfactory adjustment has been made of all just claims growing out of my past expenditures for the improvement of the grounds and buildings, and also that the matter of an assessment of four dollars for each pupil in attendance to be required of me . . . has been satisfactorily settled between the board and myself.[47]

A report that Williams had purchased the Greenville Institute in Kentucky and planned to move at the end of the session further infuriated Shannon and other trustees, who demanded that Williams "definitely and in writing to this board and without unnecessary delay" answer the rumors and send his resignation if true. Williams replied on May 9, 1856, that he would have information from Kentucky in a few days that would allow him to decide his future. Shannon lashed out at Williams with a resolution demanding that Williams give the board, as a financial accounting, a list of all pupils and rates of tuition and that a "Committee of Correspondence" be appointed to seek names of possible candidates for the presidency.[48]

Hoping for a compromise that would keep Williams at the college, Thomas M. Allen persuaded Shannon to support a resolution allowing more generous financial terms. However, it was too late. Williams turned in the accounting demanded by Shannon along with his resignation from the board and as president. In accepting the resignation, trustees produced a short and unenthusiastic resolution of respect for Williams as "a good scholar, an accomplished gentleman, and an able and successful Teacher." When the board met to elect Lansford B. Wilkes as the college's new president, a Shannon-generated resolution required that a president give at least six months' notice before leaving. The board authorized Wilkes to appoint and pay his own faculty but reinstated the requirement that he pay the board the rent of four dollars for each student enrolled.[49]

Shannon refused to allow the controversy to rest. With Williams remaining through commencement, Shannon continued his attempts to collect $548 from fees and requested a list of furniture. Williams answered with the claim that the college owed him $201.56. Shannon then inserted into the board minutes a thirteen-page tirade against Williams, rehashing the whole affair. When Williams asked permission to dispose of the buildings he had erected at his own expense, Shannon replied that Williams had erected them at his own risk and for his own benefit of collecting more tuition. Shannon then proceeded to charge $84.90 for the cost of the lumber, which Williams must pay before he would be authorized to sell the buildings. When Williams left at the end of the session, Allen resigned from the board—and was not acknowledged by the usual resolution of appreciation. Thus, with Shannon's departure from the university and from Columbia later in July, the month saw the exit of three of the college's major figures, Williams, Allen, and Shannon.[50]

Williams went on to a highly successful career. Establishing Daughters College in Kentucky in memory of his two little girls, he remained as its president for forty years while the school flourished. As a trustee of Bacon College, he helped achieve its removal to Lexington, where the college merged with Transylvania University to become Kentucky University.

The bitterness and contention surrounding the Williams administration, although highly inflammatory at the time, had little long-range impact. However, Williams's legacy became an important part of the Christian College heritage. The college benefited in its formative years from the leadership of an educator who determinedly set a solid academic tone for the future. Williams's 1855 baccalaureate address reiterated one of the concepts upon which all friends of the college could agree: "[F]emale influence . . . is the most efficient principle of moral regeneration in the world. Virtue itself . . . derives its lustre and vigor from the moral genius of Woman."[51] The college had opened the doors of opportunity for that female influence.

Williams added his own touch in other ways that have become part of the Christian College tradition. Certainly, the oft-repeated demand that students be taught to think remained an essential part of the college's teaching. Also, the treating of each student as an individual, not to be lumped together in lockstep methods, became an established tenet in the college's mission. Finally, Williams managed to reconcile that age-old dichotomy of the relationship between liberal arts and practical learning, making clear that neither excludes the other and that lifelong learning demands an appreciation and understanding of both. The tone Williams set would provide a worthy challenge for future administrations.

3

The Crucible

LANCEFORD B. WILKES: 1856–1858
JOSEPH KIRTLEY ROGERS: 1858–1877
GEORGE BRYANT: 1877–1883

In times of change and danger when there is a quicksand of fear under men's reasoning, a sense of continuity with generations gone before can stretch like a lifeline across the scary present.

—John Dos Passos

REPORTS OF "uncertainty connected with the future of Christian Female College" began as early as March 1856, with rumors that Dr. C. E. Williams planned to return to Kentucky and that President John Augustus Williams might also leave. An article in the *Missouri State Journal,* while calling the college "probably the best institution of its kind in the whole west," lamented that it "has not yet, however, been put upon that permanent basis which ensures the permanency of the present faculty. It is sustained alone by tuition fees; . . . of its continued support in this way, there is no doubt; but the property is not yet paid for, nor are the buildings completed."[1]

Conditions were, indeed, grim in the summer of 1856. When President Williams left, he took with him most of the college's furniture, more than two hundred of the three hundred books in the Mary Phelps Library, and sixteen students. Also, the Board of Trustees faced an internal upheaval of its own with the departure of Shannon and Allen, and a leadership vacuum loomed large. Henderson, who had tried so hard to move the board to greater action, remained a trustee in name only, directing his efforts to the new university at Canton. William W. Hudson, the original treasurer and loyal friend of both Shannon and Allen, replaced Allen as president of the board on July 3,

1856, only to be named president of the University of Missouri that same month, a role so pressing that he was forced to relinquish his seat as trustee by the next February. With the college thus in disarray, news came that the Baptists across town found the summer of 1856 a propitious time to lay the groundwork for a college of their own, Baptist Female College.[2]

With less than five weeks to find a replacement for Williams, the board turned to Lanceford B. Wilkes, holder of a master's degree from the University of Missouri and associate principal of the college's preparatory school, Palmyra Female Collegiate Institute. Wilkes had served the college as an agent and a trustee and had married Rebecca Bryan, daughter of trustee Lewis Bryan. He brought with him to the college his friend and colleague Joseph Kirtley Rogers. The two had shared student days at the University of Missouri and had traveled together as agents for the college. When Wilkes moved to Palmyra, Rogers opened a Christian Church female academy in St. Joseph. Rogers married Jennifer Robards, of the college's first graduating class, and was to spend the rest of his career at Christian College as a faculty member and as its president from 1858 to 1877.[3]

Despite existing difficulties, the college opened the 1856 session in surprisingly good shape. Wilkes refurnished the college for $3,500 and improved the grounds, leading a reporter to describe the school as "renovated." Although enrollment was down by 40 students, it still stood at 99, comparing well with the 108 students at the University of Missouri. Leadership emerged on the board in the person of Caleb Stone. As secretary of the university board until 1859, Stone had provided the stability needed in the early 1850s, carrying much of the load during Shannon's political and denominational feuds. At Christian College, he was blunt and fearless, offering most of the resolutions and, sometimes, colorful protests. Stone, one of the many leaders who served both institutions simultaneously, looked upon the college as the female counterpart of the University of Missouri. It was he who steered the board through the complex financial dealings in both the Wilkes and the Rogers administrations.[4]

The college's finances in Wilkes's first year centered on the urgent need for completion of the extension at the rear of the Bennett house. By February 1857, trustees appropriated seven thousand dollars, obtaining a loan with trustees as the major subscribers, thus providing funds not only for completion of the extension but also for payment toward the capital debt still owed to James S. Rollins. The board also reinstated the on-again, off-again four-dollar-per-student rent paid by the president. However, four months later, trustees realistically excused Wilkes from that obligation.[5]

As in the past, the board looked to the president to provide needed funds, and, as in the past, the attempt failed; but at least relationships remained genial. When Wilkes declined to increase his assessment, noting that he had no more ability to pay than before, the board resolved that future tuition would be set by the board. The 1857 catalog set tuition at $160, sharply increasing fees for optional studies and announcing that medical expenses would be "defrayed by the parents."[6]

The shortage of funds did not deter the Wilkes administration from making innovations benefiting the intellectual environment of the college. The most significant innovation, the founding of the Martha Washington Institute, proposed to develop student creative writing and public speaking skills. Begun by Rogers and several of his advanced students, the society became a "Department of the College proper," inheriting what books Williams had left. The University of Missouri Literary Society, a club in which both Wilkes and Rogers had been especially active as university students, served as the group's model. The men's society held exhibitions on George Washington's birthday each year, an event attended by Christian College students by special invitation. With the creation of the sister organization at Christian College, the morning program at the university led to an "open meeting" in the evening at Christian College each February 22. The 1857 catalog described weekly exercises as "various, embracing the varieties of Prose and Verse composition, Discussion, oral and written, and . . . arranged with special reference to the development of powers of thought and expression." Membership, open to juniors and seniors, became a prerequisite for graduation from the college, and the institute granted its own diploma. Partly to facilitate the efforts of the Martha Washington Institute, Wilkes proposed the acquisition of a library independent of the private collection of the faculty. The trustees approved a resolution by Wilkes for the creation of a "College Library and Cabinet" through voluntary contributions from the public.[7]

In other changes, Wilkes gave greater emphasis to normal training for those anticipating a teaching career, a move that Williams had greatly desired as president but one that Shannon had firmly blocked at the board level. Also, the addition of a class for small boys formalized the earlier practice of allowing parents and faculty the convenience of sending both sons and daughters to the college's preparatory department. Wilkes, interested in church and community activities, developed a regional reputation as an orator and logician. A famed mediator of church disputes, he made Columbia a "clearinghouse" for Disciples of Christ members by the 1860s. Wilkes loved debate. One prolonged conversation with Moses Lard went on so long by mail that Wilkes invited the church leader to campus, resulting in a six-week stay by Lard and his whole family.[8]

The persistent and prickly problem of the four-dollar fee and the inconsistency of the board's financial demands on the president led to Wilkes's resignation as president on January 28, 1858, effective the next July. To stay longer, Wilkes stated, would be "incompatible with my feelings." The board responded with an appreciative resolution that "we have the highest confidence in the learning, talents, integrity, and moral character of President

L. B. Wilkes, and that, for the untiring energy and industry with which he has administered the affairs of Columbia Female College, he is entitled to the warmest thanks of the Board." Two weeks later, after the board had tried but failed to persuade Wilkes to withdraw his resignation, it expressed its appreciation for the willingness of Wilkes to accept the presidency under such adverse conditions, noting that "the prospects of the institution are now such as to satisfy the wishes of its best friends." In a cordial arrangement, Wilkes remained as a faculty member, teaching ethics, metaphysics, and constitutional law, and joined the board as a valued trustee. His eventual role as a fund-raiser twenty years later proved his greatest contribution to the college.[9]

The college's image had improved greatly since the newspaper notices of March 1856. As early as November 28, 1856, the *Statesman* described Christian College as a "flourishing institution" of about one hundred students. The same article called attention to the Columbia Baptist Female College, which "has entered upon its first session under auspicious circumstances." In a September 4, 1856, article titled "Our Female Schools," the *Statesman* complimented Christian College: "Recently, very large and valuable additions have been made to the college edifice, by the erection of a two-story frame forty feet by sixty. Half of the lower story will be used as a dining room, the balance as rooms for the young ladies. A room forty by fifty, with a sixteen feet ceiling, is fitted up in the upper story for a chapel and for public examinations."[10]

At the February 12, 1857, meeting, the Board of Trustees, at Wilkes's suggestion, elected Joseph Kirtley Rogers as president, effective July 4, 1858. Rogers responded, "I cheerfully accept an honor which introduces me to a field of labor so highly congenial to my inclinations." In an indication of his future relationship with the board, Rogers continued, "I shall earnestly desire and confidently expect the constant and hearty cooperation of every member of the Board in my efforts to promote the interests and secure the prosperity of the Institution, over which it has called me to preside." The board then elected Rogers as a trustee, filling the seat vacated by Thomas M. Allen.[11]

Joseph Kirtley Rogers brought to Christian College the background, skills, and temperament well matched to the needs of the critical period ahead. His Marion County, Missouri, background provided him with the high level of education associated with the utopian venture in Marion City, and he attended the preparatory school at Marion College at the age of seven. From his pioneer boyhood, Rogers acquired a strong utilitarian bent. He had also witnessed the routing of the Marion City utopian abolitionists by northeast Missouri slave interests, and he learned the value of maintaining neutrality in times of turmoil. As a university student, he had thrived on debate and oratory, and he frequently acted as a mediator later in life. Deeply religious, he attended church regularly, rising at four each morning to study the Bible. He heard all the Disciples who came to Columbia to preach, sometimes attending the Christian Church three times on Sunday, going to the Baptist and Unitarian services as well. Eventually, he began to preach on his own in small towns near Columbia. When Thomas M. Allen, recognizing the young man's potential, urged Rogers to become a preacher, Rogers replied, "I will do both—teach when I preach and preach when I teach." Rogers's affable, engaging style made him an immediate social success. His biographer, Christian Church elder O. A. Carr, noted Rogers's "consummate dignity" and regal but unpretentious bearing: "His face invited and endured inspection . . . almost perfect in symmetry, indicating the well-balanced mind. . . . As there was no crookedness in the man, so there was none in his visage." One of the most essential characteristics praised by Carr, Rogers's "indomitable will," served him well in his years at the college.[12]

Although Rogers deplored materialism, family considerations motivated him to seek financial success. When his first school opened in St. Joseph in December 1854, with E. C. Davis as a partner, he made just enough money to marry Jennie Robards, daughter of the mayor of Hannibal. His determination to provide a fine home for his wife and family became a high priority. Declining his father-in-law's offer to build a school if the couple would settle in Hannibal, Rogers set out to prove himself at Christian College. Practical to a fault, he remembered the impracticality that had caused his father to lose a large brick home and 350 acres of land near Palmyra. He succeeded not only in supporting his wife and five surviving children but also in housing his mother, father, and younger brother in a cottage at the east end of the campus. He further succeeded in guiding the college through perils almost unimaginable to the founders of just a decade earlier.[13]

Serious as the college's financial problems had been in the past, Rogers faced the gravest difficulties yet. In an effort to ward off foreclosure in the summer of 1858, eight trustees held deeds of trust totaling $4,500, and the board resolved at its August 6 meeting that the college must collect all funds pledged by subscribers even if it involved suing those who had not paid. To compound their problems and frustrations, trustees found old quarrels returning to haunt them in the person of Dr. C. E. Williams, who sued the board for $1,400. By December, the embattled treasurer of the board, Alexander Douglass (Shannon's son-in-law and a university professor), had resigned. Trustees then turned to Sterling Price Jr., another Shannon supporter from the university faculty, as treasurer.[14]

With finances in a desperate state by the time of the January 12, 1859, board meeting, trustee Bolivar Head read into the minutes that "Christian College is now in debt for a larger amount of money than it can possibly be sold for . . . and will have to be sold in a few years unless adequate means be provided to meet the accruing interest on its debts." Stone made an ardent plea that the statement be withdrawn as contrary to the spirit of the founders, whose intent of permanency should remain sacred, but the will of other board members prevailed. Head sought resolution of the problem by insisting that Rogers pay the board $10 of every $165 tuition and a similar percentage of smaller tuition payments. In addition, Rogers was to pay 10 percent interest on any unpaid tuition at the end of the session. Rogers declined, refusing also a request that he pay rent of $600 a year. By the spring of 1859, trustees decided to search for sixteen citizens, each of whom would pledge $500 to liquidate the college debt.[15]

If 1859 was troubling, 1860 proved no better. The January 14, 1860, board meeting saw David Patterson Henderson "stricken from the list of Christian College trustees by reason of protracted absence." Henderson, the only out-of-state trustee, had moved to Louisville, Kentucky. The board attempted to enlarge its membership, but several of the appointees never acted as trustees, and meetings frequently aborted for lack of a quorum. Matters dragged on. After months of working to settle rents with Wilkes, now a trustee, the board finally exonerated him from any liability. Still trying in April to settle with Douglass for his period as board treasurer, trustees finally charged him $169.00. Douglass replied that the board owed him $665.35. The matter remained unresolved when, on August 4, 1860, Sterling Price Jr. resigned as Douglass's replacement. The board then named Jerry S. Dorsey as its new treasurer, appointing him to the board on August 17, 1860. A splendid choice, Dorsey served the college devotedly as treasurer until 1898. As a stopgap measure, local trustees held deeds of trust against real and personal property of the board, payable on January 1, 1861, after which time the college property would be subject to sale. Thomas M. Allen, no longer a trustee, reflected on the deepening troubles in the period before the Civil War and on how they affected not only the college but the entire Columbia area: "Times are truly tight here—money scarce—confidence destroyed—many pecuniarily ruined—no sale for anything and all at a standstill but seeking politicians—Oh, the darkness that covers the future."[16]

Local board members became the strength of the college. Judge David Gordon remained as president of the board from 1856, when he replaced Allen, until his death in 1875. Robert Lemon's thirty-year tenure also provided leadership, and other new local trustees included Walter T. Lenoir, John Machir, and Jesse Boulton. Two other loyal trustees, Moses Lard and Lanceford B. Wilkes, engaged in strenuous fund-raising and collected enough subscriptions to cover the mortgage payment. Trustees called in the liens, whose payment was due in January 1861, and transferred them as one lien to Dr. J. G. Jacobs, thus gaining another year to pay. The juggling of these debts through the war years kept the college afloat as a series of benefactors stepped up to take responsibility for the debt with liens going from Jacobs to Lenoir and then to Dorsey.[17]

Rogers's good business practices and responsible relations with the board saved the day for the college. A meticulous record keeper, he itemized personally every cash expenditure and carefully accounted for any amount the board owed him. He paid his rents to the board promptly and expected and received equally swift reimbursement of his expenses. When the first annual accounting showed that the board owed him $61 more than he owed them, trustees paid, despite the $8,000 debt, appreciative of being assured of fair and accurate accounting. Rogers consistently made the board pay its own way, submitting such items as $3.50 for moving a fence and $35.00 for blinds he left in his office at retirement. He kept the same careful accounts with the faculty, balancing costs for boarding family members and for educating faculty children so that little money actually changed hands.[18]

An accumulation of small economies kept the college running. Realizing that nearly half of the students studied music, paying fees that required no rebate to the board, Rogers raised the fee for music from $40 to $50, adding also a slight fee for penmanship and for singing in the choir. Tuition carried a penalty of 10 percent interest if not paid by the time classes started. No account was too small to collect, including those for shoestrings, ink, use of the library, pencils, and stamps. Terse notes to parents demanded payment, suggesting such alternatives as lending a slave to the college or sending fuel from wood lots or hams from smokehouses. While President Rogers kept the accounts, his wife, Jennie, as assistant matron, kept the household operating. She trained and supervised the servants, kept weekly laundry lists for the whole college, and saw to it that clothing was properly mended.[19]

Underlying Rogers's careful bookkeeping was a deep belief in the need to preserve advances in women's education, a cause making any sacrifice worthwhile. The 1858–1859 catalog elaborated on the pleas of previous presidents to educate daughters as well as sons. Referring to the university and Christian College as "co-ordinate Departments of a grand System of AMERICAN EDUCATION," Rogers deemed it "but just that while the intellectual wants of the Son had been fully provided for by the erection and endowment of our State University, some similar program should be made for the Daughter." He saw the daughter as "possessed of equal mental capacity, more resplendent virtues, and superior graces of person" than the son, and he considered the idea "that it is unnecessary to educate the female . . . a relic of the dark ages, unworthy of Republican America."[20]

Rogers's genuine respect for women emerged throughout his writings. A letter to his son included advice on the subject:

> It will be to your advantage to spend your leisure evenings . . . in the company of high-toned, intellectual young ladies; not in dancing or levity, but largely in animated, earnest conversation about persons and things, . . . things honorable, pure, and good. The young ladies ought to be fully your equals,

> in intelligence and general information, all the better if they are your superiors. . . . By all means, my son, cultivate a high regard for woman. . . . She is not perfect, she has her frailties, but she is, as a rule, a long ways better than man, purer in her thoughts, more disinterested and self-sacrificing in her life.

Rogers concluded, "Shun bad women as you would shun death and hell. Their breath is putrid, their association is leprous, and their embrace is death. . . . Whiskey and bad women have been the ruin of three out of five of our young men."[21]

The 1858–1859 catalog revealed much about the early Rogers years. He lectured parents, warning them that no "merely commercial transaction," the payment of tuition, could ever replace their obligation to be active partners in their daughters' education; monthly reports to parents should be regarded as letters from Christian College requiring answers to the college or to the daughters. With a renewed emphasis on physical education, the catalog recognized "the dependence of the mind upon the body. . . . No constitution, however robust, can long remain unimpaired, that finds not constantly new life and vigor in healthful exercise."[22]

New in the 1858–1859 catalog, the "Aurora" became a literary society for freshmen and sophomores. Members then progressed to the Martha Washington Institute for their junior and senior years. The two societies together encouraged "free untrammeled conflict of mind with mind." Graduates of the societies organized a "Literary Association" that held sessions in the chapel each year during commencement week, becoming the first alumnae group of the college.[23]

Rogers remained true to Williams's concept of education: "It is our aim, as far as practicable, to make the Course of Study and the mode of treatment a specialty for each individual case. Accordingly, our first work in the reception of a pupil, is to ascertain her age, health, previous culture, and mental aptitudes, and to select her studies, in nature and number, with special references to these peculiarities."[24]

Gathering an experienced faculty, Rogers released novices hastily hired by Wilkes. Wilkes stayed on at the college as professor of philosophy and constitutional law, while Rogers taught literature and botany. Professor William Alexander of the University of Missouri still taught drawing, painting, and guitar. Professor William Pinckney Hurt, in mathematics, brought experience, while Frederick Pannell, an Englishman, gave great distinction to the music department. Rogers hired a husband-and-wife team, John D. Dawson, who taught history and elocution, and Mary Jane Dawson, who served as principal matron, a position she had earlier held as superintendent of the Female Orphan School at Midway, Kentucky.[25]

By October 1859, the extension to the Bennett house was completed and ready for inspection by trustees. The building committee reportedly "found the edifice to be in a good state. . . . The number of pupils is already equal to that of the last session and the prospects for an increase are flattering. . . . [T]his school has been and is well sustained by public patronage during a period of unexampled embarrassment throughout the country in financial matters." The report concluded that conditions were "mainly if not entirely owing to the successful efforts of the President . . . and the prompt and faithful discharge of every duty incumbent upon each officer in the Institution."[26]

Such sanguine thoughts would soon be a thing of the past. As William Switzler wrote in his *History of Boone County,* "the school had just arrived at a happy and prosperous period when the Civil War broke out." And break out it did in Boone County, a divided county in the middle of a divided state. A secessionist meeting held on April 20, 1861, greeted the sight of the Confederate flag with thunderous applause and gave three cheers for Jefferson Davis. The crowd urged the reconvening of a recently held state convention to vote for "the immediate withdrawal of Missouri from the federal compact." A more moderate, strongly pro-union meeting of May 6 heard speeches by James S. Rollins, Odon Guitar, and Thomas M. Allen, condemning extremists on both sides and urging neutrality.[27]

By June 1861, local demonstrations had become so violent that the college ended its session with only one day of commencement activities. Rogers bid good-bye to the faculty for the summer with the warning that he could promise no pay for the next session but that he would share a percentage of whatever was left from tuition. Most would return, and Rogers made clear his own position that "continuance of the School is a certainty. Nothing . . . shall drive us from our posts." He concluded: "The hope of America is with the future; the present is lost, irretrievably lost." Rogers maintained a course of strict neutrality, refusing to mention the war even in his diary, proclaiming, "I would rather die than see Christian College go down."[28]

The board's attention in 1861 and 1862 focused on passing the debt responsibility from one benefactor to another. As of March 1861, those holding notes (for a total of $5,192.23) were Alexander Douglass, Caleb Stone, David Gordon, Robert Lemon, Walter T. Lenoir, Lanceford B. Wilkes, and Bolivar S. Head. On February 6, 1861, the board had "executed the note of the Board" to Dr. J. G. Jacobs for the same amount, due in twelve months with 10 percent interest. Recognizing the tight finances faced by Rogers, the board released him from his fees, requiring him to pay only the taxes due. The next February, the board paid what it could toward the debt owed to Jacobs, meeting throughout the spring of 1862 to discuss, but not resolve, the financial problems.[29]

If Christian College faced wartime difficulties, the University of Missouri suffered infinitely greater indignities. Union troops (a portion of Col. Lewis Merrill's mounted regiment, Merrill's Horse) were quartered on the university campus beginning in January 1862. When university curators met on March 19, 1862, they found fifty students, only thirty-six of whom were of college grade, and declared that "the use of the university building as a barracks made classes nearly impossible." By late March, the Board of Curators had closed the university "because of financial difficulties and a shortage of students." The *Statesman* reported: "The university is now in debt to the President, Professors, and Tutors of it, in the sum of $7,000, and without the means to pay it or any part of it." Although the university reopened "in partial fashion" in November 1862, the next five years continued to be a desperate struggle for survival. Misfortune for the university, however, represented opportunity for Christian College; President Rogers bought the desks of the University Literary Society at a bargain price.[30]

Physical as well as financial dangers threatened the college and the whole of Boone County as the war progressed. Pro-Southern recruits, under the leadership of Boone County sheriff John M. Samuel, formed a company, the "Columbia Greys," which suffered defeat in the Battle of Boonville in June 1861. By October, a regiment composed largely of these and other Boone Countians became part of Gen. Sterling Price's pro-Southern state troops stationed southwest of Sedalia. Since northern Missouri served as a major source of recruits for Price's state troops, Columbia and the college were very much in the line of travel for recruiting activities and guerrilla warfare directed from the southwest. Sabotage of railroad bridges and telegraph wires, along with other activities behind Federal lines, made central Missouri dangerous territory.

Gen. Benjamin Prentiss, commander of Union forces in central Missouri with headquarters in Jefferson City, visited Columbia on November 13–15, 1861, with a show of force. He indicated that he had tried to keep Federal forces out of Columbia and was eager to protect the rights of all, including secessionists, and deplored the rising tide of "marauding bands of rebels" who plundered property and threatened Union men with exile, arson, and assassination. Prentiss warned that if the lawlessness continued, he would quarter a regiment on the university campus. It was as a result of these continued clashes that Merrill's Horse took up its quarters at the university in January 1862.[31]

Another result of pro-Southern activities in Missouri was the requirement enacted by the state convention in October 1861 that all officers of government take an oath of loyalty "To support the Constitution of the United States and this state, not to take up arms against the Government of the United States, nor the Provisional Government of this State, nor give aid and comfort to the enemies of either during the present civil war." A number of prominent citizens failed to take this oath and were banished to the North. City of Columbia trustees, accused of pro-Southern sympathies, were thrown out of office on April 19, 1862, and were forbidden to exercise any of the functions of their office. Christian College would soon be affected by this same provision.[32]

Security remained a problem in Boone County throughout the war, making it difficult for Christian College students to travel to and from the college. With rural areas decidedly pro-Southern, justices of the peace remained in virtually 100 percent noncompliance with the required oath, balancing the loss of prestige and fees if they refused the oath against the probable loss of their lives if they complied. Columbians constantly feared a possible raid by guerrilla leader Bill Anderson, who pillaged nearby Huntsville on July 15, 1864, and killed more than one hundred Federal soldiers in Centralia on September 27, 1864, in the "Centralia massacre." Fearing that Price's army would move in, Columbia took on the look of a fortified town. A home guard, the "Columbia Tigers," built and occupied a log blockhouse in the middle of the intersection of Eighth and Broadway Streets in downtown Columbia. Merchants boarded up their storefronts, and R. B. Price, of Boone County National Bank, buried a major part of the bank's notes and gold in the countryside. Even the courthouse was barricaded.[33]

A guerrilla raid on August 12, 1862, posed the most serious threat to Christian College. Some seventy pro-Southern horsemen stormed the Columbia jail and released three prisoners, apparently the object of the raid. While in Columbia, "squads of them, some intoxicated, were ranging up and down the street, swearing, and hallooing at a terrible rate," while others dragged the American flag through the dust. Merrill accused Columbians of having let the horsemen know that no sentries were posted, and he threatened to burn the town and the colleges. At that point, Robert L. Todd, a first cousin of Mary Todd Lincoln, whom Abraham Lincoln had allegedly visited in Columbia during his courtship of her, took Merrill to task. According to the memoirs of Robert Todd's nephew, North Todd Gentry, Todd blamed Merrill for not having posted guards on the roads into Columbia and threatened Merrill: "Now, sir, if you set fire to our town, our university, and our schools, our friends will kindle a fire under you, and I tremble for you at the consequences." When Merrill threatened to close the two colleges, Todd allegedly reported the matter to Mary Todd Lincoln and received a letter from President Lincoln promising that he would not allow the colleges to be closed. North Todd Gentry's memoirs included a statement supporting the authenticity of the letter.[34]

Female education in Columbia had already been affected the previous February when Merrill had closed the Baptist Female College for three days. Interviewed in Columbia on her ninetieth birthday in 1941, Ida Jane Robinson Branham described that event: "My sister and I were perched atop a wooden fence that enclosed the college grounds when Merrill's Horse passed along Broadway. 'Mag' let out a rebel yell at them and waved a little black apron she had borrowed from her teacher. . . . The result was the college was closed for three days, because my sister had given vent to a blood-curdling yell."[35]

Christian College experienced its most serious problems in the 1862–1863 session. With an enrollment of fifty-six, the lowest since the founding of the college, only three students were graduated in 1862 and four in 1863. Commencements continued, but the college charged a door fee.

An extraordinary crisis occurred when trustees lost legal authority to conduct business throughout most of 1863 and into early 1864. A special section labeled "Reorganization" appeared in the February 8, 1864, minutes:

> That what follows may be understood, it is proper to remark that owing to failure, through oversight, of the Members of the Board (Mr. Machir excepted) to subscribe and file a certain oath, prescribed by the Legislature of 1862–3, by the 1st day of April, 1863, the board was induced incompetent to do business. To remove this difficulty, the Legislature of 1863–4, at the instance of Judge James Gordon, passed [an] Act, empowering the Board to organize by subscribing and filing the oath above named. Said Act and oaths are on record in the County Clerk's Office.[36]

The reauthorized trustees quickly reinstated Gordon as president of the board, naming Jesse A. Boulton as vice president, Rogers as secretary, and Dorsey as treasurer. With the college about $6,300 in debt, trustees moved to notify subscribers to pay within thirty days or be sued by the college. When the treasurer later reported little progress in collecting funds, trustees rescinded the action. They then requested that Wilkes, living in Hannibal, come to Columbia to spend six days fund-raising, but no action resulted. Trying a new device, trustees asked "the lady," Mrs. Rogers, to host a festival just before the July commencement, charging a door fee of one dollar for adults and fifty cents for children. The success of the event led to the regular use of other such fund-raisers.[37]

Despite financial crises, collegiate activities continued, although in a somewhat altered style. If Christian College students had led a sheltered life under normal circumstances, they were truly isolated during the war years. Allowed off campus only for Sunday services down the street at the Christian Church, they walked in a line, two by two, with Rogers heading the procession and faculty members holding down the flanks. On campus, concerts provided periodic entertainment, as well as some profit for the college, and the literary society meetings filled Friday afternoons and evenings. In the late afternoons and evenings, students could enjoy the freedom of the campus grounds, but even they reflected the tight finances. Potato plants lined the walks, and the gardens and orchards made the college nearly self-sufficient in food. An extremely limited social life allowed young men to be admitted to the parlor only about once each six weeks, and students welcomed the fund-raising fairs and festivals as rare opportunities to practice social skills. A group of Columbia women gained board approval to produce a series of "tableaus" in the chapel in 1864, a daring departure from tradition—Rogers had considered any theatrical production sinful, as living a lie.[38]

Daily life, described in a letter by Lizzie Brown of the class of 1865, included few frills and some hardships. Every evening but Saturday, students studied in the chapel until "Mr. Rogers would call the roll for each room and the 'Bell sheep' would take her lighted candle from the table and lead the way, all the girls following in perfect order. . . . We were supposed to be in bed by nine o'clock." Students began their day at five, sometimes by breaking the ice in the washbasins. Mornings began with a walk and a one-hour study period, breakfast, and chapel. Morning classes ran from 8:15 to 12:15 with afternoon classes from 2:00 to 4:00. Catalogs revealed no change in the demanding course requirements. If cuts were made, they were in the "ornamental" studies. Mary Louisa Caldwell wrote in her diary: "Oh how steep and arduous is the hill of knowledge."[39]

Try as he might, Rogers could never enforce a strict neutrality and isolation, and the effects of the war touched the campus from time to time. Family misfortunes sometimes forced students to withdraw from the college, and even Jennie Rogers violated the neutrality order when she loaded a wagon with blankets for pro-Southern forces, an act causing considerable embarrassment when the wagon was captured. On another occasion, Rogers's brother-in-law, Dr. Lynn Banks, had come to dine, only to be called away by a servant announcing the approach of Federal troops. Banks, first fleeing to the nearby woods, surrendered to the forces and took the oath, but he was imprisoned nonetheless, becoming the first prisoner of Union forces in Columbia. In another instance, trustee and board treasurer Jerry Dorsey "talked too much" and was temporarily banished from Columbia.[40]

The strain of the war years on Rogers showed in his diary entry blaming himself for being "harsh and refractory," sometimes disposed to "acerbity and crossness towards all around." He made a New Year's resolution "to do no scolding, . . . but after having borne with derelictions as long as my judgment says is proper, then without railing, or noisy or passionate demonstrations, to adopt the necessary remedy. The Lord help me."[41]

The college's fortunes changed for the better as the war ended. The fall of 1865 saw the biggest enrollment in the college's history with 182 students and a faculty of 9. The university at this time reported 69 students and 5 faculty members. Rogers, clearly in control of the reorganized board, offered to ease the financial burden by renting the college, an offer the board readily accepted, leasing the college for four years at $600 per year. Rogers also agreed to use income from concerts and festivals to pay the annual interest on the debt plus 5 percent of the principal. Through the vigorous efforts of its agents, the college managed by June 30, 1866, to pay all but $161.40 of its debt to Dr. Lenoir.[42]

By the late 1860s, the financial picture had improved enough to allow trustees to add new wings to the main building at an anticipated cost of $10,000-$15,000. Again, the question of funding arose, and Rogers demonstrated remarkable generosity and devotion to the college by agreeing to double the previous rent, releasing the board from paying a $1,600 debt owed him, and donating $1,000 to the building fund. In 1870, when the board decided to raise money by selling lots at the north end of the campus for $2,550 each, Rogers bought one. When the wings were finished in 1872, Rogers assumed the debt of $8,000. The college also benefited from an arrangement with the Exchange National Bank by which its account could be overdrawn up to $2,500. For the first time, a bank agreed to assume any of the college debt. The arrangement reflected the institution's greater community standing. It also meant that the bank could not afford to see the college fail.[43]

A notable event marking the end of the founding era took place with the death of Thomas M. Allen, who had left the Shannon-controlled board in 1856 when Williams resigned, departing without any resolution of appreciation. Welcomed back to the board on August 31, 1865, Allen's value to the college and the community continued unabated until his death on October 10, 1871. A heartfelt resolution honored Allen: "This board has lost one of its most highly esteemed, influential, and valuable members and Christian College one of its earliest, most steadfast, and liberal friends. . . . We recognize in him the highest type of Christian gentlemen. Ever amiable in spirit, courteous in bearing, foremost in liberality, and zealous in every good work, he endeared himself to all who know him, and in his death humanity has lot a benefactor."[44]

Allen's funeral illustrated the continuity of the college. With President Rogers preaching the sermon and elder David Patterson Henderson returning for the occasion, Allen was laid to rest near James Shannon and William W. Hudson. As Allen's death marked closure of the era, the addition of Col. William Switzler to the board symbolized the beginning of a new era. Switzler, once hostile to the college, began publishing student compositions, influenced, perhaps, by Rogers's diplomacy and by his sister-in-law's attendance at the college. With socially prominent James S. Rollins sending his daughter to Christian College and President Rogers a curator on the university board, Christian College had arrived socially as well as academically.[45]

Rogers and Rollins joined forces in their promotion of one remarkable Christian College student, the former by bringing her to the college and the latter by greatly enhancing her career opportunities and becoming a lifelong friend. That student, Vinnie Ream, entered the college in 1857 and achieved fame by the 1870s, playing a significant artistic and political role in Washington, D.C., during the Civil War and Reconstruction eras. Her fame rested primarily on her work as sculptor of the Lincoln statue in Statuary Hall of the United States Capitol, but she accumulated other remarkable "firsts." She became the first woman and the youngest artist ever to receive a U.S. government commission for a statue. With her statue of Admiral Farragut, she created Washington's first major monument to a naval officer, and, as the sculptor of Sequoia, she designed the first freestanding statue of a Native American to be placed in the United States Capitol. An acquaintance of five presidents, she allowed her studio in the Capitol to serve as a gathering place for government and private citizens, more than eighty of whom became her subjects.[46]

Ream's early years revealed her as a child of nature, a style she never wholly abandoned. Reportedly born on September 25, 1847, in Madison, Wisconsin, then a town of 632 inhabitants, Lavinia Ellen Ream played with Winnebago children but easily socialized with all manner and ages of individuals. Her father, Robert, a surveyor and cartographer, may have had the first house in Madison. He operated his home as Madison House, a stage-line terminus that became a social gathering place and a center for Democratic politics. In the 1850s, the family became acquainted with James S. Rollins, who traveled in Kansas as a land lawyer. He may have encouraged the family to send Vinnie to J. K. Rogers's school in St. Joseph when Robert Ream was stationed at Fort Leavenworth. Vinnie then went on to Christian College when Rogers took a faculty position in the Wilkes administration. O. A. Carr, writing in 1883, claimed, "Vinnie Ream owes her celebrity to the inspiration and generosity of President Rogers" who may have sponsored her financially.[47]

Ream began writing poetry in 1857, about the time she entered Christian College. One of her earliest products, "Hard Times," referring to the financial panic of the 1850s, explored the paradox of society's putting women in the role of pleasing men but then blaming them for causing men problems with gambling and an expensive lifestyle. The poem appeared in the *Statesman* on December 25, 1857, raising the question of whether an eleven-year-old student could have written such a poem. Ream's other compositions showed progressively greater artistic development as well as sensitivity to nature and to the importance of human ties among family and friends, as seen in "My Kansas Home" and in her farewell poem in 1858 to her roommate, Mary Persinger. "Heart Longings" reflected such adult themes as concern for nature and freedom for living creatures, religious self-denial, and the transitory nature of fame. Ream, writing songs as well as poems, created the school anthem and studied piano, guitar, and voice. As a student of William Alexander, she painted an oil portrait of Martha Washington for the literary society. She seemingly could have excelled in any of these fields, and the quality of her work caused doubt concerning the validity of the birth date of 1847, including the possibility that her mother may have falsified her age.

Rogers's acquaintance with her ability may have earned her special ranking as an upperclassman in the college despite her age. The census of 1850 listed her as nine years old, the census of 1880 put her age as twenty-eight, and the 1890 census recorded it at fifty-two, thus providing conflicting evidence of her true birth date. Ream's death certificate of November 1914 gave her age as sixty-seven, supporting the 1847 date of birth, the date used by Ream's biographer, Glenn Sherwood, and by her husband, Richard L. Hoxie.[48]

Ream's ties to Columbia continued when she studied at home in Washington by mail, guided by President Rogers. Her father had taken a position in Washington in 1861, and Ream became a postal clerk with the help of James S. Rollins, who wrote the postmaster general, Montgomery Blair, on her behalf. She became one of the first few women hired by the post office and upon taking the position in November 1862 affirmed that she was more than sixteen years old.[49]

Rollins, a congressman from 1861 to 1865, met Ream again in Washington and took her to the studio of Clark Mills at the Capitol to have a sculpture made of her for the Christian College library. This event changed Ream's life. Mills made her a student helper, and she eventually resigned her post office job to work as a full-time sculptor, with such notables as Rollins, Frank P. Blair of Missouri, and Ulysses S. Grant as clients. Powerful political figures gathered at the Mills studio, and Ream thought more and more about the challenge of modeling President Lincoln. Rollins and other friends recommended her to Lincoln, and Ream began going to the White House in her free time, waiting in the hallway for Lincoln to go by. He finally stopped to talk to her, and, remembering the requests, allowed her to come to his study next to the Oval Office during his rest periods. This arrangement continued for several months in 1864 and 1865, ending shortly before Lincoln's assassination on April 14, 1865. Ream shared her personal recollections of the experience in an interview much later in her life:

> At sixteen I was mature enough to grasp very well the character of the man. . . . I came for half an hour every day. I was the merest slip of a child, weighing less than ninety pounds, and the contrast between the raw-boned man and me was indeed great. . . . It seemed that he used this half hour as a time for relaxation, for he always left instructions that no one was to be admitted during that time. . . . He seemed to find a strange sort of companionship in being with me, although we talked but little. His favorite son, Willie, had just died, and . . . I made him think of Willie.[50]

Ream had nearly finished the bust when Lincoln was assassinated, and only she had been allowed to model Lincoln. As the House of Representatives began considering the commissioning of a statue of Lincoln, Ream sought support for the commission by submitting her bust of Lincoln as a specimen of her work. She testified before the selection committee, and Rep. Thaddeus Stevens sponsored a resolution to give her the commission, obtaining 178 signatures of major military and political officials, including President Andrew Johnson. Ream, still a teenager, won the commission, signing the contract on August 30, 1866. As politicians haggled over the payment of the commission of ten thousand dollars, the resentful East Coast "Boston School" of art launched a viciously negative campaign against Ream, charging that she did not do her own work, as it would require a "masculine grasp." Charges of "humbug," meaning deception, followed her for years, in spite of numerous public demonstrations of her talent.[51]

Ream's studio in the Capitol became a fashionable Washington attraction. When she allowed public display of the unfinished model, a varied list of notables came to examine her work, including Mathew Brady; Thomas Nast; Walt Whitman; Generals McClellan, Sheridan, Sherman, and Grant; Admiral Farragut; and the Supreme Court justices "as a body." Visitors included a long series of "smitten swains," and marriage proposals came even by mail. The *St. Louis Democrat* commented, "Little Ream is the Venus Victrix—She has met the enemy and they are hers."[52]

Such notoriety had its negative side in the form of attacks on Ream's art and lifestyle. She was charged with "decorating her studio with flowers, wearing long hair, attracting the men and thereby lobbying." Her detractors concluded the worst: "No girl can keep chaste and pure with three hundred wretched men around her." Through it all, Rollins remained her faithful friend, writing her a long farewell letter in March 1873 when he left Washington, encouraging her not to give up her work. George Caleb Bingham, who visited Ream's studio at Rollins's suggestion, painted a magnificent portrait of her, and she did a bust of him. This time, it was Ream who professed love, but Bingham, lamenting that he was not "20–30 years younger," gently rejected her.[53]

Much remained to be done on the Lincoln statue even after Ream completed the model, and the unveiling did not take place until 1871. Once a plaster model was made in New York, it was shipped to Italy for the work to be completed in marble. Ream left New York in June 1869, studying and visiting in London, Munich, and Florence before her arrival in Rome. She put the plaster model on exhibition in her Rome studio, attracting more than five hundred visitors, again including numerous suitors. Ream finally left Rome with the completed statue in October 1870, and, once the statue was in place in the Capitol Rotunda, she administered the finishing touches while hidden in a tentlike covering. The formal unveiling took place on January 25, 1871, to the applause of a distinguished audience.[54]

Attacks on Ream came for political as well as artistic reasons. Because her Capitol studio served as a gathering place for politicians, she had ample opportunity to use her influence to affect congressional votes. She was therefore in a position to influence the vote in the Senate when President Johnson was tried on impeachment charges.

Johnson, like Lincoln, took the position that southern states had never left the Union and thus retained their rights as states. This position created a serious split between Johnson and his fellow Republicans, the Radical Reconstructionists, who maintained that the South had relinquished all constitutional rights. When Johnson deliberately violated the Tenure of Office Act of 1867, which provided that the president could not remove any appointees whose position had required Senate approval unless the Senate agreed, the new, more radical Fortieth House of Representatives impeached him by a vote of 126 to 47. The impeachment trial began in the Senate on March 5, 1868, with Chief Justice Chase presiding.

With all twelve Democrats favoring acquittal, the Radical Republicans could lose no more than six Republican votes and still convict Johnson. The unknown factor, Republican Edmund G. Ross of Kansas, had recently arrived to fill the seat of James Lane, a suicide, with the intent that he support the Radical agenda. The Ross family, who had known the Ream family in Kansas, boarded with the Reams while finding a Washington home. Radicals, knowing Ream's sympathy toward the president, accused her of trying to sway Ross. Nonetheless, Radicals were confident of victory. The president pro tempore of the Senate, Ben Wade of Ohio, next in line for the presidency after Johnson, had already begun to select his cabinet. When Ross cast the deciding vote for acquittal, Radicals rose up in fury at both Ross and Ream. Ross later wrote, "The condition of the public mind was not unlike that preceding a great battle. Hope and fear seemed blended on every face. It was a tremendous responsibility. . . . I almost literally looked down into my open grave." House managers tried to evict Ream from her Capitol studio, but the lengthy debate about the move caused a storm of ridicule in the press. Thaddeus Stevens, slowly dying, came to her defense, preventing the eviction. Later in life, Ream stated that she had never discussed the vote with Ross and did not know how he would vote. "I was in no way responsible for his vote—of this I am certain from my knowledge of his character."[55]

The success illustrated in Ream's career coincided with increased success for Christian College. Difficult as the war years had been, the college had gained a reputation as a good place for young women to be. The *Glasgow (Mo.) Journal* of June 14, 1872, praised the college: "This school . . . has the just reputation of being one of the best schools in the United States." Conservative by nature, Rogers used a status quo policy to try to provide stability. Also, the student body grew and became more geographically diverse. Before the war, students had come mostly from river ports and county seats in Missouri and from such southern states as Kentucky, Louisiana, Texas, Arkansas, and Mississippi. The new influx from the North after the war brought students from Illinois, Kansas, Indiana, and Colorado. By the 1880s, families in New Mexico, Oregon, California, and Nebraska were sending their daughters "back east" to Christian College.[56]

With the war over, the college enjoyed a more lighthearted environment. The student social circle included a university student, Eugene Field of St. Louis, known as a cutup, who eventually became a well-known writer of children's poetry. Credited with establishing serenading at the college, Field visited Columbia years later and went to sing at the college "for old times' sake." In June 1871, he established a literary magazine at the university, the *University Missourian*. Legend attributes to Field the writing of a locally famous poem of the day, celebrating the prescribed Christian College "enormous green bonnets, with ribbons of blue."[57]

Campus facilities, described in the 1871 catalog after an expenditure of twenty thousand dollars, also suggested better times. The two wings had finally been added to the main building, each three stories above the basement, providing thirty-four new rooms for student boarders. The catalog illustration, showing a third-floor addition to the main building, was misleading, however, as that portion was still only projected. The main building finally gained a portico across the front, an addition Williams had ardently supported in 1851. On the back, a brick kitchen was added to the dining room, and rooms were provided to house Mrs. Rogers's widowed sister and her two sons. However, even these additions did not take care of crowded conditions. Rogers still used his study as a classroom, and Professor Hurt taught in the chapel while other students used it as a study hall. The cottages held the preparatory school and some faculty housing. In the new wings, some ninety to one hundred students shared space with the Rogers and Hurt families and other faculty. Even the campus pond was useful, providing a location for baptisms.[58]

With no significant curricular changes, Rogers considered the quality of the faculty his major intellectual contribution, and he led an exceptional group of individuals. Pinckney Hurt taught under the first five presidents, and Rogers made him a partner in 1870. Hurt had taught higher mathematics and sciences, and he and his wife sometimes served as domestic faculty, training students in housekeeping. In music, Frederick Pannell provided twenty years of leadership with his excellent training and fame as a composer. His contributions extended into the community, where he led the civic band and served the Christian Church. His popularity resulted in the naming of Pannell Street in his honor. While Pannell taught voice, John Prosinger taught instrumental music for ten years. Joseph Ficklin, a mathematical prodigy, gained recognition in the United States and Europe for his scholarship. With a doctorate from the University of Wisconsin, he served as a trustee and as a faculty member. In science, Dr. Andrew Walker McAlester, founder of the University of Missouri Medical School, lectured in anatomy and physiology. This tradition of sharing faculty with the university continued when Dr. Woodson Moss of the university followed McAlester as lecturer.[59]

Caroline Neville Pearre, one of the most outstanding faculty members, had taught for John Augustus Williams in Kentucky and at Christian College. She married the father of Henrietta Pearre, a Christian College student, and, in 1875, Rogers rehired her as Mrs. Pearre. She had defied tradition in 1874 by addressing a convention of men, urging support for foreign missions. A successful advocate for her cause, she went on to found the Christian Woman's Board of Missions. Her stepdaughter, Henrietta, joined the faculty upon graduation in 1875, continuing the tradition of a strong faculty in literature. Henrietta married the son of former president and trustee Lanceford Wilkes, and Henrietta's daughter, Cynthia Wilkes McHarg, taught the classics, carrying on the family tradition of excellence. Caroline Neville Pearre's sister, Virginia Neville, served as a faculty member from 1866 to 1874, teaching literature, history, and some sciences. Proud of his faculty, Rogers praised them in his retirement address to the board in 1877: "I cannot close . . . without calling to your attention the teachers who have been my collaborators. Whatever success has attended my administration is due largely to their ability and faithfulness."[60]

The star of the faculty, George Bryant, came to the college in 1872, teaching philosophy and history. A true scholar and master teacher, his importance went beyond well-taught subject matter to the impact he had on students, many of whom considered him to have greatly influenced their lives. As Rogers's health declined in the 1870s, it became obvious that Bryant would follow him. Bryant became a partner with Rogers and Hurt and would provide a vital service to the college by continuing Rogers's policies in a period of transition.

The real star of the college family remained Rogers himself, and his claim to the leading role was never in doubt. O. A. Carr wrote, "The all-pervading, all-controlling spirit in the college building, from cellar to garret, was J. K. Rogers, President. His idea was there must be one mind to give tone and direction to everything, and that mind was his." He trusted department heads to do their work and set clear rules for the students, who had "freedom to do as you please, if you please to do right." According to Emma Baldwin of Butte City, Montana,

> [L]ife at Christian College was one of almost perfect happiness. Blest with the best of teachers, the kindliest interest shown to each of us by President Rogers, and un-looked-for kindness extended to us by his wife—one of the noblest of women—how could life be otherwise than happy? . . . I cannot recall one harsh word ever spoken of President Rogers by any one. Every member of our class looked upon him as a man above reproach, one of the noblest men of any time.[61]

Rogers's popularity endured in spite of, or perhaps because of, his firm discipline. Rules were clear and fair, but rigid. He demanded that day students keep the same evening hours as board students, and he believed so strongly about the evil of dancing that he visited an alumna to reprimand her for attending dances. Never one to squander time, he decided to cancel Christmas vacation, and the 1875 catalog gave as his rationale that the Christmas holiday "with its attendant dissipation" seriously interrupted the work of the college, causing "considerable expense, diversion of mind, and frequent exposure in cold weather." He therefore "concluded to abolish it" from the school calendar except for Christmas and New Year's Day as holidays.[62]

As a result of Rogers's reputation for fairness and diplomacy, he frequently mediated disputes and chaired meetings, and he earned recognition as a financier, educator, and disciplinarian. His careful habits had brought him personal wealth, and he mingled with social leaders, helping to alleviate old tensions and reconcile old splits. With scores of friends, he was much in demand to conduct weddings. His fees ran from two dollars to one hundred, and he kept notes on marriage services. He wrote of a two-dollar wedding: "Where little is given, little will be required." When one couple paid with four bushels of corn, he called them "both young and green."[63]

Not all of Rogers's public duties reflected such humor. As he conducted funeral services more and more frequently, and, as his own health problems increased, he dwelled increasingly on the morbid aspects of life and death. Common themes repeated throughout his sermons included: life is short and uncertain; its joys are unsatisfactory and unenduring; death is certain and judgment is certain; and the business of life is to prepare for death.[64]

Rogers experienced poor health during the last five years of his presidency, and his resignation in 1877 resulted entirely from his deteriorating condition. Illness, diagnosed as "congestion of the liver," had confined him to bed for five weeks in the fall and winter of 1872, and he sent a letter of resignation to the board in February 1873. A committee of the board called on him, refusing to accept his letter, and convinced him to take a leave of absence. He recovered only by spending four weeks during the summer of 1873 in Colorado. A committee of the board went to Rogers in April 1875 "to use every argument in their power" to induce him to remain as president. Finally, by the spring of 1877, he knew that he must retire. "It almost broke his heart to leave," wrote Carr.[65]

Rogers's last words to the board typically expressed his deep concern for the college and its financial future: "My heart's desire . . . for years, has been to see the College endowed in such a sum as would place it beyond the contingencies which necessarily attach to unendowed institutions. That this end may yet be attained in the not too distant future, I have not wholly despaired of. One thing is certain, unless it is done, the days of the College are numbered, and its friends might as well prepare for its funeral." Trustees omitted the last sentence of Rogers's remarks from the minutes but included his expressions of appreciation that "your bearing towards me has ever been courteous, honorable, and just. . . . With sentiments of high regard and esteem for you individually, and with the best wishes for the institution over which you have the honor to preside, I take leave of you and it." For its part, the board praised his "eminent services, unremitting industry, and marked fidelity to duty."[66]

However, Rogers's work was not yet done. As a trustee, he continued to guide the college's financial affairs, proposing to send Lanceford B. Wilkes, president of the Board of Trustees, throughout the state as an agent. Wilkes, who had served the college as professor, president, agent, trustee, and board president, raised eight thousand dollars by 1878 to make the college free of debt.[67]

As Rogers retired to a private residence in July 1877, George Bryant began an administration characterized by preservation of what Rogers had left. A friend and supporter of Rogers, Bryant accepted the appointment as president while expressing regret at the circumstances and stating that he would "hold sacred the trust . . . and give it the best energies of heart and mind." However, Bryant, never as fully comfortable in the role of president as he had been as a faculty member, did not become a trustee and did not attend board meetings. He appointed no new trustees and kept the catalog much the same. One noteworthy change in the 1879 catalog announced the use of gas lighting, an improvement promised as early as 1871 but not in place until the late 1870s. The 1882 catalog more clearly showed Bryant's hand as primarily a teacher, listing in an appendix more than six hundred books available in the college library, a sixteen-page endeavor taking up nearly half of the catalog. Bryant concluded: "If a young lady has no other advantage in coming to Christian College than the use of these books, this alone would repay her for her outlay."[68]

Bryant's relations with the board dealt largely with routine financial matters. The ubiquitous question of rent had led the board in 1875 to lease the college to Rogers for ten dollars for each boarder beyond the first fifty. When Bryant informed the board that he did not wish to continue the lease at the present rate, a committee of the board met with Bryant at Rogers's home in a friendly interchange, resulting in an agreement to continue the rent as it stood.[69]

During the Bryant administration, a significant issue surfaced, remaining unresolved in his administration. The issue, a proposal that all faculty members be members of the Christian Church, illustrated the delicate balance between church control and academic freedom. Jesse A. Boulton, who first joined the board in 1857, offered a resolution "that all the teachers of Christian Female College shall have their names submitted to the Board of Trustees by the President for their approval or rejection before they commence their discharge of their . . . duties." Trustees postponed a vote on the resolution until a committee could confer with Bryant to see whether its passage "would embarrass him in completing his lease with the College." Negotiations resulted in Boulton's withdrawal of his resolution at the next board meeting when a substitute resolution attempted to please all parties: "Resolved . . . that as far as practicable the faculty should be members of the Christian Church." Trustees then authorized the president to select and approve his own faculty. However, they declared it his duty to submit to the board names and duties of proposed faculty members and reserved to the trustees the right to approve or reject them.[70]

The issue of the college's relationship to the church surfaced again in 1882 when the board named a committee "to consider and report on the subject of amending the Charter of the College as to bring its organic law into harmony with the suggestion made by the Christian Churches in Missouri." The suggested amendment would allow the state convention of Christian Churches "to vacate the office or offices of any trustee or trustees of . . . Christian College by a majority of the vote of the . . . delegates to the convention." A board-appointed committee amended the church's recommendation to limit the power of the church's state convention to vacate no more than one-third of the total number of trustees, while specifically allowing the Christian College Board of Trustees to remove a trustee for any cause. Although trustees endorsed the amended resolution, the Bryant administration ended before the subject reemerged, and the charter revision desired by the church never took place.[71]

Bryant, who could no longer deny his strong desire to return to teaching, resigned in February 1883. In a mutually cordial exchange, he proclaimed himself "full of regrets" at leaving, while the board responded with its gratification that the resignation came not from problems with the board but from "a call based upon the recognition of your ability."[72]

The last years of the Bryant administration saw an increasing decline in the role that Rogers was able to play. Still active in 1879 as a Christian College trustee and a university curator, he engaged in a typically generous act when he gave his blessing to Mrs. O. A. Carr, associate principal of Christian College, to become the first principal of the ladies department at the university: "I do not hesitate to advise you to accept. . . . Christian College as a *co-partner* in the great educational firm can only rejoice in your increased opportunities for good."[73]

Rogers, suffering from tuberculosis, began spending summers in Colorado for his health in the late 1870s and stayed for increasingly longer periods of time in the 1880s. He helped his two sons establish themselves in the cattle business in Colorado, spending more and more time away in 1880 and 1881, composing letters of exceptional tenderness to his wife. Finally, in the winter of 1881, Rogers became too ill to return to Columbia and spent the winter in

Colorado in close confinement. His wife, Jennifer, joined him in Colorado in February and stayed until they could both return home in April 1882. Hoping to return to Colorado to see his sons the next August, he could go only as far as Kansas City. Determined to die at home, he made his way back to Columbia on August 24 and died within a few hours of reaching home.[74]

James S. Rollins, in a memorial to Rogers, praised Christian College as well, saying that "he brought Christian College up to the highest position among the Female Colleges of the State and the West. . . . It has now a reputation not limited by the boundaries of Missouri, and which with additional means and facilities . . . will make it in the end one of the leading Female Colleges in the Mississippi Valley."[75]

Rogers had brought the college through the crucible with an extraordinary sense of duty, even leaving the bedside of his dying son to conduct commencement exercises. His leadership had prevailed through the Civil War, depression, and Reconstruction, tripling the value of the college property and ensuring an annual enrollment of more than one hundred students. A faculty member penned a fitting epitaph: "J. K. Rogers was not the founder of Christian College, nor yet its first president; but in the humble judgment of the writer, he should be called its father."[76]

4

Transition Years

WILLIAM ABNER OLDHAM: 1883–1893

Now this is not the end. It is not even the beginning of the end. But it is, perhaps, the end of the beginning.

—Winston Churchill, speech on November 10, 1942

IN THE RAPIDLY EVOLVING HISTORY of Christian College, every administration represented some degree of transition, but the presidency of William Abner Oldham marked the end of an era. Oldham was the last of the old and the first of the new. The last to have known personally such institutional pioneers as Henry White, Moses Lard, and John Augustus Williams, the last of the preacher presidents, and the last of the paternalistic figures, he was also the first since Williams not to have come from within the college ranks, thus providing a new perspective. Just as America itself seemed to be coming of age in the late nineteenth century and entering an expansionist era, the college under Oldham's leadership looked to a new century of more modern educational trends and unprecedented growth.

Oldham's arrival on the scene could not have shown more promise for the college. His nomination by the recruitment committee and election by the board were unanimous, and the *Statesman* published glowing testimonials to his worth. His introduction to Columbia society took place in the college chapel and parlors with much fanfare in settings replete with nostalgia. Sallie Bedford Robinson, the 1853 valedictorian of the first graduating class, participated in the event. For the first time, both a mother and her daughter attended as Christian College alumnae, and three founders of the Martha Washington Institute participated. Nannie J. Walker Lenoir presided. The daughter of James Shannon, she was also the wife of Dr. Walter T. Lenoir, who had become a major force on the college's board in the Civil War years.[1]

The new president determined to make the nascent alumnae organization a viable force for the promotion of the college. The "Society of Alumna" [*sic*], formed in July 1855, had normally met only at commencement each year but took on a new role with the reception for Oldham, who had orchestrated the event, including Nannie Lenoir's plea for an endowment for the college. By 1883, the college had 357 alumnae, 322 of whom were living.[2]

Oldham recognized that the college faced new challenges from the competition of five newer girls' schools in central Missouri as well as from a flourishing public school system and a now coeducational University of Missouri. As a graduate of the University of Kentucky and past principal in the Lexington public school system, he was an experienced administrator as well as a scholar, and he demonstrated his ambitious managerial style from the start. Reminding the board of past promises yet unfulfilled, he pointed out the necessity for modernization in order to be competitive. Pianos were so scattered around the campus and in such short supply that students could practice only by appointment, while bathrooms with hot and cold running water and the building of a gymnasium remained in the planning stage. As one of his first accomplishments, Oldham raised the main building and the towers to the level of the wings, making them comply with the misleading engraving previously published in the catalog. The college finally became a unified three-story structure with ornamental iron trim and a fireproof tin roof.[3]

Oldham inherited other unresolved business, including the continued threat of the Missouri State Convention of Christian Churches to endorse only those colleges that would allow the convention to approve or reject any trustee. The Christian College Board of Trustees reported on the issue at the state convention in Hannibal in October 1833. According to that report, the board had found it impossible to "so alter the charter of said institution as to make the appointment of the Board conform to the expressed wishes of the convention," because the college charter had made the board self-perpetuating. Trustees resolved the problem by submitting a statement of their good intent:

> We desire that the delay . . . to change the charter shall not be construed into a manifestation of indifference . . . and wishing to conform as far as we can legally . . . to the constitution of the convention and asking the hearty cooperation and support of the brethren of Missouri in behalf of the College, we request this convention to nominate five brethren to fill vacancies now in the Board and to receive from us the following statement of the financial and moral condition of the College.[4]

At the heart of the board's report lay the desire for continued financial support of the college despite its lack of compliance with the convention's directive. Jesse A. Boulton, who became president of the board in 1884, most actively sought the convention's approval of the college's position. As a result of these efforts, the 1884 convention amended its earlier stance, accepting the board's report as sincere. The greatly amended resolution, much less intrusive into college affairs, stated that "those colleges . . . in the state known to be conducted by men associated with our religious movement are requested to make an annual report to this body through the standing Committee on Schools and Education . . . as a matter of information to the brotherhood."[5]

Thus ended the only attempt at church control of the board. However, Oldham's efforts to prod the state convention into greater financial backing made clear his disappointment at the church's level of support. He expressed this dissatisfaction in his baccalaureate address of May 31, 1888:

> All has been endured, trusting to the generous support of a liberal-spirited constituency, that constituency the whole church of the state. If by patronage of alien schools, they are built up, and your own destroyed, upon whom shall censure fall? Who but ourselves shall reap the bitter fruit? . . . We fear that the *odium theologicum* of a supposed conservatism of the baser sort has driven some of our brethren to patronize mere catch-penny schools, ephemeral, pretentious, boastful, unscrupulous.[6]

Oldham's frustration with the patronage of Missouri Christian churches reflected his eagerness to supply the college with a more adequate physical plant. He instigated a major fund-raising campaign by the board in the summer of 1887 that, within a month, provided the five thousand dollars needed to build a new chapel. The chapel, east of the main hall, joined the east wing through a "covered chute," or corridor, on the second floor. The old east cottage, also attached to the chapel, was used for art classes. The brick chapel, completed in 1888, featured an auditorium upstairs with seating for six hundred persons and classrooms, a parlor, and office space on the ground floor. Remodeling of the old chapel then provided badly needed practice rooms. However, the college still lacked funds for furnishings, such as desks, opera chairs, curtains, and scenery for the stage. Upon Jerry Dorsey's proposal, the board borrowed the necessary money from the Columbia Savings Bank at 7 percent interest. Later, learning that funds could have been available for 6 percent interest, trustees searched for another source of funding.[7]

In its search for a lower interest rate, the trustees turned to John William ("Blind") Boone, a nationally known black concert pianist and ragtime composer who had already developed ties to the college. Boone had lost his sight as an infant when his eyeballs had been removed to relieve pressure on his brain during an illness. His mother had worked for James Shannon, and Boone had also formed a close relationship with John Lange Jr., another member of the Shannon household, who later became Boone's manager. Shannon, because of his interest in Boone, arranged for the young pianist to practice on Shannon's own square piano at the college. Boone had also studied with Anna Heuermann, a member of the Christian College faculty. By the late 1880s, the Blind Boone Concert Company had become a financial success, and it was this blind pianist, born in poverty to a runaway slave and a Union soldier, who accommodated the college. The finance committee reported on January 14, 1890, that "we have secured the sum of ($2,000) Two Thousand dollars from Blind Boone giving the note of the officers of this board for the same and due in twelve months from date at six percent interest, and have taken up note held by Columbia Savings Bank."[8]

Oldham's next request of the board came quickly after completion of the chapel. He addressed the trustees on the need for steam heating of the college, adding that the institution also needed "bath appliances" and "better water closet facilities." The board authorized ten thousand dollars to meet these needs, marking the beginning of months of careful nurturing of the installation of the systems. Oldham expressed his thanks to the board at the November 1890 meeting for the heating system that "has given us perpetual summer within the halls of the college." He then boldly moved on to another request, stating that, with the addition of bathrooms, "the cup of our earthly joy would be full." He noted that six bathtubs would cost only fifty dollars and could be placed in the west wing cellar at little expense, draining into the west pasture and that, he hoped, a bath once a week for each girl "would not significantly damage the appearance of the pasture."[9]

In addition to new facilities, Oldham brought new ideas. His remarks in the 1889 catalog, titled "Christian Womanhood as a Factor in the Moral Progress of the World," showed enthusiasm for the new roles open to women:

> The educated young woman of today may devote her talents and energies, with the utmost propriety, to callings that were closed to her grandmother. . . . Whatever tends to abolish the doctrine that a woman *must* marry . . . is to be welcomed as the friend of honest, self-respecting womanhood. I admire both the pluck and the good taste of the lady who gave as her reason for not marrying, that she was not willing to give up a sixty dollar per month job for a ten dollar husband! In medicine, in journalism, in authorship, on the lecture platform, in the schoolroom, in the mission field, and in many of the more difficult callings of life, demanding high executive ability, woman is pushing her way to the front and asking the privilege of being independent. . . . She has the right to go, on common ground of her humanity, to maintain her own independence and to support those who may be dependent on her. To refuse her this privilege and right is a perverted and antiquated view of gallantry.

Oldham agreed that some of the more mature young women could "advantageously attend well-endowed and well-officered" coeducational institutions, and concluded that the "seclusion of the boarding-school . . . cuts off the great thief of time, promiscuous company-keeping, and enables the young lady to devote her attention exclusively to work."[10]

The drive to modernize impacted the academic programs as well as the physical plant. Course names became more modern as "mental philosophy" became "psychology" and "natural philosophy" became "physics." Chemistry classes added laboratory work, and religious study became less intensive. By 1889, "Evidences of Christianity" was the only Bible course, but daily Bible readings in the chapel continued. Oldham added shorthand, typing, and bookkeeping, quoting a commencement speaker who had remarked that some of the most "womanly women have beat back the black battalions of poverty with . . . no spear more mendacious than a stenographic pencil." The most important addition, however, was the creation of a conservatory of music, with the first degree awarded in 1885. The three-year course of study included harmony, counterpoint, and composition analysis along with lessons on all of the stringed instruments and the organ. Oldham also introduced a concert series featuring nationally recognized musicians.[11]

In granting degrees, the college made a distinction between the standard baccalaureate degree in letters (B.L.) and the baccalaureate degree in arts (A.B.), providing for those who chose the "Classical Course," requiring an additional year for classes in Latin, trigonometry, astronomy, and two years each of French and German. German was very much in vogue, and the dining room included a "German table." In 1890, the only A.B. graduate listed was Oldham's daughter, Mary Frazier Oldham.[12]

In another academic innovation for the college, a new grading system, identical to that of the University of Missouri, made any grade under 60 percent failing, and designated a grade of 96 percent or better as "honors." In 1885, the board authorized a "Trustees' Medal" for the senior with the highest grade-point average over ninety who had attended the college for at least two years. Two other medals, one gold and one silver, went to the best essays written by members of the junior class.[13]

Ties between Christian College and the university continued under Oldham. Physical education at the college included a military drill performed in red coats, a practice modeled after the university girls' cadet band. In a more serious collaboration, the college quickly offered university students the use of the college chapel and classrooms after a devastating fire in 1892 destroyed the main hall of the university. The *Columbia Herald* printed the answer: "The female colleges are offered to us. They say they can embrace the entire university. And we say that, even in our demoralized and disabled condition, we can embrace them." One of the few objects saved from the fire was a portrait of Joseph Kirtley Rogers.[14]

Faculty also continued the ties between the university and the college, with Frederick Pannell teaching music in both institutions. Professor W. H. Pommer, a graduate of the Royal Conservatory at Leipzig and a talented composer, came to the college to head the new music conservatory but was hired away to chair the university music department. His replacement, Otto Tiede, married Christian College alumna Evelyn Bryant. Joseph Skinner, a Christian College faculty member, "married into" the Christian College family. A professor of Latin and mathematics, Skinner married Julia Lenoir, granddaughter of James Shannon and daughter of Nannie and Walter T. Lenoir. Skinner later returned to Kentucky to become president of Hamilton College. After his death, Julia Lenoir Skinner headed the Cincinnati Conservatory of Music.[15]

Oldham upheld the old ways rather than innovating in the area of student discipline. The 1883 catalog stated college policy: "In the moral government of the school, no system of espionage is allowed. There is watchfulness, but it is the watchfulness of guidance and protection. The government of the school is parental." The first president of the college to use the term *in loco parentis*, Oldham inserted the concept into the 1884 catalog: "Our experience teaches that evil, and only evil, comes from students paying or receiving visits. . . . With reference to calls from young men we would be especially emphatic. . . . Parents sometimes weakly yield. Please leave this matter entirely in our hands. . . . Young men and study are incompatible."[16]

Rules remained much the same. All letters except those to or from parents were subject to inspection by the president, and those students who violated the rule and engaged in "clandestine correspondence" paid the penalty of dismissal from school. The college urged parents to send a list of approved correspondents, "any or all of whom may be rejected by the President, if the interest of the pupil or of the institution so require." No student dared answer the doorbell, even for her own parents, "nor present herself at any time at the public halls or entrances without permission." Advice to parents covered even food: "Rich boxes of cake and confections bring dyspepsia, and sickness of other kinds. . . . The confections breed many unnecessary ills. They take the mind of the pupil from her studies; they lead to untidy ways and filthy rooms. Therefore, please do not send them."[17]

Despite Oldham's strictness, students remembered him with fondness, recalling that his jovial, gentle nature overcame the harshness of the rules in minor incidents. They told of his croquet contests with trustees John Conley and Robert Clinkscales—contests sometimes continuing into the twilight by lantern or in the rain under umbrellas. Oldham did, indeed, reflect the end of an era as the last of the "papas." None after him, "in the first warm days of spring, would interview each girl personally to make sure she had not taken off her long underwear."[18]

When his second five-year contract neared a close in January 1893, Oldham informed the board that he would not be an applicant for "reelection." He and the board had enjoyed a mutually satisfying relationship in which the board invited him to attend its meetings whenever he chose. The board had maintained considerable stability of membership with Jerry Dorsey still serving as treasurer and such stalwarts as John Machir, John W. Conley, Walter T. Lenoir, Lanceford B. Wilkes, and Sinclair B. Kirtley remaining active. But here, too, change came with the deaths of Robert Lemon in 1886, a board member for more than twenty years, Professor Joseph Ficklin in 1887, and Robert N. Clinkscales in 1890.[19]

The president's steady leadership had given the college a period of quiet accomplishment, and the *Statesman* regularly reported its activities with praise. An article covering the 1890 commencement called the college "ably and judiciously managed" with "a total enrollment of one hundred and sixty." Commencement "thus closed one of the most successful years in the history of the college."[20]

With more than adequate notice of Oldham's departure, the board made an intensive search for a successor, first electing Professor J. W. Porter of Hamilton College in Lexington, who came to Columbia to look at the college but declined the position. After considering a number of other candidates, the board elected Frank P. St. Clair, a former faculty member and business manager at Hamilton College, who had moved to Montrose, Colorado, for his health. A graduate of Bethany College in West Virginia (a school founded by Alexander Campbell), St. Clair continued the tradition of Christian Church presidents at the college. Unlike previous Christian College presidents, however, he had been prominent politically as a member of the State Democratic Central Committee in Colorado.[21]

After St. Clair's unanimous election by the board on May 23, 1893, he and his wife, Luella, appeared before the board to accept. The two-year contract, effective July 1, called for St. Clair to pay the board $12.50 for each full boarder at the time of registration, with a full settlement each July 1. The contract also ensured him the authority to employ whom he pleased as faculty.[22]

St. Clair's inauguration on June 3, 1893, initiated a flurry of activity during which the college's entire furnishings were sold and replaced over the summer. The excitement generated by the new administration lasted only a few months, however. St. Clair, who suffered from a heart condition, died suddenly on November 21, 1893. Although not entirely unexpected, the blow was severe, and the board lamented the loss:

> [We] cannot adequately express our deep sorrow nor formulate in words our exalted estimate of the man. He was so recently unanimously elected president of our institution. With his heart deeply touched and dominated by a laudable

> ambition and enthusiasm, he at once began his noble work, consecrating his purse, the rich endowments of a pure heart and cultured brain to the upbuilding of the cause of female education. . . . Amid our grief and tears we cannot understand why he should be so soon called away.[23]

Although faced with a crisis of the first magnitude, the college managed a smooth transition. The newly inaugurated college journal, the *Chronicle,* recalled the precarious nature of the president's health when he had arrived at the college, concluding that the writer "feared he was doomed." Only the impact of Luella St. Clair's appearance before the board assured that body of continued future leadership. The board had broken with precedent in allowing her to accompany her husband at the initial meeting and had elected him president "believing confidently that should he be taken, his highly intelligent and gifted wife would be able to carry forward the work to success."[24]

Luella St. Clair, in accepting her election as president of the college at the December 4, 1893, board meeting, proclaimed herself to be "trembling to think of assuming the labors of such a position" that "the voice of Duty seemingly demands." She became one of the first women college presidents in the United States, winning the approval of the *Chronicle:* "We believe this to be pre-eminently the age of women and where there is present the administrative and intellectual ability, that the proper head of a female institution should be a woman. . . . Christian College, now, as in the past, is abreast of the times."[25]

Thus, the leadership of the college passed into the hands of a wholly new type of president, one whose insights and accomplishments would usher in a new era of growth and progress.

5

The Torch Is Passed

LUELLA ST. CLAIR MOSS AND EMMA MOORE: 1893–1920

It is time for a new generation of leadership to cope with new problems and new opportunities. For there is a new world to be won.

—John Fitzgerald Kennedy, television address of July 4, 1960

WHEN THE CHRISTIAN COLLEGE Board of Trustees hired Luella Wilcox St. Clair as president of the college in 1893, they had reason to expect committed and intelligent leadership. However, the power and force of that leadership far exceeded anything they could have anticipated. When Luella Wilcox St. Clair Moss finally retired from the college in 1920, the original Bennett building remained, but a whole new campus had been built around it during her three periods as president of what had become a respected junior college. Beginning a whole new career after her retirement in 1920, her "firsts" as a dynamic civic leader made her a state and national figure by the time of her death in 1947 at the age of eighty-two.

Well educated for a woman of that era, St. Clair had been the only girl to receive a diploma in her Virden, Illinois, high school's first graduating class, and she led the class as valedictorian. She was graduated from Hamilton College in Kentucky after only one year, earning a teacher's certificate at the age of seventeen. She stayed on at her alma mater where she edited the college paper and where she met and married Frank St. Clair on September 1, 1886, at the age of twenty-one—a marriage that would last for only seven years until his death in 1893. When ill health forced Frank St. Clair to resign from Hamilton College, the couple went to Grandville Center, Pennsylvania, where daughter Annilee was born, moving a few months later to Montrose, Colorado, where Frank became deputy county clerk. Luella, young mother of an infant daughter, taught for three years in a country school, riding to school on horseback, sometimes in deep snow.[1]

For St. Clair, a newly widowed mother at the age of twenty-eight, the task ahead could have been overwhelming except for the support of those close to her. Her father, Seymour Bordon Wilcox, came to her aid. He was a native New Yorker and had operated a shipping business in St. Louis before embarking on a successful real estate career in Illinois. Wilcox gave invaluable advice and encouragement, overseeing the business operations of the college. However, in her second year as president, St. Clair lost even this source of strength when her father died suddenly at his home in New Orleans. Frank St. Clair's brother, W. S. "Will" St. Clair, had also come to the college to teach courses in religion and ethics, while his wife, Louise, taught piano. Will St. Clair's geniality led not only to his popularity on campus but also to civic leadership as mayor of Columbia. Certainly, a stable and experienced board of trustees lightened the new president's load. Jerry Dorsey, a trustee since 1863, continued faithfully as treasurer, and Dr. Walter T. Lenoir, whose service dated back to 1857, had become president of the board in 1891. William P. Hurt as vice president and Sinclair B. Kirtley as secretary added still more strength to the board, along with such veterans as William A. Bright, John C. Conley, and John Machir.[2]

The fall of 1893 proved a difficult time for the nation and the college. St. Clair later recalled 1893–1894 as "the year of many bank failures and widespread panic," as enormous business expansion in the United States, followed by an end of credit extension, led to a collapse of farm prices and soaring unemployment.[3]

Despite such difficulties, St. Clair responded with remarkable innovations even in her first year. She had already been a major force in renovation of the college for the opening of the 1893–1894 academic year, leading the *Centralia Fireside Guard* to comment that "everything is first-class. Christian College is acknowledged to be the leading institution in the State for the education of young ladies." Not only did the college boast new Brussels carpets, elegant oak suites, and pianos new from the factory, but also electricity enhanced the buildings and grounds for the first time. As soon as the fall semester began, St. Clair launched a college magazine, the *Chronicle,* intended to be "a faithful representation of Christian College; to reflect the thought and desire of her students and to advertise her manifold advantages. . . . The *Chronicle* should be the receptacle of all the best essays and literary efforts of Christian College girls." The practice of reprinting complimentary newspaper excerpts displayed the accomplishments of the institution, and student essays illustrated not only admirable literary style but also wide-ranging student interests. Titles included such varied subjects as "Greek Philosophy during the Athenian Supremacy," "Influence of the Russian Novel," "The Red Planet—Mars," "The Jews in Civilization," "Imperialism in American Politics," "The Decline and Influence of Chivalry," and "Studies from Dickens."[4]

St. Clair's first year brought, in addition, the creation of a new literary society, the Elizabeth Barrett Browning Society, intended to stimulate literary activity by acting as a rival to the Martha Washington Institute. Also, in line with her social, religious, and educational interests, St. Clair established a branch of the Young Women's Christian Association and added a kindergarten to the school. In a break with tradition, she ended the outdated public examinations of previous commencement weeks and organized a more active local alumnae association to further community relations.[5]

The college catalog of 1894, for the first time resplendent with photographs, revealed much about that first year. The dress code for all students specified black woolen material for fall and winter in a plain style with no trimming. Warm weather called for simple white dresses and white sailor hats with only bands of ribbon as trim. All closing exercises during commencement week required white dresses. Going beyond this customary dress, St. Clair revealed the first of changes aimed at making Christian College the "Vassar of the West." Abandoning the traditional Christian College bonnets, she introduced the use of caps and gowns, similar to those used at Smith and Vassar, as required dress whenever students appeared in public. The triangular caps, much more sophisticated than the stodgy bonnets, featured tassels dangling on each side of the face to give "a certain intellectual expression to the face." The catalog advised that no heavy wraps would be necessary, "as the students wear a university gown and cap that are both becoming and comfortable, and have been received with much favor by pupils and patrons." Uniformity required that the cap and gown be purchased at the college at $10 for the gown and $2.50 for the cap. However, "only students boarding in the College may wear the College uniform." The catalog further revealed a distinction in privileges between day and residential students in the statement that day pupils "must not enter rooms or halls of the boarding department without permission. They must not study in parlors, or reception rooms of the main building. They are required to go either to study hall or recitation rooms as soon as they come on the grounds."[6]

St. Clair's first commencement address, included in the 1894 catalog, reflected the pride she took in the year's accomplishments, referring to the college as "a Vassar in this garden spot of the West." She reflected as well the compatibility of her own personal philosophy with the imperialism of the 1890s, giving "all due respect to the Anglo-Saxon race that will ultimately master the world and wrest from Nature her most jealously guarded secrets; for this ability to cope with every obstacle is evidenced in even our indulged young people." Her own behavior provided an object lesson in coping, and a *Kansas City Times* article called St. Clair "undoubtedly the ablest president the college has ever had."[7]

Academic programs also felt the impact of St. Clair's innovations. The 1894 catalog devoted a page to the School of Modern Languages, offering instruction in French and German and announcing the creation of the "Teutonia," a German society with semimonthly meetings conducted in German. The dining room continued to promote a German table. The greatest expansion, however, came in the School of Music, already a well-known feature of the college. With Anna Heuermann as director, course offerings included harmony, counterpoint, analysis, and music history, with private lessons offered in piano, voice, violin, mandolin, guitar, and banjo. The *Chronicle* praised the creation of an orchestra, noting that the "source of this new musical inspiration is Professor Pannell, who sits like the pictured god Pan (nell) among his eight goddesses of charming sight and sound." The music program continued to flourish under St. Clair, expanding to a faculty of five with the claim that "students here have at much less expense, the same advantages, in extent of musical course and in excellence of instruction, as in the Conservatories of Cincinnati and Boston." Piano competitions held each June in the Hayden Opera House in Columbia became a major event with a thousand-dollar grand piano donated as the prize.[8]

Academic ties with the University of Missouri grew even stronger. Christian College students received "the advantages of special lectures delivered in the University chapel" and free admission to all lectures of the Bible College. Professor Frederick Pannell continued to serve both institutions, as did William A. Buckner in natural sciences, who had chaired the science department at Daughters College in Harrodsburg, Kentucky. The faculty of twenty listed in the 1894 catalog, strong enough to ease St. Clair's burdens in those early years, leaned heavily toward courses in the humanities.[9]

Demands on St. Clair's time and energy expanded steadily. She took over the college's bookkeeping when her father left in the winter of her second year, while continuing to edit the *Chronicle* and teach logic. She read to the students in the library, sewed with them, and served as an admirable role model socially as well as academically. She increasingly engaged in traveling, conferences, club work, and entertaining, becoming a much admired social leader and a special guest at numerous academic and social gatherings. As such, she attended a reception of dignitaries in January 1896 honoring the dean of the new Bible College of Missouri, a nondenominational institution of higher religious training associated with the University of Missouri. The dean, William Thomas Moore, was accompanied by his wife, Emma Frederick Moore, who at thirty-three was twenty-seven years his junior. The couple had recently returned from ten years in London where Dr. Moore had preached and edited the *Christian Commonwealth*. St. Clair's attention fixed on Mrs. Moore, an honor graduate of Wellesley and a stout, handsome woman of great energy and ability. The Moores lived just three doors south of the Christian College campus in Jerry Dorsey's former home on Christian College Avenue, and St. Clair's friendship with Emma Moore quickly evolved into a major force in the lives of both women. Moore, who had managed a school for girls in New York and personified the sophistication traditionally assumed of a Wellesley graduate, eagerly adopted the college as an outlet for her skills as a willing volunteer.[10]

Moore's helping hand proved invaluable when St. Clair, in November 1896, three years to the month after her husband's death, nearly died of double pneumonia. In addition to attending to college affairs, Moore gave devoted attention to Annilee, then a child of eight. St. Clair, having so recently lost both her husband and her father, centered on Annilee in a battle to live—Annilee, whose loving ways had been a constant comfort and joy to her mother. Writing after her retirement from the college, St. Clair recalled the crisis: "There were no hospitals or trained nurses in Columbia. My physician wired to St. Louis for a nurse, and a long battle then followed for my life. One night the nurse thought I was dying and called the physician. Although in a state of coma, I seemed to realize the efforts they were making to save me. . . . I knew that I must live."[11]

By the spring of 1897, St. Clair realized that the state of her health remained too precarious to continue at the college. Her resignation, dated March 8, 1897, was to take effect in June and was conditional "upon the acceptance by the Board of Mrs. W. G. Moore as my successor in office elected in the usual way and for the usual term of lease." In an outpouring of appreciation and admiration, trustees expressed their "wish further to record their high appreciation of the brilliant gifts, earnest labors, wise management and almost unparalleled energy which have characterized her administration, taking the work as she did in the shadow of a great sorrow." They then complied with St. Clair's bidding and elected Moore to a term of five years. Though the board may have had some misgivings about the election of Moore as president, Luella St. Clair had none. She wrote of Moore in the *Chronicle:* "In the broadest, truest sense of the word, she is a woman of affairs, fitted by rare graces of character and mind to mingle with men and women, and to understand the motives which animate them and the purposes and ends which they have most at heart." When the college made Moore its president, it acquired not only Mrs. Moore but also Dr. Moore's library of five thousand volumes.[12]

Despite good enrollments and the board's testimonial to St. Clair's success, the college that Moore inherited faced the usual financial struggles. As early as February 4, 1895, board minutes revealed the plight: "There being no money in the Treasurer's hands to pay interest on the Carter debt . . . it was ordered that the President of this Board draw an order on . . . Mrs. St. Clair for the sum of one hundred and twenty dollars to pay same."

Again, on October 18, 1895, the board tapped St. Clair's resources for $115 to pay the college's insurance premiums. Finally, on March 18, 1896, trustees consolidated the college debts through a loan of $8,500 from I. O. Hockaday, receiver for the Rollins Aid Fund. They then proceeded to borrow $1,324.18 from St. Clair to pay the deficit on the interest on the loan. Just before St. Clair's resignation became effective, the board borrowed $525 from John Black for interest on the $8,500 loan, noting, "Whereas this board has no funds in the hands of the Treasurer, . . . it is important that the interest be promptly paid to avoid a sale of the property under the deed of trust." When Oldham wrote to the board the next month, claiming that the board owed him $185, trustees understandably requested that he wait for payment.[13]

A period of transition brought leadership changes in the board as well as in the presidency. At the June 1898 meeting, Walter T. Lenoir resigned as president of the board, and Jerry Dorsey relinquished the post of treasurer, ending the era of their steadfast leadership but not of loyal board service. Lenoir remained a devoted board member until his death in 1919, although he moved to Kentucky and then Ohio in his later years and was unable to attend board meetings. Dorsey, for whom the academic hall would be named in 1911, also remained an active trustee until his death in 1909. Besides the vacancies in two major leadership posts, another blow to the board came with the death the following January of John Machir. A trustee for more than forty years, Machir "died as he had lived, one of the truest, most liberal and steadfast friends of Christian Female College . . . [and] his unexpected death has fallen upon this board and upon the institution of learning . . . with all the force of a personal calamity and is a loss which at this critical conjuncture we feel well-nigh irreparable."[14]

While the board and President Moore coped with college problems, St. Clair gradually regained her health. After her departure in June 1897, she spent several months in Europe with her sister, Maxine, "in slow and easy travel, with frequent rest periods," sending letters from Italy, France, and England. In the fall, she joined Annilee in New Orleans and visited Christian College during the Christmas holidays. Returning to New Orleans for the rest of the winter, she enrolled in course work at Tulane. However, word from the college was not good. The resignations of Lenoir and Dorsey, declining enrollments, financial problems, and reports of disrepair in the dormitory wings convinced St. Clair that she must act. By the summer of 1898, she was back as the board's "financial secretary." She resided at the college but left administrative matters to Moore while engaging in a major fund-raising effort.[15]

St. Clair's return saw almost immediate resolution of the problems. The fall of 1898 brought increased enrollments, with some applicants rejected for lack of space, convincing the board of the inadequacy of college buildings.

The board authorized a loan of fifteen thousand dollars in October, agreeing in November to erect a three-story brick building adjoining and in front of the old main hall. The new structure would include a dining room, family rooms, academic offices, and dormitory space for fifty additional students. There was even talk of moving on to build a conservatory, an art gallery, a gymnasium, and a new chapel, converting the old chapel into recitation rooms.[16] St. Clair had returned.

Just as plans were under way toward a promising future, the college's very existence in Columbia was threatened when Sedalia leaders contended for the removal of the college to their city. The *Chronicle* of November 1898 covered the story by quoting two newspaper articles, one from the *Missouri Statesman:*

> Sedalia is again on the rampage. This time she wants Christian College; wants this time-honored institution removed to the Prairie City. We have no fight to make on Sedalia's wanting it, it is something of which any city should be proud. But we will fight hard and long before Sedalia shall carry off the prize. Christian College is prospering as it has never prospered before, and with new additions, which are sure to come, and come quickly, the grand old school will continue to flourish. But she must remain at the Athens.

The other article came from the St. Louis *Republic:*

> Several prominent citizens of Columbia, Missouri, are in the city [St. Louis]. They are very much exercised over an effort that is being made to move the Christian College from that town to Sedalia. . . . [I]t is proposed by the Christian Church to greatly enlarge the college, no matter whether it remains in Columbia or goes elsewhere, also to centralize all the schools of the church.
>
> The complaint against Columbia is not on account of the local surrounding or the citizens, but because of a lack of railroad facilities from the south. At Jefferson City one can take a train in the morning to go to Columbia, and at 2 o'clock in the afternoon will find himself [in St. Louis] further away from Columbia than when he started in the morning. This is the only argument of consequence that Sedalia is using against Columbia.[17]

The effort to steal the college came to naught, but it may have been a stimulus to the citizens of Columbia to raise twenty thousand dollars in cash toward establishing a railroad connection to Jefferson City. This occurred with the completion, in the summer of 1899, of an eight-mile branch from Columbia to McBaine on the Missouri River, where it connected with the Missouri, Kansas, and Texas Railroad. The publicity also brought positive notice to the college. The January 1899 edition of the *Chronicle* quoted the *Christian Evangelist:* "Christian College is on such a boom that its trustees are planning to build a large and modern style building to accommodate its increasing patronage. Mrs. Moore's ambition is to make it the Wellesley of the West."[18]

Fund-raising to meet indebtedness, in addition to providing for the new building, proved too prolonged a process for St. Clair and Moore. The two decided to take matters into their own hands by proposing to the board that they "assume the present debt and provide the buildings necessary to carry on this work provided the property be transferred to them." A contract of May 9, 1899, between a committee of the board and the two benefactors made St. Clair and Moore copresidents and stipulated that they would assume all indebtedness of the college, amounting to ninety-five hundred dollars. Within one year of the contract, they would spend at least fifteen thousand dollars toward the construction of new buildings and improvements of its grounds. As soon as this obligation was met, the board would "convey to us the present college grounds." Additional provisions required the copresidents to "continue personally or by our agents the management and operation . . . for a period of at least ten years." Finally, when the copresidents wished to sell the college, the board would have the option of repurchasing it for no more than the copresidents had invested. Accepting immediately and unanimously, the board moved to pay all debts and to "deliver to said Moore and St. Clair the following contract for the sale of said college property and for the ultimate conveyance thereof."[19]

Trustees had some explaining to do when the church paper, the *Christian Evangelist,* requested an official board statement regarding the status of the college. Painting a dismal picture of the condition of the buildings as old and unsanitary, the June 26, 1900, report from the board noted that Luella St. Clair had "encountered the apathy which meets every worker in our educational cause" and realized that raising $50,000 "in time to save the school (if it could be raised at all) was impossible." Trustees assured the *Evangelist* readers that St. Clair and Moore had "only come into the breach temporarily" and hoped to return the property without interest and with a gift of ten thousand dollars "to some body representative of the Christian Church of this state." Noting pointedly that a church school in a neighboring state was owned by a syndicate of church members, the report issued a challenge: "[St. Clair and Moore are] perfectly willing and ready to surrender their trust whenever a suitable person or persons can be found to take their place. . . . Here is, therefore, an opportunity for some consecrated wealth among our people to be invested in a work whose Christian importance cannot be estimated. Let us hear from the church in this great question of the Christian education of our daughters."[20]

Beneficial results of the selling of the college could hardly be denied. The debt of nine thousand dollars was paid in full, and a beautiful new dormitory for 150 students was being built, equipped, and occupied at a cost of seventy thousand dollars provided for by the copresidents. Attachments to the original building were being removed, and the original college building would be retained and remodeled as a conservatory of music. What the report did not mention was that Moore and St. Clair had incurred a personal debt of forty-three thousand dollars in order to provide the improvements.[21]

Construction of the new building caused excitement not only on campus but also in the community. The *Chronicle* of June 1899 quoted a *Statesman* article: "This regeneration of Christian College is one of the three most important events in the life of Columbia within thirty years, the other two being the rebuilding of the University and the securing of the railroad. . . . The new college will be the finest of its kind in the west." The *Chronicle* referred to a covered corridor between the new building and the original hall as "The Bridge of Sighs," leading music students to thirty-two new soundproof practice rooms in the old building, which came to be called "Old Main."[22]

The 1899 academic year began with students occupying the new dormitory rooms just in front of the old west wing, rooms that had not yet been connected to the heating plant. St. Clair described the problem resulting from the early occupancy:

> A severe cold spell in September caused a telegram to be sent to Chicago to ship by express fifty oil stoves to Christian College. . . . The students were at liberty to replenish the big lamps of their stoves. We used more than a barrel of oil a day. With oil impartially spilled along the line of march of the vestal virgins, even upon the temporary wooden steps of the new building and the hallways, only a protecting providence (He would have had little help from our town fire department) could have prevented the starting of a perhaps disastrous fire. . . . Hope was in the air. Growth was in progress.[23]

Just as the exhilaration of an earlier year had been quashed by the death of Frank St. Clair, death again cast a pall, this time coinciding with the completion of the new building. Annilee, not quite twelve years old, died of inflammatory rheumatism at eleven o'clock on the night of January 24, 1900. A gregarious child with a sunny disposition, she had survived an attack at the age of seven and another in February 1899. However, an attack beginning on January 10 took her life, plunging the whole college community into despair. Letters of sympathy flooded in to the bereaved mother, and the *Chronicle* devoted its entire February 1900 issue to memorials. St. Clair described her ordeal: "I have never known any other human being with such outgoing sympathy and love for humanity. She loved and trusted the whole world. . . . For days I sat and moved about as one dazed. Nothing seemed to matter. She was gone. Thus in agony and a life-long sorrow came for me the dedication of the new building. Perhaps it is fittingly named St. Clair Hall. To me it will always mean Annilee."[24]

Thus, St. Clair Hall, originally intended to honor Frank St. Clair, came to "mean Annilee," but later generations would think of it as a memorial to Luella St. Clair. St. Clair went with her mother to New Orleans for a time but soon returned: "It gradually came to me that my one surcease was to try to do for other girls what I could no longer do for the little girl who had gone away. This I tried to do for a quarter of a century."[25]

Of all the tributes to Annilee in the dedicatory issue, the most touching may have been St. Clair's own poem dedicated to her daughter. The final verse especially reflected the mother's grief:

To my heart no brown eyed child nestles close,
　　By my side is a vacant chair;
The music of "mother" comes only in dreams,
　　but echoes are everywhere,
No swift flying feet, nor encircling arms,
　　Greet my slow coming to day,
For, until the gates of Heaven swing wide,
　　The little girl's gone away.[26]

St. Clair Hall's completion marked the approach of Christian College's Jubilee Year of 1901 and showed the college at its best. Students inaugurated the elegant formal dining room on February 20, 1900. In April, 175 invitations went out for a public reception to show off the new building, magnificently ablaze with electric lights throughout. The *Statesman* boasted: "There is but one Christian College. It leads; others may follow. The new college is a beauty and a joy forever." Again, the next month, the *Statesman* declared: "There is but one Christian College. It stands out as the brilliant head of all female educational institutions in Missouri."[27]

Student response to the improvements came in the form of record enrollments in spite of hard times for Missouri farmers. St. Clair remembered the summer of 1901 as "the never-to-be-forgotten drought summer when the ground parched day after day under a pitiless sun. There were no crops. Mrs. Moore and I assumed full financial obligations for the new building and had borrowed money for furnishings and equipment. . . . I traveled a good deal in the interest of the college." Anxiety about the impact of the drought on enrollments gave way to relief: "To our astonishment and gratitude the college opened with almost a full enrollment." The *Chronicle* hailed it as the largest enrollment in the college's history with students from eighteen states and England, totaling 135, plus a faculty of twenty-five, all under one roof.[28]

While construction continued, other undertakings moved ahead. Intramural basketball began in 1900, the same year as the first Ivy Chain. Ivy Chain was the creation of Lucy Laws, who came to the college in 1897 as "preceptress," meaning dean, when only the original building stood. She served as dean, principal of the academy, head of the English department, and librarian before her retirement in 1923. The concept of Ivy Chain may have been copied from Vassar or even from Moore's beloved Wellesley. Pictures of the earliest Ivy Chain ceremonies show circles of students bound together by chains of daisies, but later chains were of greenery. The chains, draped across the shoulders of the students, were cut between each of the participants, symbolizing the going of their own ways. The *Chronicle* of June 1900 described the ceremony, including the planting of the ivy so that it would climb the front of St. Clair Hall, as an event "to be kept up by the presidents of future classes."[29]

The tradition eventually led to such heavy growth on the brick that the practice ended some sixty years later to prevent further damage to the exterior of the building. When practicality finally demanded that the ivy be entirely removed from St. Clair Hall, one graduate complained that the college could at least have sent each alumna a piece of the ivy. Ivy Chain ceremonies continued, however, if not the planting of the ivy, carrying on the tradition begun by Lucy Laws, who wrote and delivered the first Ivy Chain oration.

One event of 1902, the demise of the *Martha Washington Journal*, reflected change as an ongoing feature of the college. The triumphant *Chronicle* gave the *Journal* an unlamented burial in a self-congratulatory editorial calling the *Journal* "out of harmony with the age of electricity. It represents the point of view and method of treatment current in the 19th century. . . . The *Journal* pined in the new atmosphere and longed for release."[30]

If the *Chronicle* writers saw the *Journal* as faulty writing, they had a rare opportunity to study effective journalism. The *Chronicle* reported in its March 1902 issue that William T. Moore had established a new department of journalism, calling it "the only school in the United States that has now in practical operation such a department." Moore's lectures included material on the history and rise of journalism in all countries, emphasizing the great daily newspapers of the world. Students studied the gathering of news, editorial departments, advertising, and mechanical features. They even produced a paper, the *Rag-Time Gazette*. Moore explained: "My notion is that nine-tenths of the journalists of the present day had to fight their ways through all sorts of difficulties. . . . A course of lectures such as I am attempting . . . will save them two to three years' hard work." His classes predated both the well-known School of Journalism at the University of Missouri, which was founded in 1908, and Joseph Pulitzer's offer to endow a school of journalism at Columbia University in 1903.[31]

Even as these activities unfolded, the copresidents never abated their drive for still more buildings. They next envisioned a new chapel built in celebration of the Golden Jubilee in May 1901. However, building the chapel by that date would not be possible. Instead, the copresidents promised that "before another commencement there would be a fine stone chapel adjoining

St. Clair Hall in the west." The Jubilee would require the completion of the chapel as an auditorium to accommodate expected guests. Thus, the date of the celebration, contingent on the completion of the building, was rescheduled for May 1902.[32]

With no new chapel yet ready, the copresidents celebrated the fiftieth commencement by signing the college property back to the Board of Trustees in the form of a trust deed. All parties signed the document "made and executed this 29th of May, 1901," providing that the college property be conveyed to trustee William A. Bright to be held in trust during the joint lives of Moore and St. Clair and during the life of the survivor. Finally, after the death of both parties, the property would be conveyed to the trustees of Christian Female College.[33]

Turning their attention to fund-raising for the new chapel, the trustees adopted St. Clair's suggestion that they raise $5,000 through selling five scholarship bonds, each educating "one worthy . . . girl." With William H. Dulany of Hannibal as the first donor, others followed, actually exceeding the $25,000 goal. Citizens, appreciative of the role of the college in the community, "showed a willingness to help in the campaign."[34]

The chapel building included not only an auditorium but also a library, gymnasium, and art studio, all connected to the west end of the main building by a breezeway. Above the auditorium, a roof garden provided outdoor exercise, recreation, and open-air programs. The cost of the building, once expected to be $25,000, reached $36,481.12. With improvements to the music hall to add thirty-four soundproof practice rooms and faculty studios, the total came to $40,568.67, leaving a deficit of $2,168.67 owed to the contractor. St. Clair again came to the rescue: "I had just received a payment on my patrimony, so I paid the $2,000. At the time it was supposed to be a loan, but I was never repaid, and it became a gift." The auditorium was first used in a celebration of its completion in March 1903 with an eighty-voice chorus singing "The Holy City." Its actual dedication took place at the fifty-second commencement in May 1903.[35]

As early as February 1902, St. Clair's reputation as a leader in women's education had led to an offer to accept the deanship of the women's department of Hamilton College in Kentucky. Tempting as the offer was for the president, student writers of the *Chronicle* confidently concluded that St. Clair "will not consider the offer as her heart and interests are inseparably connected with Christian College." St. Clair, as predicted, declined the offer, but another more enticing entreaty for her help the next year deserved more serious consideration:

> My alma mater, Hamilton College, at Lexington, Kentucky, was facing a crisis. The Board of Trustees had requested and received the resignation of the president then in charge. A number of the trustees knew me and had

> followed my work at Christian College. They authorized the president of Transylvania University in carrying out a plan to make Hamilton College the junior college for women, to write offering me the presidency of Hamilton. A long correspondence ensued. . . . Finally, after a visit from the president of Transylvania, Dr. Burris A. Jenkins, and an almost-all-night conference with Dr. and Mrs. Moore, they gave their consent . . . and the matter went to the Board, which gave an unwilling consent.[36]

The board's "unwilling consent" followed six weeks of thunderous confrontation between the board and the college's copresidents, nearly terminating the building program under way for the auditorium. Trustees charged that St. Clair, with Moore's consent, "and without the knowledge and consent of the Board of Trustees, has contracted with another school to become its president for the scholastic year of 1903–04, claiming, as the Board has been informed, that this is not a matter over which the Board has any jurisdiction." At stake was the question of who had ultimate authority, the presidents or the board, a matter left in doubt once the board no longer owned the college. Going well beyond the incident at hand and demanding a showdown on their authority, the trustees resolved that "steps be taken at once to ascertain what are the powers and responsibilities, if any, belonging to this Board." In a final thrust, the trustees resolved to cut off funds for the construction under way, instructing the building committee to enter into no new contracts until further notice from the board.[37]

If the trustees hoped to intimidate the copresidents, they met with disappointing results. In a systematic, carefully worded treatise the presidents pointing out the conditions of the 1899 agreement that made it "clear that either one, or both of us, might retire at any time from the personal management of the College, provided we secure agents to carry it on." They found no basis for the authority claimed by the board to determine when a principal could leave. "Evidently we are in no sense bound to remain in the College personally even for a single hour." The principals went still further:

> In none of the papers concerning all these transactions is there the slightest hint as to any "powers" which the Trustees are to have in the management of the College, or in anything else except to hold the property in trust for certain defined purposes on certain conditions; and finally to take possession of and manage the institution after our death, or after we have voluntarily turned over the whole control to your honorable body. . . . It was not our intention when we transferred the property to give to the trustees, or to anybody else, the legal right to interfere with or direct the management of the College during the lifetime of both or either of us. . . . We understand your position to be advisory.

St. Clair and Moore refused to believe, they wrote, that the board would embarrass them in respect to meeting financial obligations, and they suggested that the trustees might not have realized the magnitude of obligations borne by the copresidents with no cost to the college for salary or expenses except that of a home. Hoping that the board had acted "without due consideration," the women delivered the coup de grâce:

> Should the Board feel, as we understand some of them have expressed themselves, that they cannot hold their present position without the powers they are seeking, then we are reluctantly compelled to ask them to reconvey to us all rights to the Christian College property, which we may have conveyed to them in the transactions of the past. . . . [I]f the Board should decide to surrender their present trust, we pledge ourselves to constitute a new Board.[38]

The board's reply, brief, conciliatory, and somewhat contrite, came with the May 12, 1903, meeting: "While regretting the decision of the Principals, we accept that decision as legal and final and now declare the incident, so far as we are concerned, closed." The trustees further pledged their "active support" and "hearty cooperation in every worthy effort to promote the best interests of the college."[39]

Despite tensions and ruptured friendships inevitably suffered in such an exchange, St. Clair remained as secretary of the board until her departure for Hamilton College on June 1, 1903, but she would always remember the dedication of the new auditorium at the May commencement as a bittersweet occasion.

In the first year or two of the Moore presidency, Christian College seemed relatively unaffected by the change. True, Moore was harsher in inspecting the girls and put more emphasis on strictness, seeming perhaps less compassionate than past presidents. Both Moore and her husband dwelled greatly on the dangers of "attachments" to young men, imposing a somewhat severe social atmosphere. Nonetheless, board minutes of May 1904 included a resolution by Jerry Dorsey "that this Board extends its congratulations to Mrs. Moore . . . for the most successful scholastic year in the history of the college." The 167 boarding students in 1905 represented the largest enrollment in any one year, and Moore continued to make such improvements as a deep well and water tower, a large two-story brick addition to the powerhouse with a new dynamo and engine, new stables, fences, and granitoid walks.[40]

Moore met with only limited success in the academic realm. Her boldest move came in ending the kindergarten and primary school. Another change allowed a few boys to attend as day students in language, education, and music. Degrees given by the college varied from a B.L. degree granted for the junior college literary program to a B.M. degree for the four-year music courses, and postgraduate work in music, art, and oratory, all creating an "academic hodge-podge." The School of Music did produce one outstanding honors graduate in 1900, Artie Mason Carter, who in 1922 founded the

Hollywood Bowl to bring music "to every Tom, Dick, and Harry" at an affordable price. Although the faculty in the fine arts increased, academic areas such as science declined. A new department of domestic sciences was well staffed, but the best of the fifty-seven faculty members hired by Moore tended to be in the School of Music, where the college already had a fine reputation. The most outstanding member of the music faculty, Professor G. L. H. Buddeus, a graduate of the Royal Conservatory at Leipzig, had toured Europe as a concert pianist and had studied and taught in Europe for eight years.[41]

Faculty members tended not to stay long at the college, and Moore looked to the University of Missouri or to eastern schools, particularly in New York, Massachusetts, Michigan, Pennsylvania, and the Chicago area, for new faculty, forsaking the more southern sources of the past. Lucy Laws continued to make important contributions as dean and as head of the English department, but the college lost Frederick Pannell, who died suddenly in 1903 after nearly fifty years of service. Although faculty members were quite competent, Moore reported a "most unfortunate experience with one, who proved to be a real scoundrel. He was disposed of as soon as discovered, but had already done much damage."[42]

Increasing troubles marked Moore's later years in office. Misfortune struck in the summer of 1906 when a typhoid epidemic caused the cancellation of twenty enrollments after rooms had already been reserved, causing a deficit of seven thousand to eight thousand dollars. The lower enrollments continued into 1907 when the graduating class, usually more than thirty, numbered sixteen. Townspeople heard rumblings of unrest among the servants, and rigid student discipline created tension and even withdrawals.[43]

Growing dissatisfaction came to a head in a 1908 incident following a University of Missouri football victory over Texas. With spirits running high, university men requested permission to bring fireworks onto the grounds and invite the girls to join in the fun. When Moore refused, they came anyway, three hundred strong, entering the dormitory by fire escapes. Christian College students and faculty happened to be in the gymnasium for a taffy pull. Confined there until the university men left, they returned to their rooms, and almost all found some object missing—carried off as trophies. The "trophies" were easily attainable, as the student laundry had just been distributed, complete with name tags by which the looters tried to identify the owners at church the next day. The incident had gone beyond mere fun when the boys invaded the kitchen and tried to reach for taffy, only to have the cook pour the boiling brew over their hands. When the much aggrieved Moore stormed into university offices and threatened to press charges against the throng, officials suggested countersuing for harm done to the boys. The result was an unpleasant standoff, leading to even greater student dissatisfaction, and almost one-third of the Christian College students withdrew.[44]

Financial problems naturally followed the unfortunate state of affairs. Loss of revenue from a "fever scare" prohibited payment of more than the interest on the debt of fifteen thousand dollars in 1907. In desperation, Moore made an appeal in person to Andrew Carnegie for twenty-five thousand dollars for the construction of a classroom building. A response informed her that Carnegie "will be glad to pay for the erection of a College Building, at cost of Twenty-five Thousand Dollars, provided the amount of Twenty-five Thousand new endorsement is raised, in cash or realizable securities, and, further, that you first clear the existing debt of Fifteen Thousand Dollars." The board, assembled in its May 1906 annual meeting, moved to "tender its thanks to Mr. Carnegie for the gift of $25,000 and say that the Board will attempt to comply with the conditions."[45]

Although the debt, which had been forty-three thousand dollars in the summer of 1899 with the cost of building St. Clair Hall, came down to ten thousand dollars by May 1909, it had been a hard year for the college. Despite the enrollment of 168 students from eighteen states and China, a financial panic throughout the country made it impossible for some parents to meet their obligations. Trustees had increasingly pressured Moore for financial accountings after 1906, and minutes of May 17, 1909, promised that "the full report of the twelve years, as promised, will be submitted as soon as it can be compiled." However, the following fifty pages of the minutes book were left blank, and the next minutes were dated October 22, 1909, by which time St. Clair had replaced Moore as president.[46]

Word of troubles surrounding the Moore administration had reached St. Clair, whose presidency of Hamilton College had stretched into six years. St. Clair's sister, Maxine, wrote of unpaid bills, while reports portrayed Moore as a semi-invalid in her last two years as president, practically confined to her room with arthritis during her last year. In the meantime, St. Clair had performed wonders at Hamilton College after inheriting a very difficult situation in which the ousted president had opened a college just four blocks away. She "left Kentucky with a host of friends, the gratitude of the college trustees, with college buildings improved and additional real estate purchased and student enrollment doubled."[47]

St. Clair had accomplished her goal at Hamilton College, and Christian College needed her. Moore resigned, and St. Clair answered "an urgent request" to return. Elected president for the third time, she returned in June 1909 and ushered in immediate progressive changes: typed board minutes brought the records into the twentieth century; a yearbook, the *College Widow,* replaced the *Chronicle;* and student social life took a new turn. State clubs for students from each state brought friendly rivalry, and a drama club appeared, along with baseball, horseback riding, an athletic association, a junior prom (minus men), an honor roll, and an annual senior class gift.[48]

Upon returning, St Clair wrote to Carnegie to confirm that his offer still stood, and within months she had matched the twenty-five-thousand-dollar challenge. She triumphantly reported to the board in October that R. H. Stockton of St. Louis, already a generous benefactor of the college, had agreed to give the matching funds. The gift was to be used for a new academic hall as a memorial to trustee Jeremiah Spires Dorsey, who had given Stockton his start in business and had died in 1909. As a successful businessman, Stockton shared his good fortune, becoming a benefactor of Christian Church institutions as well as endowing Culver-Stockton College, the former Christian University. The board still needed to eliminate the ten-thousand-dollar debt to meet the conditions of Carnegie's gift, a feat completed in March 1910 with a check from Mrs. L. L. Culver of St. Louis for five thousand dollars for final payment on the college debt. The Christian College property was finally free of debt.[49]

The one condition still necessary for the Carnegie grant was that the college be owned by the Board of Trustees. Within a month of clearing the debt, St. Clair presented to the board a document prepared by Judge E. W. Hinton stating conditions upon which she wished to deed her life interest in Christian College back to the board. St. Clair was to be appointed president "during the term of her natural life or so long as she might be able to carry on and manage said school . . . in person, or by competent representatives" to be approved by the board. When her personal management ended, she would receive an annuity "for the balance of her natural life as may be agreed upon." At the next meeting, April 9, 1910, the board accepted the "offer of Mrs. L. W. St. Clair of a legal transfer of her life interest in the property of Christian College to the Board of Trustees."[50]

The board had granted an annuity to Moore in return for her share of the college property in an agreement in May 1909. Payments continued for thirty-six years until her death in December 1946 in Clearwater, Florida, at the age of eighty-six. By that time, the annuity had cost the college more than ninety thousand dollars.[51]

Once the Carnegie grant was ensured, plans for Dorsey Hall moved swiftly. The three-story building to the east of St. Clair Hall was to be connected to St. Clair by a walkway on the ground floor. It would contain eleven classrooms, chemistry and physics laboratories, an office, a YWCA cabinet room, a splendid gymnasium (ninety feet by forty-two feet), and above it a large study hall and a Gothic chapel. President St. Clair contributed a magnificent stained glass window in memory of Annilee.[52]

The dedication of Dorsey Hall became part of the Golden Jubilee observance in weeklong events of May 1911. Three generations of alumnae participated in activities that included a gala lawn party, followed the next day, May 23, by the unveiling of the chapel window and a banquet. As part of the celebration, valedictorians came back to speak, piano contest winners came back to play, and a tradition began of presenting oil portraits of past presidents and their wives for display at the college. Paintings presented included those of Jennie Robards Rogers, Joseph Kirtley Rogers, George Bryant, Frank St. Clair, and Luella St. Clair. Bryant returned to the college for the occasion.[53]

The excitement of the dedication became especially emotional when Mrs. Richard Shannon, the former Elizabeth Lard of the class of 1861, rose to speak. Her father, elder Moses Lard, had been a member of the original Board of Trustees and an early supporter of female education as well as a noted orator. Elizabeth Lard had married Richard Shannon, a son of Christian College founder James Shannon. Richard, who served as Missouri's superintendent of schools, had been the first pupil to be enrolled in the primary department in 1851. Elizabeth Shannon spoke quietly of her love for the college: "Hardships were many. Six of us roomed in one room. But, there was never a complaint." At that point she collapsed into her chair and was carried to one of the halls, where it was confirmed that she had died of apoplexy. St. Clair, no stranger to death, saved the day with her remarks: "For Mrs. Shannon, this was not only a Home-coming but a Home-going. It is therefore not an occasion for lamentation and tears. . . . The portals of glory have opened and a Saint has entered in."[54]

The remainder of 1911 was a positive period for the college and its president. Trustees at the May meeting extended their "heartfelt thanks" to St. Clair for "the splendid service she has rendered the College since her return in June 1909." St. Clair reported an enrollment of 244 students, up 42 percent over the 170 of the previous year. In November 1912, St. Clair married Dr. Woodson Moss, the college physician and a prominent member of the community. They married in the chapel "at high noon with hundreds of friends." The entire student body attended, and, after the ceremony, the groom kissed each student.[55]

By 1912, St. Clair Moss had begun her next project, the construction of a memorial gateway at the entrance to the campus in honor of Joseph Kirtley Rogers. Although planned as part of the commemoration of the Jubilee Year, the gateway was not completed until November 1912. Alumnae, trustees, and friends of the college contributed the $1,735.29 for the project, a copy of a memorial entrance to Princeton University. After landscaping, driveway modification, and addition of sidewalks, the Rogers Memorial Gateway was dedicated on May 27, 1913.[56]

Campus social life during St. Clair Moss's third presidency took on the flavor of the twentieth century. Christian College girls played in basketball games with area high schools, attended the Farmers' Fair at the University of Missouri, skated and boated on the new lake on back campus, and even, appropriately garbed in cap and gown, attended concerts and theater productions. When the students, again in caps and gowns, attended their first-ever university football game, the young men present stood at attention as the girls marched to their reserved section. In groups of four or more, the students could shop on their own at Miller's Shoe Store, enjoy a phosphate at Tilley and Hutton's Drug Store, and even dine at the popular Harris Café. On campus, students could receive callers once a month (once a week, if seniors), and special permission gave greater privileges to those who were engaged—or pretended to be. "The College was something between a nunnery and a marriage bureau."[57]

A St. Clair Moss innovation in 1912, the honor roll, proved helpful in promoting student responsibility. Students voluntarily signed an honor roll pledge allowing them "the privilege of walking and shopping unchaperoned." The pledge included the following standards and limitations:

> 1. To observe daily exercise (walk or gymnasium), or to report for not doing so.
> 2. To shop, or go upon Broadway or other business streets, not oftener than once a week.
> 3. Not to visit cafes or restaurants without an official chaperon. Exceptions to this are found on the bulletin board.
> 4. To limit purchases of candy to one pound per week.
> 5. Not to buy bakery goods, tinned goods, or meat.
> 6. Not to visit Postoffice, Express Office, Railway Station, Telegraph Office, physicians' or dentists' offices without a chaperon.
> 7. Not to mail any letters or packages outside the college.
> 8. Not to walk with, talk with, or make an appointment with young men while out without a chaperon.
> 9. Not to pay any visits in town without special permission to do so.
> 10. To obey all household rules, and to cooperate with the faculty members and officials in maintaining order and promoting high standards of student conduct.
> 11. In case I break one of these pledges I understand that I am to report myself at once to the College President and not wait for a teacher or official to report me.[58]

An indication that not all students observed rules came from a letter from Mrs. G. R. Clarke explaining how "Hop Alley" got its name in the 1915–1916 academic year: "In those days we were required to be ready for bed by 9:45 when the corridor teacher came by and said 'Good Night.' Since we were down the west wing [of St. Clair Hall], we could slip into each other's rooms . . . with great excitement . . . fearing we might be caught. . . . Ruth Simon of Webster Groves gave the name Hop Alley after a notorious section in St. Louis, since we too were ignoring the law." The St. Louis "Hop Alley," located near Eighth and Market Streets, was "Chinatown," where opium and "hops" were allegedly sold.[59]

The concept of an honor roll led to the creation of an Honor Roll Society sponsored by Dean Elizabeth Hall as an honorary scholastic group open to the top 10 percent of the student body. In 1926, the society became a charter chapter of Phi Alpha Theta, which, along with similar chapters at Stephens College and at Cottey College in Nevada, Missouri, formed the junior college version of Phi Beta Kappa. Phi Alpha Theta became a national society for junior colleges, the only scholastic society then recognized by the American Association of Junior Colleges.[60]

St. Clair abandoned one tradition and began another in 1914. She ended the practice of wearing caps and gowns, and students wore simple shirtwaists or middy suits. A new tradition, an elaborate ceremony, complete with pageantry and trumpeters, introduced a "May Queen" each spring as a highlight of year-end activities. In another area, sororities, which had appeared at the turn of the century, proved disruptive and were disbanded in 1915 in favor of Greek clubs. Two of the three sororities had built bungalows on west campus, and the college bought the houses when St. Clair Moss abolished the sororities. St. Clair Moss's action resulted from her belief that sororities had created bad feelings between sorority and nonsorority students and sometimes among the sororities themselves: "We are much happier without them. In place of the sororities we have three Greek letter clubs. . . . These clubs are open to every girl in school so that there is no humiliation over the fact that some of the best girls are often not invited into a sorority." The Greek letter clubs attempted to capture the best features of the literary and musical clubs while furnishing social outlets. St. Clair Moss also founded the Twelfth Night Club as an all-school social club "to crowd twelve nights of revelry into one."[61]

The decade of St. Clair Moss's last years at the college saw flourishing enrollments and new activities. The 42 percent rise in enrollment to 244 in 1911 stabilized with 243 students in 1912, 236 in 1913, and 256 in 1914. The next four years brought overflow enrollments, forcing the college to house students across the street in rental property. The coming of World War I in Europe allowed the college to be competitive in the recruitment of exceptionally well-qualified faculty displaced by wartime conditions. One such faculty member was Marcia von Wilhelm in piano, a graduate of the Royal Academy of Music in London, who came to the United States after teaching in Germany, France, and England. During the war years, Christian College students energetically supported the war effort by knitting, rolling bandages, raising money for Armenians, riding on floats in Liberty Loan parades, and adopting war orphans. St. Clair Moss was the only woman in Columbia to make war-bond speeches.[62]

Columbia College even avoided the effects of the severe pandemic outbreak of influenza that struck Columbia in the fall of 1918 shortly after university classes had begun. Parker Memorial Hospital on the university campus, intended for use by university students, was the only hospital in town and admitted as many patients as possible. In all, 134 patients were hospitalized, although hundreds more were treated. University buildings were made into hospital wards, and Stephens College transformed all of the first-floor rooms of Senior Hall into a hospital. About 125 of the 300 students at Stephens contracted the disease. Christian College, however, instituting a careful voluntary quarantine, "did not lose an hour from the regular program and escaped with only two light cases." The college assisted those less fortunate by providing supplies to emergency hospitals.[63]

In her last period as president, St. Clair Moss made one of the most significant changes of her administrations by taking the college from a four-year institution to a junior college. The junior college concept, which had its origin with President William Rainey Harper of Chicago in the 1890s, stressed the logical breaking point between the first two years of introductory courses and the last two years of upper-level work. The idea could well meet the needs of Christian College, where St. Clair Moss found it increasingly hard to maintain the upper-level standards. She first used the term in the 1910 catalog, distinguishing among the two-year junior college program, the four-year degrees, and postgraduate work. Students in the junior college program were referred to as juniors and seniors. Accustomed to working with the University of Missouri, the college as early as 1898 had made arrangements for students of the two-year program to be admitted directly into the university as juniors. The articulation agreement recognized the work at Christian College as meeting "in every respect" the requirements for admission into the university.[64]

There followed two years of visitations by university faculty to approve the various academic departments of the college, the buildings, equipment, library, and laboratories before articulation could be completed. Finally, in 1913, St. Clair Moss discarded the B.A. degree for the A.A. (associate of arts) and changed the catalog title to the "Sixty-second Annual Catalog of Christian College for Young Women: An Officially Standardized Junior College Located in Columbia, Missouri." The A.A. degree required sixty hours of credit for a student to transfer to the University of Missouri as a junior, and Christian College graduation requirements provided solid grounding in required general education courses, including six credit hours in English, five in history, ten in foreign language, three in mathematics or logic, five in physical science, and five in biological science. An expanded library resulted from a move in 1914 to a larger area adjacent to Dorsey Chapel.[65]

Once again Christian College had taken a pioneering stance, becoming one of the first few junior colleges in the United States. The standardization necessary for the articulation with the university actually increased academic emphasis, ending once and for all any sense that "being a lady mattered most." Although the new world of counting credit hours and undergoing departmental reviews seemed troublesome to St. Clair Moss, the transition reflected but another chapter in the college's long history of adapting to new trends. Indeed, Christian College students did well as transfer students, going on by 1916 not only to the University of Missouri but also to state universities in Illinois, Kansas, Iowa, Texas, and Oklahoma, as well as to Drake, the University of Chicago, and Vassar. Christian College, along with Cottey, Hardin, Lindenwood, and Stephens Colleges, formed the Missouri Junior College Union, of which Luella St. Clair Moss became president.[66]

Temporarily in failing health and overwhelmed by administrative duties required of the new regulations, St. Clair Moss again attempted to resign at the October 14, 1915, board meeting. The board declined to take action on her request but sought to lighten her burden by using the executive committee of the board to transact business between board meetings. Still more helpful was the hiring of a young history professor, Edgar Desmond Lee, to undertake some administrative duties while heading the Department of History and Political Science. Lee, originally from rural Audrain County just north of Boone County, had earned his B.A., B.S., and M.A. degrees at the university. He had taught in the Columbia Normal Academy in 1907–1908 and had served as superintendent and teacher in New London and Sikeston, Missouri, and as a field representative for Hardin and Lindenwood Colleges.[67]

The last few years of St. Clair Moss's presidency produced two more major buildings, the $25,000 state-of-the-art swimming pool and a dormitory–home economics building, Missouri Hall. St. Clair Moss gave the funds for the swimming pool, built in 1918–1919, believing that some prospective students "made their decision for or against a college on the basis of whether it did or did not have a natatorium." St. Clair Moss determined "that Christian College should have the largest and most beautiful pool connected with any institution in the Middle West, and it has."[68]

As early as 1913, St. Clair Moss had vowed to build and equip a home economics building, combining it with dormitory space. Reminding the board that women expended 90 percent of the world's income, she vowed that Christian College would teach them how to do so effectively. During the construction, St. Clair Moss "was practically the contractor, signing all contracts for materials, and finding in some way the money to pay the workmen on Saturday nights." Her sister, Maxine, brought the floor plan from Mississippi and worked with the architect. Fund-raising for Missouri Hall went remarkably well. The building, complete in 1920 at a cost of $175,000, took its name from the statewide nature of donors. In addition to a good response from the board, as well as from Columbia and Boone County, Christian College shared in the fruits of a fund drive by the Christian Church that raised $2 million for six participating schools. The first floor of Missouri Hall housed sewing and cooking laboratories, storerooms, a dressing room, lecture rooms, a lavish parlor, a practice apartment for home economics, a kitchenette, a sun parlor, and music studios. From 1920 to 1929, it also contained the apartment of Luella St. Clair Moss. Dormitory rooms on the top two floors, necessary for the overflow enrollment, provided space for 110 girls.[69]

After the completion of her last building and twenty-five years of leadership at the college, St. Clair Moss's work was finally done. In addition to St. Clair Hall, the auditorium, Dorsey Hall, and Missouri Hall, her major accomplishments, she had built the swimming pool, a central heating plant, and two cottages.

While St. Clair Moss presided over "twenty-five years of expansion, recorded in brick and stone," it was her indomitable spirit that made her accomplishments possible. Walter Williams, dean of the University of Missouri journalism school, once introduced her as "Luella St. Clair Moss, a steam engine in petticoats." Her ability to charm and her sincere dedication to duty made her an outstanding fund-raiser, and her very presence on campus seemed to create an environment of success. As St. Clair Moss wrote, "It was with great joy and pride that I turned over to my successor . . . the most complete and up-to-date junior college for women in the Middle West." Her successor, Edgar Desmond Lee, was elected president and trustee at the May 31, 1920, board meeting, when trustees made Luella St. Clair Moss president emerita, the first president to be so honored. She remained an active trustee. The pleasure of her triumph was short-lived, however, as her husband, Dr. Woodson Moss, sixty-eight, died suddenly in October at Parker Hospital after the removal of his tonsils. He had been on the university medical school faculty and a practicing physician for nearly forty years.[70]

St. Clair Moss's retirement from Christian College by no means ended her years of service to society. She turned her talents to politics and the support of women's issues, putting into practice her adage that "a woman's chief glory, next to cultivating her heart and mind, lies in society and its function."[71]

St. Clair Moss's entrance into the scene of social reform coincided with the era of the Progressive movement and its emphasis on the use of suffrage as a tool for government reform. Support for women's suffrage grew from west to east, and Missouri was right in the middle of the action. The Missouri legislature proposed a state constitutional amendment for women's suffrage in 1918, which was approved in 1919. When the federal amendment passed Congress later in 1919, Missouri governor Frederick Gardner called a special session of the legislature to ratify the Nineteenth Amendment that same year. The Nineteenth Amendment granting women's suffrage finally succeeded in 1920 when Tennessee became the thirty-sixth state to ratify it. That same year, St. Clair Moss added her talents and her voice to the cause of social change.

A list of St. Clair Moss's activities and accomplishments indicates continued fervor and commitment, marking a whole new career for the next quarter of a century. An early member of the Equal Suffrage Association of Missouri, she served as president of the local group. With suffrage accomplished, she served from 1925 to 1927 as the first president of the Missouri League of Women Voters and as a member of the national board. She served three times as a delegate to the league-sponsored Conference on the Cause and Cure of War held in Washington, D.C. She acted as president of the Missouri Federation of Women's Clubs from 1929 to 1931, becoming director for Missouri of the General Federation of Women's Clubs. In 1922, she became the first woman on the Columbia Board of Education, the only woman to serve on education boards at the local, state, and national levels. After Gov. Guy Park named her to the Missouri Library Commission, she became its first woman president. During her service as vice president of the International Convention of the Disciples of Christ, she acted also as a member of its National Board of Education.[72]

St. Clair Moss also engaged in partisan politics. A charter member of the Women's Democratic Club in Columbia, she announced at an alumnae luncheon at the Daniel Boone Tavern that she intended to run for the Democratic nomination for Congress representing the Eighth Congressional District of Missouri. She faced two opponents in the Democratic primary: Judge E. M. Zevely of Linn, a popular lawyer, educator, and officeholder; and Charles Dewey of Jefferson City, a former University of Missouri football star. In addition to giving two speeches a day, she wrote a series of articles published in every Democratic newspaper in the district. Her stand for a lower tariff won the farm vote of even some Republicans, and her victory in the primary made her the first woman in Missouri to be nominated for a national office. One of twenty-eight women candidates for Congress that year, St. Clair Moss, like the twenty-seven others, lost in the general election. She had traveled more than five thousand miles and made 109 speeches in more than fifty towns, campaigning on a platform of lower taxes for the masses, farm relief, international cooperation to end war, better moral standards in government, and economy in government administration. Despite her loss, she won significant support, including an endorsement by the *St. Louis Post-Dispatch:* "It is not sufficient to say that for thirty years Mrs. Moss has done the work of a man—it is work that only a big man could have carried out. . . . Her candidacy, then is not merely a sentimental appeal to send a woman to Congress, it is an appeal to elect a nominee of superior knowledge, energy, and resource. It is a candidacy that should by all means succeed."[73]

Honors naturally followed such a career. St. Clair Moss became the only Missouri woman to hold honorary membership in the national education society for women, Delta Kappa Gamma, and in 1937 she received an honorary LL.D. degree from Culver-Stockton College. Her name was included on a tablet in the Missouri State Capitol dedicated to women "whose courageous work opened the opportunities for complete citizenship to all women in the state." She was also one of seventy-six women honored by a tablet placed at the League of Women Voters' national headquarters in Washington, D.C., in 1930, dedicated "In honor of these leaders and others unrecorded, whose labors have won for the women of the country entrance into its political life."[74]

Luella Wilcox St. Clair Moss died in Columbia in 1947 "after an illness of many months."[75] Under her guidance, the college enrollment had grown from 50 to more than 250 students. Her construction program had created a modern campus whose buildings still stand in tribute to her vision, and her definition of a "Christian College girl" had added stature to the reputation of Christian College students as scholars and ladies. Above all, her courage and brilliance remained emblazoned in the annals of the college she so loved.

Christian College founders

James Shannon

Thomas Allen

D. Pat Henderson

CHRISTIAN COLLEGE,
COLUMBIA, MO.

THE SIXTH SESSION OF CHRISTIAN FEMALE COLLEGE will open on the ***Third Monday in September next.***

A competent and *experienced Faculty* has been selected, with reference to their ability, fidelity and moral worth.

The *Domestic Department* is fully provided for, a Lady of age and experience having been engaged to spend all her time in its supervision.

COLLEGE FEES, PER SESSION OF TEN MONTHS, AS HERETOTORE.

Board and tuition, including washing, lights and doctor's bills, in the family, (in advance,)	**$150**
Tuition for day pupils in the regular College classes, ...	**36**
Tuition for day pupils in the Preparatory Department, ...	**24**
Tuition for music—Piano or Guitar, ..	**40**
Use of Pianos, ...	**8**

Ancient or Modern Languages, Drawing, Painting, Embroidering, &c., extra, at the usual prices.

For further information address *C. S. STONE, A. DOUGLASS* or *L. B. WILKES*. *Columbia, Mo.*

L. B. WILKES,
President C. C.

July 10, 1056.

COLUMBIA
BAPTIST FEMALE COLLEGE.

THE CURATORS of this Institution hereby announce to the public that the first term of the College will open on the **1st Monday in September next,** under the management of Prest. WM. R. ROTHWELL, aided by teachers highly qualified to instruct in all the branches of Female education taught in the United States.

The College property is admirably located in the town of Columbia, Boone county, Mo., and cannot be surpassed in point of beauty and fitness for a female school. For the present the Columbia Female Academy has been secured as a school room, and parents residing at a distance can procure boarding for their daughters

Advertisement from the *Missouri Statesman* of September 5, 1856, for Christian Female College and Baptist Female College. Courtesy State Historical Society of Missouri.

John Augustus Williams, first president of Christian College, 1851–1856.

Joseph Kirtley Rogers, Christian College president, 1858–1877.

Sculptor Vinnie Ream by George Caleb Bingham.
Courtesy State Historical Society of Missouri.

Christian College 1850s.

William Oldham, Christian College president, 1883–1893, with senior class.

Turn-of-the-century art studio.

Luella Wilcox St. Clair, Christian College president, 1893–1897; copresident, 1899–1903; president, 1909–1920.

Emma Frederick Moore, Christian College president, 1897–1899; copresident, 1899–1903; president, 1903–1909.

Christian College students in caps and gowns worn on outings as originated by President St. Clair.

W. T. Moore and his journalism class, 1903.

Stained glass window in Columbia College chapel, donated by Luella St. Clair in memory of her daughter, Annilee, 1900.

Marion Hertig, holder of many titles at Christian College from 1911 to 1948.

Edgar D. Lee, Christian College president, 1920–1935.

Riding Club with St. Clair Hall in background, 1929.

James C. Miller,
Christian College
president, 1935–1965.

Mary Paxton Keeley (second from left) and *Microphone* staff, 1936.

Special train delivers Christian College students, 1930s.

Franklin Launer and Jane Froman at Christian College, 1938.

Luella St. Clair Moss after retirement.

6

Heritage Revisited

EDGAR D. LEE: 1920–1935
EUGENE STEPHEN BRIGGS: 1935–1938

It is, sir, as I have said, a small college, and yet there are those who love it.

Daniel Webster, Dartmouth College Case, 1818

IN SPITE OF Luella St. Clair Moss's pride in what she left behind, Edgar Lee faced no easy task. The college carried a debt of $135,000 from the completion of Missouri Hall, plus the expense of annuities to Moore and now to St. Clair Moss. Lee found himself surrounded by a dedicated faculty and staff—dedicated especially to St. Clair Moss—few of whom fit the description of professional educators. Immediately following Lee's name in the catalog as president of the college came that of St. Clair Moss as president emerita. Indeed, St. Clair Moss exercised continuing influence within the administration, especially with Rose Lisenby as dean of the college and within the board, where deference to her remained virtually undiminished. However much St. Clair Moss had leaned on Lee's solid academic and administrative ability in her last years, her strong style of leadership had little in common with his less dramatic but determined agenda of the professional educator—an educator who saw the need to bring the college back to a stronger academic emphasis in line with demands imposed by accrediting agencies.

Just as St. Clair Moss's talents had fit the needs of her time, Lee's strengths took the college in the direction essential for academic excellence. One of St. Clair Moss's wisest acts may have been her recognition of the need for such an educator to follow her presidency. One of Lee's first acts, upon finding that institutional records had been kept in shoe boxes, was to purchase the college's first filing cabinets.

Lee, hearty and straightforward, combined imposing good looks with a manner of simplicity, humility, and candor. Son of a Laddonia, Missouri, farmer, he spoke with the typical regional accent and prized substance over style. He had taught in rural Missouri schools before entering the University of Missouri at the age of twenty-five for his B.A. and M.A. degrees in education. At the university, he met and married Bennetta Barkley, a talented musician and Phi Beta Kappa member from Mexico, Missouri. After graduation, Lee served as a field representative for Harden and Lindenwood Colleges, moving on to nine years as a superintendent of schools in New London and Sikeston. There he gained administrative skills that earned him the position at Christian College of part-time administrator and department head of political science and history. Promoted to vice president of the college in 1919, he was the natural choice to succeed St. Clair Moss when she retired in 1920. He became the first Christian College president to receive a salary rather than to collect his pay from student tuitions, an arrangement that suited Lee well: "It will be my policy to emphasize . . . quality of work rather than expansion of numbers. . . . I believe thoroughly in the small college."[1]

Lee moved quickly to update the curriculum. While retaining the college's traditionally strong liberal arts emphasis in the graduation requirements, he reversed the fine arts dominance in favor of greater emphasis on teacher training, enabling graduates to qualify for a three-year teaching certificate. Roughly half of the graduates became teachers in the 1920s, showing education to be a practical major. Lee cut the eight art courses, some of which did not carry academic credit, to three. He scheduled recitals every other week, rather than every week, and dropped Greek, although he kept German despite its small enrollment. He discontinued the journalism program for a time, reinstating it in 1928. He also ended ornamental penmanship and relegated "pageantry" to the gymnastics program. Retaining the home economics department as one of the strengths of the college, Lee added secretarial and bookkeeping courses, granting a two-year diploma in commerce, and expanded psychology and chemistry. The curriculum became somewhat less fashionable but distinctly more academic and professional.[2]

Lee's dedication to democratic principles led him to a belief in the ability of students to act as responsible citizens in the "college community," a phrase he used widely. The 1926 catalog carried his slogan in its preface: "With 'democracy and scholarship,' the watchword of a select student body." Along with the assumption of a "select student body," according to Lee, came the obligation to provide more freedom and responsibility and to train graduates as future citizens: "School activities, both in work and play are controlled and regulated, but individual responsibility coupled with teamwork is always encouraged. This has a subtle influence upon a girl's conduct. She learns respect for the opinion of others, develops initiative and self control. The qualities count for much, and enable women to become leaders in the communities in which they live."[3]

At a time when young women could be lured by the nefarious activities of the "roaring twenties," Lee worked tirelessly to channel student energies into constructive activities. There were nine major campus organizations by the end of his second year and twenty-four at the end of his administration. Such groups included a strengthened Student Government Association; Phi Theta Kappa, the honor scholarship society; the Young Women's Christian Association; Campus Sunday School; the Twelfth Night Club, for planning social activities; an athletic association; junior and senior class organizations; department clubs in science and foreign languages; a chapter of the League of Women Voters; As We Like It Club, a literary group; an art club; the St. Cecilia Club for music majors; the Mary Arden Club in expression or dramatics; the Lineage Club, organized in 1930 for students whose relatives had attended the college; state clubs for students from the various states; and the Sextette, a vocal group in high demand at community events. In addition to such activities, assemblies took place each Tuesday and Thursday in the college chapel with one religious program each week and the other assembly featuring faculty, a club, or a visitor. A newspaper, the *Campus Coverall,* emerged in 1926 as the first to be edited solely by students. Three years later, however, it was replaced by the *Microphone,* an official campus newspaper under the guidance of Mary Paxton Keeley of the English faculty. The *Microphone* repeatedly won top awards in junior college publication competitions in Missouri.[4]

In another activity, Christian College students participated in an especially bold venture by establishing Columbia's first radio broadcasting program. The college voice and orchestra groups, at the invitation of station WOS in Jefferson City, broadcast a "coast to coast" concert by remote control, hooking up to the Jefferson City station. The city of Columbia lacked a radio station in 1923, and use of WOS as the college station finally led to the creation of a permanent remote-control studio in the auditorium, installed in September 1925. At first, programs were broadcast every Monday evening, but use of the station expanded to include such events and organizations as weekly Christian Church sermons, university choral and orchestral groups, and even the 1925–1928 university football games and the 1926 basketball games. The activity proved a public relations gold mine, with letters and telegrams of appreciation pouring in to the college. At the time of the college's seventy-fifth commencement celebration, the station featured an address by Gov. Sam A. Baker. It also broadcast other Diamond Jubilee Year events, including an alumnae reunion attended by Jennie Robards Rogers, the oldest alumna, and Lucy Laws, who had retired in 1923.[5]

In his promotion of student leadership opportunities, Lee insisted that merit prevail over privilege. Here, again, the views of Lee and St. Clair Moss diverged. When St. Clair Moss urged the admission into Phi Theta Kappa of a "lovely girl" from a "fine family," despite the student's lack of the qualifying grade-point average, Lee's shocked refusal mystified St. Clair Moss. The contrast between the two on the role of student government was equally sharp. The student government structure created by St. Clair Moss in 1914 had been self-government in name only, with a student council chosen by the faculty and responding to faculty directives, a body scorned by the students as faculty lackeys. Challenged by the spirit of change in the 1920s, Lee staked his reputation on his conviction that students deserved true self-government. The new structure created a student council composed of an elected executive committee, which then chose additional members from the student body. The council, in cooperation with the executive committee of the faculty, determined all questions of discipline and was entirely free to carry out policies and fix punishments. The student self-government structure became official with the publication in 1925 of the college's first student handbook. The handbook began with a "Grant of Power": "The faculty of Christian College . . . hereby grants to the Student Government Association, through its governing body, the right to enforce the prescribed rules and regulations, these rules and regulations to be enacted with the consent of the Executive Committee of the Faculty."[6]

Student handbooks gradually expanded their content to include extensive nonacademic subject matter such as behavior, dress, the college calendar, schedule of events, listing of churches, and information on clubs and athletic activities. Rules of behavior, though conservative for the 1920s, represented considerable relaxation from those of earlier administrations. No Christian College girl was yet allowed to ride in an automobile without permission from the proper official or she would be subject to expulsion, and she still could not enter the Western Union Office, a doctor or dentist's office, or any upstairs office without a chaperon. However, she could now go downtown alone to those stores, restaurants, and beauty shops on the approved list and could go to a "picture show" on weekday afternoons. She could even attend a Saturday-night movie if she had written permission from home. She could talk for three minutes to a young man on the street, and he could walk her home. She was allowed a maximum of seven social engagements on study-hall nights during the school year. By the end of Lee's administration in 1935, a student could make local telephone calls, limited to three minutes, and long distance calls with no time limit. An unbending rule, the local mark of a "Christian College girl" was the requirement that she wear a hat and gloves when off campus. Smoking, too unheard-of to mention in the rules until 1933, carried a punishment of six weeks' confinement to campus.[7]

The popularity of the rules changes and the use of more scholarships not only helped fill the dormitories by 1925 but also demonstrated Lee's concern for individual needs and rights, typical of his democratic nature. As much as any president before him, Lee cared deeply for the welfare of each individual, agonizing for days when a violation might result in the expulsion of a student.[8] He opened educational doors by granting scholarships when possible and by finding office jobs for further help. Later greatly criticized by some trustees for allowing too many scholarships, Lee could not bring himself to limit enrollment to full-paying students. Nor would such a practice make the college competitive in recruitment.

Lee's greatest contribution, however, may have been upgrading the faculty and attracting talented individuals whose lasting influence went hand in hand with loyal and lengthy service. As soon as possible, he dropped student assistants, accepting only applicants with graduate degrees except in the fields of physical education, dance, and music. Forsaking formerly favored southern areas of faculty recruitment, Lee relied particularly on University of Missouri graduates. Wives of university faculty, banned from seeking employment there, constituted a rich pool of talent and reinforced the old bonds between the two institutions. Once hired, faculty enjoyed a prestigious role under Lee: "I desire only that authority that is necessary in carrying out my duty and responsibility. . . . If you are sufficiently trained and broad enough to teach in an institution like this, you are capable of helping to frame the educational policy of the school and of sharing in whatever praise that may come to it." While he respected the professionalism of his faculty, Lee was demanding. Faculty were "required to make weekly reports to the Dean . . . of the standing of every student in their respective classes." Faculty were expected to be "present and prompt" at each meal—each presiding over a table—and to attend chapel. Above all, "no teacher is retained on the faculty who is not thoroughly qualified, who does not cheerfully comply with all the rules and regulations, and who is not *strictly loyal to the school.*"[9]

Talented faculty who left their mark abounded. Young Franklin Launer, brought to the college by Lee in 1925, grew not only as a musician but also as a teacher and administrator. He ended the separate status of the music conservatory and integrated it into the college structure while leading a distinguished music faculty, including Double Sextette director Geneva Youngs and pianist Anna Froman. Froman, later Anna Froman Hetzler, was the mother of Jane Froman, a 1925 graduate of the college, who went on to a dramatic career as a widely popular radio and stage singer before retiring to live in Columbia. Launer married Ruth Almstedt, head of the art department for seventeen years, who had joined the faculty in 1930. Respected by all segments of the college community, Launer retired in 1962 after thirty-six years of service. He was honored in 1972 by the dedication of the auditorium as "Launer Auditorium."[10]

Lee recruited other significant young faculty members: Margaret McMillan in history stayed for thirty-four years, retiring in 1958; Ruth Graham in home economics, coming in 1925, headed the program for more than thirty years; Esther Wagner Stearn in chemistry and bacteriology, another who stayed into the late 1950s, excelled as one of the college's most brilliant instructors; Harold Long in biology helped set the tone in the sciences for three decades; and Carolyn Reed Drew headed the horsemanship program with the same distinction she lent to her work as director of the Missouri Horse Shows Association and superintendent of the Missouri State Fair Horse Show. Drew's daughter, Shirley Hardwicke, a Christian College graduate, directed horsemanship at Stephens College for more than thirty years.[11]

One of the more colorful faculty members, Mary Paxton Keeley, came to the college in 1929, founded the *Microphone,* the college newspaper, and taught creative writing for twenty-three years. A native of Independence, she grew up next door to Bess Wallace, attended high school with Wallace and Harry Truman, and became one of Margaret Truman's two godmothers. Keeley enrolled in the University of Missouri School of Journalism when it opened in 1908 and became its first woman graduate in 1910. During World War I, she worked in the YMCA Canteen Service in France, and in 1919, she married Edmund Burke Keeley. After her husband's death in 1928, she returned to Missouri for an M.A. degree in journalism. She retired in 1952 but went on to edit the *Missouri Alumnus* and write for the *Kansas City Star.* A prolific writer, her plays, poetry, fiction, newspaper columns, and radio scripts entertained two generations of readers before her death in 1986 at the age of one hundred. As Keeley remarked in 1983, "I've always prayed to God for an interesting life. God may have overdone it."[12]

In the administrative area, Rose Lisenby, brought to the college by St. Clair Moss in 1912, continued as dean of faculty and sponsor of Phi Theta Kappa. Promoted to her position just months before Lee's coming to the presidency, she had previously served as head of the English department and principal of the academy, and her devotion to the former president remained unswerving.

Most important of those faculty already at the college, Marion Hertig served from 1911 to 1948 in a wide variety of capacities: 1911–1919 as head of the preparatory department and a physical education instructor; 1919–1920 as a field representative; 1920–1926 as an assistant in English, history, and the Bible; 1925–1941 as editor of the *Christian College Alumnae Bulletin;* 1928–1946 as sponsor of the yearbook, the *College Widow;* and 1933–1948 as the alumnae secretary. Known by all to be a person of extraordinary character and unfaltering ideals, she exerted a lasting influence on almost four decades of Christian College students. Her imperious air, straight-backed stance, and the ever present black-velvet neck band belied a softness known to the many students who found solace in

"Mrs. Hertig's room." Alma Hill, a former student who later became a faculty member, remembered Hertig as "a little old lady with the beauty of a cameo and the strength of a steam roller." It was Hertig who greeted students at their first assembly, chose the big sisters for each new student, set the tone in the dining room, and initiated each generation of students into the college's traditions. An excellent organizer, she founded the Lineage Club, created the May Queen Pageant, planned proms, and oversaw all manner of special events. Dear to her heart was rehearsing students for baccalaureate, where all present would rise to sing "Jerusalem the Golden." Although the rendition of the difficult hymn sometimes left something to be desired, Hertig asserted: "I love that song so, I want them always to sing it while I am here." They did.[13]

Hertig's career at Christian College could not have been more unlikely in view of her earlier life: her grandfather had been a trouper with Van Ambugh's Circus; her father owned the first Magic Lantern Show in Union City, Michigan; and her mother excelled at doing readings at church programs. Born of this entertainment background, Hertig made her stage debut as Little Eva in *Uncle Tom's Cabin,* went to Boston to study expression, and performed as "Marion Willis, Dramatic Reader." After an impulsive marriage to "handsome, intellectual, ne'er-do-well" Roland Hertig, she and her two baby boys, living a life of poverty, were abandoned, and she managed to obtain enough education for a teaching career in order to support her two sons. Tragically, her older son was killed in a high school episode, and the younger boy, a high school valedictorian, committed suicide after suffering a nervous breakdown. Beginning her new life at Christian College in 1911, Hertig exemplified the values of a small college in her devotion to student welfare. Sometimes a fun-loving cutup, but always possessed of great dignity, the "Mrs. Chips of Christian College" was finally moved to a convalescent home in Columbia in December 1946 where she remained until her death in 1949.[14]

Lee also brought into his administration Julia Spaulding, hired as principal of the academy and then becoming the first real dean of women in 1923. Known for her sound judgment, loyalty, and scrupulous fairness, Spaulding served as dean until 1933 and headed the mathematics department from 1921 until her retirement in 1949. Recognizing new needs to meet contemporary competition, Lee also hired the college's first full-time recruiter of students, an innovation later stimulating considerable debate in board meetings. The recruiter, J. Kelly Wright, highly effective in bringing students to the college, had worked for the Missouri State Board of Agriculture, addressing more than two thousand farmers' institutes, and had traveled in all counties of the state. He and the other "educational counselors" who joined him in the recruitment effort played a significant role in furthering the reputation of the institution.[15]

A special member of Lee's staff, Maurice Wightman grew up helping his father, Harry Barnett Wightman, superintendent of buildings, tend to the physical needs of the campus. As part of the college community, he became a close friend of Lee's son, Desmond. Born in 1900, Wightman first went on the college payroll in 1915. He took over more and more of his father's duties, and when his father died in 1936, Wightman had already been acting as superintendent of buildings for several years. He remained on the payroll for sixty-two years, almost certainly longer than any other college employee, and was considered "as much a part of the college as the foundation." He earned the admiration of administrators, faculty, and students for his dedication to the needs of the college community as well as for his skills and unflappable good nature. A bachelor and a favorite with staff women, Wightman found his future wife when Louise Yeager joined the college as dietitian in 1941, replacing Agnes Funkhauser, who had held that position for twenty years. The couple married in 1945 and lived in an apartment in St. Clair Hall. Louise Yeager Wightman was to become a highly effective manager of the dining services during the next administration. In 1968, the college maintenance building was dedicated as the "Wightman Building" in Maurice's honor, and in 1972 he went into semiretirement, becoming fully retired in 1976, eight years before his death in 1984. When the maintenance building was razed to make room for a new art and classroom facility in 1995, the new maintenance building on east campus became the second "Wightman Building."[16]

Lee's most important appointment, the naming of James C. Miller as dean of faculty in 1927, had enormous implications for the future of the college. Miller, inseparable from the college's academic achievements in his era, became acting president from January to August 1935 and served as president from 1938 to 1956.

With the help of capable personnel, Lee brought enrollments to new heights. After a large increase in registration in 1922, at least partly the result of the work of J. Kelly Wright as a field representative, the total enrollment reached 363 by May 1923, adding another 58 by May 1924. Deteriorating economic conditions led to a decline in enrollments by May 1925, but by May 1926, a gain of 38 students brought figures back up to 341. Lee, reporting that the college's finances were in excellent condition, planned to pay off any remaining debt.[17]

Despite the successes of Lee's early years, he met a severe challenge in the growing dissatisfaction of St. Clair Moss with his policies. An innovator in her early years as president, St. Clair Moss could once have agreed with Lee's statement at the beginning of his administration that "the college that regards itself as having reached the limit of improvement is in a dangerous way. The advance in the general educational ideas, changes in the position of women in the community, the recent granting of suffrage to women, all call for reconsideration and readjustment of our educational program." By 1926, however, St. Clair Moss had begun to consider Lee's changes alarming and even looked upon Lee himself, whom she had once admired, as too unpolished. Adding to Lee's troubles, the presence on the board of the new pastor of the Christian Church, Walter Haushalter, represented quite a different image. A sophisticated novelist who had studied at Yale and at Columbia University, Haushalter had promotional plans that matched St. Clair Moss's new idea of leadership.[18]

The emerging conflict between the old and the new involved not only Lee's democratic views but also opposing concepts of how the board should function. Trustees, though quite satisfied with Lee's reduction of the debt from $135,000 to $50,000, bristled at his attempt to instruct the board. Whereas St. Clair Moss had spared the trustees too many financial details, Lee brought such details to the board and asked them not only to help in decision making but also to accept more financial responsibility. At its March 30, 1923, meeting, the board authorized Lee to use his own judgment on improvements under $1,000 but required him to submit to the board any expenditures over that amount. In a change of policy the next July, the trustees allowed Lee to have full authority and responsibility for all matters of policy and management of the college "except in questions of finance, which shall be settled by conference with Mrs. Moss acting in her official capacity of Secretary of the Board of Trustees." This requirement included salaries, furnishings, grounds, and buildings. Any items more than $1,000 would be submitted to the executive committee.[19]

Outstanding issues between Lee and St. Clair Moss came to a head in March 1926. Lee, in Chicago at a meeting of the convention of the American Association of Junior Colleges, had just been elected vice president of that organization on March 17 and returned to campus to find that St. Clair Moss and other trustees had met in his absence. The *Columbia Tribune* reported Lee's resignation:

> [I]t is understood by those close to his office that he decided to leave the college because of long-standing friction between him and influential members of the Board of Trustees over certain school policies. The Board called a meeting last week. Several members took exception to certain administrative policies. . . . Upon his return home, Mr. Lee was informed of the sentiment of certain board members and his resignation immediately followed. Mr. Lee's policy in school life had been to encourage democracy and to develop self-government. He believed in placing responsibility on the young people and in developing leadership through school activities. School government in Mr. Lee's regime reached the highest degree of efficiency and school spirit in the seventy-five years that the institution has been in existence. The enrollment today is the biggest in the history of the school.

The article closed by noting that the 1926 yearbook was dedicated to President Lee.[20]

Lee informed the board at its March 22 meeting that he would not accept reelection when his contract expired June 1. The board voted to accept Lee's "declination" and chose a committee to recommend a name for his successor. The committee was composed of Haushalter, St. Clair Moss, and one of Lee's staunchest supporters, R. H. Emberson.[21]

The *Columbia Missourian* quoted Lee as stating that he had "been thinking of quitting the school business for several years" and would "probably enter the business world." Like the *Tribune* article, the *Missourian* praised Lee for achieving the largest enrollment in the school's history and applauded his accomplishments.[22]

The announcement of Lee's decision to leave brought an immediate reaction at a student convocation. Supporters circulated a petition to be given to Lee for presentation to the board, and all presidents of all classes and campus organizations signed. Students pointedly gained permission from the board to present the college with a three-quarter-length oil portrait of Lee.[23]

Because the committee to submit a name for the presidency failed to produce a viable candidate, another committee met with Lee to discuss conditions for his possible return, reporting at the May 10 meeting. The committee, including Fred Harris, William A. Bright, and Emberson, reported that Lee, after a lengthy conference, had "stated that if it were for the best interests of Christian College for another person to be selected president, the Board should feel free to do so." However, further negotiations produced agreement that Lee would be willing to resume his duties under four conditions. First, he would be reemployed for a term of three years. Second, his salary would remain the same for the coming year and would be determined by the board after that. Third, he specified that "all authority as president of the College be lodged in him for which he alone should be responsible." Finally, an election on the conditions stated by him must be unanimous. Not only did the trustees meet Lee's demands, but they also increased his salary by five hundred dollars and passed a resolution by Emberson that "from this time on all faculty members and officials shall be nominated by the president of Christian College and that election shall be by the executive committee of the Board." Further, the executive committee "would be expected to keep in close touch with the interests of the college." His position protected, Lee retired from membership on the board.[24]

When Harris, as chairman of the board, announced Lee's retention at a student convocation in Dorsey Chapel, the surprise announcement was "greeted by an enthusiastic demonstration on the part of the students." Harris stated that every member of the board was "squarely back of Mr. Lee" and wanted "to give him all of the assistance" possible. Dean of Women Julia

Spaulding had tendered her resignation when Lee resigned, and Lee told the students: "I think I will be perfectly safe in announcing at this time that Miss Julia Spaulding will be our next dean of women." J. Kelly Wright, who had also resigned in protest, also returned. St. Clair Moss's close friend Rose Lisenby resigned as dean of faculty.[25]

Lee's victory could not have been more complete, and he was free to move ahead vigorously with increased prestige. Vice president of the 250-member American Association of Junior Colleges since March, Lee became its president on December 1, 1926, in Jackson, Mississippi. His influence in the junior college movement brought increased attention to Missouri's leading role, organizing in 1912 the Missouri Junior College Union of all private women's junior colleges in the state. Lee credited the role of the University of Missouri in the junior college movement and the influence of the private junior college for the state's progressive stance. Well ahead of his time, Lee recognized the divergence of interests between private and public junior colleges, with the private junior college emphasis on providing the first two years of a four-year degree, and the newer public or "community college" more likely to provide the terminal degree and place less emphasis on the liberal arts. In recognition of Lee's leadership in the junior college movement, the American Association of Junior Colleges elected him as its president in 1926, and he became a member of its Hall of Fame for his innovative teaching methods and for involvement of students in the decision-making process.[26]

After the resignation of Rose Lisenby, who joined the faculty of Texas Women's College in Fort Worth, filling her position demanded Lee's immediate attention. He presented the name of Louis A. Eubank as Lisenby's successor, for the first time bringing to the college a professional educator as dean of faculty. Coming to the deanship in May 1926, Eubank advanced rapidly in his career, staying only until the next May. He resigned to become dean of faculty at Northeast Missouri State Teachers' College in Kirksville, where he served with distinction as a major force in Missouri higher education. Eubank recommended his longtime friend James C. Miller as his replacement. Eubank and Miller had grown up together in the small Ozark town of Spring Garden, and both had attended Central Missouri State Teachers' College in Warrensburg. Miller had lived in the Eubanks' home from 1913 to 1915 while principal of the Otterville High School, where he later became superintendent of schools. He entered the naval reserve and served nine months in Europe before finishing his undergraduate work. Later, as a graduate student in education at the University of Missouri, he knew both Eubank and Lee and moved to Columbia in 1926 to act as principal of the elementary school of the university. He came to the deanship at Christian College in September 1927, continued his graduate work, and finally earned his doctorate in 1930.[27]

Lee's choice of Miller as his dean had major implications for the college where Miller would serve as acting president in 1935 and as president from 1938 to 1956. Lee and Miller worked well together as mutually appreciative professionals, both becoming well known in the field of education.

Another major academic influence in the mid-1920s, the "Reeves survey," was a thorough examination and evaluation of all aspects of the college. The Board of Education of the Disciples of Christ instigated the survey as part of an evaluation of the work of all Christian Church–related colleges. The study, begun in 1925 and completed in 1926, was directed by Floyd W. Reeves, head of the research department of Kentucky State University at Lexington. One of the best-known college evaluators in the country, Reeves had directed more than one hundred surveys and was used by the North Central Association of Colleges and Secondary Schools as an examiner. Reeves looked into the administration, finances, plant, faculty, equipment, catalogs, and cost of education. Lee, wise enough to understand the great benefit of such a study in preparing for reaccreditation and secure enough not to feel personally threatened, welcomed the study.[28]

Survey results proved useful and gratifying—especially in their recognition of the college's worth:

> In general the survey staff received the impression that conditions in the college are excellent both as regards the educational efficiency and financial practice. We are of the opinion that few of the colleges of the Disciples of Christ receive greater educational returns for the amount expended per student for strictly educational purposes than Christian College. Christian College is the only institution of those surveyed which has succeeded in financing its educational program without either incurring an annual deficit or having available for use an income of considerable amount from productive endowment or other outside sources.[29]

Appreciative of Lee's innovations in student government, Reeves stated that "students have accepted this Grant of Power with enthusiasm and as a result have many more social privileges than formerly, and the college has much less trouble administering its social regulations. . . . The Student Government Association is functioning in a very wholesome way at Christian College."[30]

Reeves did have specific criticisms, most of which could be remedied reasonably soon. He found it a "serious mistake" that no minutes of any faculty meeting had ever been preserved. Finding faculty salaries only 76 percent of the average for comparable institutions, he suggested a salary schedule as an incentive to faculty. His conclusion that the immediate goal of the college should be the acquisition of an endowment of at least two hundred thousand dollars, preferably five hundred thousand dollars, would prove a more difficult challenge.[31]

Lee found the study so valuable that he took the opportunity to retain Reeves as an administrative and educational counselor in the fall of 1927. Reeves agreed to make one-month visits to the college at frequent intervals and to advise the administration on policy while cooperating with the faculty to study the curriculum. He had a threefold mission: to help the college gain maximum efficiency for the money expended in the educational program, to help faculty develop a curriculum to meet the specific needs of young women, and to help direct a program of faculty improvements. Reeves worked so well with the administration that in 1929 he enlisted the services of Dean Miller to help survey the Baptist colleges of Kentucky.[32]

While Lee found himself juggling several major issues simultaneously in the 1920s—internal factionalism, recruitment of an effective dean, and the flurry of administrative activity attendant to the Reeves survey—none approached the magnitude of his most critical challenge, that of securing continued accreditation from the North Central Association of Colleges and Secondary Schools. The setting of standards for Missouri colleges dated back to the efforts of President Jesse of the University of Missouri in 1893, and Lee fully recognized the importance to Christian College of meeting those standards. Missouri had helped charter the first regional accrediting association, the North Central Association, in 1895 to standardize both public and private institutions. In 1912, Missouri became the first state in the nation to apply such standardization to private junior colleges through use of an "approved list," with which Christian College complied. After the North Central Association first accredited the college in 1923, the accrediting agency established standards for junior colleges. The only standard posing difficulty for Christian College was Article Eight on finances that the "minimum annual operation income for the educational program of the junior college should be at least $20,000 of which not less than $6,000 should be derived from stable sources other than students' fees, such as public support or permanent endowments."[33]

In February 1925, Christian College received notification that the college would be dropped from the accredited list of junior colleges by the North Central Association; such denial of accreditation would almost certainly be the death knell of any college. Lee appeared before the North Central Association as the representative of the American Association of Junior Colleges to ask for an interpretation of Article Eight. After lengthy discussion, the association voted that any school on the accredited list that met all requirements other than Article Eight should continue on the accredited list for one more year. Christian College was safe for the moment. However, in 1926 the association increased the money required from outside sources to a minimum of ten thousand dollars, and Christian College was put on probation to be "surveyed" at the end of one year. Not only did the college lack the prerequisite endowment, but it also needed to spend more income on such mandated requirements as better-balanced teaching loads, higher salaries, and better library and laboratory facilities. Lee turned to Reeves for help in launching an endowment campaign. He also persuaded the trustees to add to their membership two men in education: A. G. Capps, a professor of education at the University of Missouri, and Claude A. Phillips, a writer of accrediting specifications. As with the hiring of Reeves, Eubank, and Miller, Lee again attracted strong professionals to the service of the college.[34]

The 1927 survey by the North Central Association resulted in a recommendation that the college be accredited for only one year with an intensive review to take place March 1, 1928. The fourteen-page report defined steps to be taken to correct deficiencies. According to the report, the faculty was "markedly underpaid," and too many faculty members had received their degrees from the University of Missouri. The report also found the library deficient in science and the science laboratories in need of better lighting. Finally, there must be a better institutional accounting system.[35]

When Miller held his first faculty meeting after coming to the college on September 1, 1927, only six months remained to prepare for the North Central visitation the next March. In his appearance before the faculty, described as "brilliant, witty, to the point," Miller laid out the starting points. There would be two faculty meetings per month, with one entirely focused on the profession of teaching, including discussion of the best current literature on the subject. Faculty must also plan a uniform system of grading and compose a mission statement. Miller also announced his intention to visit classes and discuss the teaching performance with each instructor. His strategy hinged on the one loophole in the North Central report: "If any factor can be cited in lieu of endowment it probably should be found in a comprehensive program for the maintenance of effective teaching." The faculty would be asked to save the college in the absence of sufficient endowment.[36]

Intense activity to prepare for the visitation resulted in swiftly implemented changes and heated faculty meetings. Frances Heckman, the college's first professional librarian, weeded unwanted volumes from the shelves and ordered new reference works in the most significant enlargement of library holdings in years. Faculty enrolled in graduate programs and experimented with new methods in the classroom, especially in testing. New wiring provided more light in science laboratories. In a new system of cost accounting, expenditures of the college were separated from those of the high school, making it clear that the high school must go; the last high school classes were held in the 1927–1928 academic year.[37]

The much anticipated accreditation visitation took place on March 2–3, 1928, with George R. Moon of the University of Chicago holding the inspection at the request of the Commission on Institutions of Higher Education of the North Central Association. Moon concentrated especially on the classroom experience. He called the academic work done "easily the equivalent of the first two years of any of the so-called four-year standard colleges" and concluded: "I have never seen better teaching in Junior College work. The teachers are enthusiastic, alert, and are well versed both in their subject matter and in methods of putting it across. I believe that the faculty, along with the teaching which is being done, is the . . . strongest point about Christian College at the present time."[38]

Moon found the classes, ranging in size from five to thirty-four, with most in the range of fifteen to thirty, to conform to "the spirit of the North Central Association requirements." He also found "no observable dead timber in the library" where "practically all of the books are first class college material." The chemistry and botany laboratories had been improved, and the home economics department was "well-equipped and . . . exceptionally well taught." Dealing with finances, Moon stated: "Christian College does not meet the requirements of the Association in this regard. It has very little permanent endowment. . . . However, there has been an available income for the past five years . . . from the Missouri Churches. . . . The entire accounting system is being revised under the direction of Mr. Reeves. . . . The new scheme is one of the best which I have seen in any of the colleges visited."

Moon then concluded that the administration "has made a consistently conscientious effort to carry out every recommendation of the Survey Committee of last year. . . . The students are receiving an unusually high grade of training. On the basis of the unusual standing of Christian College in all of the requirements aside from endowment, I recommend that the school be accredited."[39]

Christian College won not only the battle but also the war. The North Central Association report of September 1933 recognized that the original standards of the association "have concerned for the most part the material and physical features of the institution. They were founded on the assumption that a superior school plant turned out a superior product. Now educators are realizing that this is a false assumption." New standards dropped the prescribed amount of endowment.[40]

Trustees celebrated the successful accreditation effort with the formal establishment of a Permanent Endowment Fund. With a gift of twenty-five thousand dollars from R. H. Stockton and five thousand dollars from Frank and Ella Hughes, the board determined that "there should be some regulation governing the handling of the endowment fund." A board resolution of May 28, 1928, set forth procedures for funds.[41]

Optimism abounded in 1929 at Christian College, as in much of the country. In line with long usage, a charter revision officially dropped the word *Female* from the college name. The revision also clarified the property title, explaining annuities paid to Moore, to ensure unchallenged bond ownership by the college. Also encouraging, enrollments flourished, forcing faculty who had lived on campus to move. By October, even St. Clair Moss had left her suite in Missouri Hall, her rooms in demand for more space for Conservatory of Music students. Only the Lee family continued to live on campus, occupying the family bungalow enlarged by two bedrooms and a bathroom to provide fitting presidential quarters. The endowment fund had grown to seventy-five thousand dollars, and Lee proposed an expansion campaign of three hundred thousand dollars for a new residence hall. Trustee Berry McAlester called the president's January 1930 financial report "the best he had ever heard since he had been a member of the board." With Lee's contract due to expire on May 29, the board named him president for life, in place of the usual three-year contract, an honor previously bestowed only on St. Clair Moss.[42]

The college also prospered academically with Dean Miller continuing the goal-setting activities so successful in retaining accreditation. In his second year, Miller emphasized research and publication, unleashing a creative wave of faculty articles published in the *Junior College Journal, Education,* and the *Missouri School Journal,* among others. The focus for the third year was on the preparation of a course syllabus for each class, laying out the course content, teaching methods, objectives, and bibliography. The syllabi were then bound into a 330-page volume as a standard for incoming faculty. In the fourth year, Miller, by now an acknowledged expert on the role of the junior college, set as a goal the study of the junior college curriculum. Faculty agreed that the junior college courses should concentrate on general education and academic repair with a curriculum emphasizing general survey courses. Finding that only half of junior college graduates continued on to receive a four-year degree, the faculty defined the functions of Christian College in the 1931–1932 catalog:

> 1. PREPARATORY, in that the graduates are qualified to matriculate with junior standing in senior colleges and universities.
> 2. GUIDANCE, in that all aspects of college life, such as academic, religious, recreational, and social are under the careful supervision of a faculty selected on the basis of appropriate training.
> 3. TERMINAL, in that graduates are prepared to assume both vocational and civic duties.
> 4. CULTURAL, in that the graduates have acquired new appreciation of the finer things of life.[43]

To implement the preparatory function, catalogs in the 1930s carried entrance requirements for junior standing at other institutions most attended by Christian College graduates, including universities in Missouri, Arkansas, Colorado, Illinois, Iowa, Kansas, Kentucky, Nebraska, Oklahoma, Tennessee, and Texas.

The institutional focus for 1932–1933 concerned the development of student personality and character, followed in 1933–1934 by a study of the proposed new standards of the North Central Association. The emphasis in the early 1930s shifted more and more to student guidance, reflecting Miller's own counseling specialization. The Christian College program, advanced for its day, emphasized personal attention and individual needs. Preentrance guidance began with a study of the student's high school record information form, interests, and plans. A tentative student program based on this information and the assignment of a faculty advisor then led to a conference between the student and advisor at registration time. By 1934, the college had adopted placement tests, regular conferences with the advisor, and an early-warning system, all emphasizing the college's traditional role: "The real center of interest is not units of subject matter or credits, but the individual student. A study is made of each girl as an individual, and every effort is made to help her to realize all of her possibilities." The years of study led to a publication, *Christian College,* printed in May 1934 as a supplement to the catalog. The demand from other educators quickly sent the publication into a second printing and further secured Miller's reputation as an authority on guidance and matriculation.[44]

The illusion of prosperity at the college, as in the country as a whole, was shattered in 1929. After "Black Tuesday," October 24, 1929, the stock market took until mid-1932 to reach rock bottom, and the Great Depression reached its most critical stage in 1932–1933 with the downward spiral in prices, production, employment, and world trade. When the unemployment rate reached 25 percent, defaults on installment payments increased, including unpaid bills in education. Christian College began to feel significant effects of the depression in 1929 when 71 of 310 potential students canceled by fall. By May 1930, the minutes reported that "unless the net income of the College justifies present salaries and operating expenses . . . at the end of the year, or any time in the future, the Board shall feel free to reduce salaries and expenses." By December, the administration had managed to decrease expenditures by $15,209.98, but a cut of at least $30,000 more was needed, which would still leave a deficit. Lee reported that it was more and more difficult to collect accounts. Even with previous cuts, the March 1931 minutes reported a further reduction of $29,000, and Lee was forced to go to a local bank for a loan to meet the March payroll.[45]

With hard times came controversy. Ever since Lee had hired Wright in 1921 as the first recruiter, the roll of the field representatives had been a subject of debate within the board, debate that had intensified by 1931. A board resolution of January 1928 had decreed that "all field agents be required to submit monthly reports of places visited, work accomplished and expense accounts." As enrollments declined, the trustees decided to use the carrot as well as the stick, turning to the use of a bonus in addition to salary. The two women recruiters each received a salary of $1,800 and expenses, plus $75 per student for any over twenty-five. The bonus for the three men, with a salary of $2,400 each, was $75 for every student over thirty-two. By the 1930s, competition for students had become so intense that colleges routinely relied on such measures.[46]

Another issue, the college's relationship to Moore, resurfaced with financial problems. Realizing the need to refinance the college by issuing bonds, the trustees hoped to clarify Moore's contract, which had called her annuity payment a rental. Although Moore did not hold a first mortgage, trustees feared that she "could create a situation very embarrassing to the college." With Moore living in Florida, the college worked through her lawyer in Springfield, Missouri. Trustees offered to put a portion of the bond issue in escrow to secure continued payment of Moore's annual income from the college in return for her agreement to relieve the college from her first lien on its property. Moore, professing willingness to cooperate, prolonged negotiations by her reluctance to agree to the college's terms, terms recommended by her lawyer. The trustees finally decided to lay the issue to rest without completing a new contract and instructed their attorney to proceed no further with the negotiations.[47]

The refinancing plan proceeded quickly in the summer of 1931 with the issuing of bonds totalling $83,000 at 6 percent interest. The ten-year bonds, secured by a first mortgage, provided for payment of overdue notes and other obligations. However, matters grew worse in the following months, and Lee, forced to borrow to meet the payroll, faced a debt of $70,000 by the fall of 1931, the date once proposed for the completion of a new dormitory. With enrollments down to 277, Lee cut salaries by one-third, and released some faculty and staff. The income for 1932–1933, down 25 percent from the previous year, brought on the same type of juggling of debts that had been necessary during the Civil War. Indeed, the crisis was no less dire than that of the 1860s. College-owned bonds were in default with no interest collected after January 1, 1932.[48]

The stress of meeting day-to-day obligations took its toll, and, by commencement week of 1932, Miller, suffering from "nervous exhaustion," could barely come to campus to work for a few hours each day. Refusing to give up, he became so weak that it required a major effort for him to go from the front gate to his office. Once back home, he found it impossible to eat or rest well. Lee did his best to shelter Miller from demands over the next two years, impressing his dean with the need to recover, until Miller began to regain his strength by the fall of 1934.[49]

Demands on Lee, however, remained unrelenting. Short-term borrowing continued, and enrollments dipped to 188 students, 206 counting part-time students. The college even resorted to a form of barter in 1934 when Lee made a contract with Dale Wild of the Sarcoxy Nursery for landscaping in exchange for two years of tuition for his daughter, Lillian. The next October brought 26 cancellations, but, even though enrollment increased by 45 students, Lee's darkest days were just ahead.[50]

When President Lee made his financial statement to the board at the December 18, 1934, meeting, he knew it was the end of his presidency and that he must step aside. With characteristic simplicity, Lee addressed the board: "Gentlemen, I have done the best I could. I've worked hard. I've been honest. But in the face of times like these, my best has not been good enough."[51] Lee's presidency had become a victim of the depression. At an emergency meeting the next day, the trustees failed to convince Miller to accept the presidency. Miller, believing that his training was appropriate to the deanship rather than to the presidency, also emphasized his physical limitations in declining the offer. Finally, Miller did agree to accept the title of acting president after Lee left at the end of the semester in January. He insisted, however, that he would stay only until June 30, 1935. The administrative change was announced at an assembly on January 10, 1935, and Lee left on January 21, moving his family to University City in the St. Louis area.[52]

Conditions forced the trustees to rally to save the college, an action Lee had urged during his administration. The board worked closely with Miller, who retained the title of dean of faculty while acting as president. Two long-serving trustees, accustomed to weathering storms, were no longer with the board. Slater E. Lenoir, a trustee for almost forty years, had died in 1929. William A. Bright, who had joined the board along with Lenoir and had been invaluable in his service as treasurer, died in 1933 after forty-four years as a trustee. There was still St. Clair Moss, who refused to give up, and W. W. Payne, whose wife and daughter were graduates of Christian College, devoted and effective as a trustee. Barton Robnett had come on the board when his father, David A. Robnett, president of the board for fourteen years, had died in 1921. Every generation of his family had given either a board member or a student to the college, contributing generously in funds. Harris, president of the board, added stature as lieutenant governor of Missouri, and a lawyer in his firm, Lakenan Price, served as financial advisor to the board. E. C. Clinkscales was another trustee with long family service, and R. H. Emberson remained active. Clarence E. Lemmon, pastor of the Christian Church, worked especially well with Miller and helped convince other trustees of the need for action. Filling out the local board were Newton D. Evans, John M. Taylor, and E. E. Evans, a generous donor. Local trustees fully accepted their responsibility in the time of crisis, as they had in the past and would again in the future.[53]

Desperate as the situation seemed, 1935 brought improving conditions. The college began the year with $2,900 in cash and a debt of $93,587.50, and trustees estimated that they would need another $42,000 by September for expenses, payments on current indebtedness, and necessary repairs. With no way to increase the indebtedness, only one source remained—the endowment fund. Selling securities where possible, the board issued a new series of bonds in April 1935 for $100,000 and a series of second mortgage bonds for $20,000. Local banks agreed to furnish money to operate until the end of the year if the trustees would raise enough funds to settle all local debts by March 1. With almost all local financing, the college consolidated all debts and became a cash customer for local business. It had come through the worst of the depression years, and even Moore agreed to reduce her annuity from $2,500 to $2,000.[54]

Early in 1935, the board began to identify policies to be changed. Audits revealed uncollected student accounts of $52,800 for 1934–1935, most of which could no longer be recovered. Vigorous collection of accounts became a prime goal, and by 1935, as the nation began to recover, efforts met with some success. However, the policy most faulted by the trustees looking back at the Lee administration was the president's recruitment of students from families with incomes insufficient to support full payment. As critics saw it, the granting of scholarships and other benefits, such as part-time work in college offices, resulted in too much time spent on lower-income prospects at the expense of recruiting full-paying students. The trustees saw Lee's eagerness to maximize opportunities as bad business, and Miller repeatedly ordered field representatives not to deal with those prospective students who could not afford the expenses: "Don't waste our literature, stationery, postage, and foremost your time and effort upon impossible situations." Because the bonus feature could lead recruiters to enroll those who might later default on expenses, instructions clearly forbade the promising of any scholarships other than those stated in the current catalog. Miller adopted the practice in January 1935 of issuing a weekly letter to college field representatives, and his letter of March 16, 1935, decried "the evils of unprofessional, unprincipled, methods now being employed in student promotional work" to lure prospective students who had already decided on another college. He reported to the May 1935 meeting of the board:

> High pressure salesmanship, propaganda, and cut-throat business practices are the results of this frenzied effort to maintain numerical enrollments as tangible evidence to the public of financial stability. Inducements in the guise of so-called scholarships have been held out to depression harassed parents as a bait to lure them from one college to another until the public has become scholarship conscious, and the scholarship business has become a racket.[55]

Miller viewed recruitment in purely business terms, concluding that the only way to fill the college by the fall of 1935 was to "divide the number of new students we want by twenty-five and then see that we have that number of representatives in the field." He hired two additional representatives for 1935, making a total of seven, the largest number thus far utilized by the college.[56]

Just as Lee had brought professionalism to the academic operations of the college, Miller hired the first business manager, Roscoe A. Miller, who had served as a bank examiner with the State Finance Department and had worked for the National Refinance Corporation headquartered in St. Louis. Eager to live in Columbia again, R. A. Miller accepted the offer, coming in April 1935. He was elected secretary to the board and business secretary, and the college provided his family with the south bungalow, complete with utilities.[57]

James C. Miller had served valiantly in filling the role of president in 1935, but he knew that his health would not permit him to stay under such stressful conditions. He wrote to Robnett: "I have repeatedly been reminded of my condition of three years ago. I am convinced I cannot stand the wear and tear that it is going to take for the next three years here at Christian College. I hope the Board of Trustees will feel that I have given my best." Miller agreed not to announce his departure until August, and by September he had become dean of faculty at Northwest Missouri State Teachers' College in Maryville.[58]

At the July 24, 1935, board meeting, Harris recommended the election of Eugene Stephen Briggs as president. Born and reared in Fayette, Missouri, Briggs had received his Ph.D. degree from Columbia University. He had served in the public school systems of Moberly, Carrollton, Slater, and Trenton, Missouri, as well as in Oklahoma, where he became president of Southeastern State Teachers' College. He returned to Missouri in 1934 as state supervisor of adult education, resigning that position to take the presidency of Christian College in August 1935. An elder in the Christian Church since 1917, he was active in civic and church affairs and had written widely on education. Briggs brought with him to the college his wife, Mary Gentry Briggs, whom he had met in Moberly, where she was teaching music and art. His elaborate formal inauguration, arranged by Marion Hertig, took place on February 19, 1936.[59]

Coming as president when the deepest lows were behind the college, Briggs enjoyed almost immediate success. By October, he had achieved a 40 percent reduction in "self-help" students, with the expectation of reaching and maintaining 250 full-paying enrollments. His major project, in response to North Central concerns, was the addition of nearly one thousand volumes to the library, a task in which he hoped alumnae would participate. Like Miller, he emphasized the importance of the role of college representatives, hiring nine in all.[60]

By the end of Briggs's first academic year, he had put before the board an extensive list of recommendations. He would limit enrollment to 250 full-paying students—150 first-year and 100 second-year students—with the addition of twenty day students. He introduced a scheme of state quotas for each state traditionally sending students to the college, including quotas for specific high schools. His plan called for fees and tuition to be raised to a total of $775 for 1936–1937, while the budget for promotion would be reduced by 20 percent within two years. At the same time, he would restore faculty salaries by 20 percent, noting that the college ranked "too near the lower level of salaries paid in the North Central area." In spending for student services, he targeted the library for $2,500, proposing also $15,000 for a health unit and $150,000 for a fine arts building. Briggs's wife, Mary, continued her interest in the arts, activating the art club to sponsor weekly art shows and bringing in noted artists, including Thomas Hart Benton. Briggs reported considerable redecorating and anticipated that income and expenditures "would very nearly balance the next year." A natural promoter, he urged the board to launch a campaign for an endowment fund of $250,000.[61]

The outlook continued to be upbeat. Enrollment for the 1936–1937 academic year pushed the college to its limits despite the tuition increase, giving "a feeling of confidence and optimism," and faculty received a 10 percent salary increase. Briggs urged that a new dormitory be built by the fall of 1938 at the latest to provide for some applicants being turned away. Proud of the recruiting efforts, he reported that the college was "making a determined effort to place our promotion campaign on a high ethical plane. Many schools are responding to our consideration. It is my opinion that we are in a better situation regarding other schools who might be called competitors than we were a year ago."[62]

Briggs further expanded the professionalism of the staff by hiring Portia Penwell Stapel as alumnae secretary. Stapel's goals included the organization of an active alumnae file of at least twenty-nine hundred up-to-date addresses and the creation of permanent alumnae clubs. By May 1937, clubs were active in Denver, Springfield (Missouri and Illinois), Los Angeles, St. Louis, Kansas City, Jefferson City, and Mexico and New Haven, Missouri, with a dozen more planned by the end of the year. Stapel installed a "future file" of children of alumnae and organized class reunions for annual homecomings. Briggs expressed his "honest conviction that a small budget appropriated for the cultivation of the alumnae work will yield the largest returns of any single projects to be undertaken."[63]

Changes in the academic program emphasized both practical programs and the fine arts. Briggs added courses in interior design, personal grooming, sculpture, and statistics. The dance program expanded from three courses to seven, making Christian College the only junior college in the United States to offer a major in dance. Degrees in secretarial studies and education remained popular, as well as a broader preprofessional curriculum in business, commercial art, home economics, journalism, library, nursing, physical education, and social service. Briggs relied on his dean of faculty, Robert

Sala, to carry on the faculty studies begun by Miller. Sala, who held a Ph.D. from the University of Chicago and had studied for one year at the Union Theological Seminary in New York, had come to the college in April 1936.[64]

Despite his energetic measures, Briggs never achieved as comfortable a "fit" with the college as he would have liked. He had always been committed to coeducation, with a special interest in adult education. Rumors circulated of offers to Briggs, whose frequent speaking trips expanded his contacts. Finally, he announced in December 1937 that he had accepted the presidency of Phillips University in Enid, Oklahoma, a coeducational Christian Church–related college in the state of his choice.[65]

With Briggs's resignation and his desire to be released to his new position by January 31, trustees wasted no time in contacting James C. Miller in Maryville. By January 28, 1938, local papers carried the announcement of Miller's election by the board as the college's next president. Miller, who wanted no ceremony, was informally installed at the regular noon assembly hour on February 3, 1938.[66]

The coming of Miller to the presidency owed much to the influence of Lee, who had originally brought him to the college. The two had worked together in what had been the darkest times since the Civil War and shared similar goals and policies. At the time of Lee's death in 1955, Miller fondly remembered his friend in a memorial tribute, professing a "deep and personal respect and obligation" and recalling particularly Lee's helpfulness and consideration at the time of Miller's own illness in 1930. He noted Lee's outstanding talent for working with people and his intellectual ability that had led to his election as an honorary member of Phi Beta Kappa in 1932. Miller concluded: "Edgar Desmond Lee was a good man."[67]

Ironically, Lee, whose financial acumen had been faulted by his critics, had moved on to a highly successful business career in St. Louis. Through his son, Desmond, Lee met John Rowan, the father of Desmond's friend Jim Rowan. The Rowan family had begun a manufacturing company specializing in hangers and trouser creasers, later expanding to become pioneers in the field of organizational storage products and closet accessories. Edgar Lee became a cofounder and partner in the Lee-Rowan Manufacturing Company in 1939, serving as vice president of the company until his death on January 29, 1955, at the age of seventy-five. Desmond Lee had attended Hickman High School in Columbia with Sam Walton, and the Lee-Rowan Company later formed a lucrative relationship with Wal-Mart as a retailer of its products. The Lee-Rowan Company eventually expanded its sales to include England, Japan, Germany, and South America, becoming a subsidiary of the Newell Corporation in 1993.[68]

Edgar Lee's business talents, carried on in the company by his son, Desmond, and the continued success of the company made it possible for Desmond to contribute tens of millions of dollars to educational and cultural charities. Desmond Lee, called "the Spirit of St. Louis" by William Danforth, former chancellor of Washington University, was named "Man of the Year" in St. Louis in 1996 for his generous philanthropic projects. He also became a trustee, benefactor, and valued friend of Columbia College.[69]

Although Edgar Lee's financial success came too late to rescue Christian College from its crisis during the depression, what he did leave to the college proved more lasting. The academic integrity that he instilled in the curriculum remained in place, carefully nurtured by Miller. The democratic principles by which he operated reflected the principles of 1851. Further, he had the ability to inspire others to strong leadership without feeling threatened by their achievements. Above all, a generation of students and faculty would remember Lee for a special quality—his very humaneness.

7

One Life to Give

JAMES C. MILLER: 1938–1956

Influences unpredictable and immeasurable take over the spirit of the headwaters of civilization, and, after their destructive sweep, we follow in the backwater to repair and improve and hope to build with such permanency and force as to offstand the headwaters which will surely come again.

James C. Miller, "Some Concerns of the Junior College," 1941 speech

THE JAMES C. MILLER WHO returned to Christian College as president in 1938 had been irrevocably marked by the past. His success as dean of faculty at Northwestern Missouri State Teachers' College had given him the confidence he had lacked when first offered the presidency in 1935, and he had developed an assurance and polish well suited to his role as a promoter of the college. However, the trauma of his health problems in the 1930s and of the college's struggle to survive the depression had instilled in him an anxiety that surfaced repeatedly throughout his presidency, despite his unqualified achievements.

Success surrounded Miller as he began his presidency. He had become a recognized educational leader in Missouri as the result of his specialization in the philosophy of education. His best-known statement of the subject, "A Philosophy of Education for Elementary Courses of Study," became the foreword of a work used by all elementary school principals in Missouri, reprinted as a leaflet by the Missouri Department of Education. Miller also brought financial success to the college. The first year of his administration showed a balance of $30,468, a satisfying $6,000 increase over the previous year, and a $4,500 Carnegie grant provided for expansion of the library's holdings. By his second annual board meeting, Miller reported gifts of $4,500 in addition to $25,000 generated by a Chamber of Commerce drive on the college's behalf. Just four years later, the college managed to go through the summer with no short-term borrowing, and its gross income was the largest in the institution's history.[1]

Even with this auspicious beginning, Miller's feeling of physical insecurity led him to add a note, "A Personal Matter," to his midyear report in September 1940. He reminded trustees that he had left a state university that provided a retirement plan and had received overtures from other colleges. Stating that he would be forty-nine on November 14 and possessed very modest savings, he appealed to the board: "With a few more years of service here at this college, I shall not be good for any other position and I think it only fair that I look after the interests of myself and family. . . . If the Board adopts the plan I shall feel entirely free to cut all the bridges behind me and give my best efforts to this job for the next sixteen years if I can last that long." Miller's plan, as adopted by the board, established a pension fund that he would begin to draw at age sixty-five. His wife would receive one-half of the pension if she survived him. This introduction of a pension plan became even more important when it was extended to the entire faculty in 1945.[2]

Academic leadership, in the hands of Miller and Dean Robert Sala, continued to be strong and effective. Sala had come to the college in 1936, serving under Miller until enlisting for military service in 1942. He chaired the history department while serving as dean of faculty and taught American History and American Government. Sala practiced what he preached. Elected to the Columbia City Council in April 1942, he commented, "I have always felt that those who teach American Government should have first-hand experience with its operation. The teacher is not only a teacher, but a citizen and should carry his responsibility as a citizen."[3]

Together, Miller and Sala created the Missouri Association of Junior College Administrators. Sala wrote to administrators of other Missouri junior colleges and received enthusiastic and unanimous response in favor of forming an organization "to bring the junior college administrators of the state closer together to study . . . matters pertinent to the field of junior college administration." At the first meeting, held at Kemper Military School in Boonville in January 1938, Sala became the group's secretary.[4]

Curricular changes under Miller saw continued emphasis on meeting the needs of a women's college. The October 1938 *Bulletin* announced the addition of a new home-management degree program including not only homemaking but also problems of marriage, philosophy of life, hygiene, and child care. With Theta Holmes Wolf heading the program, courses such as "Marriage and the Family" and "Textiles and Merchandising" filled rapidly. Personal-presence courses taught by Josephine Dillon were especially popular. Dillon came to campus in 1940 to supplement the work in speech and drama while heading the radio program. Best known as the first wife of actor Clark Gable, she had coached such stars as Irene Rich, Nelson Eddy, Marion Talley, and Lily Pons. She was a graduate of Stanford University and of the Sorbonne in Paris and was a well-known lecturer and author with more than twenty years of experience.[5]

In academic areas, emphasis continued on political science, especially American government, and on the traditional liberal arts offerings. However, Miller dropped the education courses, convinced that the college's offerings could not compete with those of the university. He supplemented religion courses with an annual "Religion in Life" week, begun in 1943 on all three campuses in Columbia.[6]

Miller, like Lee, retained and attracted a number of faculty members who would become stalwarts of the college. Carrying over from the Lee presidency, Robert Abram, in religion and sociology, remained a loyal and effective instructor for thirty years until his retirement in 1948. Sue Gerard, who came to the college in 1935 as an instructor in physical education, taught aquatic sports, lifesaving, and recreational leadership, winning recognition for her lifesaving techniques. After her retirement in 1972, the college dedicated the pool in her name, rededicating it in 1995 after renovations. Gerard placed articles in national magazines as a freelance writer and produced a book, *My First Eighty-four Years,* in 1998.[7]

Other continuing faculty included Ruth Almstedt in art, Franklin Launer as head of the music conservatory, Ruth Graham in home economics, Mary Paxton Keeley in English, Harold Long and Esther Stearn in biology, and Margaret McMillan in history, all gradually becoming the "old hands." Marion Hertig still served in a variety of roles, writing publicity, contacting alumnae, and editing the *Bulletin*. New recruits who would also have a long-range impact included William Bedford in music, Ellen Dahl in textiles, Margaret Tello in piano, Esther Heppel in Spanish, Hazel Perryman in German, and Hortense Davison in French. A husband-and-wife team, Burnett Ellis, hired in 1949, and Jessie Ellis, coming in 1954, served in geology and geography until their retirement in 1991. Dora Johnson, in mathematics, became Miller's first dean of women, followed in 1941 by Margaret Habein, one of the first new faculty members hired by Miller. Habein received high praise from Miller: "No person on the campus is more respected by the students and by associates than Miss Habein."[8]

Of the faculty new in 1951, Sidney Larson, in art, stood out from the beginning. In a report to the board at the end of the 1951–1952 academic year, Miller's description of Larson's work proved prophetic: "The art instructor, Mr. Sidney Larson, has proved himself to be an excellent teacher and a fine influence among our students. He has gone far beyond the ordinary teaching and counseling responsibilities in attempting to stimulate interest in art. He has an excellent reputation in this part of the Middle West and certainly shows promise as being the type of teacher who will attract art students to Christian College."[9]

Larson worked with Thomas Hart Benton, becoming a personal friend and colleague of the well-known Missouri artist and acting as his resident assistant on the Truman Memorial Library mural. Larson earned a national reputation in the art world for his own murals, completing thirty-one panels in nine mural projects in three states. Appointed in 1961 as fine arts curator for the State Historical Society of Missouri in Columbia, he also established himself as an accomplished conservator and restorer of nineteenth-century paintings. He treated the artwork in the Missouri State Capitol, the Truman Library in Independence, the Missouri Supreme Court Building, several museums, and the Thomas Hart Benton murals at Indiana University. Writing and lecturing extensively, Larson became a recognized authority on the art of George Caleb Bingham and of Benton, while exhibiting his own paintings nationally and internationally. The college chose him to execute oil portraits of Presidents Lee, Freeman, Kelly, Hill, and Brouder.

With the longest tenure of any faculty member in the history of the college, Larson determined to match his tenure from his hiring in the centennial year of 1951 to the sesquicentennial of 2001 before retiring. Largely through his efforts, the art program, which he chaired for twenty-nine years, grew from a one-person department to a program rivaling those of well-known universities in creative talent and teaching ability.

Larson's honors included the Distinguished Service Award from the State Historical Society of Missouri in 1989, two commendations by the Missouri Senate, and a 1991 award from the Missouri State Council on the Arts "for significant contributions in art." He also received the prestigious Arts and Science Distinguished Alumnus Award granted by the University of Missouri–Columbia in 1999, capped in 2000 by receiving the University of Missouri 2000 Faculty Alumni Award. Despite his many awards as an artist, Larson's most significant contribution may have been, however, as a devoted and effective teacher. Not only did he become "Missouri's Outstanding Professor" in 1987, but also the Council for Advancement and Support of Education named him "National Professor of the Year" bronze medalist that same year. In addition to these and other activities, Larson remained in frequent demand as an art judge and critic and as a tour conductor for art seminars in the United States and Europe. With the completion of the new art center in Brown Hall in 1996, the college showed its appreciation of Larson by dedicating the art gallery in his name in appropriate ceremonies during Alumni Reunion Weekend.[10]

One innovation of the Miller administration, Faculty Fall Conference, consisted of a weeklong series of meetings and workshops during which faculty and administrators launched the new academic year with guest speakers, committee meetings, and planning sessions. The gathering brought the "college family" together in a way possible only in a small college and provided orientation for new faculty as well as stimulating participants to renewed educational efforts in the coming academic year.[11]

Miller's leadership in off-campus activities matched his impressive impact on campus. Like Lee, he served as president of the American Association of Junior Colleges, elected at the Chicago meeting of the association on February 28, 1941. He became a prominent spokesperson for the 610 junior college members and an authority on the role of junior colleges in American education. Although supportive of junior colleges' ability to respond flexibly to vocational programs, he warned of the dangers of going too far in the vocational direction: "My personal conviction is that the junior college movement will have its permanent recognition in the educational scheme made more secure by adhering to the thought that college, after all, is an intellectual enterprise." Miller served also on the executive committee of the American Association of Junior Colleges and became the first representative of a junior college to be elected to an office of the North Central Association of Colleges and Secondary Schools. His election as vice president of that organization in March 1946 automatically made him a member of the executive committee, the fifteen-member governing body of the association. Also a leader in the Christian Church, he acted as a member of its Missouri Educational Commission and of the Board of Education of the Disciples of Christ.[12]

In his role on campus, Miller's primary focus became the recruitment of students or, as he called it, "promotional work." Constantly preoccupied with enrollment figures, he worried about the economy, farm crops, or any other factor that might affect student numbers: "I thought I would spend 90 percent of my time teaching and 10 percent administering. Instead, I found it was 10 percent educating and 90 percent keeping up the enrollment." Miller worked closely with his "educational counselors," as he called the field representatives, bringing them back to campus for a week each fall for orientation through visiting with faculty, attending classes, and learning sales techniques. He set quotas for the field-workers, publishing recruitment results in his weekly newsletters. The newsletters, "To the Educational Counselors," began in April 1941 and became detailed, multipage, folksy communications describing events on campus. They also included inspirational comments and advice. Miller periodically instructed his recruiters on behavior:

> As a long-time policy, I am sure you will be better off if you adopt the Golden Rule toward your competitors. Today I have had a letter from the president of a junior college for young women in which he speaks of very unpleasant and very uncomplimentary remarks made of his college by a representative of Christian College. . . . You misjudge the intelligence of your prospect and her

> parents when you think you can run down the other school and still command the respect of the person to whom you are talking. It simply does not work. The very fact that this person will go and tell on you is evidence that you have offended her intelligence.[13]

Competition for students grew more pronounced and complex each year in the period before World War II. Prospective students tended more and more to make multiple applications, choosing which college to attend only after having been accepted by several institutions. Miller first referred to this practice in a 1938 report to the board. He complained that "what appears to be a *bona fide* reservation which carries the clause that room reservation fees will be refunded, provided the college is notified on or before the first day of August," may lead to an increasing number of cancellations. With 311 students signed up for the 1938–1939 academic year, 71 canceled, and 10 were reinstated. Although 1939 brought a "prospects" list larger than ever, parents were waiting later and later, a pattern of behavior exacerbated by the approach of American involvement in the war. Miller complained that "various types of inducements" and "elaborate publicity programs" had become necessary. Fortunately, good retention helped keep enrollments up, reaching a high of 327 students in 1940–1941, but the struggle for new students merely worsened: "Still the greatest problem of the administration in the private school is that of promotion. . . . Each year new inducements, decoys, and, may I say, bribes are offered to highschool graduates."[14]

A loyal coterie of field representatives served the college well, headed by J. Kelly Wright, the first full-time professional field representative, and Mary White, also an effective and longtime representative. The college engaged in national advertising and produced promotional booklets for prospective students. Miller himself sometimes took to the field, driving the Double Sextette ensemble all over Missouri and Iowa. In a blow to the recruiting effort, word came that Wright had suffered a stroke at his home in Columbia in November 1941. Miller's newsletter informed the representatives of Wright's death on December 4. In his twenty years of service, Wright had brought more students to the college than any other representative, and the board established a scholarship in his memory.[15]

Regardless of struggles, enrollments increased so steadily in the late 1930s that Miller considered the construction of a new dormitory to be imperative. From an enrollment of 246 when he took office, the numbers grew to 263 in 1938–1939 and to 288 in 1939–1940. However, with college buildings already encumbered by mortgages, borrowing was out of the question, and Miller resorted to stopgap solutions. He first placed students in the two-story brick house across the street from campus on the southeast corner of Rogers Street and Christian College Avenue, the present Tenth Street. The home had been purchased for $5,500 in 1937 during the Briggs administration from

J. S. Stephens for use as an infirmary. Miller moved the infirmary upstairs to provide student housing on the first floor. In addition, the college obtained the deed in 1939 to the white frame house on the southwest corner, directly across the street. Former president Moore had relinquished the deed to the college in return for a payment of $200 per month. Especially popular as a small dormitory, it had housed St. Clair Moss for a time, earning the sobriquet of the "Moss House" or the "White House."[16]

Prospects for building a new dormitory brightened as the result of a bequest from Frank Hughes, a merchant and banker from Liberty, Missouri, who served as a trustee from 1931 until his death on October 17, 1937. Hughes and his wife, Ella Vaughn Hughes, had been lifelong friends of St. Clair Moss and became generous benefactors of the college. Hughes, who had already given the college $15,000 in memory of his wife after her death in 1936, willed the college $30,000 plus one-fourth of the residue of his estate, a total expected to exceed $100,000. Anticipation of the bequest and confidence in Miller as president moved the board to announce a $125,000 expansion program with completion of the dormitory on the southwest corner of the campus expected by September 1939. The trustees voted to name the new facility Hughes Hall. Although costs allowed construction of only one of two intended wings, the hall opened in September 1939 with sixty-six students.[17]

Miller increased the board's willingness to proceed with the dormitory through a bold move, calling a faculty meeting at which he asked for evidence of moral and material support to take to the board in the form of pledges of one month's salary. Pledge cards, eventually representing virtually all of the faculty and staff, brought a total of $4,700.[18]

By March 1941, Miller had greatly improved the college's physical plant. In addition to building Hughes Hall, he had repaired and refurnished St. Clair Hall, repaired all campus buildings, and installed modern kitchen equipment. In a cost-saving move when the heating plant threatened total breakdown, Miller saved $468 by purchasing two Heinie boilers and stokers discarded by the State Capitol's heating plant in Jefferson City for $1,500. The purchase became the brunt of numerous jokes, especially when misconstrued in later years that they had come from the state penitentiary.[19]

Despite such improvements, Miller's own ten-year plan never saw fruition. The completion of the second part of Hughes Hall took top priority in his plan. Also, he had requested a "nice" home for his wife, Nell, and their three daughters, feeling it should compare well with the homes from which students had come. In addition, he had planned for a fine arts building behind the auditorium with music studios, a radio studio, and offices on the first floor and practice rooms, a recital hall, and drama facilities on the second floor. The third floor would have accommodated the visual arts. Finally, and dearest to his heart, was the dream of constructing a library between Missouri Hall and the swimming pool. He had envisioned a beautiful small building with a large entryway worthy of housing a museum of the college's history. His tenure would see only the acquisition of the president's home, coming in 1944 with the purchase of a fine brick house two doors south of the "White House."[20]

Miller shelved his ten-year plan, turning his attention to national and international affairs. As the newly elected president of the American Association of Junior Colleges, he represented a major force in American higher education. As such, he received an invitation to attend a July 1941 conference in Washington, D.C., of college presidents and representatives of national associations in higher education, sponsored by the Subcommittee on Military Affairs of the National Committee on Education and Defenses. The conference, held to discuss the relationship of colleges and universities to problems of national defense, included War and Navy Department officials, leaders of the Office of Production Management and of the Office of Civilian Defense, and members of the United States Information Service, the Civil Service Commission, the United States Employment Service, and the Office of Emergency Management. Miller participated in meetings attended by New York mayor Fiorello H. La Guardia, Harvard president James B. Conant, University of Illinois president A. C. Willard, and eighteen other college and university presidents. Although discussion centered around the subject of how colleges could assist in a national emergency, conclusions were tentative with the United States still not a belligerent, and officials instructed educators to keep their institutions operating normally.[21]

Miller's newsletter of December 12, 1941, reported that word of the coming of war reached him when "Mrs. Hertig came rushing in, in her usual brusque fashion, and announced that Japan had fired on the possessions of the United States." Miller and Sala spoke to students at a special assembly, and Miller, in his next newsletter, wrote of his views, a mix of patriotism and promotion: "We believe we are . . . in a state of readiness for any service. . . . I do not wish to be commercial, [but] . . . I do think it is fair, however, to point out that the geographic location of our college makes it about the safest spot on earth today."[22]

Miller returned to Washington in late December to participate in a conference called by the Committee on Military Affairs and the War-Time Commission. Participants acted as a preparatory group in planning for the National Conference of Institutions of Higher Education to be held in Baltimore on January 3–4, 1942. The January conference was attended by more than one thousand college and university presidents, and Miller acted as one of the ten sectional leaders, presiding over the session for junior college officials. He also served on the ten-member Committee on Recommendations that put before the conference sixteen recommendations on acceleration of learning, utilization of manpower on campus, deferment of students, morale, and introduction of pertinent subjects into the curriculum. Miller's term as president of the American Association of Junior Colleges expired in 1942, but his leadership role in the conference, the largest group of college officials ever assembled at that time in the United States, provided him with invaluable experience: "It was the most stimulating and consequential experience that I have had since I have been in the school-teaching business."[23]

Upon his return to campus, Miller made the war effort a major part of his activities. He acted as dean of faculty for a time after Sala left for military duty in 1942, cutting back on faculty meetings and writing occasional letters to the faculty in place of "so many meetings." He chaired the Missouri State Speakers' Bureau on World War II, touring the state to promote war-bond drives and other war-effort programs.[24]

Activity on campus also emphasized the war effort. As early as September 1941, the *Microphone* reported that the college was the first in the United States to have organized a chapter of the Red Cross on its own campus, and blood drives became regular events. *Microphone* editorials advised students on "Things You Can Do for Defense," such as buying defense bonds and stamps, saving tinfoil and razor blades, conserving paper and sugar, saving canceled stamps, and being well informed. The college cooperated with the Office of Transportation by canceling spring break in 1942 and holding commencement early. Also in an effort to avoid peak travel times, a long Christmas vacation from December 15 to January 13 complied with government guidelines. Most important, the college's war effort included the War Service Program, a carefully designed plan implemented by Sala and a faculty committee, requiring all students to complete the standard Red Cross First Aid course, granting them certification from the American Red Cross. All students also enrolled in a two-hour elective "war service course" intended to prepare them to participate in the war effort in their own communities as secretaries, morale officers, recreation leaders, or volunteer nurses. The courses, offered for no credit, included classes on lettering, typing, filing, business machines, nutrition, family purchasing, home nursing, community recreational activities, and library aid. A point system rewarded students for such activities as helping out at ration boards, working the war-stamp booth, engaging in Red Cross and other drives, and rolling bandages, and student vocal and dramatic groups performed for civic organizations and traveled to Fort Leonard Wood to present programs. The college cut back on other usual club activities to provide more time for war-effort participation.[25]

Cooperative wartime programs continued the traditional intercampus relations between Christian College and the University of Missouri. The college allowed second-year students to participate in two university defense courses for Christian College credit. The offerings, taught evenings and Saturdays, gave students a choice between an engineering drawing course and a radio technician course. The engineering course qualified students to enter the civil service immediately upon completion of the course, whereas the radio technician course concentrated on requirements for students to be employed in industry or the United States Army or Navy. Another course (in cooperation with Wiggins Air at the Columbia Airport) provided the ground-instruction portion of aviation training, preparing students to pass the ground requirement for a pilot's license.[26]

The college suffered the loss of a number of faculty to the war effort, the draft, and marriage. When Sala enlisted in July 1942, he had been dean of faculty for six years and had just been elected to the Columbia City Council. His experience qualified him to be an instructor in the Army Air Corps and led to a variety of special assignments, culminating in his appointment to a position entitling him to a seat on the four-power board governing Berlin. With Sala's plans still indefinite, Miller, operating with acting deans since 1942, finally hired a permanent replacement.[27]

Wartime conditions led to some unanticipated side effects at Christian College. In one innovation, Louise Yeager began the use of students as dining room servers. When male help became almost impossible to find, Miller reluctantly agreed not to stand in the way if a planning group could sell the idea to students. Yeager presented her plan at a meeting of the student body, asking students who wanted to participate to bring a sign-up card to breakfast the next morning. When 85 percent of the students returned cards, Yeager established a system of teams and captains, inaugurating a highly successful operation. Even well-to-do students enjoyed an opportunity to earn money on their own and gain practical experience. Students received a twenty-five-cent-savings stamp for serving a breakfast or lunch and two stamps for a dinner.[28]

Whereas one change began a tradition, another ended a tradition, as Miller reported in his newsletter of March 26, 1942:

> On Saturday afternoon at 5 o'clock, March 21, in the year of our Lord, 1942, a second Emancipation Proclamation was posted to become effective Monday, March 23. Christian College students will be permitted to go to town without hose and hats until 6 o'clock in the evening. . . . Students have been urging this change for some time. Many parents had appealed to us in the name of economy, and almost in the name of patriotism, saying that silk hose are expensive.[29]

Despite some dislocations and hardships, Christian College prospered during the war years. Miller, whose preoccupation with enrollments never ceased, wrote in August 1943 that "still they come. Almost daily we receive special delivery letters, long distance telephone calls, or telegrams stating 'Is it too late for us to enroll our daughter in Christian College?' " Advertisements in *Good Housekeeping, Cosmopolitan,* and *National Geographic* the previous March had had an impact and, by April 1944, enrollments closed at 334 students. Miller wrote that women's colleges are "having a field day. How long it will last is anyone's guess." In the mid-1940s the college was filled to capacity by February with a long waiting list to replace any cancellations. Gross income doubled in a decade, from $150,000 in 1933–1934 to $302,000 in 1943–1944, and short-term borrowing ended. The college, becoming more selective, began giving entrance examinations for the first time in 1947, a practice routinely continued until the use of standardized testing began.[30]

As a result of prosperous times and growing space needs, the college began to acquire additional property south of the campus. The college purchased the home of S. M. Stevenson in the spring of 1944, a property third from the southwest corner of Rogers Street and Christian College Avenue, redecorating it to give the president the type of home he had been wanting. The "White House" on the corner, finally purchased outright from Moore, became the "Senior Annex" for twelve students. On the main campus, the former home of the president housed another ten students. The purchase of the Willett Funeral Home, the middle house between the president's home and the Senior Annex, consolidated college property on the west side of Christian College Avenue. The Willett property included two brick apartments over a four-car garage in the rear available as rental property. Most important, the purchase allowed the college to move the music conservatory from Missouri Hall, where it had been located at the end of the St. Clair Moss presidency. Miller described the "storm and strife . . . between those in charge of living conditions in Missouri Hall and those in charge of the music studios. . . . When the studios are in operation, along with the choral room with a class in music theory, music ceases to be music and becomes an annoying noise." In Miller's final property expansion, the college acquired Eagle Park Farm, site of the Drew Riding Academy. A fifty-one-acre property, the farm bordered Highway 63 east of town and had already been in use for the college's riding program.[31]

Prosperity also permitted the college to expand faculty benefits by finally enacting a faculty pension plan, especially helpful since Social Security did not yet cover faculty in private colleges. The Disciples of Christ plan, authorized by the trustees and put into effect July 1, 1945, provided an annual income one-seventieth of the total income during the time the contract was in force, granting a death benefit before retirement age for active members. Retirement was optional at sixty-five and mandatory at seventy. Reflecting the thinking of the times, female faculty contributed 4 percent with 4.5 percent contributed by the college, and male faculty put in a 5 percent personal contribution and received a 5.5 percent college contribution.[32]

Small improvements marked the later 1940s. A "friend of the college" made a gift of chimes for the auditorium in 1946, and, at the same time, Miller and the board engaged in creative planning to provide improved pipe organ access. Upon learning that the Christian Church intended to replace its older organ with an up-to-date model at a cost of $20,000, the college offered to contribute $2,000 toward the purchase. In an agreement for the "purchase of organ service," the college bought limited use of the new church organ and acquired the old organ for student practice in the conservatory. According to the formal contract, the college organist would have access to the church organ for recitals, demonstration purposes for students, programs by concert organists invited to the college, the training of students in service playing, and recitals by exceptional students. Practice hours were to be held to a "reasonable amount."[33]

The Christian Church had also been helpful financially, designating a portion of funds raised by "A Crusade for a Christian World" to go to the college. With a fund-raising goal of $14 million, the church allotted $150,000 to the college, but the total amount by 1953 reached barely half of the projected goal. Nonetheless, the sum contributed to a good financial report for the end of Miller's first decade in office. Fixed assets had risen from $732,293 in 1938 to $1,116,502 in 1948, and current assets had increased from $32,830 in 1938 to $99,596 in 1947. In March 1949, the college announced its largest gift ever by one individual, a $100,000 bequest from William H. Dulany, whose uncle, William H. Dulany, had served on the board from 1901 to 1914.[34]

A high degree of student satisfaction coincided with stable financial conditions. A survey of the class of 1950 recorded the graduates' impressions one year after they had left the college. With an 89 percent response, survey results showed that 68 percent of respondents considered their training at Christian College to be superior, while 25 percent regarded it as better than average and 7 percent as merely adequate. Of those responding, 76 percent had gone on to a senior institution, 85 percent of whom lost no credits in transferring.[35]

A potentially dangerous, but fortunately minor, episode occurred when St. Clair Hall suffered a fire on January 13, 1945. Just before dinner on a Saturday, two students gave the alarm after discovering that a fire had started in the trash chute and spread to the attic. Students evacuated the hall in three minutes, and the fire department, arriving in five minutes, had the fire under control in half an hour. The effectiveness of the fire department kept damages to a minimum, with losses set at $8,733.50, all of which insurance covered. All but a few of the students who took shelter in other dormitories had returned to their rooms by the following Monday, and three rooms requiring redecorating were completed in a few weeks.[36]

Despite favorable conditions, Miller's apprehension repeatedly colored his reports to the trustees. He wrote in September 1946 that "it is destined to be a difficult year." By June 1947, he again predicted trouble: "I anticipate some financial reverses; also I am looking for the drought which is long past due." A September 1948 report continued: "There are those who think that we are to be overtaken with a depression soon. . . . I still wear the scars that I received . . . during the depression that followed the boom of 1929."[37]

Enrollments did dip temporarily between 1949 and 1952, but the fall of 1952 brought the highest enrollment yet with 425 students. Miller noted that applications were obtained less easily by late 1948, and, by the fall of 1949, the college opened without capacity enrollment. Uncertainties related to the Korean War made recruiting more difficult, and the trustees directed Miller to hire an assistant for student recruitment work. Miller, who had personally directed the admissions program since the death of Wright in 1940, hired Neil Freeland as the college's first director of admissions in August 1950. Freeland, a former high school principal and Missouri state supervisor of secondary education, spent half of his time as director of admissions and half in fieldwork. Four full-time recruiters worked in Oklahoma, Texas, Arkansas, Kentucky, Tennessee, Indiana, Ohio, and Michigan, as well as in Missouri.[38]

As early as 1950, Miller's anxieties led him to think more and more of retirement: "While the retirement plan that we have worked out for me is to be effective at age 65, which would be 1956, I now seriously question the advisability of trying to continue that long." Predicting that college administration would be more difficult in the days ahead, Miller called for "fresh new vigor, a new outlook and some modernization of the total program." He went on to consider the possibility of hiring a woman president, as was typical of women's colleges in the East. He added a final note:

> During the past thirty years I have given my entire time and effort to the position at hand with the result that I have accumulated a relatively small amount as one looks to living costs now and in the future. However, if the right person should show up, I would recommend that we seize upon the opportunity, and I would hope that some kind of an arrangement might be worked out in view of my more than twenty years of service with the college that would at least keep me off the bread line.[39]

As Miller's anxieties about the future increased, the board experienced the loss of several longtime leaders. Frank G. Harris, who had joined the board in 1905 and served as its president from 1922 to 1940, died in 1945 after forty years as a trustee during the presidencies of St. Clair Moss, Lee, Briggs, and Miller. W. W. Payne, who died in April 1947, had just resigned after forty-one years as a trustee and six years as board president. In 1946, David Barton Robnett, a trustee since 1922, replaced Payne as president. William Henry Dulany, a St. Louis businessman and philanthropist, had joined the board in 1922 and served until his death in March 1948. The college had honored Dulany in 1947 as the recipient of the first Distinguished Service Award. Dulany's two sisters were Christian College graduates, and his father, W. H. Dulany, had contributed funds to the construction of the auditorium and had been a Christian College trustee. Also, the death of St. Clair Moss on August 18, 1947, marked the end of her fifty-five years of service to the college.[40]

New leadership replaced the losses, especially with the coming of Hartley G. Banks to the board in 1945 and his election as president of the board in 1947. His father, Hartley H. Banks, also a trustee, had lived on campus and had attended the "small-boys class." Banks's great-uncle, Christian College president Joseph Kirtley Rogers, had given his sister, Mary Banks Rogers (H. H. Banks's mother), a home on campus after the death of her husband. Hartley G. Banks, one of the most successful and respected trustees in the college's history, served as president for nineteen years. In 1960, a new dormitory on the northwest corner of the campus was named Banks Hall in his honor. William Frank St. Clair, a nephew of Luella St. Clair Moss, also joined the board in 1945. His mother had taught music at the college, where his father was bursar. Other trustees, experienced and effective after years of service, continued their duties into the next presidency. They included J. C. Mundy, Louis P. Blosser, Haden H. Bright, E. S. Haynes, Artic Mason Carter, and especially C. E. Lemmon, whose guidance and loyalty had been invaluable since his joining the board in 1931 upon becoming the minister of the First Christian Church in Columbia.[41]

One of the more touching losses to the college during the Miller administration occurred with the death of Marion Hertig on November 28, 1949. Hertig and Miller had worked closely together, and Hertig had made an unusual request of the president in 1938: "There will come an end and I have a request to make of you. The members of my family are all gone. When the end comes, I want my body taken back to Union City, Michigan, and placed on the family lot beside my mother. . . . I want you to go along to see that it is done properly. Will you promise that you will do this for me?" Miller fulfilled that promise on December 2, 1949: "As I . . . watched the casket being lowered I thought, 'here is one who has run the gamut of most of life's experiences. Here was a life that will lie for many, many years in the hearts and minds of former students. Now I bid goodbye to a great woman.' "[42]

Personnel changes also affected administrative positions, especially in the case of the dean of faculty office. With Sala's enlistment in July 1942, Stella Meyer, who had come to the college in 1919 to teach Spanish and French, served as acting dean until 1946, when Miller named Kenneth H. Freeman as dean. Freeman had taught in the public schools in Everton and in Columbia and had been an assistant superintendent of public schools and dean of the junior college in Washington, Iowa. He had married Martha Katherine (Kay) Warnick in 1940, who had also taught in the Columbia public schools.

Freeman, clearly a young man on the rise in 1946, resigned as dean in 1948 to become director of elementary education in Rochester, Minnesota. He would return to Christian College in 1956 as Miller's chosen successor as president. With Freeman's resignation, Julia Spaulding, hired by Lee in 1921, became acting dean until her retirement in 1949. Miller turned next to Thomas T. Blewett as dean of faculty. He remained as dean until the summer of 1956, taking a leave in 1952 to accept a Fulbright Scholarship to teach English in Greece. William C. Bedford, a faculty member in the music conservatory since 1938, became acting dean for the 1952–1953 academic year until Blewett returned. Bedford, editor of the *Bulletin* after Hertig's retirement until 1952 and a future dean of faculty, was praised by Miller as "a scholar and a gentleman" with a "keen intellect, a basic culture, a pleasant and courteous manner with students, and above all, a will to succeed."[43]

The Centennial Celebration of 1951 became the major occasion of the 1950s. Miller targeted Charter Day on January 18 and commencement activities in June as dates for special events: "For we must launch Christian College into its second century with its sails so gibbed that it will weather the storm." The college hired Raymond Derr, a journalist, as director of public relations, and Bedford utilized the *Bulletin* to keep alumnae informed of plans and stimulate participation. Compilation of an alumnae directory, the first since 1911, served as a historical document while also resulting in correction of alumnae records. The directory included all known alumnae, living or deceased, since 1851, listed by year of graduation. Although a modest fund drive had as it goal the dedication in the memory of St. Clair Moss of an organ for the chapel, Miller firmly avoided tying any other fund-raising to the celebration.[44]

With the coming centennial, trustees agreed in February 1950 to employ Allean Lemmon Hale to write the college's history. Hale, daughter of C. E. Lemmon, minister of the First Christian Church and a trustee, had been a student of Mary Paxton Keeley and a 1933 graduate of the college. Completing a degree in journalism at the University of Missouri, Hale went on to write award-winning plays. The original intent that she write a brief account led eventually to the publication of the college's history from the time of its founding. Her carefully researched and authoritative work, *Petticoat Pioneer*, published in 1956 and updated in 1968, became the first serious examination of the pioneering role of the college.[45]

Pressures on Miller built steadily as activity increased in the month before the centennial Charter Day, and the strain took its toll on his already weakened heart. Miller first observed numbness in his right hand and side on November 15, 1950, but felt better in several days. The major attack struck on December 27 when his left leg would not support him, and on December 29 a "rather excruciating chest pain" began, lasting forty-eight hours, accompanied by "smothering spells." Despite the diagnosis of angina pectoris and orders to enter a hospital, Miller merely reduced his activities, rested at home as final preparations continued for Charter Day, and returned to his office in three days.[46]

Just before the Charter Day commemoration, the First Christian Church held a Recognition Day to honor trustees, friends, and descendants of the founders who had helped create and maintain the college. Ethel Robnett Estes of Columbia, a 1902 graduate, represented sixty relatives who had been students or trustees. W. Ed Jameson of Fulton represented his grandfather, an incorporator of the college, and his mother of the class of 1856. Edmund Wilkes of Kansas City represented his grandfather, President Lanceford B. Wilkes.[47]

The academic procession on Charter Day, an unseasonably balmy January 18, included representatives of nearly 150 colleges and universities and thirty learned societies from as far away as Maine, California, and Florida. Congratulatory remarks by University of Missouri president Frederick A. Middlebush noted the close ties between university presidents Shannon and Hudson and Christian College as evidence that the university, in the early days, always considered Christian College as "its distaff side." Floyd Shoemaker, secretary of the State Historical Society of Missouri, brought greetings, and Gov. Forrest Smith reaffirmed the college's role as the first women's college chartered in Missouri, characterizing the college as "small, select, serious in purpose," a phrase to be much used in later years. The featured speaker, Sen. James William Fulbright, had been president of the University of Arkansas and was a member of the Senate Foreign Relations Committee. Best known for creating scholarships for the exchange of teachers and students between the United States and foreign countries, Fulbright was a former Rhodes scholar. His address, "The United States and World Affairs," brought extensive newspaper and radio coverage in central Missouri, St. Louis, Kansas City, and Fayetteville, Arkansas. Reporting went beyond the events of the day to bring attention to the history of the college, and the *Columbia Missourian* published a special twelve-page section on the college. The day also included a celebratory luncheon, an afternoon reception for delegates and guests, and guided tours by Lineage Club members in period dress. However, the occasion was not without its ominous note. Former president Lee suffered a heart attack after arriving in Columbia that morning, and former president Briggs, who had accepted an invitation to participate, was too ill to attend. Miller remarked that "the honors of being a college president were well balanced by its tendency to be fatal."[48]

As activities in preparation for the June events proceeded after Charter Day, Miller took the time off that had been urged earlier. His doctors called his symptoms "warnings" and ordered him to leave campus for sixty to ninety days and then to reduce his workload by 50 percent. Miller went to the Mayo Clinic for six days of tests and to Texas for recuperation, leaving Blewett as acting president. Although his condition gradually improved, Miller never fully regained his health. The *Bulletin* carried a note from him in April: "Upon my return, I must reduce what I have been doing. My greatest consolation stems from the fact that we have an excellent organization. A number of people have complimented the smooth and efficient way our Charter Day Centennial was carried out. This was due to splendid team work." Concern for Miller's health was inevitable, and the board in June authorized the executive committee to act "in case of any unusual circumstances during the year."[49]

A major portion of the preparations for June involved alumnae work, and the college turned to Hale to handle alumnae affairs, drawing her away from progress on the college history. In October 1951, she became alumnae correspondent, a position that involved working on the *Bulletin,* corresponding with alumnae clubs, and handling publicity. With a lapse in alumnae work from 1939 to 1951, Bedford, Hale, and Verna Mae Edom of the alumnae office engaged in a yearlong effort to complete the alumnae directory. The only active alumnae clubs had become inactive after Stapel left in 1938, and clubs in Kansas City, St. Louis, Indiana, and Columbia were reactivated by June 1951. Other clubs were being formed in Memphis, Chicago, and Kentucky, with seventeen clubs existing by 1954.[50]

The long-anticipated climax of the Centennial began on Friday, June 1, with the registration of eight hundred alumnae for the reunion and another two hundred attending. Alumnae came from twenty-nine states and Canada with thirty-one from Texas alone. The St. Clair Moss organ was dedicated in the chapel, and the banquet the same evening featured the presentation by the Indiana Club of a portrait of Hertig. While alumnae gathered, husbands and fathers attended a smoker-barbecue in honor of the "small-boys class," which had been discontinued about 1905. Saturday featured class reunions and a business meeting, all leading up to the climactic event, the Saturday-night concert by Jane Froman, the 1926 graduate whose singing career had become a permanent point of pride for the college. The gala concert, held on the floodlit front steps of St. Clair Hall at eight-thirty, had an audience of four thousand and drew rave reviews.[51]

Events of the Centennial affected the college in a number of ways. Renewal of spirit that comes with rededication, widespread publicity, and more active alumnae all were positive results. All manner of historic items, a total of more than four hundred sent by alumnae and friends of the college, formed displays in a temporary museum and remained in safekeeping for possible future use. Another outgrowth of the Centennial was the publication of the history. Hale gave up her alumnae work in 1953 to devote herself exclusively to completion of the book. Although she moved to Iowa City in 1954 when her husband, Mark, relocated to the University of Iowa, she completed her history two years later.[52]

Just as the Centennial drew attention to the college for its century of achievement, the Froman concert highlighted the singer's incredible career, a career that would eventually bring her back home to Columbia in 1961 as a productive citizen and trustee of the college.

By sheer grit and talent, Ella Jane Froman had turned a troubled childhood and early career struggles into a life of admirable achievement. Born on November 10, 1907, in University City to Anna and Elmer Froman, she experienced the separation of her parents in 1912 when her father left, never to make future contact. From that time on, Froman coped with stuttering. Her mother soon moved with Jane to Clinton, Missouri, where she entered her daughter into a convent school.[53]

Froman was twelve when her mother joined the music faculty at Christian College. She attended high school in Columbia, becoming an outstanding voice student at Christian College before her graduation. Despite her stuttering, she entered the journalism program at the University of Missouri, admittedly to participate in the department's annual musical revue. She excelled as a star of the revues, but not as a student, and her mother sent her to the Cincinnati Conservatory of Music in the fall of 1928. Froman convinced conservatory officials to grant her a scholarship as a freshman, an award usually available only to seniors. She supported herself by singing at social functions, and Powell Crossley, head of radio station WLW, heard her and gave her a job. Froman performed twenty-two programs per week for WLW, with a schedule ranging from eight in the morning to one in the morning. When Paul Whiteman, well-known band leader for NBC, heard her on the late-night shift, he added her to his group until NBC gave her a band of her own. After working in Cincinnati and Chicago, she went on to star in the Ziegfeld Follies and other Broadway musicals, performing with singers James Melton and Bing Crosby and with orchestras of Frank Black and André Kostelanentz. Froman sang especially the works by George Gershwin, Cole Porter, Richard Rogers, and Irving Berlin. In 1938, she recorded the *George Gershwin Memorial Album* and sang with the New York Philharmonic in 1942 in an all-Gershwin concert. Performing in nightclubs, theaters, and a Warner Brothers movie, she had reached the peak of her career by the early 1940s.[54]

Later in life, Froman proclaimed herself to be happiest when singing for the armed forces: "Once you've done something like that, you're spoiled for any other audience." Before Pearl Harbor in 1941, she sang with the first USO group at Fort Belvoir, Virginia, and at Camp Dix, New Jersey. Returning to Christian College, Froman performed in the college auditorium in a war-relief concert sponsored by the Victory Drive for the "I Pledge America" week. She was the first to volunteer when President Franklin Roosevelt asked for volunteers to put together a USO program for entertainment of American troops overseas. Leaving New York on February 21, 1943, with sixty-eight others on a Pan American seaplane to tour England and North Africa, Froman was one of only fifteen people to survive the plane's crash in Lisbon's Tagus River the evening of February 22. Too badly injured to stay afloat, she was supported until help arrived by John Burn, the pilot, despite his own broken back and skull fracture. Her extensive injuries prohibited normal functioning for the rest of her life; she suffered a broken right arm, a compound fracture of the right leg, gashes to the bone below the crushed left knee, and bits of steel and wood embedded in her body. Fighting to prevent amputation, she underwent twenty-five leg operations before she could walk at all without crutches, spending three years confined to a wheelchair. Over the years, she endured thirty-nine operations in all and wore a leg brace the rest of her life.[55]

Determined to continue her career despite the seriousness of her injuries, Froman performed mostly in nightclubs where she could appear in a wheelchair, then later on crutches, and eventually standing on a motorized platform. Struggling to pay her medical bills, which totaled nearly a half-million dollars, she sang in major clubs throughout the United States. Dubbed "soldier in greasepaint," she went to Europe in 1945 on the USO circuit for a thirty-thousand-mile trip, wearing a cast and using crutches. She gave ninety-five shows in nine countries during a three-and-a-half-month period.[56]

By 1947, Froman's life appeared for a time to be improving. She had her own radio show for Coca-Cola, and her relationship with Burn, who had saved her life, had become serious. In February 1948, she divorced Donald Ross, a fellow performer she had met in Cincinnati at WLW, and her marriage to Burn took place in Coral Gables, Florida, on March 12, 1948. The next October, Froman returned to Columbia as the "Coming Home Queen" for the University of Missouri homecoming. However, the physical and emotional strain of the past five years had taken its toll, and Froman suffered a breakdown in 1949. Friends took her to the Menninger Clinic in Topeka, Kansas, and paid her expenses while she slowly recovered during the next nine months. While at the clinic, she worked toward overcoming her stuttering problem, although it never ended entirely.[57]

After 1949, Froman resumed her career with success, known as "the girl who wouldn't give up." She starred in her own television show, *USA Canteen,* in 1952, renaming it *The Jane Froman Show,* broadcast on CBS television until 1955. With her career on track again, she returned for the Christian College Centennial in 1951, receiving the college's 1951 Honor Service Citation. In 1952, she established an annual Jane Froman Award in honor of her mother. That same year, Susan Hayward starred in the movie version of Froman's career, *With a Song in My Heart,* for which Froman performed the vocal parts. Froman delighted in the filming: "I feel as though I have lived three lives—one before my accident, another since, and the third watching the two lives brought to life again so entertainingly, tunefully, and truthfully."[58]

Although Froman appeared on major television programs, the difficulty of maintaining her career led to her divorce from Burn in 1956 and, ultimately, to her retirement and return to Columbia in 1961. Her health had declined by 1957, leading to spinal surgery and then back surgery. When her "good leg" required yet another operation, she decided to go home, feeling that it was time to retire in order to preserve her artistic integrity.[59]

Froman returned to Columbia and lived with her mother, the widow of W. J. Hetzler, a Columbia mayor who had died in 1945. Froman faced recovery not only from the surgery but also from pneumonia. She soon renewed a friendship with Rowland Smith, whom she had known at the University of Missouri. A widower, Smith was a newspaperman who had become associate director of the Office of Public Information at the University of Missouri. Smith and Froman married on June 20, 1962, and Froman began a new phase of her life.

Free of career demands, Forman indulged her natural inclination toward charitable work. She had already served as chair of the New York State Easter Seal Campaign in 1953, and in 1956 she had established the Jane Froman Foundation at the Menninger Clinic for the support of emotionally disturbed children. Serving as a trustee on the Board of Governors of the Menninger Foundation, she received the Lifetime Achievement Award from the foundation in 1977. After her retirement, she also chaired the 1967 Missouri Easter Seal Campaign, and, in 1971, she hosted an Easter Seal Gala in Kansas City and was elected to the Board of Directors of the State Easter Seal Society. Also in 1971, she received the Missouri Mental Health Association Annual Award. Christian College honored Froman in 1964 with its Distinguished Alumnae Award in appreciation not only of her career but also of her role as a friend of the college. Froman brought outstanding performers to the campus over the years, including actors Helen Hayes and Vincent Price and opera star Rise Stevens. In 1976, she became a Columbia College trustee.[60]

Froman received varied and numerous other honors throughout her career. As early as 1934, she became the number-one female singer in radio and in 1954 was named "Woman of the Year" by the Boston Press Club. She received an honorary doctorate in music from the Cincinnati Conservatory of Music in 1951, the first given to a singer of popular music. The National Alumni Association of the University of Missouri named her to the Board of Directors in 1963 and in 1970 honored her with its Faculty-Alumni Award. The Missouri Squires inducted her into their ranks in 1971 at a luncheon hosted by Gov. and Mrs. Warren Hearnes. Clinton, Missouri, held a "Jane Froman Day" in 1973, and a historical marker placed by the Henry County Historical Society identified her childhood home there. One of Froman's most meaningful awards, however, came from the USO National Council in Dallas at a dinner in her honor on March 28, 1963. Froman received a specially crafted USO Gold Medallion with a citation: "For her gallant pioneer effort to bring the sight and sound of home to our American troops in World War II, for her exceptional example of courage and devotion to duty despite personal sacrifice, this citation is awarded to Jane Froman with great admiration and deep affection by the USO in the name of the American Armed Forces of three generations who have not forgotten."[61]

In one of her last projects, Froman collaborated with Jay Turley to establish a music camp at Arrow Rock, Missouri, near Columbia. She appeared in musicals written and produced by Turley and acted as a fund-raiser, enabling Turley to purchase and remodel the Old School House, which became the Jane Froman Music Center in 1969. Two years later, Christian College acquired the facility, renaming it the Jane Froman Arts Center and utilizing it as a center for student retreats and summer programs. Turley, as president of the center, attracted a series of performers, but the project ended in 1977. Froman's last public performance took place on October 28, 1971, at the National Press Club in Washington, D.C., in celebration of the 150th anniversary of Missouri statehood. In the presence of state officials, and with Jack Buck, announcer for the St. Louis Cardinals, as master of ceremonies, Froman appeared last on the program to a tumultuous standing ovation.[62]

Froman died of cardiac arrest on April 22, 1980, at the age of seventy-two. Her life had been well defined by Burn in 1952:

> It would seem as though every possible obstacle was interposed between the girl and the thing she sought to attain as though she were being submitted to a trial, infinite in its severity. She accepted such conditions; further, she imposed the strictest ethics on herself. She must fight at all times honorably, ask little of others, and at the same time fulfill every obligation in a fuller measure than is asked of those not so burdened as she.[63]

The last five years of the Miller presidency ran their course quietly. Miller called the academic year of 1951–1952 "the most satisfactory year since the beginning of World War II" in the areas of student morale, extracurricular activities, and educational progress. "Promotional work," a heading in every report to the board, had, to Miller, always meant admissions work, and enrollments appeared promising. Indeed, the next year would see the largest enrollment in the college's history with an overflow crowd of 425 students. As for promotion of the college in the form of fund-raising, the president preferred to leave that to the board: "We as a Board know that I am not adept as a money-raiser." Although there was some discussion of hiring an "agent," the Miller presidency ended with no such action.[64]

Breaking the calm of the early 1950s at Christian College, "panty raid fever" struck in May 1952. Dozens of colleges, especially major state universities, experienced "panty raids," brought on, according to one official, by "sex, simple-mindedness, and just a means of blowing off steam before final exams." Roughly two thousand University of Missouri men raided dormitories and sorority houses, hitting all three Columbia campuses, on the night of May 19. Christian College students, "armed with plumbers' plungers, wet mops, and brooms" fought back the crowd, and "the battle was joined" at the stairs ascending from the dining hall basement level. The girls managed to repulse an attempt to enter the main level of St. Clair Hall. When raiders forced open the door to the Wightmans' ground-floor apartment, Louise Wightman "vigorously railed at them" with a blackjack, driving them off. Meanwhile, another mob stormed the main front steps, unhinged the massive wooden doors, and threw rocks at the windows while Christian College students in turn threw hot water and Coca-Cola bottles out the windows. As students and housemothers stood their ground at the front door, the acting police chief, J. L. Parks, appeared at the top of the steps and averted more serious trouble: "Boys, you have torn hell out of Columbia. Now go home and go to bed." The National Guard had been put on alert but fortunately was not needed. Gov. Forrest Smith happened to be in Columbia and witnessed a portion of the turmoil from his limousine, reportedly remarking that "boys will be boys." He later realized the seriousness of the situation and denounced the conduct.[65]

Loss of personal property suffered by Christian College students occurred largely in Missouri Hall, where some of the intruders managed to force entry. Damage to the campus consisted mainly of broken windows and screens and ruined shrubbery. Miller, at the instruction of the board, wrote a letter of commendation to Dean of Women Dora Johnson for the "loyal, courageous, and justifiable manner" in which she faced "a difficult situation." He also praised Blewett, acting president while Miller was out of town, for his "straight thinking, sane appraisal of the temper of the raiders, and the knowledge that mob emotion spends itself if given time." Certainly, the destructive event failed to dislodge the good relationship between the college and the university. Miller met with university curators at their request in a cordial exchange of views, recommending that "we not allow this one episode to disrupt or mar future cooperation." The Committee on Student Conduct at the university dismissed three of the participants in the raid, making them eligible for the draft in the Korean War. Seventeen others were disciplined.[66]

In 1952, Miller again turned to the matter of his own retirement and the need to find a successor. Expressing disappointment at his inability to manage the workload he had hoped to carry after the passing of a year, he announced to the board that he had withdrawn from all civic affairs and off-campus professional activities except for membership on the church board.

By "putting in a shorter day, followed by rest and occasional diversion," he had been able to get along fairly well. Miller left the choice of action to the board: "I shall be glad to have the Board of Trustees express freely their observations and their judgments relative to my work at Christian College. When the time comes that the interests of Christian College will be better served by a change in the administrative head, we as a Board must lay aside all personal consideration and act positively. Seriously, I say, if the time is now, let's face it."[67]

As Miller curtailed his activities, the faculty augmented its role. September 1954 saw the beginning of an intensive faculty study of student retention in which the faculty explored the need to improve educational services in all areas of the college. Eight faculty committees, each specializing in a specific area, launched a study discussing, analyzing, and evaluating existing conditions and suggesting improvements. Since it was evident that solutions would require board action to be effective, study committee heads met with the executive committee of the board on September 15, 1955, to report on and discuss their findings.

Recommendations of the several committees gave a good indication of the condition and needs of the total program in the mid-1950s. The Curriculum Committee recommended remedial help for students with low reading and writing skills, a need many colleges were beginning to recognize. The report also urged more efficient class scheduling, abandoning the practice of allowing some faculty members to set their class times for personal convenience. The Committee on Improvement of Instruction made a survey of needed equipment and suggested that the college operate its own bookstore. It also recommended that new students arrive on campus early for orientation and testing. Student orientation would soon become a routine feature for first-year students, but the idea of a college-owned bookstore received little serious attention.[68]

Particularly revealing in its indication of institutional needs, the report of the Committee on Finance proposed somewhat bold changes: the creation of a joint committee of board and faculty members to implement a program for the improvement of educational facilities, an investigation of fund-raising procedures, and the hiring of an educational consultant through the United States Office of Education or the State Office of Education to conduct a complete efficiency survey. The report also advocated the adoption of a salary schedule to help faculty members anticipate future pay along with the creation of a faculty handbook comparable to those of other colleges. Fringe benefits sought by faculty included some regular provision for sick leave, tuition-free education for children of faculty members, and some remuneration for professional travel. The impact of this committee later became evident in the adoption of a number of the recommendations in the 1960s.

The Committee on Physical Plant, with a list of fifty-five items, centered its report on improving the function of physical facilities in classrooms, laboratories, dormitories, and administrative offices. Almost as lengthy, the report of the Committee on Recruitment and Public Relations emphasized the need to increase staffing for public relations and alumnae activities and to develop better communication among public relations staff, alumnae staff, and the rest of the college administration. The report urged a more active role for alumnae in recruiting, public relations, and fund-raising. It proposed launching a fund-raising program and hiring a professional fund-raiser to approach foundations and industries on a regular basis.

By the mid-1950s, plans moved ahead for Miller's retirement. Although he was eligible to serve until June 30, 1957, Miller preferred to leave no later than February 1, 1957, at the beginning of the second semester. His successor would take charge the previous September. With a full enrollment expected, the college would be well positioned for a new administration.

On August 9, 1956, the board met to interview Kenneth Freeman and voted unanimously for his election as president of the college. Although his term was to begin on February 1, 1957, Freeman was to visit the campus on November 19, 1956. As the result of his deanship at Christian College from 1946 to 1948, Freeman was well acquainted with the college, and, having broadened his experience since 1948, he was a logical choice for the presidency. He had chaired the Department of Elementary Education at the University of Nebraska from 1949 to 1951 and served as dean of faculty at the State University Teachers' College in Geneseo, New York, from 1951 to 1953, where he also became acting president.[69]

The college seemed to have reached the end of an era when Banks presided over an assembly on September 28, 1956, to announce Miller's coming retirement. Bedford had just been appointed acting dean of faculty to replace Blewett, who had left in July for an administrative position at Chico State College in California. Also, Roscoe A. Miller had retired in the summer of 1956 after twenty-one years as business manager. Banks had words of high praise for James C. Miller: "The trustees regret that retirement time has come for Dr. Miller. He holds the affection of all those who have worked with him. Under his direction, the college has reached the best period in its 105-year history with improvements in the physical plant and its educational services that have never been attained before."[70]

The board held a rather exceptional meeting on November 14, 1956, Miller's sixty-fifth birthday, and presented him with a unique gift. The college had taken out a five-thousand-dollar insurance policy on Miller in 1940 "as a protection to the College" in the event of Miller's death. Banks stated that, as of that date, Miller had arrived at retirement age and that the policy had served its purpose. He requested that the board consider "the proper distribution of it." The board then presented the policy to Miller "as a gift of appreciation." Two days later, the president was dead, and his close friend, Lemmon, described that last board meeting:

> It was a really happy meeting—he made it so. We could sense his satisfaction. The College was filled with a fine group of young women—the largest enrollment in its history. He had an excellent staff of colleagues in whom he took pride. The fiscal situation at the College was satisfying. The school year was progressing well. His successor had been chosen who in a few weeks will take charge of the College—a successor who had once been on the College staff and whose selection he warmly approved. He was happy on Wednesday of this past week, and we were happy with him.[71]

James C. Miller died of a heart attack at 4:18 P.M. on November 16, 1956, at his home after spending a normal working day with his staff. Tributes in local newspapers and letters of condolence all reflected the deep affection of those in all areas of the college who had worked with him. Lemmon, in his remarks at the memorial service for Miller, ranked him with Rogers and St. Clair Moss in importance to the college, praising him for his combination of idealism and realism and for his self-depreciatory manner with the board: "College administration is a difficult art, piled high with problems—economic, personal, intellectual, emotional. It is not an easy life our friend led." Trustees paid him tribute: "His long tenure, his singleness of mind, his devotion to education and his integrity of character, will live in the history of Christian College and mark him as one of the few men who have indelibly placed the stamp of their lives on this institution for which we hold mutual responsibility."[72]

Never had there been a greater outpouring of affection at the leaving of a president of the college. Not only had Miller built for himself a national reputation in educational and church circles, but also his own stature had enhanced the reputation of the college and brought it academic and financial stability. Like St. Clair Moss and Lee before him, he had brought to campus the man who would carry on his work. His accomplishments as an educator had continued the progress begun by Lee, and he left an institution of which he could be justly proud but one not yet embracing modern administrative techniques. As his successor, Freeman would bring a new era of administrative sophistication to the college he envisioned as "small, select, serious in purpose."

8

Small, Select, Serious in Purpose

KENNETH FREEMAN: 1956–1965

There are mountainous, uncomfortable days, up which one takes an infinite time to pass, and days downward sloping, through which one can go at full tilt, singing as one goes.

—Marcel Proust, as quoted by Kenneth Freeman
in a report to the Board of Trustees

THE COMING OF KENNETH FREEMAN as president represented a sea change for Christian College. In place of Miller's cautious, sometimes dire, outlook, protective of and comfortable with what was in place, Freeman's innovations threw caution to the winds. He was appalled at the state of the salaries, equipment, and methods he found and complained of the college's "stubborn complacency that tends to permeate its various constituencies as well as its collective entity." He called for "an open-minded willingness to explore the new" as "essential to success—perhaps to survival." Freeman echoed the tenet of the college's founders that relevant education must reflect social change: "In periods of greatly accelerated change, like the present, there is some possibility that the gap between social reality and a college's complacency may become so great that the educational program loses much of its value."[1]

The major "social reality" sparking Freeman's concern was the growing discomfiture of Christian College as a junior college. In contrast to the situation in 1913, when the college became one of eleven junior colleges in the United States, by 1930 it was one of some four hundred junior colleges, only half of which were private. By the 1960s, with the advent of the large nonresidential, publicly funded, two-year community colleges—serving a strongly vocational and adult-education function—few junior colleges were either private or oriented to the liberal arts. In the face of daunting competition from coeducational and four-year institutions, Freeman concluded that a small, residential junior college must distinguish itself by rising above the commonplace, offering an excellence that would entice outstanding students. Taking up the centennial theme of "small, select, serious in purpose," Freeman defined the terms more fully. By "small," he envisioned maintaining the present size whereby "maturity is obtained in an intimate group setting where environmental conditions can be more carefully controlled." "Select" meant the need "to choose students who can and want to profit from a college education: Some colleges must make for these gifted students a primary place in the total educational scheme of things. Christian College proposes to do its share." The "serious in purpose" emphasis downplayed "extracurricular activities and a general setting of gracious living," stressing that "the basic part of its program is a sound collegiate education."[2]

Taking office on November 21, 1956, Freeman was formally introduced to Columbia on March 17, 1957, at an inaugural reception attended by 450 guests, including local, state, and national officeholders. Within months, the theme of change became apparent. In July, Freeman presented two alternatives to the board: improve the present plant or build a whole new campus at the site of the horse farm. Estimating the cost of renovations at $2,500,000, Freeman preferred the option of a new campus at $3,775,000 as cheaper in the long run, fearing that St. Clair Hall might not be strong enough to withstand extensive rehabilitation. He proposed that the college hire an engineer to evaluate the existing buildings for safety and duration of service, obtain professional planners to appraise the suitability of the campus and other possible locations, and authorize a survey to determine the potential for a fund drive. The same meeting resulted in a two hundred dollar tuition increase and allocation of two thousand dollars for a fund-raising survey by Clifford King of the National Fund Raising Company. The King Survey Report of June 1958 considered it vital to educate the community "as to the urgency of the projected need for remodeling, renovating, and expanding college facilities." Freeman even thought the unthinkable. The first president to cast doubt publicly on the appropriateness of the college's name, he charged that it inhibited enrollments and deplored "the difficulty Christian College has in attracting students to it because of the name 'Christian.'"[3]

Going beyond a general emphasis on change, Freeman targeted specific areas for action in a series of "firsts" for the college. In alumnae affairs, he instituted the first annual homecoming in May 1958, using the May 3 banquet as an occasion for unveiling the official oil portrait of J. C. Miller. That homecoming, attended by 350 alumnae, led to the first annual alumnae fund drive in 1959 and the hiring of the first full-time alumnae secretary. Although the alumnae goal of $30,000 for 1959–1960 was not close to realization, total giving of $11,000 far surpassed contributions of $3,414 the previous year. In 1962, Freeman hired Jane Canedy Crow, a Christian College alumna, as director of alumnae affairs, and a vigorous alumnae program evolved. Under her leadership, graduates formed the National Alumnae Association, and the first Alumnae Workshop took place in October 1963, creating the Student Recruitment Committee within the association.[4]

Part of the new Christian College public image was the work of a revamped public relations office. Peggy Phillips, well experienced in public relations, became the college's first professional director of public relations and development in 1959. She changed the *Bulletin* into a larger and glossier piece, the *Alumnae Magazine,* and the yearbook, the *College Widow,* took on a more professional look. A more attractive college catalog featured the symbol of two C's back to back, one looking backward and the other looking forward, resting on an open book. Phillips brought the college national publicity with articles in *Mademoiselle* (August 1959), *Glamour* (November 1962), *Seventeen* (November 1963), *Look* (December 1960), the *Junior College Journal* (January 1963), and the *New York Times* (March 7, 1965). The *Look* article, in an issue of 6.3 million copies, was reprinted and widely distributed by the American Association of Junior Colleges and by the National Education Association. In development work, Phillips helped conduct the college's first community capital campaign since 1938, quickly raising $106,000 in 1959 toward the construction of a new dormitory. The college also initiated parent involvement in fund-raising with the first Parents' Weekend, held for both systematic giving and academic consultation between parents and faculty members. When Phillips resigned in June 1964 to take a position in Washington, D.C., the college granted her an honorary degree.[5]

In 1961, development became a separate function under Freeman, who argued that "Christian has for years had no organized development program which included a continuous volunteer fundraising group to obtain funds to support capital additions, replacements, and improvements. This is a must. The faculty is at work developing a blueprint for the future, and definite recommendations will be placed before the board." Freeman named Bill Winstead, a member of the social sciences faculty since 1953, as head of the first development office, making him responsible for the alumnae fund drive and the capital campaign of 1961. Under Winstead, the college made a start toward acquiring federal loans and foundation grants, although foundations tended to give scant attention to two-year women's colleges. With the work of the office well under way, Winstead resigned in 1962 to return to teaching and was replaced by George W. Shirley.[6]

In admissions, Freeman hired Louis Lewis to replace Neil Freeland, who was in turn replaced by Ken Serfass. Dissatisfied with the performance of some admissions counselors, Freeman replaced older ones as soon as possible and hired better-paid young men. By the 1960s, Freeman resolved to be more selective in admissions and established the first formal Admissions Board to scrutinize applications and deal with problems in admissions policy. The board consisted of Serfass, Bedford, and Robert Montaba, who had joined the faculty in 1959, primarily to update the guidance and counseling program. Montaba instituted systematic use of Scholastic Aptitude Test (SAT) verbal scores and high school grade averages, comparing the credentials of Christian College students and applicants with national averages. Montaba, later director of student personnel with supervisory authority over the offices of the registrar and dean of women, also directed the faculty advising program and residence hall counseling.[7]

Another innovation by Freeman came in replacing the college's own dining hall employees with a catering service, Slater Food Service, with the advantage of quantity purchasing at a savings of twenty to twenty-five thousand dollars per year. Slater began its contract with the opening of classes in the fall of 1957, causing quite a stir among students by using white-jacketed university men as waiters. Slater had achieved prominence during World War II by servicing industrial plants and soon had contracts with 90 colleges and universities as well as with 15 hospitals and 210 industrial firms. In 1962, the college gave birth to a new corporation, Catering Management, when William Bratrud and Ernie Goldsmith resigned as managers for Slater Food Service to create their own company. They too succeeded in growing into a multicampus caterer, keeping the original contract with Christian as their centerpiece. In another food service change—one lamented by many—the personal preparation of snacks by Nettie Ashlock in the Tea Room ended in 1960 to be replaced by vending machines. Ashlock, too valued as an employee to be released, moved into the role of operator and supervisor of the college's first telephone switchboard system.[8]

As professionals replaced amateurs and secretaries replaced student help, the staff size, carefully contained by Miller, tripled during the Freeman administration. Under Miller, the registrar had served as administrative secretary to the president and to the dean of faculty. The public relations person had written brochures, edited the alumnae magazine, supervised the yearbook and the *Microphone,* and taught journalism. The college had operated with eight administrators and a support staff of seven. Assembling his own administrative staff, Freeman hired Beuna Lansford, an instructor of secretarial courses, to replace Lillian Keene as registrar in 1960, and Warren Conner replaced R. A. Miller as business manager in the fall of 1956. Bedford, who was acting dean of faculty in 1956, became dean with the understanding that he must complete his Ph.D. degree as soon as possible, regularly reporting his progress to the board.[9]

Following through on his intent to improve the physical plant, Freeman obtained authorization from the Buildings and Grounds Committee of the board to hire the architectural firm of Hellmuth, Obata, and Kassabaum of

St. Louis to prepare a master plan. The firm's study revealed that Hughes Hall, Missouri Hall, and the swimming pool were structurally sound, but that the other buildings on campus needed to be replaced. As a result, the Twenty-five-Year Master Plan approved by the board in July 1958 put forth a six-phase building program intended to serve a campus of 700–800 students:

> Phase I—Build a new dormitory in the northwest corner of the campus, housing 160 students.
>
> Phase II—Build a new dining hall and student union to the north of the new dormitory and a second new dormitory north of the dining hall and social center.
>
> Phase III—Build a new academic building north of St. Clair Hall to include all classrooms, fine arts, library, and administrative offices. Tear down Williams Hall, then called Practice Hall or Old Main.
>
> Phase IV—Demolish St. Clair Hall, Dorsey Hall (except for the swimming pool), and the maintenance building. Build a new gymnasium adjacent to the swimming pool on the east side with room for dance and lockers.
>
> Phase V—Build a round chapel and bell tower as a campus focal point in the space formerly occupied by Dorsey Hall.
>
> Phase VI—Build an infirmary at the extreme north end of the campus and a third new dormitory to house 120 students.[10]

With the master plan in place, fund-raising began for the new residence hall. Although the second unit of Hughes Hall had never been added, a wholly new dormitory would be built; the survey of the physical plant had concluded that the expansion of Hughes was not feasible in light of advances in dormitory planning. Estimates placed the cost of the new building at $760,000, and the college turned to the use of federal funds along with a capital campaign. An application for a loan of $671,000 was approved in January 1959, and the capital campaign set a goal of $150,000. For the first time, the college used professional fund-raising services. One contribution of symbolic importance came from the University of Missouri Athenaean society, a speech organization that had learned of the university's use of the Christian College chapel for fourteen months at the time of the university fire sixty-seven years earlier.[11]

Even as the new residence hall took shape, college officials scrambled for increased funds when faced with a budget shortfall in the 1959–1960 academic year. The enrollment of 380 had fallen short of projections, and renovation of older dormitories and debt service on the government loan combined to produce a deficit. Emphasizing how closely the college's destiny rested on student numbers, the college paid recruiters one hundred dollars for each enrollment over their quotas. Board minutes of February 1960 reported that Christian College relied on tuition for 98 percent of its operating income, compared with a general figure of 58 percent. The cost of building a "new Christian College" would be overwhelming, but Freeman and the board stood firm in their determination to construct an ideal campus environment. In June 1960, the board increased tuition from $1,675 a year to $2,500, a 67 percent increase, making future enrollment projections still harder to achieve. The college also sought to augment funds from the Christian Church by participating in its Unified Promotion. The board approved an agreement of participation with the church calling for reports by the college on its objectives for the decade and on annual goals and objectives, but the end result did little to improve funding.[12]

In the midst of intense financial activity, the board faced the threat of losing their president when the University of Texas offered Freeman a chairmanship in its School of Education at a salary higher than his contract at Christian College. Freeman, although pleased with his role at the college and with his location in Columbia, set three conditions for staying: a substantial salary increase and an indication of his salary for the next four or five years; an agreement that, if terminated, he would be paid for the year in which he was terminated and for the year following termination; and modernization of the kitchen in the president's home. The board, in full agreement that Freeman had done an excellent job, increased his salary for the next fiscal year, making future salary adjustments contingent upon operating results. Although agreeing to modernize the kitchen, they declined to meet the second condition, concluding that relations between the board and the president rested upon "mutual respect and consideration."[13]

Not only did the new residence hall open as scheduled on December 18, 1960, but it won national honors for architectural design. Hellmuth, Obata, and Kassabaum received the Residential Award Citation in the Sixth Annual Design Awards Program sponsored by *Progressive Architecture,* a national architectural magazine. Rooms opened onto a balcony or patio, and built-in desks and dressers added a functional touch. The residence hall was dedicated as James C. Miller Hall on May 5, 1962, in a ceremony featuring Miller's close friend C. E. Lemmon as speaker.[14]

As Phase I of the master plan moved to completion, collateral moves fell in place. Hertig Hall, the building south of the White House, became a dormitory. The Conservatory, formerly housed in Hertig Hall, was relocated to Practice Hall (Old Main), the college's original building. As students began to use Miller Hall, the rooms vacated at the east end of the second floor of St. Clair Hall became faculty offices. The planned razing of Practice Hall was postponed, partly in response to appeals from alumnae who established a fund for its upkeep. The board finally decided in September 1961 to keep Practice Hall and to remodel rather than replace the heating plant, modifying Phase I of the master plan.[15]

Changes in top administrative positions accompanied other activities under way. Problems in the business office led to the hiring of Donald Wyss as financial secretary in July 1960, but Wyss left the college in July 1961, leading to the hiring of Charles M. Chrisman and the change in title from financial secretary to business manager. In the dean of faculty position, Bedford continued to work toward his doctorate, receiving an extension of the deadline for its completion, followed by a leave of absence and yet another extension of the deadline. His deanship remained in doubt as Freeman continued to press him for the establishment of policies for sick leave, tenure, merit ratings, vacations, promotions, salary increases, and eligibility for the pension fund as well as a constitution for the organization and operation of the faculty and administration. Development of such policies, never fulfilled in the Freeman years, would see fruition in the later 1960s.[16]

As in other areas, Freeman's presidency brought major changes in the faculty. Those role models of a generation earlier were reaching retirement age in the 1960s; one-third of the faculty had been at the college for twenty to forty years. Faculty members leaving included Franklin Launer, Geneva Youngs, and Margaret Tello in music, Ruth Graham and Ellen Dahl in home economics, Esther Stearn and Harold Long in science, Mabel Buckner and Cynthia McHarg in English, Hazel Perryman in German, Robert Abram in religion and social studies, Carolyn Drew in horsemanship, and Margaret McMillan in history, who had also served as librarian. Faculty continuing from the Miller administration included Burnett Ellis, who pioneered in the teaching machine field, creating his own "learning laboratory" for geology while also serving as the audiovisual supervisor. He and his wife, Jessie, constituted the geology faculty until their retirement in 1991. Also carrying on with significant contributions were Hazel Kennedy in English, Sue Gerard in physical education, Hortense Davison in French, Allene Preston in speech, and Sidney Larson in art.[17]

In addition to the continuing talent of earlier years, new faculty members were to help shape the future of the college. Dan Hoagland joined the faculty in mathematics and astronomy in 1958, becoming one of the most popular and respected faculty members of that period. He took on major assignments in the Freeman years, helping to create the college's first honors program and to plan the return to a baccalaureate curriculum. Ill health forced his retirement in 1985.[18]

Another new faculty member, Paulina (Polly) Batterson, also came to the college in 1958. Batterson's teaching specialty in American government led her to active political involvement as well as the creation of eight new upper-level courses and a special interest in the role of faculty governance. In addition to acquiring internships at the state and national levels for students, Batterson conducted periodic study tours to Washington, D.C., and brought such national figures to the college as Roselynn Carter while she was the first lady, journalists Roger Mudd and Tom Brokaw, Joan Mondale, and FBI director William Webster. Batterson published extensively and acted as a frequent speaker, panelist, and radio and television commentator. A Missouri Humanities Council grant funded her eight-part radio series in 1984, carried by the local station KOPN and made available by satellite to National Public Radio. In addition to serving as a member of the Missouri Humanities Council Speakers' Bureau, Batterson coordinated political campaigns, acted as chair of the Boone County Democratic Central Committee, and received gubernatorial appointments to state commissions. On campus, she served as president of the local American Association of University Professors (AAUP) chapter, contributed leadership to major college committees, and wrote the first Columbia College *Advising Handbook* before retiring in 1996 after thirty-two years of teaching at the college.[19]

However, it was Batterson's husband, Jack, who "would exert the most consistent, long-term influence of Freeman's appointees." Replacing his wife when she left temporarily to become a full-time mother, he then moved to a vacancy in American history just before his wife was reappointed to the faculty in American government in the spring of 1965. A few months later, when Dean Hill had become president, he named Batterson to become acting dean of faculty and, later, dean of faculty. Batterson remained as dean for eleven years until his love of teaching drew him back to the faculty ranks until his retirement in 1996.

Jack Batterson's impact was almost immediate and grew throughout his years at the college. Freeman and Bedford singled him out in his second year to chair a committee charged with one of the most important academic overhauls in the college's history. Under his leadership, the Curriculum Committee engaged in an intensive and long-range study of all aspects of the college's educational programs, concluding with the strengthening of the liberal arts offerings. Batterson would eventually serve on every major committee of the college and repeatedly represented the faculty as a member of the Board of Trustees. Also active in faculty governance, he was a cofounder and first president of the college's AAUP chapter and served on the committee to create a constitution for the Faculty Association. As scholar and teacher, he created eleven upper-level courses, pioneering especially in oral history and in the history of American business. The board awarded him a research grant for study at the Library of Congress in 1963, the first such grant made by the college, and he became a research associate at the University of Illinois.

As dean of faculty from 1965 to 1976, Batterson brought about major changes in the role of the faculty, strengthening their professional standing and organization along the lines urged in vain in the past. Under his guidance, the four-year curriculum was created and accredited in the crucial changes of 1970 and after. When he left the deanship, the board honored him with the college's only Distinguished Educator Award. As chair of the

History/Government Department after 1976, he and the department faculty made the major one of the most challenging and respected at the college.[20]

The Freeman administration saw the coming of several other talented faculty members who made the college the cornerstone of their careers and influenced minds and events. Dennis Grev, especially active in stimulating student research, guided the first Christian College student to present findings at the Missouri Academy of Science. Other students followed, performing at national meetings of the science honorary society, Sigma Zeta, whose local chapter Grev sponsored. The faculty elected Grev as president of the local AAUP chapter and to repeated terms as the faculty representative to the Board of Trustees. In addition, he received the Governor's Award for Excellence in Teaching.[21]

Penelope Carroll Braun, coming to the college as a personnel assistant in the residence halls in 1963, went on to act as assistant to the dean of women and as acting dean of women when Dean Elizabeth Kirkman went on leave to complete her master's degree. Carroll (later to become Braun) joined the English faculty in 1966. During a sabbatical leave in 1978, she became a Recognized Student with faculty privileges at Magdalen College, Oxford. She also received two National Endowment for the Humanities junior college teachers' fellowships for work at Indiana University, Denver University, and the University of California at Los Angeles. She taught the first coeducational class in 1969 when students from Christian College and Kemper Military Academy in Boonville joined forces for a class that met alternately on the two campuses. Especially active in faculty governance affairs, she served as president of the Faculty Senate, as faculty representative to the Board of Trustees, and as the college's affirmative action officer, completing a faculty equalization study that resulted in the upgrading of salaries for women faculty at the college. As campus sponsor of Alpha Chi, the scholastic honor society replacing Phi Theta Kappa, she served as regional president and a member of its national council. After twenty-eight years at the college, Braun resigned to pursue a business career.[22]

With Launer's retirement in 1963, William D. Brown became director of the Conservatory of Music. Under his leadership, the Double Sextette became a polished vocal group, representing the college in an active touring role, and the Conservatory continued to produce a full recital and professional concert program. The faculty chose Brown, along with Grev, as the first faculty representative to the Board of Trustees in 1966 when that position was created. Always concerned with institution-wide matters, Brown was highly successful as director of admissions during the Hill presidency. He brought professional business and sales procedures to the admissions staff, creating an efficient and well-motivated corps of recruiters. Promoted to vice president in 1972 and to executive vice president in 1973, Brown became a major force in directing the development of the college's Extended Studies Program at sites across the United States before he left the college in 1977 to engage in other business activities.[23]

Long and effective careers in teaching and mentoring had typified many Christian College faculty members throughout the college's history, and faculty in the Freeman years continued that tradition. In addition to those teachers already noted, others who displayed significant service and concern for student welfare included Glenna Mae Kubach in accounting, who joined the faculty in 1960 and taught until 1990, and Norman Reves in English, who taught for thirty years before retiring in 1994.

Whereas the faculty role in teaching and scholarship had long been outstanding, previous administrations had seen neither an institution-wide role for the faculty nor the need to define the role of the faculty in relation to the rest of the college. Faculty committees in the Miller presidency continued to function in academic areas only. In contrast, Freeman, from the outset, began involving faculty in institutional planning. As early as 1957, he named Larson as chair of the Plans and Projects Committee to study the needs of each department in upgrading facilities. More ambitious assignments continued when Freeman used faculty and trustees on the same committee, while pressing Bedford for creation of a formal organizational structure.

Also early in his presidency, Freeman determined the need for a clear statement of the college's beliefs and objectives, requesting that board president Hartley Banks appoint a special committee, the Committee on General Philosophical Positions and Goals, to compose a statement. Banks named Larson and trustee William Bradshaw as cochairs of the effort, ultimately creating a committee of fifteen: three trustees, two administrators, two students, two alumnae, and six faculty members. The committee, under Larson's leadership, began its deliberations in December 1961, presenting its findings to the faculty the next April. After faculty approval by a vote of thirty-three to two, the board adopted the final draft on March 20, 1963.[24]

The final document of the Committee on General Philosophical Positions and Goals, written by Dan Hoagland and labeled "Profile and Purpose," became the college's official statement. In a tone of reaffirmation of the college's traditional beliefs, the statement remained true to the motto of "small, select, serious in purpose":

WE BELIEVE
that in a world ever more worshipful of sheer size,
there is yet a place for the small college;
that in a world ever more devoted to specialization,
there is yet a place for broad liberal education;
that in a world more tolerant of mediocrity,
there is yet a place for excellence.

The statement pictured as its model a two-year women's college, primarily residential, small in size, with a program "strongly centered in the liberal arts." Heavy emphasis on the "personal relationship between teacher and student" as the "primary educational tool" would lead to student success. "'The student who actively avails herself of these manifold opportunities will leave the College with both the preparation and the desire for that life-long quest which *is* education, in the truest sense of the term."[25]

The statement to the faculty included a section of notes intended to explain the committee's deliberations. The notes, influential in molding future policy, suggested that "small" be limited to a student body of approximately seven hundred students and that students be the products of "the total college environment"; the introduction of "an appreciable number of non-resident students would tend to break down the present cohesiveness of the student body, and this would be undesirable." In its remarks on the role of the liberal arts, the report urged that "vocational and pre-professional programs . . . be set against a background of broad liberal education" and recommended that "the granting of specialized degrees be discontinued, and that all graduates meet the requirements for the Associate in Arts degree." Though recognizing the importance of spiritual values, the notes concluded that "required attendance at church services is of dubious value and should be terminated." The text called attention to the college's relation to the Christian Church as "largely one of tradition and sympathy" in which "any formal strengthening . . . could lead to conflicts with the spirit of the charter and the College's present philosophy." In a hint of future policy, the comments suggested that the college's name posed difficulties for admissions work but refrained from recommending a change. Finally, the notes supported a policy of more selective recruitment: "Economic strictures of the recent past have brought about the enrollment of a significantly large number of students who are probably not college material in any sense of the term, and who are in any case patently unsuited to the college which we wish to become."[26]

With the completion of the "Profile and Purpose," it fell to the Curriculum Committee to implement the newly written philosophy into sweeping curricular changes. Jack Batterson, as committee chair, reported to the faculty at the fall conference in September 1963: "A perusal of the college's catalogs of the past fifty years offers some insight into where we have been but does not tell us very much about the direction in which the college wants to go." Patterns in the 1920s showed a steady growth of general survey courses well adapted to the junior college curriculum, a de-emphasis of vocational and terminal work, and an emphasis on liberal studies with a requirement of thirty-four hours of general education. However, by 1963, general education requirements for the A.A. degree had been reduced in a retreat from the college's traditional liberal arts stance. According to Batterson in his address to the faculty, "The Present Curriculum: A Revision in Need of Revising," the 1923 requirements were "more in line with the stiffening demands of most of the universities to which our graduates transfer than are our present requirements." A comparison of the requirements for graduation bore out this conclusion. Of the sixty credit hours required for graduation in 1923, thirty-four hours of required courses included English composition, history, foreign language, mathematics or logic, and physical and biological sciences, leaving twenty-six hours of electives. In 1963, with sixty-two hours required for graduation, twenty hours of required courses included English composition, history or social studies, humanities, any science (no laboratory required), and physical education, leaving forty-two hours of electives.[27]

The curricular reform of 1964, effective for students entering in the fall of 1965, required sixty-two hours for graduation, thirty-three of which were in required courses: English composition and literature or exposition, nine hours; laboratory science, five hours; social studies (history, government, sociology, economics, anthropology, or geography), nine hours; humanities (religion, philosophy, art, literature, music, or language), eight hours; and physical education, two hours. Students had the remaining twenty-nine hours as electives.[28]

Yet another faculty committee, this one headed by Dan Hoagland, crafted an honors program approved by the board in July 1961. The program, effective in the 1961–1962 academic year, provided for graduation with honors for students completing an honors paper. Nomination of candidates in the second semester of the student's first year allowed the candidate to choose a research topic in consultation with an advisor in the field of the chosen topic.[29]

In another innovation, Hertig Hall became a French-language dormitory, *La Maison Française,* housing sixteen students under the supervision of Hortense Davison, a native of France. The experiment required the use of French in day-to-day living, allowing "English hours" for study time in non-French-language courses. Even residence hall meetings took place in French, and, after the first six weeks, residents ate at French-language tables in the dining hall.[30]

In line with his respect for faculty leadership, Freeman enhanced the faculty's professional conditions whenever possible. With the completion of the new dormitory, former student rooms in St. Clair Hall became faculty offices, vastly improving the opportunities for faculty advising and mentoring and for professional activities. In another "first" for faculty members, Freeman paid them for participation in a six-week in-service training program in the summer of 1962. Two-thirds of the full-time faculty took advantage of the opportunity, with sessions held in the new air-conditioned Miller Hall. Facilitated by outstanding educational leaders from across the country, faculty members investigated developments in modern teaching materials and devices, effective measurement and evaluation of instruction and learning, independent study programs, and principles and procedures of guidance and counseling. The workshop produced more and better visual aids, better examinations, and refined advising skills. It also heightened a sense of camaraderie among faculty members and provided a setting for interdisciplinary exchanges and reflection on larger educational issues. Throughout, the emphasis continued to be on the liberal arts, as stated in the "Profile and Purpose." Faculty morale received even more bolstering in the fall of 1962 when the college provided faculty lounges, first segregated between men and women but soon integrated. In addition, the Board of Trustees, although still lacking any systematic sabbatical-leave policy, took initial steps in that direction by providing one-semester paid leaves for Larson and Winstead and a summer stipend for Jack Batterson. In 1964, trustees initiated a policy of free tuition for daughters of Christian College faculty and administrators.[31]

The one area of retrenchment during the Freeman presidency brought the elimination of the horsemanship program. Although financial considerations weighed heavily in the decision to end the program, Freeman and the trustees also saw horsemanship as inconsistent with the college's image as a "place of the mind." An administrative study indicated that few students had come to the college specifically for that program and the ones who did tended to be not academically strong. The college had put as little of its resources as possible into upkeep, and a committee of trustees found conditions deplorable, requiring at least fifty thousand dollars just to put the barn in good repair. Although only fifteen or sixteen students entered the college each year for the program, an enrollment of seventy-five to eighty students, taking riding as an attractive physical education credit, put too great a demand on the number of horses available. With fewer and fewer colleges offering such a program, Freeman expressed a desire to move away from the "horsey set." The announcement of April 1964 that horsemanship would be discontinued at the end of the school year came as no surprise, and the college eventually realized a gain of ninety-two thousand dollars from the sale of the horse farm.[32]

Changes included modifications in the social area. The student population, somewhat more urban, upper-middle-class, and diverse than before, represented eighteen religious backgrounds and a generally conservative political outlook. Discipline remained strict. Students could not enter the living quarters of a man without official permission and the presence of a chaperone, nor could they be absent from the dormitory or campus without permission. Although they could not keep or rent cars while in Columbia, they were allowed to ride in cars within the city limits but, if at night, only to places approved by the college. A resident student who married must withdraw immediately, and if a town girl married, she must leave at the end of the semester.[33]

Students who broke college rules were sometimes penalized with what was called a "campus," which could take a variety of forms. Typical terms of a two-week campus applied to one student who had left campus at an unauthorized hour:

> You are not to leave the campus.
> You are not to use the telephone for local calls; you cannot make long distance calls and you cannot receive them. All long distance messages must be relayed through the head resident or some other college official.
> You are not to associate with boys.
> During quiet hours you cannot leave your room.
> You must attend church; no church cut may be taken.
> You may not attend any Special Event on campus.
> You must sign in and out in the campus book in your dorm each time you leave it for any reason except for meals in the Christian College dining hall and for classes.
> You may have no guests, local or out-of-town.[34]

Student expenses other than tuition remained modest. A room key cost fifty cents, books and supplies were roughly forty dollars per year, gym clothes were ten dollars, and room decorations typically amounted to fifteen dollars. Dues were one dollar for the Student Government Administration, three dollars for class dues, and two dollars for a dormitory fund. The *Student Handbook* set a guide for parents: "For personal expenses, we recommend not more than ten dollars a week, and we do not recommend charge accounts at all."[35]

In the academic area, all graduates received an associate in arts degree, but before 1957 the degree could take several forms: associate in arts; associate in fine arts; associate in fine arts in music, art, drama, and speech, or dance; and associate in arts in commerce. Although the college offered no majors, the catalog set forth a proliferation of sample course programs for an emphasis in such usual subjects as art, education, various sciences, business courses, English, history, political science, speech, and nursing, as well as an array of specialties less common for a liberal arts junior college: camp counseling, dental hygiene, library science, medical technology, occupational therapy, and airline hostess.[36]

By 1964, in response to the college's "Profile and Purpose," discouraging specialized courses and calling for graduates to receive only the associate in arts degree or the associate in arts with honors degree, sample program selections became more realistic and appropriate for a junior college. They included pre–elementary education, pre–secondary education, pre–physical science, pre–social studies, secretarial training, art, and home economics. Special-interest areas were offered in literature, drama, and design.[37]

Other changes brought college procedures more up-to-date. An early acceptance program, begun in January 1959, guaranteed space and acceptance to a student in the top third of her high school class based on her seven-semester record. Students who sought early acceptance must cancel applications to any other colleges and make a fifty-dollar nonrefundable deposit on tuition. Also, the college began to use the Educational Testing Service to identify a student's strengths and weaknesses and for indications of potential career fields. Students took tests in reading, writing, mathematics, social studies, and science upon entering college and again in April of the senior year for use in guidance and for national comparison. The college also began using the American College Testing (ACT) program, gaining access to student information from high schools as part of ACT scores and profiles.[38]

In an updating of the grading system, the old E, S, M, I, F grades gave way to A, B, C, D, F, and Incomplete, and graduation demanded a grade point average of 150 (on a scale of 400 for an A). The attendance policy, already strict, grew even more stringent. Students must be present for all classes and at weekly assemblies and special events. With no system of "cuts," only illness justified an absence. Any unexcused absences during the twenty-four-hour periods immediately preceding and immediately following a vacation period or at the beginning of the second semester added one hour of credit to a student's graduation requirements.[39]

With an overall emphasis on academic standards, Freeman sought better-qualified students through the extension of scholarship programs and the expansion of honorary scholarship societies on campus. He ended courtesy scholarships for daughters of ministers and teachers and increased merit-based funds. The college offered twenty William Dulany Scholarships, totaling roughly thirteen thousand dollars, for those students with high ranks in their high school graduating classes, and, in 1963, the board established fifteen "trustee scholarships" granting full tuition, room, and board to the most outstanding applicants. Local chapters of national honor societies in subject matter areas proliferated, with organizations available for honor students in music, art, drama, science, languages, and secretarial subjects. Phi Theta Kappa continued under the leadership of Hazel Kennedy of the English faculty, boasting its own chapter room, used by members as a study and reading room as well as for meetings and official ceremonies. Social organizations abounded, with the Twelfth Night Club still taking responsibility for planning major social functions. Other popular clubs were for Spanish, French, home economics, choral, St. Cecilia (for music students), the Student Organ Guild, the Drama Guild, and the Popular Piano Club. Recreational groups included the Women's Recreational Association, Bowling, Dolphin, Dance, Modeling, Riding, and International Relations. Students also contributed to such publications as the *College Widow* (the yearbook), *Microphone* (the newspaper), the *Student Handbook,* and the *Alumnae Bulletin.* For those students who could afford the cost, the college offered an opportunity for an extended European tour each summer, beginning in 1962.[40]

Every segment of Christian College felt the thrust of Freeman's determination to redefine the college as a bastion of excellence, and the board was no exception. Freeman put before the trustees a vision of two different types of colleges and asked which one trustees wanted Christian College to be:

> 1. A college that exists in an "aura of genteel poverty" and draws its *raison d'etre* from the "glory of its past"—under-financed to the point that it is impossible to perpetuate this "past glory" in its second century of existence—exploiting its momentum from the past by using underpaid, inadequately-trained faculty, by often admitting inferior students for reasons of economic necessity, by allowing plant deterioration—until in 15 or 20 years it passes out of existence.
>
> 2. A college whose faculty, students, plant and program compare favorably with the best, having a program based on solid and continuing research, a challenging curriculum constantly updated to meet current needs and attracting national prestige and recognition, with no need for apology for any phase of its program or for any part of its physical plant—all of this under-girded with a stable income that will permit the realization of "the bright promise of the future."[41]

Offering no middle ground, the choice was as optimistic in the second vision as it was unfair in the first depiction, giving the trustees little choice. Freeman then challenged them to define their own role. Consequently, the board named James M. Silvey, president of the MFA Mutual Insurance Company in Columbia and father of a Christian College student, to chair a committee to define "Trusteeship at Christian College." The resulting forty-page booklet explored the importance of trusteeship to the college, duties and responsibilities of trustees, personal requirements, organization of the board, criteria for selection of trustees, and rewards of trusteeship. The challenge of financing the president's visions also led to the creation of the Development Committee of the board under the leadership of John M. Allton of Columbia, and the board hired Gonser, Gerber of Chicago as development consultants.[42]

Freeman inherited a strong and committed fifteen-member Board of Trustees, all but three of whom still remained on the board at the end of his administration. Even so, new appointees outnumbered the carryovers, with eighteen trustees added in the Freeman years. Those members remaining from the Miller presidency included board president Hartley G. Banks Sr., Frank Hollingsworth, William St. Clair, Roy M. Shelbourne, William L. Bradshaw, C. E. Lemmon, Louis P. Blosser, L. S. Nickell, Thelma Underwood Marx, J. C. Mundy, Mrs. Berry McAlester, and Artie Mason Carter. Only Hollingsworth, Mundy, and Lemmon were lost to the board in the

Freeman presidency, and it was Lemmon's death that was most deeply felt. His thirty-four-year service spanned the terms of four college presidents and four board chairmen, and he acted as a link between the college and the church. "This man and his family have made an enduring contribution . . . which will continue in many ways as long as the college exists. . . . His example will be one to which we can and will aspire, working together for the common good."[43]

The board gained strong future leadership with the appointment of B. D. Simon Jr., who would replace Banks as chair and remain on the board until 1990. Other important new members included E. C. Adams, J. M. (Tom) Allton, James M. Silvey, and Sidney Neate of Columbia and Garth Clinkscales of Boonville, all of whom brought outstanding business leadership to the board. Elizabeth Gentry and Leta Spencer devoted themselves to furthering alumnae activities and solicitations. Both Louis A. Eubank and Sterl Artley provided expertise in higher-education administration, and Glynn Burke joined the board as Lemmon's replacement at the Christian Church in Columbia. Other new board members included Dorothy Heinkel, a generous benefactor, and Robert M. White, a former editor of the *New York Herald-Tribune* and publisher of the *Mexico (Mo.) Ledger.* Margaret Robnett, Vivian Fiske, Robert C. Lanier, William O. Lee, Walter E. Bixby Jr., and Elizabeth Coppedge completed the group. Several trustees had strong earlier ties to the college. Simon's mother was a Christian College graduate, and Clinkscales, whose mother was also an alumna, followed his father, who had served on the board for fifteen years. Allton's two daughters had attended the college. Elizabeth Gentry, an alumna, chaired the new National Advisory Committee on Alumnae Affairs for the board and, in 1962, received the Alumnae Achievement Award for "the tradition of interest in and loyalty to Christian College which has extended throughout five generations of her family."[44]

Once the board had accepted Freeman's vision of a college "attracting national prestige," the acquisition of funds to move ahead with the master plan became a top priority, making student numbers crucial. A strong enrollment of 409 students in 1960–1961 resulted in a surplus of $49,000, the first in several years. In a daring move, the board increased tuition to $2,500 in 1960, and an increase to $2,600 for 1965–1966 set costs at almost double the 1956 price of $1,345 when Freeman became president. Problems emerged in July 1961 when a higher cancellation rate and lower retention rate revealed a drop of seventy-one enrollments.[45]

When the retention rate, as high as 69 percent in 1957–1958, fell to 46 percent in 1961, Freeman, refusing to blame tuition costs, lashed out at institutional causes for the decline. He reported to the board that of 436 women high school graduates contacted, only 7 would choose a women's college, 6 of whom wanted a four-year women's college. Two-year women's colleges ranked at the bottom of the list of preferences. He thus cast doubt on the future of Christian College as a single-sex junior college, just as he had already called into question the marketability of the college name. In his frustration with continuing recruitment problems, Freeman blamed poor instruction, the inability to establish credit by examination, a poorly administered honors program, inadequate counseling, and overly strict campus regulations. He found fault with development and alumnae personnel for not meeting his fund-raising targets and with the admissions staff for their failure to recruit his projected goal of 400 students. Despite the college's dependence on tuition, Freeman proposed to eliminate lower-ability students to increase retention. In 1958, 60 percent had come from the top one-third of their classes and another 30 percent had come from the middle third. However, by 1961, 57 percent of entering students came from the bottom half of their classes. According to Freeman, "concern for quality must precede concern for numbers. The financial value of numbers, achieved by taking students of doubtful ability, may ultimately prove to be more imaginary than real. In fact, the long term effect may be dangerous."[46]

Despite recruitment and retention setbacks, Freeman remained adamant on the need to move ahead with the building program as a means toward attracting more and better students. Plans for the dining hall and social center, on the drawing board for Phase II of the master plan, were reduced to only a dining hall but held firm for a facility to accommodate 700 people. Freeman informed the board that enrollment must go up to at least 500 students for the operation to be economically feasible and projected an income based on an enrollment of 425 for 1962–1963 and 475 for 1963–1964 as a start toward the goal of an enrollment of 700. However, the budget, based on a proposed resident-student enrollment of 425, resulted in a deficit of $200,000 when only 356 students entered in the fall of 1962. Noting that the error in enrollment estimates resulted from higher than normal cancellations, Freeman concluded that the "financial condition could best be improved by obtaining ninety additional students for the next year." He announced that Frederick E. Frazier would replace Winstead (who would return to teaching) as director of development and Ken Serfass would serve as director of admissions under development. He set the goal for 1963–1964 at 450 students.[47]

In response to the financial problems, Freeman set forth a Ten-Year Plan in 1962 to bring financial goals in line with the previous Twenty-five-Year Master Plan for building. The Ten-Year Plan, adopted by the American Association of Junior Colleges and the Ford Foundation as a case study for a planning conference, further enhanced Freeman's reputation as a planner. The document, which Freeman called "bold and visionary," projected an enrollment of 800 students by 1972 and capital expenditures of $5 million. In line with the recently passed "Profile and Purpose," it ruled out "transient trends" toward specialized courses and reaffirmed the high admissions standards: "This college can also communicate its purpose to those students it should admit and make intelligent refusal of those whose goals and character make them unlikely to mature under its instruction."[48]

Freeman's optimism proved misguided when figures in late June showed 282 students enrolled for 1963–1964, and, by October, the administration faced a crisis. A deficit of $160,000 for 1962–1963 and possibly of $340,000 for 1963–1964 could reach the half-million-dollar mark by June 1964. In response, Freeman continued to project larger enrollments, setting a goal of 450 students for 1964–1965, which would permit a reduction in the deficit of approximately $200,000. He insisted that continuing the enrollment figures of the Ten-Year Plan would allow removal of the deficit in two years through careful management. Freeman presented trustees with a report, "Required: A Massive Effort," as his solution: "The next two or three years will determine the direction, perhaps even the destiny of Christian College. . . . Let us pray for brave hearts to give us courage and confidence in the massive effort. . . . [T]otal amelioration of budget problems, recruitment problems, and educational problems is not in sight.[49]

A combination of factors had led to the enrollment shortfalls, according to Freeman. He pointed to a stock market decline beginning in May 1962, a lack of new summer enrollments, and problems in the admissions office. An inexperienced admissions staff (all but three of the eight counselors were new), a new director, resignations, and sickness all compounded the problem. Further, tightening of academic requirements had led to the rejection of seventy-seven applicants, three times as many as in the previous year. As a result, the enrollment of 306 students in 1963–1964 fell well short of the projected 450.[50]

Freeman described the challenge ahead as a need to increase enrollments almost 50 percent in one year to 450, develop a new curriculum, raise capital for a new instructional building, and build and furnish the new dining hall. He predicted "some mountainous uncomfortable days ahead." The college did receive 56.6 percent more applications by November 1964, and the board hired Machin Gardner as a consultant. Changes led to an enlarged admissions staff with redefined territorial assignments, and counselors received better salaries and engaged in a three-week training program. With a strengthening of the academic program by a new dean of faculty, Freeman expected that high morale would bring good retention. He noted that a study by the American Council on Education in May 1963 had predicted an increase in the supply of female students by 20 percent in 1963–1964 and by 30 percent in 1964–1965. In response, the trustees reaffirmed their support for holding to the higher academic standards, concluding that a good image with high school counselors would bring better students and fewer dismissals. Trustees, still hopeful that the college would reach an enrollment of 450 students for the 1964–1965 academic year, held fast to "the need for the Christian College Dining Hall . . . as presently designed and its capacity utilization within the year after construction."[51]

Much of the optimistic outlook rested on confidence in Machin Gardner, hired as a consultant in the fall of 1963 and promoted to dean of admissions in March 1964 when Ken Serfass left for other employment. Gardner had spent ten years as director of admissions at Stephens College and was a past president of the Association of College Admissions Counselors. His reputation, along with staff changes, encouraged the trustees to consider construction of a new 150-bed residence hall to be built in 1965–1966 for occupancy in September 1966—a construction considered necessary for the contemplated enrollment increase to more than 500 students. Projections set residential student figures at 545 for 1967, 585 for 1968, and 625 for 1969. Although these higher projections followed a failure to meet past goals, Freeman anticipated that future enrollments would erase the 1964 deficit: "The ability to gain increased enrollment with higher tuition is based on the assumption that we can continue successfully with our master plan for improvements in staff, facilities, and programs."[52]

Admissions efforts suffered a severe blow when Gardner resigned for health reasons in June 1964. Freeman turned next to Howard Kelley, hired in August 1964 as assistant to the president in charge of admissions, public relations, and church relations. Kelley came to the college from Chapman College in Orange, California, where he served as director of admissions and alumni activities and as assistant to the president. Kelley, more experienced than previous admissions directors and working with a staff of eight full-time counselors, held an intensive ten-day workshop in September. Counselors at the workshop received a handbook of information, ideas, and instructions. In addition to supervising counselors, Kelley visited high schools himself, but he could do little in the way of fund-raising in his role in church relations. The college continued to receive less than 1 percent of its annual income from the church in the 1960s. By that time, the student body included more Methodists than any other denominations, with Presbyterians, Episcopalians, and Disciples coming next.[53]

Despite financial concerns, plans for the college building program continued. A $738,000 bond issue approved at the October 17, 1964, board meeting, combined with federal loans, led to the successful completion and furnishing of the new dining hall, one of the more elegant structures thus far built on campus. At the same October meeting, Freeman presented plans for a fine arts building—plans based on an enrollment of 800 students. With the proposed date for a new library and administration building at least five years away, the administration resolved space problems by moving the library from the second floor of Dorsey Hall to the former dining room facility in the basement of St. Clair Hall. The new dining hall, put into service in January

1965, was dedicated on February 21, 1965, as William H. Dulany Hall in honor of Dulany's thirty years of service and generosity to the college. During the construction of Dulany Hall, workers unearthed a four-foot boulder, a pink quartzite erratic deposited by glaciers some 7 million years ago, according to Burnett and Jessie Ellis. Although scientifically significant, it was too large to be moved intact and was broken into pieces. The college placed two of those pieces outside Dorsey Hall, then the location of the science laboratories.[54]

In a spectacular turnaround, Kelley's leadership of the admissions program brought an enrollment of 447 students in the fall of 1965, the largest in the history of the college and an increase of 151 students over the 296 in the fall of 1964. Residence halls were full, and, by July 21, 1965, the college had a waiting list. Numerous changes had brought about the impressive increase. There were more applicants (530 as an all-time high) and fewer cancellations, but the greatest change came in the smaller number of rejections. Kelley used the services of three college admissions centers, providing more than one thousand names of potential students. Also, his contacts with Christian churches across the nation produced additional names, and alumnae throughout the United States held social activities for prospective students. Under new procedures, applicants paid a thirty-dollar fee, refundable only if they were rejected. In addition, Kelley began the use of a rolling admissions plan whereby an applicant would be admitted as soon as she qualified rather than waiting until the end of her seventh high school semester. No student was rejected before the end of her eighth semester. The college required a nonrefundable advance tuition payment of three hundred dollars immediately upon admission, previously not required until May 15. Students returning for the second year at the college were required to pay an advance tuition of three hundred dollars in March rather than in May.[55]

By the end of the Freeman presidency in 1965, reasonable prospects for continued healthy enrollments looked good despite the deficit of $354,000. The college had survived the lean times largely through the efforts of Hartley Banks, who organized all of the Columbia banks under his bank's sponsorship to create a sizable loan for the college. B. D. Simon, who replaced Banks as president of the board, later hailed his accomplishment: "This was not a prudent loan [for the banks]. It was really a statement of respect for Hartley and the prestige of some of the board members. . . . It was a disastrous situation. . . . What Hartley did was a Herculean task, a Herculean effort. Christian College would have gone the way of many single-sex private colleges of that era."[56]

As the Freeman administration drew to a close, future leadership evolved. Elizabeth Kirkman, "the glue that held tradition together" at the college, completed her M.A. degree at the University of Missouri by taking a semester's leave and then settled into a long and successful tenure as dean of women. Kelley continued as assistant to the president and director of admissions, with Frazier as director of development. A major change for the future came in the dean of faculty office where Bedford went on leave in January 1963 for continued graduate work. In June 1963, he terminated his leave and his employment with the college. The relationship between the president and his dean had deteriorated when changes in the office had not come fast enough to please Freeman, who also faulted Bedford's judgment in hiring. Winstead, who had just returned to the faculty from his director of development role, interrupted his teaching again to become acting dean of faculty but soon decided to complete his doctorate with a fellowship from the University of California at Berkeley. The search began for a permanent dean. The product of that search, W. Merle Hill, served two years as dean until 1965 when his elevation to the presidency began one of the most significant administrations in the history of the college.[57]

Hill, a 1950 graduate of Oberlin College with a B.A. degree in German and French, completed his M.A. degree in German at the University of Cincinnati. After earning his Ph.D. degree in psychology, German literature, and education at Purdue University in 1961, he spent the next year as a Fulbright exchange teacher in Germany. He had gained administrative experience in the military as commanding officer of a Military Intelligence Reserve Unit from 1957 to 1961 and as section chief of a Prisoner of War Russian Interrogation Team.[58]

In his short time as dean of faculty, Hill reorganized that office to include the registrar's office and the dean of women's office. With such a large jurisdiction for the dean of faculty, an assistant to the dean of faculty became necessary. In 1966, when Beuna Lansford left the college after six years of devoted service to students as registrar, an assistant to the dean of faculty took on the duties as registrar, handling Hill's new preenrollment process as well. The first assistant, Robert A. Craig, helped carry the work of that office through the transition to a new dean when Hill became president of the college in 1965. Hill, in addition to restructuring the academic administration and introducing an improved preenrollment system, also guided the creation of *La Maison Française* and added an academic dimension to student orientation by requiring that new students participate in discussion groups, each led by a faculty member, evaluating a preassigned literary work.[59]

With Freeman's outstanding academic reputation, the college regularly risked losing him to other institutions. He resigned on March 16, 1965, effective June 30, 1965, the day before he was to become president of the Metropolitan Junior College in Kansas City. His leaving evoked a fond farewell from the college family. The board gave him his presidential car and a color television "in recognition of outstanding national leadership in the junior college field." A farewell dinner in his honor was a campuswide event. His portrait, painted by Sid Larson and dedicated at Hill's inauguration, depicted Freeman holding the blueprints of the campus he had envisioned in his master plan. In 1967, Freeman accepted the presidency of Illinois Valley Community College, leaving that post in 1969 to become director of the Higher-Education Department at Texas Tech University in Lubbock. After his retirement at the age of sixty-five, Freeman returned to live in Columbia until his death on September 30, 1998. His ties to the college remained close, and he acted as a consultant and fund-raiser for the college.[60]

Freeman's leadership role in higher education brought credit to the college throughout his administration. He had become president of the Missouri State Teachers' Association in 1958 and went on to serve as president of the Missouri Association of Junior Colleges in 1961 and of the American Association of Junior Colleges in 1964–1965. In 1962, the University of Missouri College of Education awarded him a citation as a distinguished educator. He was instrumental in the founding of the Council of Midwestern Women's Colleges, an organization consisting of Christian, Stephens, William Woods, Monticello, and Lindenwood Colleges, a group working to educate the public about the advantages of women's colleges and to gain recognition from foundations and high school counselors.[61]

Providing the faculty with more professional conditions became one of Freeman's major contributions to the college, and his willingness to grant the faculty an important role in institutional and curricular planning led to philosophical and academic changes marking his administration. His work in adding new personnel for residence hall guidance and in the use of testing programs brought the college into a whole new range of activities necessary to become competitive in the 1960s. These actions, in addition to his provision for faculty offices and leaves, the summer workshop, and a virtual doubling of faculty salaries, contributed to the retention of strong new faculty members who made the commitment to devote their careers to the college. According to Jack Batterson,

> President Freeman was determined to build a competent and stable faculty of men and women dedicated to the type of teaching expected at Christian College rather than depend on "swallows of passage" whose first loyalty was to their doctoral work at the University of Missouri. He made great strides in this direction during his tenure. . . . The growing professionalism of our faculty has been accompanied by an increased unity and comradeship.[62]

Although the master plan in its six phases proved far too ambitious for completion in Freeman's years, a first-class physical plant would come about through renovation and building in future years. In his years at the college, Freeman never reached the top of the mountains he had depicted in his Proust quotation, and he was well acquainted with "uncomfortable days," but he showed the path for others to follow. His early desire to see Christian

College move beyond junior college status, relegated to a low priority in the crush of more immediate needs, failed to materialize but would reemerge as a major consideration in the next administration. His willingness to rethink old assumptions and to insist that the college be relevant to the society it served would soon bring greater changes than even he could have envisioned. Just as St. Clair Moss had responded to new trends in the early days of the rise of junior colleges, Freeman and Hill saw the needs of a later era. The days of the college as single-sex, two-year "Christian College" were numbered, but Freeman's insistence on high standards of excellence, his emphasis on a liberal education, and his expanded use of a dedicated faculty reinforced the traditions set more than a century before.

9

Change and Continuity

W. MERLE HILL: 1965–1973

There is nothing in this world constant but inconstancy.

—Jonathan Swift, *A Critical Essay upon the Faculties of the Mind*

IF KENNETH FREEMAN'S ADMINISTRATION represented a sea change for Christian College, Merle Hill's presidency corresponded to an earthquake, shaking the institution to its very foundation while preserving its roots and heritage. Described by the president of the board as "young, innovative, and aggressive," Hill seemed bigger than life in both his strengths and his weaknesses, resembling St. Clair Moss in the force of his leadership. He undid much of what St. Clair Moss stood for, taking the college back to four-year status, admitting men, and renouncing the name "Christian College," but these changes never abandoned the college's basic concepts of expanding educational horizons and responding to social needs in an environment of personal attention.

Hill, coming to the presidency at the age of thirty-nine, had spent two years as dean of faculty. He had taught for twelve years before becoming an administrator and considered himself student and faculty oriented. Valuing practicality over theory, he urged all constituencies of the college to think in new terms for a new era. More unconventional than ceremonial, he played the trumpet in the faculty combo and jogged at the high school track with faculty members, activities unimaginable in earlier presidencies.[1]

The new president's inauguration held overtones of both continuity and change. Traditional in all its trappings, the celebration featured a lecture by the noted British historian C. Northcote Parkinson, followed the next day, October 19, 1965, by an inaugural luncheon, the inauguration ceremony, and a reception in the Missouri Hall parlors. The college's past was on display in the historic re-creation in St. Clair parlors of a turn-of-the-century drawing room, student room, and president's office, along with a photography exhibit. The line of procession at the lavish inauguration included representatives of 114 colleges and 18 learned societies and organizations. Two new features of the inauguration began their own traditions. A ceremonial mace, carried by the most senior faculty member, Hazel Kennedy, as marshal, began a tradition continued by Sidney Larson at Kennedy's retirement. Also, Hill wore the new Presidential Seal of Office, a medallion, leading to his observation, "I note, by the way, that the Board of Trustees and the Inaugural Steering Committee made certain that there was plenty of chain on this medallion for me to hang myself."

Whereas tradition had its place in the inaugural, Hill's address stressed change. He spoke of "a sense of accomplishment at having finally reached the entrance of St. Clair Hall in 1966. In 1946 . . . when I hitchhiked from Oberlin College to visit a Christian College student, Dotty Rowe, now Dotty Rowe Hill, and arrived about 8:00 A.M., I was thrown off the campus by the janitor of Missouri Hall. In those Dark Ages, young men were not permitted on campus until late afternoon."[2]

The inaugural speaker, Donald A. Eldridge, vice president of the American Association of Junior Colleges, represented nearly one thousand junior colleges. He praised the junior college movement as "the most dramatic educational movement of the past quarter century . . . the most significant development since the free American high school." Although Eldridge lauded Christian College as a "special place" in its small and selective environment, Hill's remarks foretold different priorities: "We shall not be afraid of change and experiment . . . [and] we shall reject the parochial and that which is consistent only with the culture that was. We shall work, instead, for a program that will create an educational mind capable of coping with the polycultured world of today." He had already produced a catalog that, for the first time in more than half a century, left out the words *junior college* on its front page and defined Christian College as a "non-sectarian two-year liberal arts college for women."[3]

The administrative team upon which Hill would rely also represented both continuity and change. Elizabeth Kirkman as dean of women, Howard Kelley as director of admissions, and Jane Canedy Crow as alumnae director continued from the Freeman years. Don Landers, new to the college late in the Freeman administration, would become an invaluable part of the team as business manager. His immediate grasp of the college's financial crisis and his quick bonding with the institution provided him with insights and influence belying his twenty-six years. He met with bankers constantly "to resolve the college's long term and short term debt," later remembering that "good people kept things going." Also new, Charles Mai joined the administration in October 1965 as director of development. Persistent, patient, and knowledgeable, with a background in sales and education, Mai was to lay the groundwork for bequests that would serve the college well in future years.[4] The new administrator who would have the most profound influence throughout Hill's presidency, however, was Jack Batterson, chosen as acting dean of faculty after an unsuccessful search for a dean to replace Hill. Batterson's more cautious nature as a traditional but open-minded educator worked as a counterfoil to Hill's sometimes impatient enthusiasm for change. This balance, temporarily disrupted in the late 1960s, led to fruitful progress for the college in the early 1970s.

The excitement and optimism of the new administration became evident during the faculty fall conference of September 1965. In the first few months of his deanship, Batterson had joined with Hill to draft the college's first *Faculty Handbook.* Wanting faculty involvement as early as possible in the process, Batterson appointed a Faculty Handbook Committee at the start of the fall conference, providing for faculty input before the handbook was submitted to the trustees for approval the next month. The committee became a permanent feature of faculty governance, setting the precedent that faculty would pass upon and commonly originate handbook revisions. Opening with the "Profile and Purpose," the handbook empowered faculty, as the legislative body of the college, "to approve the curriculum, to fix the calendar, to nominate students for degrees, and to dismiss students from the college." Committees created by the handbook reflected a broad scope of faculty action.

In addition to a long-overdue statement of academic structure, the *Faculty Handbook* for the first time guaranteed faculty such traditional academic benefits as tenure, sabbatical leaves, leave to attend professional conferences with college aid, and academic freedom, bringing the college more in line with standard practices. Acceptance by the board of the concept of academic freedom gave faculty the protection of the American Association of University Professors guidelines on freedom of research, freedom of discussion of subject matter in the classroom, and freedom as citizens. The handbook also guaranteed nondiscriminatory hiring practices and a more comprehensive benefits package for medical insurance. With the benefits came responsibility, as the document established a compulsory and thorough system of faculty evaluation based on teaching performance, counseling and advising, professional activities, research, and contributions to the college and the community.[5]

Another product of Batterson's early months, the "Proposed Academic Regulations," went to the same October board meeting for approval. This document set forth formal procedures for such academically related activities as admissions, readmissions, acceptance and evaluation of credits, graduation, grading, scholastic honors, unsatisfactory academic progress, registration, academic programs, classroom policies and instruction, and appeal of polices.

Thus, a few short months of work had produced many of the changes necessary for a more professional academic environment, and faculty morale flourished. In response to an expression of amazement that an *acting* dean of faculty should be so bold, Batterson responded that he took the title to mean that he should "act like a dean." A memorandum from Batterson to Hill described the productive working relationship between president and dean: "Your patience, understanding, and example have aided and sustained me during my apprenticeship, and I truly am grateful. Christian College will flourish under your creative and progressive leadership." Hill's statement at the end of the academic year when he granted Batterson tenure while serving as dean indicated the effectiveness of the first year's teamwork: "The applause at yesterday's faculty meeting manifests the esteem in which you are held by the faculty. Your leadership has enabled me to forget almost entirely about the academic program and concentrate on other needs of the College."[6]

Hill, although constantly prodding the faculty to be more creative and productive, acted as their champion and publicist in his early years. He convinced the board not only to allow full scholarships for faculty daughters but also to provide for full tuition for faculty sons for their first two years at the University of Missouri. At his urging, the board added two elected faculty representatives to its membership. Hill and Batterson worked together to begin a summer school program in 1967, seeing the program not only as an opportunity for students to upgrade skills and earn additional credits, but also as a means by which faculty could supplement their income. Hill, concerned about the low level of faculty salaries, quoted figures to the trustees, comparing Christian College salaries with national averages in a campaign to double faculty salaries within ten years. Granting a raise of 6 percent in 1965, he managed a 7 percent increase in 1966 and 10 percent in 1967. Hill noted that only 25 percent of the Christian College budget went for the educational program, in contrast to a 60 percent average at other colleges, and vowed that whatever else of the college's master plan might not progress on schedule, faculty salary increases would. Insisting that "massive injections must be made immediately if Christian is to retain its strong faculty," Hill recommended that "such increases be made even if deficit financing is required to carry the additional expense."[7]

The president pointed to the quality of the faculty in response to a question about what made Christian College different: "I have concluded that outstanding teaching is our main reason for being. . . . The best thing we have to offer is the faculty. . . . We cannot hope to compete with more affluent schools in buildings and settings . . . but on faculty we can compare with the best."[8]

The faculty of thirty-nine in 1967, evenly split between men and women, was young but experienced, sharing the common denominator of dedication to their profession and college. They averaged thirty-eight years of age, six years at the college, and ten years of teaching experience. With the faculty lounge as a gathering place for faculty discussions, Dan Hoagland described the academic environment:

> Its academic community is a close-knit entity. . . . Either because of a subtle selection process which operates before the teacher comes to Christian or more explicit influences on campus, no one on the faculty is only a specialist. . . . In the faculty lounge, a typical conversation may involve a chemist, a musician, and a specialist in English literature. Under these circumstances, it is difficult to avoid a growing sense of the essential unity of our purpose—that of human knowledge itself.[9]

Christian College had benefited throughout its history from the loyalty and excellence of its faculty, leading many acquainted with that history to wonder what might explain the phenomenon. Sid Larson told why he stayed at the college: "Columbia College provides unique satisfactions. . . . Somehow, in spite of human fallibility there is distilled here a delicate essence of meaning and purpose which permeates all of us. . . . The uniqueness I refer to is the *degree of total involvement* which our faculty assumes as its role." Batterson also identified several characteristics of the faculty that brought real strength to the college: "[T]hey are dedicated to Christian's philosophy that the most meaningful education for young women during the first two years of college is one in the liberal arts. They believe that of all the scholarly pursuits, teaching is the most important accomplishing the stated goals of the College. Finally, they are convinced that effective teaching must not and cannot be confined to the classroom."[10]

The college suffered the loss of three older faculty, Hazel Kennedy in English and Tina Armstrong in Spanish retired in 1974, and Hortense (Petie) Davison, who had led the French House venture since its inception, died of a heart attack in June 1975 while vacationing in the Northwest. Others continued the tradition, including Larson in art, Hoagland in mathematics, and Polly Batterson in government. Another, Penny Carroll, an assistant to the dean of women under Freeman, joined the English faculty in the Hill administration. Eldon Drennan had joined the faculty in philosophy in 1959 and, like Jack Batterson and Bill Brown, would become an administrator under Hill.

Still others joined the faculty to become part of the tradition of excellence. New in music in 1965, pianist David O'Hagan remained active as a performer, also frequently accompanying Elaine Karnes (to become Grev) in voice recitals. O'Hagan served three terms as a faculty trustee, received the Missouri Governor's Award for Excellence in Teaching, and was named a director of the Paul D. Higday Mozart Music Trust, which brought performing artists of international fame to Columbia. He also remained active as an adjudicator of music competitions until his retirement in 2000. Grev, also a competition adjudicator and performing soloist, came to the college in 1966 and combined her teaching with directing campus vocal groups, before transferring to the Evening College administration until her retirement in 1998.[11]

Coming to the history faculty in 1967, Dianne Berry (to become O'Hagan) acted as sponsor of Phi Theta Kappa, serving as regional sponsor and receiving the National Sponsor of the Year Award in 1970, the year in which the National Phi Theta Kappa Congress took place on the Christian College campus. Twice a faculty trustee, she was also the founding sponsor of Alpha Chi, the national honorary for four-year colleges that replaced Phi Theta Kappa. Leaving teaching in 1981 to become director of alumni affairs, she fostered closer communication between the college and its traditional alumni while also integrating the new Extended Studies graduates into the system. Also coming in 1967, Larry Dunham in English served on major committees and as a faculty trustee before his death on June 22, 1976. Shocked by the sudden death of the popular instructor, the trustees dedicated Dunham's budgeted salary to the Dunham Memorial Scholarship Fund.[12]

Another faculty member new in 1972, Joann Scrogin (to become Wayman) became director of the fashion department and implemented the bachelor of science degree in fashion merchandising and the bachelor of fine arts degree in fashion design. She later joined the business department and became its chair, playing a major role in the development of a master's degree program in business administration. Active in faculty governance, she twice served as president of the Faculty Association, organized in 1993, and twice as a faculty trustee.[13]

Christine Cotton joined the faculty in English in 1975, taking an active role within her profession and in faculty governance at the college. A Fulbright scholar, Cotton became the faculty advisor for Alpha Chi and an honorary member. As Alpha Chi regional president, she hosted the society's regional conference on the Columbia College campus. She also served as regional president of Pi Lambda Theta, an honor society for educators, and represented that organization at international conferences. Especially active as a presenter of conference papers on literature, some of which have been published, she has served as a speaker at public forums and on civic boards and committees. On campus, Cotton served as area coordinator for the humanities and worked to strengthen the honors program as it evolved into "Graduation with Distinction." She served as president of the Faculty Senate and later chaired the Faculty Governance Committee, a group responsible for writing a constitution for the Faculty Association, which became the faculty governing body.[14]

Novelle Dunathan joined the faculty in 1974, later becoming director of the teacher education program and chair of the education and psychology department. Active in professional organizations in education, she also received the Missouri Governor's Award for Excellence in Teaching. When Dunathan left teaching to serve for a five-year period as vice president for student life, she initiated the Freshman Experience Program, a course to orient students to college life. Returning to teaching in the 1990s, she led the department's work in creating a graduate program, becoming director of graduate education for the M.A. in teaching.[15]

In science, William Houston began his career at Christian College in biology in 1966. He chaired the Biological Sciences Division of the Missouri Association of Junior Colleges and led the faculty as president of the local chapter of the American Association of University Professors in 1968–1969 when such leadership was crucial to the college's future. Houston left the college in 1981 to pursue a business career.[16]

New members of the art department included Ed Collings in 1969, Tom Watson in 1971, and Ben Cameron in 1974, all adding strength to the rapidly growing program. All contributed to national and international exhibits. Collings, in photography and ceramics, became department chair in 1989, giving steady leadership to the program. For twenty-five years after 1972, he maintained a summer pottery shop of his work at Arrow Rock, a popular tourist village near Columbia. Watson, who considered himself primarily a teacher rather than an artist, introduced and maintained the computer graphics program in the art department while continuing to teach the foundation courses. Cameron initiated "Paper in Particular," an annual juried national exhibit, bringing to the college a national show of works on paper.[17]

Numerous other faculty members during the Hill administration gave long years of dedicated and outstanding service, including Helga Huang, who created the major in sociology, Grace Baker in biology, Vera Coats and Sandra Schubert in fashion, Suellen Wells in dance, and Joanne Macher in physical education.

In another area, improved physical facilities enhanced campus conditions. With basement space in St. Clair Hall freed by the relocation of the dining room to Dulany Hall, the library could leave its cramped quarters on the second floor of Dorsey Hall. In a remarkable show of spirit, faculty members and administrators contributed their services on a September Saturday in 1966, moving virtually the whole library in one day. A chute from a second-floor window to a basement-level window was fed by a well-disciplined brigade passing books to the window, down the chute, and into the new quarters. Turning the former dining quarters into a library required total renovation at a cost of sixty thousand dollars, quadrupling the library space. The "new" library included private study carrels, a listening room, and a seminar room, creating a handsome and functional facility. The old library quarters became a dance studio with mirrored walls, providing an ideal environment for the dance program. With additional space still left in the basement, the art program expanded into what had been the kitchen, doubling the space for that program, which enrolled more than half of the student body in 1966.[18]

More serious expansion came as part of an aggressive building program. A new residence hall, completed in less than a year, opened at the northwest corner of the campus in January 1967. Students doubled up in St. Clair, Missouri, and Hughes Halls until the 108-bed facility could open. The project fulfilled the third step in the master plan of the Freeman administration, a plan destined for major revision in the future. The second major construction, a student health center, resulted from a gift of seventy thousand dollars from Mrs. E. L. Spence (Mittie V. Robnett) of Kennett, Missouri. The first major gift since the Dulany gift in the 1940s, the building was the first ever given entirely by one family. Construction at a site between Hughes Hall and Dulany Hall began in the spring of 1968, with groundbreaking ceremonies on May 9, 1968, followed by dedication on May 20, 1969, and occupancy in September. The dedication of the Robnett-Spence Health Center reflected the strength of family ties at the college. The family of Mittie Robnett Spence had included either graduates or trustees of the college in every generation since 1851, when Mary Robnett had become one of John Augustus Williams's first seven students. More than seventy of Mittie Spence's relatives had either attended Christian College or served on the board, including her daughter and her brother, Dudley A. Robnett, the college physician in the 1930s.[19]

In another type of expansion, Hill began the process of acquiring property in the campus neighborhood. Progress toward this goal came partly through the efforts of a group, "Dual Associates," composed of eight Christian College faculty and staff. The group invested in rental property adjacent to the campus with the intent that the college could later purchase the properties as funds allowed. By October 1968, the college had bought four houses bordering the college and held an option on another property.[20]

As expansion continued, Hill determined that there should be names for all buildings on campus still lacking such identification. The original building, the old Bennett home, had been called at various times Old Main, Practice Hall, and the Conservatory. In 1968, it became Williams Hall in honor of the college's first president and was appropriately restored through tuck-pointing, painting, and refurbishing. The hall had begun to gain attention as the oldest women's college building west of the Mississippi River, having been in continuous use since 1852. Landers then pointed out another building lacking a name—the maintenance building—suggesting that it be named the Wightman Maintenance Building in honor of Maurice Wightman, longtime superintendent of grounds. Also in a well-deserved tribute, the new dormitory, first called simply "North Hall," became Hartley Banks Hall upon Banks's retirement as president of the board in 1971 after twenty-four years of service as a trustee. The next year, the college honored Banks with an honorary doctor of humane letters degree, the first honorary degree given by the college. Finally, the auditorium was dedicated as the Launer Auditorium in 1972, ten years after Launer's retirement as director of the Conservatory.[21]

Through the president's proclivity for change, student life regulations became "consistent with society in general." Hill asked Kirkman to appoint a student committee, which she would chair, to "propose sane dress regulations for Christian College students both on and off campus." Such regulations, according to Hill, "should be based on good grooming, cleanliness, and appropriateness of dress and not on ideas of what was appropriate at Christian College five or ten or fifteen or fifty years ago." As the result, students were no longer required to "dress" for dinner. With acceptance of regular classroom dress for dinner, student attendance at the evening meal rose from 42 percent in 1968 to 68 percent in 1969.[22]

In a more controversial policy, Hill's alleged "permissiveness" in dormitory privileges raised some parental eyebrows but brought the college more in line with practices of the 1960s. In a letter to parents on March 27, 1967, Hill proclaimed the end of the old rule that a "Christian College student may not enter the living quarters of a man without proper permission and chaperonage." Hill informed parents of a new rule: "A Christian College student may not enter the living quarters of a man without parental permission." The letter enclosed a permission form for parental signatures. The ultimate concession, granting key privileges to second-year students, came as a victory for the Student Senate and Campus Council. Administrators placed prudent limitations on the policy, requiring the permission of parents or guardians and attendance at an orientation program, while denying the privilege to any student on probation. Convinced that the old rules were punitive rather than educational, Hill preferred letting students learn by their own mistakes, emphasizing "mature responsibility and self-discipline."[23]

Other areas felt the impact of Hill's innovations. He introduced more regular prospective student weekends and changed the college's payment policy. He found that of seventeen junior colleges for women, Christian was the only one requiring full payment of tuition and all fees by September 1, and that almost all of the others had refund policies. Henceforth, Christian College policy would require a deposit of three hundred dollars when a student was admitted, with 60 percent payable by September 1 and 40 percent by January 10.

Student government took on a more complex structure. A Student Senate acted as the legislative body, while the Campus Council, consisting of Hill, Batterson, and Kirkman, approved acts and heard appeals from the Student Conduct Committee. Each dormitory chose a hall council and a hall judicial, and an Interdormitory Council was composed of all hall presidents.[24]

Despite Hill's eagerness to make the college a place "where the action is," the student body remained relatively sheltered from the disruptions of the 1960s and somewhat disinclined to embrace controversial issues. Deploring that "we have become a haven for young women of the more affluent class," Hill proposed that the board offer one-half fee remission for 25 or more students of lower socioeconomic backgrounds in exchange for work performed on campus, hoping that a more diverse student body would become more politically and socially aware. Faculty members did their part by scheduling panel and group discussions and by sending 150 student volunteers into weekly service at local agencies.[25]

One student, Deborah Bryant, personified the traditional ideal of Christian College. A top student, highly respected by faculty and students alike, Bryant used her modeling experience to become Miss Kansas and then Miss America, crowned September 11, 1965, just months after her graduation from Christian College. She had held a Trustees Scholarship and served as the president of Phi Theta Kappa. Her natural beauty and genuine personality led one observer to remark, "I didn't know they were still making girls like her, and if they spoil her, I will know there is no defense against the forces that have made girls like her so rare." Bryant's triumphant return to the college on Friday, March 25, 1966, brought a whirlwind of activity. Mayor John Longwell proclaimed "Miss America Day in Columbia," presenting Bryant with the key to the city. Events included a press conference, a president's luncheon for community leaders, an alumnae tea, a student assembly, and a "Miss America Day" banquet. The college honored Bryant with the Distinguished Alumnae Award for Special Achievement for "her achievement in being selected as Miss America of 1966, for her personification of the highest ideals and purposes of Christian College and for her embodiment of the desirable attributes and potentialities of the young American woman." In return, Bryant presented the college with an endowed award, the Phi Theta Kappa Scholarship, for incumbent club presidents and club vice presidents. The national president of Phi Theta Kappa, Rick Wilson of Lawton, Oklahoma, attended the banquet, giving Bryant an engraved president's pin.[26]

With the coming of popular changes, student numbers soared. Enrollments climbed from 296 in 1964 to 467 in 1965, 559 in 1966, and 566 in 1967. According to Batterson, "across the country parents in increasing numbers are beginning to see the educational value of the type of education we can provide here . . . looking for the best type of learning environment where teaching is primary, classes small, and the approach individual." However, part of the increased enrollment resulted from more liberal admissions policies adopted in 1961 and again in 1964 after Kelley joined the admissions effort as well as from substantially greater expenditures for the admissions program. Certainly, the admission of some students of lesser ability called for safeguards. Borderline students could be admitted only if they attended a summer school program and successfully completed at least five hours of credit. Also, those students with weaker high school records were admitted as "limited load" students, permitted to take only 12.5 hours of credit. Only those who proved themselves on this basis could become regular full-time students. Any student with a grade point average below 1.50 was placed on academic probation and had to achieve a 2.00 (a C average) to avoid becoming ineligible to return.[27]

Such compromises on student quality accompanied a national pattern of declining enrollments. Of thirty-four private women's colleges represented at a Philadelphia meeting in 1968, only seven reported an enrollment increase that year. Lindenwood College in St. Charles, Missouri, was down more than 100 students from the previous year, whereas Park College in Parkville, Missouri, went down 160 resident students. Westminster College in Fulton, Missouri, closed a 60-bed residence hall the following year. At Christian College, tuition increases of 1960–1961 had a devastating impact on enrollments, but the more generous admissions standards would later lead to higher student numbers. Student quality was suffering by 1968, but the record high enrollments brought budget surpluses for three years straight.[28]

Clearly, higher enrollment brought progress in debt retirement. When Freeman left in 1965, the college was borrowing against the next year's tuition, with a $350,000 loan necessary for operating expenses for the 1965–1966 academic year. By the summer of 1966, however, there was a $65,000 operating surplus, and the total indebtedness was reduced to $248,000 in 1966 and to $150,000 by September 1967. With development funds increasing from $71,584 in 1965 to $108,351 in 1967, no short-term borrowing was necessary by the summer of 1968, and the college was able to start the new academic year with no notes payable.[29]

Despite the encouraging environment continuing into 1968, Hill became more and more restive, worrying that the college was out of step with modern trends. Having spent "tremendous sums" in admissions work while lowering admissions standards, Hill wrote to the board: "We must face the fact that an even smaller proportion [of prospective students] chooses a two-year college for women; we must face the fact that many colleges, segregated by sex, are becoming co-educational or are establishing coordinate institutions; and we must face the fact that many two-year colleges are becoming four-year colleges." Hill later added: "After three and one-half years of stubborn refusal to even listen to talk about a name change, I am now convinced that the College name is the biggest drawback to our program. In our recent admissions tour, I found myself starting each presentation with an apology for our name." The president proposed that the college try to interest an individual in a naming gift, but that if such a move were unsuccessful, the board should move within two years to change the name anyway. Finally, on

June 4, 1968, the trustees voted unanimously that a donor be sought but that even if none came forth, the name would be changed.[30]

Hill, plagued by back surgery in May 1968, became increasingly critical of conditions impeding the ability to "sell" the college, including the role of the faculty. At this point, Kelley put forth his plan for the admissions effort. In a memorandum to the president, Kelley described "the use of faculty, alumnae, students, etc., in our admissions program." The Kelley proposal stood out in the degree of control he would exercise over all constituencies, "that we [must] have an adequately structured and directed program—one that is firmly in my control and not in the control of someone who has little or no identification with the admissions program." Kelley described the role of the trustees as he viewed it: "What we need here mostly is the prestige of their office. . . . And *whatever* they do, it must be directed by the *Dean of Admissions.* These people cannot be permitted to grab the ball and run with it (the same principle applies to every group discussed)." Trustees, Kelley believed, could be useful in providing their homes for entertainment of groups and signing letters to key people—letters written in the admissions office—"as long as control resides in the admissions office. (I keep referring to this because I feel it fundamental to any acceptable use of persons other than the admissions staff.)" Kelley stated that "if properly trained they can help some with interviews, high school visits, etc."[31]

Faculty, according to Kelley, could develop a series of programs for various publics and sign letters describing their areas of specialty, "produced in my office over the signature of the faculty members involved." Faculty would also be expected to use vacations, trips, and holidays to call students or "arrange some type of gathering." Kelley further proposed arranging "cultural exchanges with selected high schools" and informing high schools that "our faculty are available for career and college day (or night) programs in the schools." Similarly, ambitious programs were included for alumnae "*if they were adequately trained.* This I insist on: *Adequate training, on campus* of any alum so involved."

After Hill forwarded Kelley's memorandum to Batterson for comment, the reply from Batterson showed evidence of growing strains between the faculty and the admissions staff. Agreeing "wholeheartedly with Kelley's statement that such a program must be 'adequately structured and directed,'" Batterson disagreed "with his contention that the suggested faculty programs should be under the control of the director of admissions." Batterson continued: "This is not only contradictory to the administrative organization of the college, but I would argue also that the present organization of the admissions office, coupled with the mood of the faculty toward that office, would preclude any close cooperation between the two. In this regard, I fear that the faculty would rebel at any attempt at control by the admissions office." Batterson responded positively to the idea of developing a series of programs using faculty talent and interests for school assemblies, church groups, and service clubs. He stated that much along those lines was already being done, but that "again . . . such a program cannot be the servant of the admissions program, nor should it be under the control or direction of the admissions office." He concluded:

> Remember, our purpose is to retain not only students but faculty members. . . . [T]o place the faculty at the service of the admissions office or to place it in any way under the control of the admissions office . . . seems unwise at the very time the faculty is facing greater academic expectations and demands. . . . It is up to the president of the college whether the work of the trustees "must be *directed by the Dean of Admissions*," but the dean of faculty must insist that the faculty remain "firmly in my control and not in the control of someone who has little or no identification with the" academic program.[32]

Absent from the campus for six weeks during the summer of 1968 to lead a student group on a European tour, Batterson returned to find an escalation of Hill's criticisms of the faculty. He found also increasing pressure that the curriculum and teaching methods should "sell" the college. Hill's remarks to the faculty at the fall conference suggested such a course: "Automobile dealers do not sell their cars because of a strong chassis but because of imaginative styling: creative, sound engineering; and, of utmost importance, good financial potential. . . . There is a great need for imaginative teaching, soundly engineered in-depth courses with obvious relevance to today's problems, and an educational program that has financial potential." Exhorting the faculty to tailor their teaching to "our particular clientele," Hill called for a teaching style to accommodate those students of lower ability already being recruited by the admissions staff:

> We must forget transfer courses. . . . We are perhaps too frightened of and intimidated by those big-college registrars who count credits and semester hours. Let them continue to waste their time counting credits and semester hours, but let us . . . forget about the pages covered. . . . When you start any job, enroll in any course, or teach any subject, a certain amount of background knowledge is expected. If you don't have it, it is up to you to get it. So be it! If our students have not mastered certain concepts before they leave us, they must make their acquaintance elsewhere.[33]

Faculty, skeptical of adapting the academic program to admissions practices, feared that the approach urged by the president would not only sell student needs short but also amount to "selling out" the academic standards of the college. Praised by the president just months earlier as "the best thing we have to offer," faculty members, stunned and apprehensive, resisted such admonitions as interference in academic matters.

Throughout the fall, as administrative meetings continued to focus on adopting programs and teaching practices on the basis of ongoing admissions demands, Batterson began to see serious trouble ahead in the relationship between the faculty and the president. Particularly alarmed about a meeting that was an outgrowth of "an earlier meeting held with the admissions people," Batterson urged the president to receive faculty input on "programs and practices outside the education area. . . . There have been frequent and long discussions between you and admissions people regarding all aspects of our program. I have been negligent, however, in not bringing faculty comments, ideas, and criticisms to you regarding important matters outside the educational realm." Batterson continued:

> Since your discussions with the admissions people have stimulated and influenced your thinking on the educational program, the living program, the social program, etc., perhaps similar discussions with instructors would shed new light on the admissions program and its practices. My purpose is to explore in depth all reasons why the college is not selling before launching a major change in what everybody seems to recognize as a sound educational program. . . . Let us instead spend this coming year in a similar in-depth analysis and study of our sales department—the admissions office.[34]

What followed was a family quarrel of the first order—a battle for the very soul of the college. Overall, the faculty could agree with the president on the major changes under consideration: a name change, a return to the original four-year status, and the introduction of coeducation. In fact, a number of the faculty enthusiastically welcomed such changes. The real points of disagreement between many faculty members and the president centered on faculty control of the academic program and teaching methods and on the practices of the admissions effort.[35]

Disagreement intensified in December when Hill proposed "A Different College." The document began on a positive note, arguing effectively for coeducation and praising the faculty as "getting stronger every year," reiterating that it "compares favorably with the best." Hill faulted the faculty, however, for their refusal to adjust adequately to the type of students being admitted along with the traditionally strong students:

> Teaching methods must change. The lecture method will almost disappear, and increased emphasis will be put on supervised study for the less-than-average students and on independent study for the average or better students. . . . If a science course is necessary for today's young woman, and I believe it is, then it must be a different science course for the less-than-average student. . . . We pioneered in 1851 but recently have drawn our educational wagons around ourselves in a circle.[36]

Deeply troubled by the president's academic vision of the future of the college and by his repeated criticisms, faculty members reacted with a strongly worded response composed by members of the college's chapter of the American Association of University Professors:

> At present our program does offer extra assistance to slower students in the form of limited loads, basic courses, help sessions, how-to-study programs, and individual conferences. However, if we accommodate our standards to the abilities of the poorest students, we will immediately bring about such a debasement of our ideal of academic excellence that our program will "sell" to no one—certainly not to the best students or faculty. For Christian College to adopt programs that would offer "post high school" courses would put the college in direct competition with community colleges. Such competition would price Christian College entirely out of the market. . . . Other colleges have attempted to make this change, sometimes with disastrous results. We do not want to be known as Parson's Little Sister, nor do we want to suffer that school's fate![37]

Denying faculty inflexibility and pointing to the academic program's "amenability to change and its capacity for growth," the statement continued: "Furthermore, our faculty is relatively young, and most have come rather recently from other institutions where they received modern training or experience using modern methods. It is not as though our program were debilitated by age or crusted over with conventions." Furthermore, a perceived threat to academic freedom had become an issue:

> We were given every assurance that the basic principles of academic freedom were upheld by the administration. We are alarmed by the present threat to these principles. We know of no reputable institution where the acknowledgedly competent faculty members are not given full freedom to choose and execute their methods of teaching and standards of evaluation as they see fit, subject to the guidelines of a faculty handbook. While we cannot and should not agree on methods, we are in perfect accord on one point: no one should have the prerogative to determine what methods must be used in any class other than his own.

Taking the offensive, the faculty criticized the admissions staff for "their constant anxiety to forsake our program in favor of nostrums." Battle lines were drawn: "It is the consensus of the chapter that at least part of the problem lies with admissions practices. Through our contact and cooperation with the admissions office, we have gained and confirmed the impression that the college's representatives lack sincere faith in its avowed purposes and program and also lack accurate information about them."

In his "Different College" presentation, Hill had advocated giving "outside consultants" an opportunity to study the Christian College program and make recommendations. Accordingly, he hired Arden K. Smith of Davis-MacConnel-Ralston, Inc., in Palo Alto, California, as a consultant. Smith visited the campus on January 13–17, 1969, producing a report for the Board of Trustees. He shared his findings at a faculty meeting before leaving campus, basing his dire conclusions on national trends that "may prove too overwhelming to stand against." Smith discounted the role of faculty dedication, commenting that "sincere and dedicated faculties exist in literally hundreds of colleges." His answer was to "change practically every aspect of the College," especially with the "package deal" of four-year, coeducation, and name-change reforms. Taking aim at the trustees, he charged that they were "ultimately responsible for the lack of necessary activity during a crucial period and must bear the burden of making a life-or-death decision concerning Christian College." They must provide funding "far in excess of the amounts which the Trustees have previously given."[38]

Much of Smith's report reiterated Hill's previous statements, but, striking out on his own, his findings reflected less understanding of education in the Midwest than in California. He pointed to California as an example of the dwindling role of private education, with 80 percent of college freshmen and sophomores already in public institutions and 20 percent in private schools. His figures did reflect accurately the California scene, with its vast expenditures on a statewide network of tax-supported public junior colleges. However, his conclusion that "the very states in the Midwest from which Christian College draws the majority of its students are engaged in a significant expansion in the areas of public junior colleges" implied a more serious threat than the faculty were willing to accept. Indeed, support for private higher education continued unabated in Missouri. (In 1998, 42 percent of Missouri undergraduate students in higher education were in public institutions, and 58 percent were in private institutions, figures relatively unchanged since the 1960s.) The faculty also doubted Smith's understanding of private education in Columbia when he concluded, "Stephens [College] is unalterably embarked on the road to coeducation." Smith, who had been introduced both in person and in correspondence as "Dr. Smith," was a graduate student working for the California firm while he completed his degree.

Hill's letter of transmittal in sending the report to the board recognized negative faculty response to Smith's findings: "Because Dr. Smith is younger than many faculty members (he is only thirty-three), some of them have refused to believe many of the things they heard from him." Actually, of the forty-seven faculty members, thirty-three were in their thirties or younger, and twenty had been hired within the last five years.[39]

Although Smith's report remained highly controversial, it did emphasize a need for the college to overcome the rift between the president and the admissions personnel on one hand and the faculty and other administrators on the other. Hill's letter to Batterson of February 1, 1969, offering the next year's contract, suggested possible regret for some of his recent attitudes:

> Although it is Saturday and I am typing contract-accompanying letters for all administrator contracts, I especially want to type this one. There is no position at the college now that is more important than that of the dean, the leader of the academic program and the supervisor of so many other aspects of the total living and learning environment; and I want you to realize how eager I am to have you continue in this leadership role. I have never been one to offer praise, even when it is very much deserved, and I realize how difficult it is to work with someone as brusque as I tend to be much of the time. I do not expect anyone to agree with my ideas all of the time and am very aware that I need someone to act as a brake to my sometimes over-enthusiastic plans for a program in which I see tremendous merit. I am confident that our differences of opinion about how best to proceed with our educational program can be minimized and that both of us are interested in the same ultimate goal.[40]

Batterson replied: "I appreciate your confidence, past and present. Well aware of the adverse tasks ahead, I am interested in continuing to serve Christian College as my ability and conscience will permit and in the capacity you believe to be most helpful to the future of the College. Thanks for many things."[41]

Despite good prospects for Hill and Batterson to return to an effective working relationship, the president remained painfully aware of his lack of support among much of the faculty. On February 20, 1969, to the shock and dismay of many, he submitted his resignation to the board:

> At a meeting this morning with Mr. Banks, I submitted my resignation as president of Christian College, effective June 30, 1969. There has been a growing gap between what I feel education should be and what many Christian College faculty members and administrators believe it should be, and I now find myself in a position where the leader has too few followers to be effective. I am convinced a new leader may be able to bridge the gap I cannot.[42]

At Hill's resignation, administrators other than Hill and Kelley (who had resigned when the president did), assisted by ideas from six faculty members, produced "A Case for Survival," a collaborative work intended to present to the board a more balanced view than that of the Smith report. It argued against the ideas set forth in "A Different College," hoping to convince the board that changes could be made for survival without jeopardizing the college's academic reputation and liberal arts program. The document, divided into sections on development, admissions, finance, public relations, the academic program, and the social and living program, attempted to present within each section evidence of strength, potential for progress, and recommendations for change.[43]

One idea put forth in the "Case for Survival" was, in the light of the intended name change, to place advertisements in the *Wall Street Journal, Forbes,* and *Fortune* offering to rename the college in return for a $5 million gift. Some found it embarrassing, seeming to put the college up for public sale, but the concept was far from new and would have been viewed more kindly if the ads had borne fruit. The report also advocated a full-time director of admissions, in contrast to Kelley's role that had at times combined those duties with his work as assistant to the president, representative to the Christian Church, and supervisor for student service projects and of the office of public information. The study again reflected distrust of the role of the admissions staff, noting the drop in high school visits from 1,950 in 1966 to 1,532 in 1968, while applications dropped from 528 in 1966 to 433 in 1968. The report expressed support for the idea of coeducation, despite a student vote of 307 to 72 against such a change. In defense of the academic program, it pointed to such efforts as team teaching, independent-study options, interdisciplinary approaches, honors classes, collegewide and departmental honors programs, and how-to-study sessions, as well as opportunities for slower students as already mentioned in the AAUP document. Possible future approaches and techniques, along with potential economies in the academic program, were suggested. Indeed, the board minutes of the May meeting reflected such cutbacks as the release of five full-time faculty members, maintenance workers, and some maids, while two full-time faculty members went to three-quarters time.[44]

With Hill's resignation due to take effect at the end of June, Banks appointed a joint trustee-faculty presidential selection committee. The group prepared criteria for the position and by early May had received the names of thirty applicants or recommended candidates. Although the committee had chosen three finalists to invite for interviews, it first asked Hill to reconsider his resignation. On June 4, 1969, the board reappointed Hill, whose resignation "had never been accepted by the board" and who still enjoyed more support from trustees than from faculty and administrators. At the same time, a press release announced that Hill would be spending two months of the summer in Germany working on translations (he also spent a portion of each day answering college correspondence and racewalking mountain trails). Another announcement named Bill Brown, director of the Conservatory of Music, as director of admissions to replace Kelley, who had returned to Chapman College in California as director of admissions.[45]

The board meeting of May 21, 1969, may have been one of the most significant since the founding of the college. At that time, the trustees, who had already agreed to a name change a year earlier, voted unanimously to accept a limited number of male students in 1970–1971 and to make initial moves in the direction of a four-year program.[46]

Batterson's comments represented the general sense of the faculty in welcoming the board's actions, calling the changes educationally sound and financially beneficial: "There seems to be almost universal agreement also among the immediate members of the College family on the need to change the College's name in order to convey a more accurate image of the College."[47]

Meanwhile, in the midst of internal controversy, and with a president who had resigned but had not yet left office, the college faced a reaccreditation visitation set for April 28–29, 1969, by a team representing the North Central Association of Colleges and Secondary Schools. At the end of the visit, the review team presented its report: "In spite of these problems, Christian College is providing for its students the kind of education it professes to give and doing a good job of it. The faculty is relatively strong and, to a man, dedicated to the College and the students. The students are wide awake though by no means radically active, and morale is good."[48]

The report also complimented the well-managed business office, the new buildings, and the promising increases in development. However, the lack of an endowment still represented the most serious concern, presenting a severe financial problem despite the greatly reduced debt. The report faulted the high cost of the admissions program and the lack of previous training of the new director of admissions, recognizing that the pressure on admissions would "certainly add to the educational dilemma which the faculty and more serious students find difficult to accept." In the area of academic affairs, the report noted a problem already recognized by the dean: "The Dean of the College carries so wide a range of responsibilities and is so much involved with . . . all aspects of administration that he has not been able to provide the academic leadership the faculty must have if Christian is to find its distinctive difference."

The report was to be reviewed and voted upon in Chicago by the North Central Association's Commission on Colleges and Universities on July 22, 1969. With Hill on leave in Germany for the summer, it fell to Mai and Batterson to represent the college. Mai, director of development and acting president, stated the college's case, and Batterson conveyed the final vote to Hill:

> The Executive Committee voted to continue the College's full accreditation as an A. A. degree-granting institution. However, we are being placed on Private Probation. This means that the College will not be listed as being on probation in any of the association's listings, announcements, or informal materials. It is a private and confidential matter between the institution and the commission. It means also that the college will be re-visited in about three years . . . [and]

> the knowledge that we have three years to meet certain expectations should provide the proper motivation to work together to remedy our short comings and weaknesses. I understand that it is not too unusual for the North Central to re-visit after one, two, or three years; and the fact that this is happening to us can spur all faculty and staff to new efforts.[49]

In explaining the commission's decision, Batterson stated that "Joe Semrow [executive secretary of the North Central Association] . . . informed me in person that the major area of concern was the College's precarious financial status and its need for a firmer financial base." Hill later agreed, emphasizing that the reason for the decision to revisit the college was financial, not academic.[50]

With historic decision making and the North Central visitation behind it, the college entered into one of its most constructive and fruitful eras, carrying out the mandate of the board, moving quickly to implement a name change. A faculty committee, an alumnae committee, and a trustee committee all worked first separately and then together. Names under consideration included such past leaders as Williams, Rogers, and St. Clair along with Charter College, Midwest College, Smithton College (the original name for the town of Columbia), and College of Columbia. Absent from the early lists, the name Columbia College proved the choice of the board and was adopted on October 25, 1969, effective in July 1970, on the motion of Darrell Eichhoff, a dynamic new trustee from New York.[51]

The name Columbia College, intended to reflect the close ties between the college and the community, allowed the college to retain the "CC" initials. Less popular than some other choices, the name lacked the negative features present in those choices. It proved a comfortable fit in later years, especially when the community tie became even closer with the development of the "Evening College," leading to the sobriquet of "Columbia's College."

Amid the rush of activities in implementing the board decisions, a loss to the college came in October 1969 when Landers left his position as business manager. Landers had made himself an integral part of the college from his earliest days in office. Leaving to establish his own accounting firm, he remained a champion of the college and returned as a trustee in 1995.[52]

Fastest of the three major changes to implement, acceptance of male students, began in just months. Male students were not entirely new to the college. The first male student, James Shannon, son of the founder of the college, had entered in 1851, and a number of sons of leading families had attended the small-boys class. The first and only male resident student to come in the fall of 1969, Kirk Williams, occupied the former Town Girls' Room. He shared "pioneering" honors with 4 area residents attending as day students. With 6 additional male students enrolled for the second semester, "coeducation at the College, if not terribly obvious, was indeed a reality."

As the male population increased, men were housed in Banks Hall and on the second floor of St. Clair Hall, which actually became a coed dormitory with women housed on the third floor. The presence of male students grew at a gratifying rate, numbering 54 in the fall of 1970, 198 in 1971, 254 in 1972, and 380 in 1973 with a total enrollment of 987.[53]

Appropriate title changes reflected new realities. Kirkman, formerly dean of women, became dean of students. Batterson's requested redistribution of responsibilities allowed him to concentrate solely on academic affairs, and his title reverted from dean of the college back to dean of faculty. Mai, in a move to enhance his development role, became vice president for development. Emil (Bud) Menzel followed Don Landers as business manager.

The change most difficult to implement—and for many the most exciting—was the development of the four-year degree programs. Faculty members, singly and by committee, along with administrative staff members, spent many hours studying programs at institutions similar to their vision of the future Columbia College, concentrating on student interests and already-present curricular strengths of the college. Deciding early to offer at first only those programs feasible in limited curricular areas, the college avoided the pitfall of spreading resources too thin.[54]

Clearly, upper-level courses could not be offered immediately. Possible coordination with Stephens College had already been discussed with President Seymour Smith the previous March when Christian College was considering its options before the May 1969 board decisions. Stephens College, moving toward a four-year program since the mid-1960s, was just far enough ahead of Christian College to be of help. By the fall of 1969, the Christian-Stephens Coordinate Program produced the opportunity for sixty-eight Christian College students to enroll in sixteen courses at Stephens and for sixty-one to take eighteen courses the second semester. More than half of those third-year students were also enrolled in courses at Christian College, where twelve new courses were added by the second semester. In a very limited and brief coordination with Kemper Military Academy in Boonville, Kemper students enrolled in art courses at Christian College while Christian students took courses in personal finance and business at Kemper. By the fall of 1971, no Columbia College students were enrolled at Stephens, and more and more students were spending their third year on the home campus.[55]

Although the coordination with Stephens College ended relatively soon, the more significant coordination with the University of Missouri reinforced traditional ties between the two institutions. Both Stephens College and the University of Missouri agreed to accept seniors who had completed three years at Columbia College, and the popularity of spending the senior year at the university greatly enhanced recruitment for Columbia College. The advantages of "College Town U.S.A." provided attractive opportunities.[56] In another advantageous agreement, the university granted Columbia College students access to the university library, just a few blocks away from the Columbia College campus, an arrangement still in effect.

In one way, the cooperative ventures led both Stephens College and the University of Missouri to follow the lead of Columbia College. As early as 1968, Batterson had introduced an innovative calendar that began the semester in late August, completing it before the Christmas break rather than at the end of January. The college returned to the traditional calendar in 1969 for purposes of coordination, but, in 1970–1971, Stephens agreed to adopt the early calendar. University officials, appalled at the idea in 1968, adopted a similar calendar in 1971–1972, making the three Columbia institutions among the earliest in the Midwest to make such a move.[57]

Freed from all but academic responsibilities, Batterson focused on creating a four-year curriculum by building on identified areas of strength and responding to current academic practices. Academic activity proceeded at a feverish pitch with faculty and student enthusiasm high. Some 40 new courses introduced in the 1970 catalog combined special training with studies in the liberal arts. The 1972 catalog included nearly 150 more courses. A new executive secretary program required two years and two summers to complete, granting an associate of arts degree and a certificate. A travel administration program began with 37 students in 1971 and grew to 105 in 1972. In 1971 alone, 63 new courses represented "probably more than the combined total of new courses added at the college in the past twenty years." New programs in fashion design, industrial administration, child study, banking and finance, computer programming, and commercial art proved popular as well. Faculty provided internships in many areas, including such traditional programs as social work and government, and many of the new courses resulted from the social activism and new interests of the 1960s. These courses included black culture, the role of the individual in politics, the community in social action, the future and social change, man in ecological crisis, the contemporary novel and films, South American culture, and Asian history. Popular in the community, a dinner-theater program began in the summer of 1971 with a company of thirty-three, including Columbia College students along with University of Missouri graduate students. A self-sustaining program, it required students to pay for summer school credit, and ticket sales were brisk.[58]

With curricular expansion came a feasibility study for the initiation of an accredited baccalaureate degree. Trustee Charles Koelling of the University of Missouri Department of Education chaired a committee of trustees, administrators, and faculty, and, by November 1971, the college was ready to request an evaluation visitation. Also with the benefit of Koelling's guidance, the college entered into an agreement with the university to help the college plan and develop a teacher education program. The program, approved for teacher certification by the State Department of Education, granted a two-year certificate even before the college's accreditation of the baccalaureate program. After accreditation, the two-year certificate was converted to a life certificate upon the completion of eight hours of graduate work in education.[59]

A more appropriate academic structure took shape by the end of 1972 with the creation of five divisions:

> Division of the Arts—art, dance, interior design, music, theater.
> Division of Communication—English, foreign language, journalism, speech.
> Division of Science and Mathematics—biology, chemistry, mathematics, geology, computer programming.
> Division of Behavioral Sciences and Social Studies—psychology, sociology, social work, history, government, education, philosophy.
> Division of Community and Vocational Education—child care, fashion, physical education, business education, travel education.[60]

The Academic Policy Committee, the vehicle through which the structure and its programs were implemented, ensured a strong role for the faculty, meeting weekly to handle the accelerated pace of change. Other faculty committees evolved, including the Honors Committee, the Library and Audio-Visual Committee, the Artist Series Committee, the Board of Student Publications Committee, the Tenure Council, the Social Committee, and the President's Advisory Committee. Further faculty governance also took place through regular faculty meetings, the Faculty Senate, and the AAUP chapter.[61]

In another major effort, the dean of faculty, division chairs, and faculty created a new "Statement of Institutional Purpose" to bring the college's mission in line with the many changes:

> Columbia College in the 1970s sees itself as a rapidly changing institution in a rapidly changing world. It is very much aware of its strong heritage as a liberal arts college, but it is especially aware of the need on the part of its ever-growing student body for educational programs which prepare not only for concerned and knowledgeable citizenship but also for productive participation in the world of work. As it moves toward full baccalaureate degree status, it will maintain the acknowledged strength of its two-year liberal arts program and at the same time introduce carefully-selected curricula of an occupational and professional nature. The College would hope to attain a size which would assure its students academic diversity and institutional stability yet to remain small enough to preserve the personal atmosphere which has been an essential part of its nature for more than a century.[62]

Changes in academic policy addressed the needs of each student on an individual basis, giving each advisor complete authority over the advisee's schedule. New general education requirements replaced the more structured plan of 1964–1965, requiring only three hours of English composition for an associate in arts degree, along with at least sixty-two hours of credit and a minimum grade point average of 2.00. The bachelor of arts degree required at least 120 credit hours with a minimum grade point average of 2.00, six hours of English composition, forty hours of upper-level course work, and completion of the requirements in the area of concentration (forty-five credit hours for art, seventy-two for fine arts, forty-five for history/government, twenty-four for psychology, and fifty-six for social work). Another option—one especially reflecting new national trends—was a bachelor of arts degree in individual studies. A completely unstructured program for nontraditional students, its only requirements were 120 credit hours and a minimum grade point average of 2.00.[63]

Other academic changes also reflected the trends of the 1960s and 1970s. Innovations included allowing credit by examination, ability to register for one course a semester on a pass/fail basis, expansion of independent study opportunities, and a drop policy. Safeguards were built into the new policies to protect academic standards. For example, the "drop policy" allowed a student to drop a course without penalty anytime during the semester or up to thirty days after the end of the semester, but the proper form had to be signed by the course instructor. The form stated that the student "must show evidence of a sustained effort in the class before the instructor will sign the petition." The policy gave the instructor the "prerogative of dropping from the class roll any student who has been reported as being excessively absent and/or has shown a lack of sustained effort. Instructor-initiated drops are recorded as F's on the student's permanent record." Independent study contracts, subject to review by the Academic Policy Committee, required a detailed learning contract and the completion of at least twelve hours of previous credit. In a strict attendance policy, students were "expected to attend all classes," which replaced an earlier policy automatically allowing a specified number of class absences. A strict suspension policy also accompanied the changes, all of which granted new options and more freedom to students while continuing to demand high standards of performance.[64]

The November 1972 self-study for the upcoming North Central visitation testified to the "abilities, ideas, and flexibility of the faculty and academic staff" and the "environment of progressive cooperation," resulting in "substantial, and sometimes dramatic, progress in the academic program since the last review by the North Central Association."[65]

The development of baccalaureate degree programs also generated a study of faculty status, leading to the adoption of a system of faculty rank. Problematically, such a system could discriminate against the so-called junior college faculty, many of whom were outstanding teachers with many years of experience but lacked terminal degrees. A plan ultimately formulated to fit the needs of a college in transition provided that candidates for the senior ranks of associate professor and professor must have tenure and possess the doctorate or the highest degree normally required for their teaching fields in a four-year institution *or* have "comparable qualifications." Those faculty with outstanding qualifications, although lacking the doctorate, could thus be considered for the upper ranks, but evaluation of "comparable qualifications" was stringent. The plan, adopted by the board in November 1977, led to the assignment of initial rank in the spring of 1974.[66]

Student and faculty activities and accomplishments in the early 1970s provided a stimulating environment. Service opportunities for students placed in local social work programs took the name of "Operation People," and political interest increased with the greater activity of the College Republicans and Young Democrats. Internships could be more challenging with upper-level course work as preparation, and extracurricular credit rewarded participants. The summers of 1971 and 1972 saw a forty-five-day "French Civilization" tour, the beginning of dinner theater, a bicycling tour of Europe, a "Spanish Civilization" tour, a comparative fashion tour of Europe, and a "Campus on Wheels," utilizing twenty-six-foot mobile homes in an eight-thousand-mile trip through the West. As proof that real change had come to the college, Rusty Ford became the first male president of the freshman class in 1971 and the first male student government president the next year. Even dormitory intervisitation between men's and women's dormitories became a reality. The student editor of the *Microphone* took appropriate notice of events: "Slowly, almost every antiquated restriction has fallen . . . and Columbia . . . has a smile. . . . Changes still must come. Columbia is just one small private institution among many that are dying every month because they are stagnating—they resist change and oppose progress. . . . The difference is that this is one little college that plans to stay alive THROUGH change and not in spite of it."[67]

Adding to the excitement of the period, Larry Young, an art student on an athletic scholarship and a future sculptor of international reputation, made headlines as a racewalker. In addition to winning gold medals in the Pan American Games in Canada in 1967 and in Cali, Colombia, in 1971, Young won bronze medals at the 1968 Olympics in Mexico City and the 1972 Olympics in Munich. Hill, who had personally granted Young the scholarship, made it possible for him to create a foundry on campus with the help of the art faculty. After his graduation from Columbia College in 1976, Young received grants to study in Italy, acquiring the training that led to his highly successful career in casting large-scale bronzes. He later established his own foundry near Columbia, and his works have appeared in collections throughout the United States as well as abroad.[68]

Activities on campus continued at a rapid pace in 1973. The college continued to develop the Fine Arts Center in nearby Arrow Rock at the Jane Froman Center, while the Double Sextette embarked on a USO tour of Labrador, Newfoundland, Iceland, and Greenland. The dance group, formerly known as the "Ivy Girls," became an integrated "Forward Motion" jazz dance group under Suellen Wells. The college gained a cheerleading squad, a pep band, and a mascot—the Centaur—as a sports program took shape. Eldon Drennan, who had taught philosophy since 1959, became director of men's affairs and helped establish basketball, baseball (which he coached), soccer, swimming, tennis, and golf. Joanne Macher, the swimming instructor, coached women's basketball as well. By 1974, the Centaurs had won their first trophy in intercollegiate varsity competition in soccer, with a record of 12–4–1. With recruits from St. Louis, the "hotbed of the nation for soccer," the team competed against such teams as Kansas State and the University of Missouri.[69]

One cloud on the horizon for Columbia College in the early 1970s resulted from a brief sanction against the college by the American Association of University Professors. The case involved a University of Missouri faculty member, Bill Wickersham, who had taken a leave of absence to work in the peace movement and had received a terminal contract upon his return to the university. Hill, acting entirely on his own, signed an employment agreement with Wickersham in the fall of 1969 by which Wickersham would act on a consulting basis until he could become a full-time faculty member in the fall of 1970. Problems arose when the University of Missouri became one of many campuses erupting in student protests in May 1970 after the U.S. invasion of Cambodia. The deaths of students engaging in protests at Kent State and Jackson State College led to further student protests in May, with some 350 colleges being closed by campus disturbances.

Wickersham, active in the movement to cut off funding for the war in Southeast Asia, returned to Columbia on May 7, 1970, from a Washington, D.C., meeting of the New Democratic Coalition. He joined a large group of students in the university chancellor's office trying to solicit a statement on political issues and became involved in a mass rally on May 11. When protestors ignored a police order to stop their activities at the rally, Wickersham was one of thirty-two demonstrators arrested. Released without being charged, he became useful as one who could quell the potential violence of the crowd of three thousand, managing to persuade the students to disperse. As a result of these events, university officials accused Wickersham of neglect of his duties and reduced his pay for "the forcible blocking of the Chancellor of the Columbia campus in his office . . . and explicit refusal to abide by the University regulations relating to attendance at classes."[70]

Concerned about community pressures, Columbia College trustees refused to honor the agreement between Hill and Wickersham. The case came before the Committee on Academic Freedom of the AAUP, and the committee, concluding "that the proposal offered by the president and accepted by

Professor Wickersham . . . constituted a bona fide appointment," placed the college on the association's censure list. When the AAUP held its conference in St. Louis the next year, officials censored the University of Missouri for its handling of the 1970 protests. They then removed Columbia College from the censure list, even though "to get censure removed in just one year, as Columbia College did, is a rarity." The college had reached an agreement with Wickersham, which expedited the lifting of the censure. Many faculty members, in the light of Hill's failure to use regular procedures for hiring, had little sympathy with the case and resented the AAUP censure. Indeed, the censure contributed to the eventual lapse of the local chapter. One AAUP investigator remarked, "Present conditions of academic freedom and tenure at the college seem generally good."[71]

As Columbia College worked toward baccalaureate accreditation, changes by the board and in admissions practices resulted in sharply higher enrollments. Brown sought professional sales people who were older and more mature and gave each the title assistant director of admissions. He increased the number of recruiters to thirteen and continued to base them in the field rather than in Columbia. Aided by the major changes of 1969–1970, the use of effective Prospective Student Weekends, cooperative programs with faculty members, and new advertising techniques, enrollments went from 494 students in 1970 to 686 in 1971, 754 in 1972, and 987 in 1973. Hill boasted in 1971 that "we are probably the only college in the country where the application rate is up sixty percent." Batterson added, "[T]he College also holds the distinction of being one of the only, if not the only, college to offer 80 new courses in their curriculum within the last eighteen months."[72]

In 1972, Hill rewarded Brown by naming him vice president of the college and giving him new duties as supervisor of admissions, public relations, alumni activities, and development. When the Hills left the president's home to move to an area more removed from the campus, Brown and his family moved into the former president's home and became even more actively involved in campus life. By the end of 1972, the college could claim a seasoned administration, with Hill in his eighth year in office, Brown in his fourth, Batterson in his eighth, and Kirkman in her fourteenth.[73]

Financial concerns continued with the costly changes, but the year 1970 brought a degree of stabilization, and the next year saw a minimally balanced budget. Cost-per-student went down with the four-year enrollments and with a larger student body, but financial aid costs escalated from $25,000 in 1962 to $255,000 in 1971. In one advantage, the college benefited greatly from the Missouri Grant, a tax equalization bill passed by the state legislature in 1972. The bill, intended to remove pressure from state universities (and the need to build), provided need-based state aid for students to attend colleges of their choice, public or private. Payments went directly to the colleges, and 250 grantees attended Columbia College by the end of 1972. Also, Hill could report that gifts in 1972 of $247,166 had doubled over the previous year. In 1973, the college received a $100,000 bequest from the estate of Alice Boone Kirtley, a 1912 graduate who had taught English in the Columbia public schools for thirty-six years. At the suggestion of Hartley Banks, Hill designated $50,000 of the bequest to go to the library, which then became the Kirtley Library.[74]

The ultimate test of the college's changes came with a visitation by the North Central Association team on May 2–4, 1973. After the visitation in 1969, the college had been scheduled for another evaluation in 1971. However, this changed when Hill in 1971 notified the association of the college's desire to apply for a visit to "examine the state of readiness to offer a baccalaureate degree" and sent an institutional profile to indicate progress since the last visitation. In response, North Central officials agreed to forego the 1971 review in favor of a baccalaureate preliminary accreditation visit in 1973, a move Hill called "a real morale booster."[75]

After its May 1973 visitation, the North Central team submitted its review of the college's strengths and concerns. It reported an efficient administration, dedicated trustees, supportive and satisfied students, and a harmonious relationship among students, faculty, and staff. Many problems noted in 1969 had been solved, and the team noted an active and effective student government, an attractive health center, good residence halls, and a good but cramped library. Concerns still remained, especially with 87 percent of the income still coming from tuition and fees. Calling the rapid growth of liberal arts and occupational programs a "curricular hybrid," they found the mission statement "unclear." They also found unresolved problems remaining in enrollment and retention, promotional publications promising too much, faculty spread too thin and too heavily weighted toward University of Missouri graduates, and still too little financial support for the library. Once again, the college's precarious financial situation was the greatest concern.[76]

Hill and Batterson went to Chicago for the accreditation hearing to take place on the morning of Wednesday, July 18, with the final decision to come on July 20. Hill recounted that "Wednesday afternoon loomed long, so we went to Wrigley Field and saw the Cubs beat San Diego. . . . After the good news was received on Friday, July 20, we thought the six and one-half-hour-long drive back to Columbia just flew by." The college had been fully reaccredited for the associate of arts degree and approved for the baccalaureate degree with a follow-up visit to come in 1976. North Central recommended the use of a consultant during the three-year period. Batterson phoned the news to a packed faculty lounge, and Kirkman called the occasion "one of the happiest days on campus." Hill drafted a letter to be sent to all students:

> The good news we have all been waiting for came from Chicago just five minutes ago: Columbia College has been given permission to offer a four-year degree to eligible students as early as December. This means that in addition to the present fully-accredited two-year degree, the Associate in Arts, the College will offer the four-year degree programs—bachelor of art in art, history/government, and psychology; bachelor of social work; bachelor of fine arts; bachelor of individual studies; and bachelor of art in education for elementary and secondary teaching.[77]

By September, enrollment swelled to 828 resident students (987 total full- and part-time students), 43 percent of whom were males. Student lounges were temporarily converted into dormitories to contain the overflow, and the increase from 296 in 1964 to 987 in 1973 taxed all campus facilities. The president stated that "in short, we have invaded ourselves to the limit." By the next January, the *Columbia Daily Tribune* boasted of the college's success:

> Columbia College had a crisis of its own a few years ago. Like other private, two-year female colleges, Columbia College was in a money crunch supreme. . . . There was talk about selling the college, . . . or otherwise eliminating the problem. . . . But there was also talk about succeeding, and President Merle Hill conspired with top aides and the governing board to make some rather drastic changes. . . . It's a symbol of true accomplishment these days when small private colleges are under such strain.[78]

In three short years, the college family had come together to create yet another "new" college. It had transformed a "single-sex, two-year college with a misunderstood name and a declining enrollment into a dynamic coeducational Columbia College with a growing enrollment which provides the strength required for baccalaureate status."

The return to four-year status after the junior college years represented a return to the college's original educational goals. The college once again responded with bold and realistic initiatives, accepting the challenges and excitement of expanding its educational programs. Faculty and students could enjoy a four-year relationship rather than two, and school pride swelled. Women students, who in 1851 met new challenges merely by being allowed entrance to a college education, now met the new challenge of competing with men in an academic environment more relevant to contemporary society. The name change repaired what some, even in 1851, had considered a mistake subject to misinterpretation.

Although all three changes conformed to the college's heritage, two conditions continued that heritage by remaining unchanged. The institution continued to be a liberal arts college, combining, as had always been the case, more practical opportunities with the liberal arts emphasis. Also, the standards of academic performance, staunchly upheld by a determined faculty, preserved a level of achievement intended by the founders. Once again, the college had ensured continuity through essential change. The challenge ahead would be to secure the college's financial future.

Kenneth Freeman, Christian College president, 1956–1965, shown in oil painting by Sidney Larson with blueprints for his twenty-five-year plan.

Sidney Larson with Thomas Hart Benton and student, 1952.

Jane Froman on Hollywood set with Susan Hayward who played Froman in *With a Song in My Heart*.

W. Merle Hill, Christian College and Columbia College president, 1965–1977.

Deborah Bryant, Miss America of 1966, as a Christian College student.

President Hill giving away the bride at Deborah Bryant's wedding.

Christian College faculty moving the college library, September 1966.

Sue Gerard, physical education faculty and author.

Dan Hoagland, mathematics faculty, Christian College's "Renaissance Man."

Sidney Larson, national professor-of-the-year finalist.

Jack Batterson, history faculty, later dean of faculty and dean of the college.

William Brown, director of the Conservatory of Music, later director of admissions and of the college's Extended Studies Division.

Howard Kelley, director of admissions, 1964–1969.

St. Clair Hall in 1960s before removal of ivy.

Williams Hall as it appeared in the 1960s.

Williams Hall undergoing restoration in 1968.

Williams Hall dedication as a Boone County Historic Site, September 28, 2000.

First Lady Rosalynn Carter at Christian College for her last appearance in the 1980 presidential campaign. President Bruce Kelly appears at the left.

Larry Young, renowned sculptor and Olympic medalist, at his Columbia foundry.

Bob Burchard, athletic director and basketball coach.

Donald B. Ruthenberg, Columbia College president, 1984–1995.

President Ruthenberg's hot air balloon at the General Assembly of Christian Churches in Iowa, August 7, 1985.

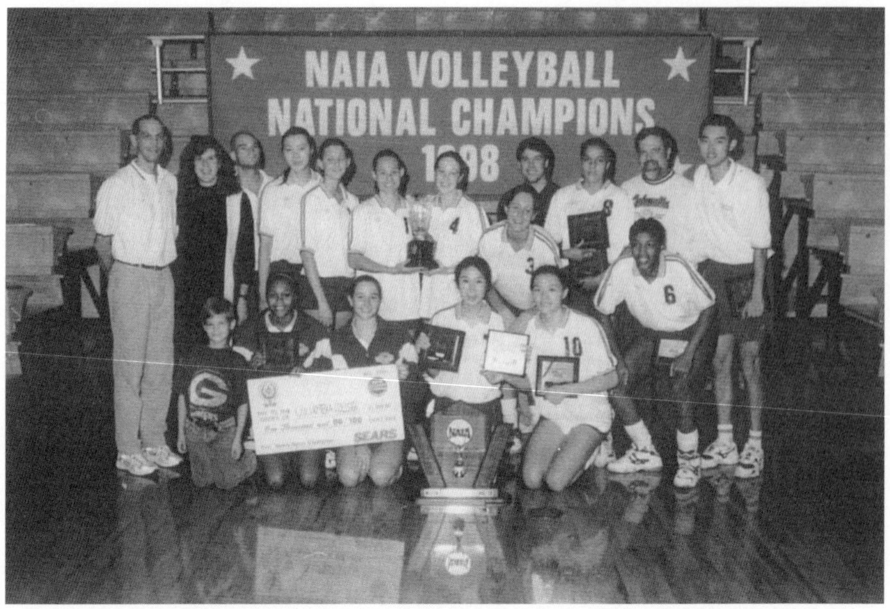

Columbia College volleyball team, 1998 NAIA national champions.

Gerald T. Brouder, Columbia College president, 1995–present.

10

A Living Endowment

W. MERLE HILL: 1973–1977

He that will not apply new remedies must expect new evils; for time is the greatest innovator.

Francis Bacon, "Essays"

There is nothing more difficult to take in hand, more perilous to conduct, or more uncertain in its success, than to take the lead in the introduction of a new order of things.

Niccolo Machiavelli, *The Prince*

IN THE FALL OF 1972, Ted Messick, a United States Army education services officer walked into the office of President Hill, initiating a dramatically different future for the college. His request for educational opportunities for an army recruiter would ultimately lead to the development of Columbia College campuses on military bases throughout the United States.

The contact with the college was routine, but discussion soon turned to other possibilities. The officer had come to campus to arrange for the enrollment of an army recruiter, stationed in Jefferson City, to complete his college degree. As the conversation progressed, the officer became especially interested in sales management courses that could be useful for other army recruiters in the St. Louis area. When the officer visited campus again in January 1973, he sought further opportunities for a recruiter who could not come to the Columbia campus. This time, he asked Hill if it might be possible to take courses to this individual and to any other personnel who might be interested in a degree-completion program—a program especially tailored to the needs of recruiters.

With an all-volunteer army, military emphasis on self-improvement made the availability of degree-completion programs particularly important. Military expectations for higher-quality personnel and for a smaller force meant that noncommissioned officers needed A.A. degrees and commissioned officers should have B.A. degrees to avoid becoming victims of a reduction in force. Within two months of the January discussion, Columbia College faculty members were driving to the Troop Support Command Headquarters (TROSCOM) in St. Louis to teach evening classes to the first students in what eventually became the Columbia College Extended Studies Program. Hill and Bill Brown accepted an invitation to the United States Army Recruiting Command (USAREC) at Fort Sheridan in Illinois to discuss how the college's program in sales management might upgrade the sales skills of recruiters. Military officials also requested that liberal arts courses be included for degree completion in a balanced program. Such courses as U.S. social history, American social problems, psychology, human relations, and the counseling process soon supplemented the business management program. The curriculum would allow military personnel to complete A.A. degrees or bachelor of arts in individual studies (B.A.I.S.) degrees. Soon military recruiters were driving from as far away as Cape Girardeau, Missouri; Springfield, Illinois; and Columbia to attend the classes offered in St. Louis on Monday through Thursday evenings.[1]

The college had no intention of offering programs beyond the St. Louis area, but, as word spread within the military of the opportunities offered in St. Louis, requests for programs at other locations multiplied. By mid-April, a second program had begun in Springfield, Illinois, taught by faculty recruited by the college in the Springfield area. By June 15, Hill informed college trustees of locations being established in Bloomington, Illinois, and in Cape Girardeau, Missouri, with others planned for Kansas City and for Wausau, Wisconsin. By August, sites began in Topeka, Dayton, Cincinnati, and Iron Mountain, Michigan.[2]

So it was that the college's first baccalaureate commencement since 1910 took place in St. Louis on August 31, 1973, just after North Central accreditation of the four-year degree. Hill and Batterson attended the ceremony, awarding twenty-five A.A. degrees, five B.A.I.S. degrees, and one B.A. degree to military and civilian personnel. Students in the Columbia College Active Duty Program consisted entirely of military personnel who came to the program largely through self-generated contacts within the military, whereas the more traditional Veterans Program recruited prospective students who attended with veterans' benefits. The college's first December commencement, held in Launer Auditorium in 1973, awarded forty-seven B.A. degrees and thirty-eight A.A. degrees. The program, distinctly degree-completion in nature, did not attempt to provide full undergraduate offerings but rather accepted previous college work as well as experiential learning credit for nontraditional experiences, requiring that the final twenty-four hours of credit be at a Columbia College site. Those entering the program included students who had never attended college before, college dropouts, servicemen who had attended military service schools, and some students very near graduation. Filling new educational needs in an imaginative format, the college offered courses in eight-week sessions for the convenience of the frequently transferred personnel.[3]

The new venture inevitably brought administrative changes. The attempt to handle the program through an additional assistant in the dean of faculty office proved completely inadequate. In April 1974, Hill separated the off-campus programs completely from the on-campus administration, placing Brown in charge of the total off-campus effort. Beginning with a staff of four in the summer of 1974, Hill and Brown introduced new procedures and employed a staff to parallel the on-campus program. They created the position of dean of extended studies, hiring as its first dean James Preston, a captain in the Missouri National Guard, who had been employed by the University of Missouri. Preston "brought control to the chaos," and an enlarged staff with three assistant deans aided in the process. One assistant dean, Frazier Moon, a ten-year army man, had just received a degree from Columbia College and would serve for twenty years in the program. Another, James Moore, was a retired lieutenant colonel with twenty-six years of army time. The third assistant dean, George Parker, also a retired lieutenant colonel, had served twenty-one years in the air force and had been elected to the Missouri House of Representatives for three terms. The staff, in addition to the dean and three assistant deans, exploded to include an assistant registrar, three evaluators, an administrative assistant to the dean, a director of admissions, an office manager, an assistant public relations officer, and twenty-two clerical workers.

Guidelines controlled program quality, responding to the demands of the Veterans Administration Office in Jefferson City. Prospective adjunct faculty submitted résumés, along with three letters of recommendation, and each hiring required the approval of the Extended Studies dean and the college's president. Textbook availability was to be ensured before the start of any class, and sites could offer only those courses listed in the college catalog unless approved by the Academic Policy Committee, the academic dean, and the president.[4]

As the program grew, its accompanying problems escalated. Paperwork mushroomed as sites proliferated, and, with the increase to seventy-five sites by late 1974, the college began to turn down requests for new locations. Trustees' concern for quality control led to a ban on opening of new sites from October 1974 to January 1975, providing a period of consolidation, standardization, and planning.[5]

A serious cash-flow problem had prompted the board's moratorium on new locations. Minutes of the October 24, 1974, Finance Committee meeting revealed that the "discussion of the entire meeting revolved around billings, collections, and other financial aspects of the Extended Studies programs off-campus." Trustees discovered that many students already enrolled in classes had not yet been billed and that collections were delinquent, resulting in a cash drain of $234,122. The grouping of Extended Studies records made it impossible to determine individual site records, and it was also difficult to determine which expenses resulted from off-campus or on-campus operations. Veterans benefits were paid to individuals and sent by the individuals to the college, causing a delay of eight to ten weeks in recovering expenses. To resolve the problem, the trustees demanded that a "power of attorney system of paying for classes must be initiated immediately for all to whom it applies. Pay-now-or-sign-the-form will be required for all regular duty military personnel utilizing the G. I. Bill."[6] With this approach, government checks could be sent directly to the college rather than to the student.

Hill accepted responsibility for the excessively rapid expansion and resultant problems:

> I must take the blame for any unresolved or unanticipated problems that could precipitate a crisis. I have not permitted the staff to slow down growth in Extended Studies, and it is a too rapid growth that has created most of our current problems. As early as last October, staff members encouraged me to "shoot in the leg" the advance man [Ted Messick] responsible for program promotion and starts. Weekly, from January 1974 to date, Bud Menzel had tried to get me to give a "slow down" signal because of cash-drain problems. Until ten days ago, I refused to heed these admonitions in spite of cognizance of the financial strain.[7]

Two aspects of the paperwork accounted for most of the holdup in the process. The college had to certify each student for eligibility, sending the evidence to the Veterans Administration so that payments could be made. Also, transcript evaluations of credit granted for previous studies required many hours of work. Each night, staff took home stacks of transcripts, working literally night and day calculating transfer of credits. By the spring of 1975, work still overwhelmed the enlarged staff, and there was no relief in sight from the tedious procedures. After a visit in April 1975 to St. Joseph's College in Rensselaer, Indiana, to study their computer system, Hill finally convinced the board to purchase the college's first computer. Paul Wellman, who had supervised the system at St. Joseph's, became the college's new business manager, and Hill reported that the college was going on-line in July 1975.[8]

The summer of 1975 saw significant changes leading to more stability in Extended Studies. Hill created a new office for Brown, who had served as vice president and director of admissions. Brown became executive vice president, and, in 1976, a separate director of admissions supervised the work of the twelve assistant directors of admissions. Brown turned his attention wholly to the Extended Studies Program, working with its dean. When Preston left in June 1975 to join the Missouri State Department of Higher Education, Don Foster, who had come to the college in 1974 as associate dean of faculty and registrar, became the new dean of the Extended Studies Program. Foster would serve the college in a variety of administrative positions over a period of almost twenty years, becoming dean of faculty in 1977, director of administrative services in 1979, and director of the Kansas City Extended Studies site in 1987 until his retirement in 1993. A career military man, Foster had become one of the army's youngest lieutenant colonels at age thirty-five. He possessed extensive military experience and, according to Hill, an "innate ability to foresee problems."

Foster faced not only a heavy workload but also a space crunch. The offices of the program had grown from one room to a few rooms in St. Clair Hall and then moved to the second floor of the Child Study Center and eventually to a nearby building at 613 Ash Street. Even that building proved grossly inadequate, providing twenty-two hundred square feet to accommodate work requiring at least six thousand square feet. Finally, with the lease expiring in 1976, the college acquired a spacious headquarters of eighty-six hundred square feet a few blocks from campus in the building that had been the former home of the Farmer's Mutual Hail Insurance Company. The company pledged $42,000 toward the purchase price of $342,000. With space to spare, the facility housed the college's development offices as well as the Extended Studies Program.[9]

As dean, Foster brought to the program one of its most conscientious and able employees. In a discussion with Brown and Hill, Foster happened to mention Frank Westling, with whom he had served in Vietnam, as one of the two "gentle men" he had known in the army. Much to Foster's surprise, Brown responded that Westling was teaching for the college as an adjunct faculty member at the Fort Sheridan, Illinois, site. Foster called Westling and asked whether he might consider retiring from the military and coming to work for the college. Westling, hesitant about new orders for a Paris assignment, did retire and served the college with distinction until his death in 1987. Supervising the hiring of adjunct faculty for the program, Westling worked well with on-campus faculty in a relationship of mutual respect. Westling and Frazier Moon, according to Foster, did much to bring quality control to the program, and Foster himself deserved no little credit.[10]

By the summer of 1975, the Extended Studies Division (ESD), as it came to be called, reached its peak of 155 locations with almost three thousand students in more than thirty states. The Active Duty Program held classes first in recruiting stations, army reserve centers, and National Guard armories and later operated largely on military installations where classrooms used for military instruction during the day became available for college courses in the evening. The Civilian Program, another arm of the Extended Studies Program beginning in 1974, held classes in business colleges or high schools. By the spring of 1975, Hill reported that the "gross revenue from ES now exceeds on-campus revenue."[11]

With the college preparing for renewal of accreditation in 1976, outside consultants recommended by the North Central Association proved invaluable. George N. Rainsford, president of Kalamazoo College in Kalamazoo, Michigan, visited the college December 9–11, 1975, returning January 11–13, 1976, just before the visitation took place. The other consultant, Robert F. Ray, dean of the Division of Extension and University Services at the University of Iowa, came to campus October 13–15, 1975.

Rainsford reported to the North Central Commission on Institutions of Higher Education: "My general impression was that of an institution approaching some difficult problems in non-traditional ways with an air of excitement, optimism, and high morale based on some significant success in dealing with these problems." Recognizing that the college was both a traditional institution with a liberal arts curriculum and an institution with a nontraditional program requiring a different approach, Rainsford stated that it should be seen as "an institution in transition in the sense that trends may be as important as actual results." He correctly predicted that the nontraditional elements of the program would be more difficult to evaluate both for the North Central Association and for the college.[12]

Rainsford praised the on-campus admissions program for its organization, procedures, controls, and evaluation mechanisms, calling it "one of the best run admissions programs I have ever seen. . . . It could be a model for numbers of other colleges with much more difficult enrollment problems. Columbia College has simply accepted earlier than most institutions the necessity of spending significant money to generate the student tuition income." He found "genuine concern for the institution and the instructional program," while students exhibited "considerable enthusiasm for the school and particularly relations with the faculty." Indeed, in 1974, the college continued the same enthusiastic activities typical of the period of preparation for the four-year accreditation, as baccalaureate status encouraged the offering of greater educational opportunities with the benefit of upper-level courses. Forty students spent the summer in the Swiss village of Appenzel in a combined art and travel administration program. Another group of students experienced unusual opportunities on an intensive spring break study tour in Washington, D.C., where interviews included a Supreme Court justice, top White House officials, senators and congressmen, lobbyists, and journalists, and State Department, embassy, and Pentagon briefings. Also, on campus a full slate of sports now included baseball, soccer, tennis, and golf teams.[13]

In contrast to the earlier North Central report critical of the college for recruiting faculty too heavily from the University of Missouri, Rainsford concluded that "the close involvement with the University of Missouri provides a real source of strength through part-time faculty and consultants. Columbia College would be a considerably less strong institution if it existed by itself . . . without the immediate access to a large prestigious university."[14]

Turning to the new Extended Studies Division, Rainsford praised the "exciting program of experiential learning based on the belief that not all learning takes place in the classroom. Therefore, the institution has validated certain kinds of employment experiences as equivalent alternatives to classroom learning of the same subject matter." He added, "[T]he college has very wisely planned not to count on its significant income resources from the extension division to last more than another five years. By which time the competition for those program dollars will have become intense with other institutions." Rainsford concluded: "Columbia College has come a long way in the past four years and has established a truly impressive record of accomplishment in the face of severe obstacles. There are lessons here for many institutions."[15]

Ray's visit focused entirely on the college's Extended Studies Division. Patricia Thrash, assistant executive director of the North Central Association, had recommended Ray and Rainsford, and they directed their reports to the association. Ray's mid-October visit in 1975, just a month before the college submitted its self-study to the North Central Association, served as an invaluable preliminary for the visitation scheduled for the next January. Ray's assessment, though noting concerns, recognized the merits of the program: "It would appear, in general, that the program has experienced good relations with the Veterans Administration, state approval agencies, and . . . [army] education officers. The program is clearly designed to meet genuine needs by military officers and enlisted men. The program and the college are administered by capable leaders, and the faculty shares the apparent desire to have programs of high quality."[16]

The report applauded the service done by the college through the breadth of the educational program it provided to individuals who would not ordinarily be touched by an academic experience. Ray also praised improvements in the proposed guidelines for experiential learning, along with the "aggressive interest" of the staff and its willingness to work with the academic program. He leveled his most serious criticism at the unstructured nature of the B.A.I.S. degree and at the separation between the structures of the on-campus and off-campus programs. He reminded the college that "as a condition for eligibility for membership in the NCA . . . an institution must . . . include general education at the post secondary level as a prerequisite to or an essential element in its principle educational program." The college's lack of a general education requirement for the B.A.I.S. degree assumed that advising would take care of that need, but Ray recommended that an "eligibility requirement . . . be given prompt attention" along with the requirement of upper-division work. Faculty had devised the program with the on-campus student body in mind, but its use at off-campus sites made such requirements all the more important. Ray further urged more on-campus involvement in adjunct faculty hiring and the regular use by adjuncts of on-campus course syllabi. He also recommended the routine use of base or public libraries at ESD locations and cautioned that the college needed to "take all necessary steps to assure an off-campus enterprise that is indistinguishable from its campus program from the standpoint of quality."[17]

The second Rainsford visit and report, coming in early January 1976, provided a final review of the college's programs prior to the arrival of the North Central review team later that month. Rainsford's familiarity with the college made his assessment on the eve of the visitation especially meaningful. He agreed with the new objective "to expand the number of students in each location rather than significantly expand the number of locations." He reported:

> The college has also initiated significant quality control measures in ES. All operations throughout the United States are now certified to be legal and meet the licensing requirements of each state. All locations are on the same schedule allowing predictability of course timings and therefore faculty needs, allowing for advance time for recruitment. A standard operating procedure has been established for all locations. The [ESD] Dean of the college through his review of credentials of Extended Studies faculty has recommended that some faculty be dropped from the program and they have been dropped. The Dean has also recommended that the Extended Studies program require student evaluations of faculty which can be part of the review process in addition to the current vita and letters of reference. The Academic Policies Committee of the college has also turned down some proposed courses. The faculty evaluation of experiential learning credit is now done by a faculty committee . . . and has resulted in the reducing of the average credit granted for experiential learning from seventeen to between eleven and thirteen credit hours. . . . The guidelines for experiential education have been strengthened and credit is now given by level rather than generally. The syllabus of on-campus courses has been circulated to the off-campus centers and forms the basis of the off-campus course offerings. The . . . Dean subsequently reviews all off-campus course syllabi. The pool of qualified faculty for the off-campus program is being increased slowly with a better review of credentials and references by the on-campus administration.[18]

Also helpful to the college in the North Central review, Rainsford noted that $639,000 of short-term general fund debt was retired because of the Extended Studies Division, and that only capital indebtedness remained.

The college's self-study detailed the financial and logistical aspects of the Extended Studies Division. It explained that the use of adjunct faculty, free access to military facilities, and lack of any need for student financial aid allowed low overhead at the sites. Thus, the budget of $4,279,670 could be used for administrative and other academic needs of the nontraditional aspects of the program. As the self-study explained, files for applicants for employment as adjunct faculty members now went through the dean of faculty office to on-campus faculty members in the corresponding subject matter for comment. The faculty evaluation then went back to the dean of faculty office for transmittal to the dean of the Extended Studies Division. Also, by 1976, arrangements had provided all locations with the use of nearby academic or public libraries. Further, course offerings had been expanded to include banking administration, business administration, sales management, English, foreign languages, geography, history, government, humanities, mathematics, philosophy, psychology, science, sociology, social work, and speech. Courses offered on campus but not at Extended Studies sites included art, education, dance, drama, fashion, hospitality management, interior design, journalism, music, travel administration, military science, and physical education. Available degrees, with requirements identical to the ones on campus, included the A.A., B.A.I.S., and B.A. degrees, with majors in English, history/government, business administration, and psychology.[19]

The North Central visitation of January 26–28 resulted in an encouraging report. The team chair, William R. Hazard, was professor and associate dean of the School of Education at Northwestern University, and other team members came from the University of Michigan, Augsburg College, and Oberlin College. All agreed that the "financial crisis of a few years ago is over," largely as the result of the burgeoning Extended Studies Division. By the time of the visitation, the college had 2,450 students in the program, with 20,000 enrollments per year and 250 instructors in its one hundred locations. The team reported, "The ESD leadership and the college officers recognize and are moving to solve problems in student advisement, monitoring instructor performance in the off-campus sites, library needs of students and instructors, and numerous other academic quality issues."[20]

The team's evaluation of the on-campus program also recognized progress: "Columbia College . . . with substantially increased enrollments and increasing financial surpluses, has the opportunity to review its mission and consolidate its strengths. Much progress has been made in many areas since its initial accreditation at the four-year baccalaureate degree level." Praising the dedication of the faculty and the system of faculty evaluation, self-evaluation, and evaluation by the dean of faculty, the team also reacted positively to the creation of the Faculty Senate and to high faculty morale: "Faculty confidence in the Academic Dean is high and this respect and trust extends generally to the entire administrative team. . . . The Dean of Faculty appears open and ready for increased faculty participation in decision-making, which provides favorable ground for potential improvement in the area of governance."[21]

The team reported that the "student body on the Columbia campus appears to be a reasonably authentic cross-section of the regional population. . . . The students engage in the expected range of cultural, social, and service activities of a typical college." Further, "more responsibilities are being given to students for their own activities, reflecting the view that it makes better educational sense to help people learn to regulate their own lives than to regulate them for them." The conclusions praised the serious efforts by the college to respond to a diverse clientele and the college's use of North Central consultants and prompt response to their counsel. Particularly important, the team believed that "broad recognition that proposed degree requirements are needed" could lead to the stronger general education requirements already desired by many faculty members and the academic dean. The report also recognized the improved career placement and student counseling areas and the positive student-faculty relations. Although the library budget was still "inadequate," the team acknowledged improvement, especially in the library's professional leadership.[22]

Shortcomings appeared in the areas of planning structures and processes, limited development opportunities for faculty, and inadequate fiscal budgeting and reporting mechanisms. Also, some unresolved problems still remained in reporting on quality control mechanisms in the Extended Studies Division.[23]

The visitation team recommended to the North Central Association that accreditation be continued for the B.A. degree-granting status. However, they attached three conditions: that on-site reviews be conducted of a select sample of Extended Studies sites in a focused review of quality control, as there had not been time for such a focused study by the team; that the college continue the use of qualified consultants in financial planning and in degree-program development; and that a total review be held in another three years. Because of the rapid expansion of Extended Studies locations and the need to ensure quality control, the team mandated that no new locations begin in the future without prior approval from the North Central Association.[24]

Once again, a Columbia College administrative team traveled to Chicago for the final decision. Hill, Brown, Batterson, and Wellman met with the fifteen-member Review Committee of the Commission on Institutions of Higher Education on Sunday, March 28, 1976. As Hill reported, "Vice-President Brown and Dean Batterson carried the ball in the one-hour meeting. . . . We were well represented by these two gentlemen, and all questions were answered to the satisfaction of the Committee members." When word came the next morning of the continued accreditation at the baccalaureate level, Hill expressed his delight to the board: "We knew this was going to happen, but it was more of a thrill for us than was initial accreditation in July 1973." The college, under truly adverse conditions, had created and solidified a baccalaureate degree status and an Extended Studies

Division, both meeting the demands of the North Central Association. Administrators had no doubt that a solid foundation had been laid and that necessary modifications could satisfy future concerns of the North Central Association.[25]

Thus, a small private college with limited financial means had, through a creative and determined effort, blazed new trails in the scope of its offerings, but not without facing and overcoming formidable hurdles. The confidence reflected in Hill's attitude carried the college through repeated unexpected setbacks. Such a setback occurred in April 1976 when a Veterans Administration directive informed the college that all extension courses outside the state of Missouri must be approved by the State Approval Agency in each state and that the college must set up a whole administration at each site. Although realizing that "most of our programs faced extinction due to costs of administration at each site," Hill had begun to comply when the Veterans Administration issued another directive that courses on military bases or courses offered specifically for active duty military personnel were exempt from the requirement, but only if the activity had a Memorandum of Understanding with the commander of the students in the course. Hill was amazed: "We had never heard of a Memorandum of Understanding." Hill and Brown drew up such a memorandum, sending a copy to each commander, only to find that they must meet with military educational authorities and base personnel to convince them of the validity of the programs. The problem affected thirty-one sites, and the college lost only three in the process. Hill reported to the board that the college had the approval of everyone required: state licensing, the Missouri State Approval Agency, the Veterans Administration, base education officers, the North Central Association, and "even students." However, the April Veterans Administration directive did not exempt the college's eight civilian locations from its requirements, and all eight had to be closed.[26]

The structure of the Extended Studies Division illustrated its complexity. With Brown as its head, there was an extensive administrative staff: dean of the Extended Studies Division; assistant dean for administration; two assistant deans of adjunct faculty; assistant deans for western locations, eastern locations, and the Civilian Program; ten Active Duty Program coordinators; and eight Civilian Program directors.[27]

Hill appreciated the effort needed to put such a program in place: "Without Bill Brown's dedication and will to make our off-campus efforts succeed, it may well have gone down the drain on several occasions during the past year." Of Dean Foster, Hill remarked: "This position demands more of an individual than most can give," noting that Foster had spent more than 40 percent of his time on the road "to hold our program together." In the course of refining the program to meet Veterans Administration regulations, and for greater efficiency, the college dropped the sites from 155 to 104 and then to 87 in 1976 and to 70 in March 1977, intending to consolidate the program into fewer but larger locations for more effective administration.[28]

On campus, college officials struggled to house the overflow enrollment. Board discussion of erecting temporary classrooms moved instead to rental of three classrooms from the junior high school across the street from the college for the 250 students in the college's new on-campus evening program. The Evening College, beginning in March 1975 with 60 students, another arm of the Extended Studies Division, would become a major asset not only for the college but also for the community. Traditional day enrollments also expanded with the move to a coeducational four-year program. Dormitory lounges doubled as classrooms through the day as enrollment climbed to a total of 1,134 students on campus in the fall of 1976, and some students even found temporary quarters in faculty homes and in motels. Once again the college had a waiting list.[29]

After the difficult years of establishing both the four-year program and the Extended Studies Division, the hard work seemed to be bearing fruit. At the October 1976 board meeting, "Mr. [Marvin] Owens [chairman of the Finance Committee] reported there was an increase in the fund balance," and Hill pointed out that "in three years the fund balance went from a deficit of $629,000 to a surplus of $1,337,215. Notes payable dropped from $699,000 to zero at the end of June." On September 1, 1976, the college finally repaid $83,500 to the endowment fund that had been "borrowed many years ago." Also, the college was one of eight private schools approved by the Missouri Coordinating Board of Higher Education to participate in the Missouri Student Grants program. On another positive note, John Foley, who had replaced Paul Wellman as business manager in 1976, reported on changes producing greater efficiency in the business office.[30]

Improved financial conditions went hand in hand with other improvements on campus. The art program moved into expansive quarters in the building of the former Allton auto dealership downtown on Broadway at Hitt Street and added another smaller building nearby on Orr Street. The large open-studio format provided room for drawing, painting, jewelry, ceramics, commercial art, and photography along with an art gallery, and the facilities included a bronze furnace, a large kiln, lapidary equipment, airbrushes, and a darkroom. A Columbia College art student created a new logo for the City of Columbia, and freelance work for local businesses carried class credit, as did art study tours both in the United States and in Europe. In addition, a new classroom building on back campus was to be ready by mid-October 1976.[31]

Academic improvements kept pace with other developments. New majors added from 1975 to 1977 included English, public relations, public administration, administration of justice, social work, science, psychology, dance, fashion, music, and education. Also, the faculty increased general education requirements, effective January 1, 1977. In addition to the forty hours of upper-level course work, graduates must have completed six hours of credit in English composition and eight additional courses, or the equivalent, distributed among at least three of the following academic divisions: Division of the Arts, Division of Communications, Division of Social and Behavioral Sciences, and Division of Science and Mathematics. The change, approved by the board at the meeting of April 23, 1976, was a first step toward more stringent requirements to come, as trends moved away from the less structured practices of the 1960s. The board also reinstated sabbatical leaves, which had been suspended temporarily, and entered into a tuition exchange program. The program allowed eligible children of Columbia College faculty members to attend any of 143 other private colleges in the agreement with no tuition charges. Also, the college was accepted by the other four-year institutions into the Mid-Missouri Association of Colleges and Universities (MMACU), including the University of Missouri–Columbia, William Woods College, Westminster College, Central Methodist College, Stephens College, and Lincoln University. The agreement provided for cross enrollments of students attending Columbia College, Stephens, and the University of Missouri–Columbia and included library privileges on all campuses.[32]

With the Columbia College academic program in a positive mode, Batterson stunned the college family on April 14, 1976, with the announcement of his resignation from the deanship to return to teaching. He had "envisioned a two- or three-year deanship," but "new sets of challenges kept coming up to delay" his ultimate goal of going back to the classroom. Hill reacted with a memorandum to Batterson:

> You could have knocked me over with the proverbial feather this morning. . . . Your impact on the curriculum and the perseverance/dedication required to accomplish what you have done, especially in the past seven years, will always be the keystone for the baccalaureate at Columbia College. . . . I shall miss your cool head you always had on your shoulders but trust that you will be available for advice from your position as a senior faculty member.[33]

Batterson replied, "[E]veryone should have sometime in his life the kind of day I had on April 14. An important personal and professional decision, followed by a steady flow of gratifying expressions by many friends and colleagues. None was more satisfying to me, however, than your generous response to my request and your kind personal and public remarks."

In a letter to faculty before any public announcement, Batterson looked both ahead and back at his tenure as dean:

> The administrative and managerial rewards of the deanship have been substantial. The opportunity to work closely with one of the most far-seeing, innovative, and articulate college presidents in the country has been exciting. The

> opportunity to work harmoniously with other staff members, and especially with faculty and students, in the development of the baccalaureate degree programs has been a career in itself. The promotion of faculty benefits and development has been most satisfying. The knowledge that I am turning over an expanding and firmly-accredited academic program is not least among the rewards. None of these rewards, however, can match the joy and excitement of the prospect of returning to my first professional love—classroom teaching and scholarly activity.[34]

Hill and the trustees showed their appreciation of Batterson's eleven-year stewardship of the academic program at a crucial period in the college's history by honoring him with the only Columbia College Distinguished Educator Award ever granted by the college, given for his "dedication and diligence guiding the college through a time of change and growth."

Despite the general sense of satisfaction among administrators in 1976, the college faced an extraordinary challenge lasting over a period of months in 1976 and 1977 with a North Central focused visit to specified Extended Studies Division sites. The North Central team, again headed by Hazard, would include visits to eleven sites, including one or two sites within each of six accrediting regions of the United States. The North Central Association had specified that sites visited should include both active duty and civilian locations, on-base and off-base locations, sites with large enrollments and small, and sites with permanent Columbia College staff along with those sites with part-time staffing. North Central officials and Columbia College staff selected sites to be visited by a "core team" of North Central evaluators along with evaluators from the particular regional accrediting agency of the site visited. Regional agencies included the New England Association of Schools and Colleges, the Middle States Association of Colleges and Secondary Schools, the Southern Association of Colleges and Schools, the Northwest Association of Secondary and Higher Schools, the Western Association of Schools and Colleges, and the North Central Association. "Minireports" for each site reflected information, observations, and evaluative judgments based on five factors: initial conferences with the on-site director, course instructors, and Columbia College administrators; observation of classes; group interviews with students; review of personnel files and program-related materials; and exit conferences with on-site and Columbia College personnel. The process, with site visits beginning in July 1976, would be completed in April 1977.[35]

Hazard's report lauded much about the Extended Studies Division. He praised the board's emphatic demand for quality, the time and effort put forth by Columbia College administrators, the "attractive well-maintained headquarters" near campus, the evident intent of increased academic supervision, and the wisdom of offering only a limited number of programs.

He reported strong support of the program from on-base Military Education Service officers, enthusiastic and committed students and faculty members at Extended Studies locations, a systematic effort to maintain personal contact with site staff and faculty, and a commitment "to making college-level courses and programs accessible to civilian and military personnel who are often excluded from the traditional, campus-based programs." The greatest concern remained the degree of separation of the Extended Studies Division's operations from the academic structures and processes of the Columbia campus. The college had yet to develop a system of regular involvement by on-campus faculty in hiring and consulting with adjunct faculty members. The team also expressed disapproval of the use of the B.A.I.S. degree off-campus, aware that its use on campus could be guided by faculty advising. Instructional support services, resources, and facilities were not yet comparable to the ones on campus, resulting in a lack of comparable counseling and advising. Finally, evaluation processes still needed better implementation, and the disparity of library resources remained unresolved.[36]

The report recommended continued accreditation at the B.A. degree level including all Extended Studies sites in operation in April 1977. However, the college needed more time to complete implementation of quality control mechanisms, especially in the area of demonstrating comparability of academic outcomes on and off campus and in the integration of Extended Studies Division staff into college decision-making structures. Therefore, after Hill, Brown, and Westling met with the Commission on Institutions of Higher Education in Chicago on April 12, 1977, the commission placed several requirements on the evolving program. Official written notification of North Central action from Thurston Manning, director of the commission, specified three requirements. First, a comprehensive evaluation, including ESD, was to be scheduled for 1977–1978. The second requirement resulted from the college's intent "that the ESD programs be comparable to the campus programs." Therefore, "it is to develop in consultation with the Commission staff a satisfactory evaluation process including, but not limited to, a study of academic outcomes . . . and to report its findings." Finally, no new ESD sites were to be opened after April 13, 1977, "until further action by the Commission."[37]

Although ESD had been reaccredited in a unique and intensive review, the innovative nature of the program and unprecedented complexity of site reviews caused more and more board concern. The trustees, willing to retrench, if necessary, to ensure quality control, became increasingly uneasy with the speed of expansion.

The board, which in 1969 had followed Hill's lead in creating a four-year, coeducational Columbia College, was less willing to give the president free rein in the Extended Studies Division. By 1977, the trustees expressed skepticism of new courses being introduced into the program and of the financial management of the program. One of the strongest and most significant boards in the college's history, its members were typical of past trustees in their dedication to the institution, and some would remain to see the college through the turmoil of the major changes to a period of stability and prestige by the later 1980s.

Of the trustees during the Hill years, B. D. Simon, who had joined the board in 1963 and followed Hartley Banks as chairman of the board in 1971, carried the heaviest load. Well experienced in board affairs from his roles as secretary and vice president of the board before becoming its president, Simon exhibited dedication and attention to detail, devoting countless hours to institutional matters. He was proud of other outstanding trustees whom he had brought to the board, including Marvin Owens, Tom Atkins, Andrew Bass Jr., David Rogers, and Darrell Eichhoff. Owens joined the board in 1975, becoming chairman of the Finance Committee at a time when his guidance may well have been the salvation of the college and earning the profound respect and admiration of all associated with him. Simon was to refer to his addition of Owens to the board as "perhaps the outstanding feat of my chairmanship. Marv spent time over and beyond the call of duty getting the college back on a firm financial footing." Atkins, husband of an alumna, came to the board in 1976, having chaired fund-raising committees for the college's Columbia campaign for two years, including the first Columbia campaign. It was Andy Bass who interested Atkins in becoming involved with the college and who served as Atkins's mentor. Atkins would play a major role in the college's history, chairing the board from 1982 to his retirement in 1999. Among the many expressions of appreciation at the time of his stepping down as chairman of the board (although remaining as a trustee), the National Alumni Association named him an honorary member. His steady, skillful leadership guided the college through completion of many changes to stabilization and one of its most successful eras. Rogers, son of a Christian College graduate, joined the board in 1972 and served as its chairman from 1980 to 1982. The son-in-law of Hartley G. Banks Sr., who had served as chairman from 1947 to 1971, Rogers carried on a long family tradition of association with the college. Bass came to the board in 1966 and became a trustee emeritus in 1996, three years before his death. In 1988, the college awarded him an honorary doctor of humanities degree for his outstanding service. Bass Commons, dedicated in 1978, honored Bass's mother, Mary Machir Dorsey Bass, the oldest living graduate of the college at that time. Her grandfather John Machir had served on the college's board from 1857 to 1899. Bass continued in this tradition, and his "stamp is on the board as it has been on any group that he has been with." Eichhoff, husband and father of college alumnae, had acted as president of the Parents Association. He joined the board in 1967, becoming its vice president in 1971. According to Simon,

Eichhoff "added strength to the board and had a long-range outlook that at least kept me going."[38]

Some of the more active of the thirty-two trustees coming to the board during Hill's twelve-year administration included Virginia Southwell Singletary, Evelyn Schrom Estes, Sidney B. Neate, Isabel B. Browning, George Miller, Charles Koelling, Donald A. Reid, and Peggy Price. Singletary's numerous gifts, including a million-dollar challenge pledge to the college in 1980, proved nothing short of providential. She also served on the board of the National Alumnae Association and received the college's Distinguished Alumna Award in 1982. Estes came to the board in 1970 as an alumnae representative. She had helped to organize the National Alumnae Association in 1962 and served as its president. She and her husband, Alex, counted some one hundred relatives associated with the college, several of whom were trustees. Continuing on the board from the Freeman administration, Elizabeth Gentry of the class of 1920 became the first president of the National Alumnae Association. She was honored in 1970 as the Distinguished Alumna of that year. Her great aunt Sallie Bedford was valedictorian of the college's first graduating class in 1853, and Gentry could claim fifty relatives in five generations who had attended the college. Her uncle North Todd Gentry had attended the small-boys class. Koelling, whose daughter was a graduate of the college, guided the cooperative programs with the University of Missouri as Columbia College evolved into a four-year institution and gave academic strength to the board from his experience as a professor in the University of Missouri–Columbia College of Education. Peggy Price, her mother, and three sisters were alumnae, representing the family's five straight generations of ties to the college.[39]

By early 1977, several issues put the strong-willed president and this equally determined board at odds. The continued inability to collect debts owed the college in the Extended Studies Division particularly concerned the board. At a meeting of April 15, 1977, trustees learned that some accounts receivable went back to 1975 and that a new law would compound the problem, causing the college to close seventeen locations with seventy locations still in place. Public Law 94-502, effective as of October 3, 1976, specified that Veterans Administration funds could not be used to pay for education at an institution or branch if that location had not been open at that site for two years. It also provided that no more than 85 percent of students enrolled in any such class as the Extended Studies courses could pay for their educational experiences with federal funds. Most detrimentally, the law prohibited the use of the power of attorney to encourage recipients of federal funds to pay their bills. Brown informed the trustees that accounts receivable amounted to $1 million "since we can no longer use the power of attorney." Hill explained to the board that some states had pushed the legislation through to keep "foreign corporations" (meaning out-of-state entities) from offering programs in competition with local institutions. Hill stated that the college could not "put new students in the program because of Public Law 94-502; however, next year we will at some locations become a two-year program . . . and will, at that time, be able to put new students into the program."[40]

As Hill and Brown sought other nonmilitary off-campus programs, their leadership aroused board concern when they began to provide a series of courses not offered on the home campus and not yet approved by the Educational Policy Committee. Classes in "bionutrition" opened in Kansas City on October 2, 1976, with 62 students, most of whom were chiropractors, osteopaths, and nurses. With 13,000 more prospective students contacted by mail, 192 students had attended a second session in Kansas City. Despite growing board disagreement with the program, Hill and Brown planned to begin further sessions in Los Angeles in March 1977. Because Brown wanted the program taught on campus in the fall of 1977, an ad hoc committee from the Institutional Planning and Policy Committee, composed of two faculty members, one student, and four administrators, approved the bionutrition program. A majority of the corporate faculty then approved the recommendation of the committee. Bio-Nutrition 401, a program consisting of twelve modules, would "treat basic biochemical function, the role of nutrients in the biochemical malfunction, clinical procedures, laboratory analysis, and medical office practice." As Hill continued his advocacy of the program over the objections of trustees, the board responded unanimously: "Resolved: It is directed by the Board of Trustees that all courses in Bio-Nutrition now in session may be completed. No person not now in the course is to be admitted under any circumstances. Under no circumstances are additional courses of study to be started in this program." In what had become a test of authority, Simon demanded that the Educational Policy Committee of the board be advised of all academic procedures, including new courses. When Hill objected that this tactic had not been used for at least fourteen years, Simon replied that "for fourteen years Columbia College had been offering courses on campus."[41]

In addition to curricular concerns, financial prospects became more disturbing, and the trustees continued to insist on a balanced budget. The faculty pension plan, begun in the 1940s by Miller, fell victim to budget cuts when changes in federal guidelines made the plan too expensive to continue. In another change, the college faced termination of funds from the Christian Church unless the board approved a new twelve-point covenant with the church by November 1, 1977. Hill and the board agreed that the requirements of the new covenant would in no way interfere with "recruitment of students, faculty, or general support of the institution," and the board adopted the document on April 15, 1977. The covenantal relationship between the church and the college became a permanent part of catalog statements.[42]

The covenant was the last point of agreement between Hill and the board. Trustees disagreed with Hill's choice of a statistician for a study of comparability of student learning in off-campus and on-campus courses, and when the trustees intervened in the firing and hiring of business managers, Hill complained that they were assuming responsibilities normally the province of administrators. Later recalling the tense relations of 1977, Simon believed that Hill "got to the point that he was doing everything without us, and we felt that one or the other didn't need the other." What Hill, looking back, saw as "internal meddling by the board . . . anathema to education," Simon saw as the board's right to be informed and give direction. The final breach came in an exchange of letters between Simon and Hill. With Hill on the road visiting a Springfield, Missouri, alumni chapter, his secretary read him a letter from Simon setting up a meeting between Hill and local trustees. Hill dictated his response:

> On this date I have submitted my resignation as President of Columbia College to B. D. Simon, Jr., Chairman of the Board of Trustees. I have suggested that the effective date be August 31, 1977. I should like to express my appreciation to you for your past support in our common endeavor. What was a two-year college for women with a misinterpreted name, a declining enrollment of fewer than 300 students and little hope for survival is today Columbia College, an accredited coeducational baccalaureate institution with nearly 1,400 students attending class in Columbia and hundreds more at the ESD sites. All of this, accomplished in what was perhaps the worst period in private higher education's history, is an amazing feat.
>
> Thank you, good luck and *Auf Wiedersehen*.[43]

With Hill's departure, the board named Bruce Kelly, director of admissions, as interim president in July, making his appointment permanent at the fall meeting. Kelly had served as director of student loan programs, assistant dean of students, dean of men, and director of financial aid at his alma mater, the University of Illinois at Champaign, and at its Chicago medical center. He had also been the assistant regional director of the nine-state Midwest Region of the American College Testing Program. Coming to Columbia College in 1975 as an associate director of admissions, he advanced the next year to director of admissions. Kelly, with sixteen years of active duty and army reserve service, continued in his reserve capacity.[44]

After leaving Columbia College, Hill continued his academic career as dean of the School of Consumer and Family Services at Purdue University in 1977, moving the next year to Washburn University at Topeka, Kansas, to serve as vice president of institutional advancement. In 1983, he became executive director of the Kansas Association of Community Colleges, a position he held until shortly before his retirement to Sarasota, Florida, in 1997.[45]

Although the legacy of the Hill administration was not immediately clear, it laid the foundation for the modern Columbia College. That college, after troublesome growing pains, would flourish as a baccalaureate coeducational institution. Meanwhile, the off-campus program became a twentieth-century educational pioneering venture, serving as a "living endowment" to supplement the on-campus program.

The college's mission of bringing educational opportunities to off-campus sites proved an ideal fit for the needs of the military personnel who first sought its services in 1973. The program, evolving from their request, not only was mutually beneficial but also continued the college's tradition of relevancy. Foster reflected on the Extended Studies Division after his 1993 retirement: "It is a program in which anybody who has ever been connected with it can take a great deal of pride. It is part of the flexibility the college has always demonstrated. It started that way—so far it has always continued." Don Landers, as a trustee in 1998, sought to describe the spirit of the college in much the same way, referring to its "ability to face reality, to change" and to some mysterious quality that "made good people willing to stay involved." However, the quality Landers put above all others permeating the college's history was its "HONESTY—honesty in its dealings with others and in its recognition of its needs and obligations." These qualities served the college well in the many challenges of the Hill years, a period testing the institutional will and convictions no less than any other in the college's existence.[46]

11

Guarding the Heritage

BRUCE KELLY: 1977–1984

There are all sorts of good vocational schools, graduate schools, and industrial training programs that can develop practical and salable skills in their students, but no other institution in American society that can train balanced, mature, and wise future leaders as effectively as the liberal arts college.

Peter W. Stanley, dean of Carlton College, quoted by Jack Batterson in "Realistic Response," April 12, 1982

THE JOURNEY OF Christian/Columbia College from a single-sex junior college to a coeducational baccalaureate institution with branch locations from coast to coast involved struggle and success, trauma and triumph. The first seven years of that transition ended in 1977 with the departure of Merle Hill. The second seven years, in some ways the most trying of times, would reveal the Extended Studies Division to be a two-edged sword capable of either saving or endangering the college as the speed of the program's early growth threatened the academic reputation of the college itself. The changes brought a seemingly endless parade of North Central Association teams to campus before both the college and the accrediting agency could resolve the program's considerable growing pains. Meanwhile, cash-flow problems added to the drain. Despite these concerns and a decline in national enrollment patterns, the Columbia campus, the heart of the college, prevailed. From this core component the new off-campus sites and the on-campus Evening College gained the academic strength necessary for quality programs.

In this evolution, Bruce B. Kelly presided over the second seven years of the college's transformation. The first president since St. Clair Moss to take seriously the obligation to make fund-raising his prime priority, he faced a faltering national economy and an institutional controversy that came close to costing the college its liberal arts heritage. The trustees expected the new president to settle some rather stormy seas and provide stability after Hill's sudden departure in the summer of 1977, and Kelly's move from interim president to president at the September 24 board meeting occurred without a national search. Kelly's inauguration on April 23, 1978, featured James I. Spainhower, Missouri state treasurer and chairman of the Christian Church Division of Higher Education, as the main speaker.[1]

Far from the stability anticipated, the Kelly administration suffered a rapid rotation of senior staff. One of Kelly's first steps was to establish a structure recommended by his assistant, David Williams. Hired by Hill in 1976 as an institutional planner and assistant to the president, Williams had become acting dean of faculty after an unsuccessful search to replace Batterson. Promoted to full dean by Hill in January 1977, Williams became assistant to the president again after Hill left in July. In the structure devised by Williams, associate dean of faculty Benelle Reeble became acting dean in July 1977, with Don Foster serving as associate dean for the Extended Studies Division.[2]

In other areas, Robert Godfrey carried over from the Hill era as director of admissions until John Bart replaced him in 1980. Allan Rodgers continued as dean of student life, replaced in 1978 by former philosophy instructor Eldon Drennan, who had served as director of men's activities since 1970. Novelle Dunathan, of the education department, followed Drennan in student affairs in 1981 and remained in that position during the rest of the Kelly presidency. John Foley, brought to the college late in the Hill presidency to improve business office procedures, left in August 1979 to take a position in Wisconsin. Barbara Scobee replaced Foley, succeeded in 1980 by Kay Kanger. Kanger had previously served the college in the admissions department, in student personnel services, as associate dean of faculty, and as acting dean of faculty. Jane Crow remained as director of alumni activities until 1981, when Diane O'Hagan assumed that position and Crow became director of alumni records.

The plethora of overall administrative changes, however, could not come close to matching the turnover in the dean of faculty office. After Williams ended his brief period as dean of faculty, Reeble served for part of 1977 until Foster became acting dean later that year. Foster left the deanship in 1979 to fill a newly created position of dean of administrative services. Associate Dean Kanger served temporarily as acting dean until replaced by Jerry Harris in 1980. John Henricks, previously director of the Evening College, replaced Harris in 1982 until another search resulted in the 1983 hiring of Robert

Evans. When health concerns forced Evans to leave early in 1984, Henricks again stepped in briefly as acting dean.

The position of director of development went unfilled for the first five years of the Kelly administration, a period of great need for fund-raising. Kelly optimistically chose to function as development head, "in the interest of husbanding our resources." As a result, he was off campus as much as 65 to 70 percent of the time, tending not to be greatly involved in the college's day-to-day affairs. Actually, lack of involvement in the origin of issues fit well with his style of command reminiscent of his military experience. Kelly disliked confrontation, preferring to stay above the fray. His organizational structure allowed administrators to work out problems, leaving it to him to make a clear-cut yes-or-no decision following staff work.[3] This management style tended to work reasonably well for most of the first year until accumulated problems began to take their toll.

The Kelly presidency began with considerable accomplishments. As early as August 1977, Kelly announced to the executive committee of the board that "in an attempt to be in compliance with Federal Regulations," he was naming a Title IX coordinator and that "Penny Carroll had been appointed to this position." Title IX of the Civil Rights Act of 1964 had mandated equal employment opportunities on the basis of sex as well as race, a requirement widely ignored in some organizations. Although Kelly informed the board at the time of the appointment that "no other action was required," neither he nor the board had allowed for the diligence of Carroll, an English professor, who took her assignment quite seriously, making Columbia College an exemplar of full compliance. As a result, the college made "a substantial equity [salary] adjustment for women . . . in January 1978."[4]

In another constructive move, a slight upgrading of the still weak general education requirements specified that the eighteen semester hours of course work in three of the eight academic departments must be earned outside the department in which the student was majoring. The strengthening of student quality, begun in 1976, continued, and the grade point average of entering freshmen in 1977 stood at 2.89, comparing well with the 2.7 average for Missouri high school graduates. The ACT score of 19 for incoming Columbia College freshmen also exceeded the national average of 16.22. Kelly pleased faculty members by rescinding Hill's ruling that staff with B.A. degrees were eligible to vote in faculty meetings—meetings usually attended under Hill by major administrators and heads of support services as well as by faculty. Kelly asked Foster to place the item on the September 12, 1978, agenda: "I feel that only *teaching faculty* should attend and vote at corporate meetings. I do not feel that possession of a Bachelor's Degree by anyone in the employ of Columbia College qualifies that individual as a faculty member with voting privileges."[5]

In curricular changes, the faculty added a technical writing major and phased out public relations and journalism. Also, the addition of a performing arts major in drama, music, or dance strengthened the theater program. A local newspaper article reflected the success of one production: "This is a rare review. If you don't like superlatives don't read any further. The Columbia College production of *The Matchmaker* is, if not the best theater that will be done in town this season, surely one of the best evenings of drama to come along in a month of Sundays."[6]

Nor were student interests neglected. With enthusiasm building for sports under Drennan as acting dean of students, the basketball and baseball teams made the Ozark Collegiate Conference playoffs in their first year of organized play, and the soccer team ranked second in the NAIA district playoffs, placing three players on the All-Midwest team. In another morale builder, trustee Prentice Gautt headed a new Student-Trustee Coordinating Committee, providing a venue of lunch meetings for students and trustees to exchange views. Although students expressed concerns about such matters as food, intervisitation hours, and the desire for a multipurpose building, they regularly reflected strong confidence in the faculty and the academic program.[7]

The Extended Studies Division also continued to improve. Following a suggestion of the North Central Association, the program merged its organization with the on-campus structure under the office of the dean of faculty, putting both components under one administration. The college began to close smaller sites, concentrating on the ones large enough to hire full-time staff, reducing locations from forty-five to thirty-five. On-campus staff meanwhile began testing Extended Studies classes for course outcomes, comparing results with similar tests to be performed on campus. With preparations under way for another North Central Association review in 1978, Kelly was confident that "the College will get through the accreditation process with flying colors."[8]

Final plans for the spring visitation began in January 1978 when Kelly, Foster, and Williams met with North Central officials in Chicago to discuss use of an evaluation instrument to test general comparability of learning at off-campus sites and on campus. At that time, North Central participants in the meeting described the upcoming visitation as a "comprehensive sequential evaluation" to take place in three phases. In phase one, the North Central team would visit the Columbia campus and several Extended Studies sites: the Columbia Evening College, Fort Leonard Wood, Kansas City, and St. Louis. In the second phase, two-person teams would examine ten other sites in four accrediting regions from Seattle to Miami. The last phase would bring the entire team back to Columbia to write the final report. By the time of the April visitation, Foster reported that "the result of the comparability testing accomplished in the first semester which showed no significant difference in the learning outcomes of off and on campus students, increases our confidence about the validity of our program."[9]

The North Central team report included wide-ranging concerns and strengths. Dealing with the admissions effort, the report indicated "a need to study carefully the student recruiting and admissions practices," especially the practice of paying the associate directors of admissions a salary plus a "variable" based on the number of students recruited. Kelly heeded the advice and put all recruiters on fixed salaries in the next budget.[10]

Faculty-related concerns included the need to increase the proportion of faculty holding terminal degrees, a problem inherent in the recent move from a junior college to a baccalaureate institution. The report called the general education requirements at the college "ineffective and not comparable with criteria and standards generally accepted . . . in the United States nor with some of the institutionally-stated goals." However, the report noted that general education nationally was showing only "the first signs of emerging from the doldrums into which of recent years it has fallen," and the college was still evolving in this matter. The team considered teaching loads excessive, the library budget inadequate, and the faculty still not filling their proper role in governance. It also deplored a "retrenchment" in liberal arts offerings: "The Humanities do not possess the critical mass of faculty necessary to carry the responsibilities they ought to have in a Bachelor of Arts degree granting institution, and they have in addition a monitoring function which the home campus is beginning to provide the Extended Studies programs."[11]

Regarding the Extended Studies Division, the team urged more control by home campus faculty over course content and library usage. It also faulted the program, in something of a surprise, for not showing "adequate substantial intellectual exchange and all elements of cultural and social growth commonly related to collegiate education"—a need not commonly associated with adult education. The report issued a stern warning: "The management of an off-campus program, which ranges from Florida to Washington and New York to California, when that administration and faculty have serious on-campus difficulties to resolve, may present an unmanageable problem." On the positive side, experiential learning procedures were found to follow general recommendations of the Council for the Advancement of Experiential Learning, with better controls coming into place.[12]

Strengths were just as wide-ranging. The report took note of a renewed confidence in the administration by the Board of Trustees, faculty, and students and recognized improved communications. It praised the equity adjustment for women, good leadership in the financial area, substantial improvements in the plant and grounds, consortiums for library use at ESD sites, and development of a four-year business program. The report commented favorably on some aspects of the Extended Studies Division: its integration into the total college program under the control of the dean of faculty, faculty review of the ESD faculty and instruction, the elimination of weaker sites, and improved evaluation of experiential learning. The report described students at off-campus sites as "upwardly mobile, high-achieving, moderately able . . . and highly appreciative of their opportunity and determined to make the most of it."[13]

Immediate results of the April visitation were encouraging, and evaluators "sounded very favorable toward Columbia College" at the exit interview. The report recommended continued accreditation, including all off-campus sites, with the next evaluation to come in three years. It stipulated that annual reports be sent to the North Central Association by July 1, 1979, and July 1, 1980. Those reports were to demonstrate significant progress in three areas of serious concern: completing the transition from a two-year to a four-year institution, ensuring minimum standards for the Extended Studies sites, and achieving appropriate fiscal planning and management, faculty compensation and benefits, and independence of the Columbia College campus from Extended Studies funds. At no point did the report fault the academic program or the teaching performance of the home campus.[14]

When the Commission on Institutions considered the report at its summer meeting on July 24, 1978, it agreed to the stipulations of the visiting team on improvements needed, continuation of accreditation for a three-year period, and limitation of Extended Studies sites to the ones operating at that time. However, to the shock of all constituencies of the college, the commission recommended to the executive board that the institution be placed on public probation for the three-year period until the next review. Although the college did meet criteria for accreditation, the commission based its action on the continuing concerns of present and prior teams and on the history and nature of the problems. The action, above all, would serve as guidelines for the next review.[15]

If the problems facing the college seemed severe early in 1978, the announcement of public probation greatly exacerbated the institution's troubles. On-campus day enrollments, standing at 1,033 in 1977 and 1,055 in 1978, plunged to 842 in 1979 and 807 in 1980. Foley reported to the October 20, 1978, board meeting that Extended Studies income had fallen $844,223 with the closing of nine locations. By January 19, 1979, board records showed a drop in income from $8,424,000 in 1977 to $7,001,000 in 1978, with a projected income of $6,790,000 for 1979.[16]

Nevertheless, the college, in what may have been its lowest period since the depression of the 1930s, rose to the occasion in one of the finest achievements of its history. Stunned by the unexpected action, all constituencies of the institution acted decisively and effectively, refusing to accept the onus of public probation for the allotted three-year period. In action after action, faculty and administration attacked the concerns of the 1978 report and acted on recommendations of the North Central Association to turn the situation around in nine short months. Friends rallied to help the college, as in the case of University of Missouri chancellor emeritus Herbert Schooling, who volunteered to help resolve the North Central concerns.[17]

Issue after issue came under examination with swift results. Board action in October targeted the need to increase terminal degrees among faculty by providing that, for the next three years, sabbaticals be given only to faculty members pursuing such degrees. That same month, faculty approved a statement on the meaning of a baccalaureate degree in higher education. The statement emphasized: development of both written and spoken language skills; general education requirements amounting to no less than one-fourth of the total hours; development of precise, critical, analytical thought and of the ability to adapt to change; development of philosophical and moral values; and a planned, upward progression of learning.[18]

Faculty approved three proposals to strengthen academic requirements within all majors: all departments offering a major must require at least twenty-seven hours in the major, with fifteen of these being at the upper-division level; all departments must require that at least twelve hours toward the major be earned at Columbia College, with at least six hours in upper-division course work; and all departments must require that at least one-half of any major requirement be earned in the classroom. Faculty also tightened requirements for academic bankruptcy, allowing a student to petition for such relief only once in an academic career. In addition, new general education requirements passed by the board in May 1979 would go into effect on January 1, 1980. They included six credit hours of English composition, fifteen hours of social and behavioral sciences in three disciplines, twelve hours of humanities in two disciplines, and six hours of natural science and mathematics in two disciplines. All general education courses must be in areas outside the major, selected from an approved list.[19]

Faculty action also dealt with the Extended Studies Division, adjusting guidelines for students to participate in graduation with honors to the time frame of the Extended Studies program. Also, a particularly significant step forward came with action by the Curriculum Committee and the full faculty to establish criteria for creating new sites or reviewing existing sites. Creation by Kelly of an Extended Studies Sites Committee composed of faculty, administration, and staff provided a vehicle for application of the following criteria: evidence of a valid educational objective at the location; an adequate supply of students; sufficient local resources, financial support, and government structure; legal authorization; and institutional approval.[20]

In an attempt to improve the college's financial base, administrators trimmed the on-campus curriculum, cutting French, geology, instrumental music, and majors in dance and drama. Kelly also convinced the board to cut the number of associate directors of admissions, once a total of thirteen, to three in the field and three in the home office. Intended as a cost-saving action, this counterproductive move would cost the college a well-established network for locating prospective students that had been nurtured over many years.[21]

Another administrative move, the drafting of a five-year plan, responded to a North Central recommendation that the college engage in institutional planning. However, the lack of faculty involvement brought strong negative reactions to the plan's top-down approach and to the radical nature of its changes. The document, formulated at the request of the president, was the work of Tim Donovan, an unsalaried University of Missouri intern in institutional planning who had retired after a military career. In providing options to make the college financially stable, Donovan proposed "the transition of the college from a four-year liberal arts college to an adult institution with emphasis on occupational training." Criticized by the *Columbia Daily Tribune* as the "virtual abandonment of liberal arts studies," the plan provided for year-round operation with eight-week "minimesters," creating an adult education and seminar center either with no residential students or with residence halls operated as motels by students in a hotel-motel management program. The food service would be used to train students in a food management program.

Although Kelly emphasized that "any actual changes would not be unilateral but would entail further study by the faculty and administration," the faculty's shock at the revelation of the plan indicated a serious communication gap. The *Columbia College Columbian,* the 1979 successor to the *Microphone,* faulted the administration for its failure to utilize faculty knowledge. The plan may have been mere speculation, but it came to represent the first step toward more serious breaches between administration and faculty on issues of the faculty's role in curricular planning and the possible abandonment of the college's liberal arts emphasis.[22]

Although the North Central Association had stipulated that the college complete its first progress report by July 1, 1979, administrators requested that the first report be received by the association in April. They further requested that the on-site visit, due in three years, be scheduled in May of the first year, permitting early removal of the probationary status at the July 1979 meetings. North Central agreed to the dramatically escalated review, setting May 7–9, 1979, for a focused visit on the 1978 concerns. The team would monitor progress made since April 1978, consider any new concerns, and recommend whether to remove the probationary status from the college's accreditation.[23]

The 1979 team found very little in the way of new concerns and reported good progress in redressing the 1978 issues. The team report criticized inadequate staffing in development, citing the hiring of "an experienced and able chief development officer as an absolute necessity." It also expressed concern "that the liberal arts and fine arts elements of the mission have lost appropriate emphasis." It suggested: "If the shift away from liberal and fine arts should continue, appropriate changes should be made both in the college's definition of the baccalaureate degree and in its own statement of institutional purpose."[24]

In a report distinctly sympathetic in tone, the 1979 team responded to the concerns raised by the 1978 review, issue by issue, showing the college's satisfactory performance, especially in academic areas. They found good progress toward increasing library holdings and in the operation of the library and computer center, which had "improved rather remarkably over the last year." They also expressed satisfaction in faculty acquisition of terminal degrees, recognizing that the process would take time. The team viewed the new general education requirements and the statement on the meaning of a baccalaureate degree as "a step in the right direction." They concluded that "excellent progress" had been made in the area of general education and that the college was completing the transition to a baccalaureate institution. They examined upper-class course content and held discussions with faculty members, concluding that it was essential for those faculty with commitment to the traditional academic disciplines to "continue to bring expertise to bear" on curricular matters. In reference to administrative plans to eliminate dance and drama and to reduce intercollegiate athletics, the team warned: "Further reductions, especially in the arts and humanities, will push Columbia further toward a vocational rather than a liberal arts orientation and probably will prove counter-productive as regards enrollment."[25]

Indeed, the report expressed unqualified support for the academic program, confirming that its quality had not been an issue in the 1978 action:

> There was little or no criticism in the 1978 report of the academic program itself. Discussions with faculty and students and review of committee reports all suggest that Columbia students are receiving an education of good quality, especially on campus in Columbia. The performance of faculty and students in the context of an academic program of improved quality is fundamental to the team's judgment that institutional purposes *are* being realized.[26]

In all other areas, the team found further compliance with North Central standards. They described the promotional literature and admissions program as "efficient, effective, and entirely forthright in presenting the College to its publics" and saw the administration as highly collegial with widespread support. The financial area also received approval: "Columbia has made significant progress in addressing the financial management concerns contained in the 1978 NCA report. . . . [The] present system is quite sophisticated and provides for considerable faculty knowledge and participation." The report called the computer system "inefficient" but disagreed with the 1978 team's judgment that it was "inadequate."[27]

As usual, the team paid great attention to the Extended Studies Division. They commended the closer ties between site personnel and on-campus faculty that allowed faculty to be involved in "recruitment, screening, and appointment of site directors and adjunct faculty as well as in sending of syllabi and recommended textbook lists." It noted that the *Standard Operating Manual* for the Extended Studies Division "codifies organization and functioning, defines the relationship between Extended Studies Division sites and the Columbia campus, and specifies responsibility for processing forms, student records, and reports." The team was "satisfied that general management is much improved. . . . Positive initiatives have been taken to bring ESD under proper control of on-campus faculty and administrators." The report also replied to the concern of the 1978 team relating to elements of cultural and social growth commonly related to a collegiate education: "The nature and objectives of adult students differ markedly from those of 18–22 year olds and it might not be appropriate or necessary for adult degree programs to provide significant cultural and social comparability. . . . The college has made considerable progress toward an appropriate definition and implementation of its ES program."[28]

Stating that the college had responded well to the 1978 stipulations, the report concluded: "The College has successfully weathered difficult times before, has met new conditions in flexible fashion, and has evolved over the years in constructive ways. Vulnerability to external forces is no more extreme than with most small private colleges with few endowment resources." With all criteria "fully met," the team recommended removal of probationary status. They suggested that the next comprehensive evaluation come in the fall of 1981 with a report on the college's financial condition to be made September 1, 1980, followed by an on-site evaluation no later than December 1, 1980; accreditation would continue for a maximum of thirty-six sites. This time, the recommendations were accepted by the Commission on Institutions of Higher Education, and Thurston Manning, director of the commission, notified President Kelly on July 31, 1981, that the three-year probationary status was cut short by more than two years.[29]

In 1980, the college experienced a financial turnaround as well. Fortune smiled on the college in the person of Virginia Southwell Singletary, an alumna who had come to the college as a student in 1937 and who remained a loyal supporter throughout her life. In June 1977, Singletary contributed $150,000 for "Southy Building," an athletic complex dedicated to John N. Singletary, her recently deceased husband. As a trustee, Singletary watched the college scrape through the lean years of the late 1970s, never abandoning her faith in its mission. She agreed in April 1980 to contribute $1 million, the largest amount in the history of the college, making the first of six payments later the same month. The college announced the gift at a press conference on May 9, 1980:

> After having weathered a stormy decade that saw the transition of the school from two-year to four-year, from all women to coeducational, from a dwindling to a stabilized enrollment, from accreditation concern to academic solidarity, and from deficit to balanced budgeting, the Columbia College community was ready for a bit of smooth sailing. Mrs. Singletary's extraordinary gesture was exactly the breath of fresh air the school needed to unfurl its sails proudly.[30]

A faculty resolution expressed appreciation for the gift: "That the faculty applaud the financial commitment demonstrated by the generous gift of $1,000,000 by Mrs. Virginia Singletary. We appreciate her realistic grasp of the problems facing small, private colleges, and her leadership in meeting these realities . . . toward an increasingly high quality of education for our students."[31]

Singletary's gift resulted not only from her abiding loyalty to the college but also from her close relationship to her cousin, trustee and alumna Marty Toler, and her confidence in Marvin Owens as chairman of the board's Finance Committee. Atkins later described that influence:

> We give full credit to Virginia Singletary, but I don't think too much can be said about the support that Marty Toler gave . . . on our behalf. . . . If Marty hadn't had faith in us, I guarantee that Virginia Singletary wouldn't come up with a million dollars and continue to do more. . . . Virginia Singletary had complete confidence in Marv Owens and she felt . . . if she gave a million dollars to Marv Owens, the college would spend that million dollars and make it worth probably two, which he did.

Testimony to the value of Owens as a trustee, going far beyond the Singletary event, came years later from fellow trustee Don Schubert: "The real reason that Columbia College still exists today is Marvin Owens. . . . He has respect near to awe. . . . I think probably today that more of our board members understand what it really takes to operate a college than most boards of directors because of what Marvin has done.[32]

In addition to the 1980 pledge, Singletary in 1983 made a challenge gift and traveled widely to help recruit other donors. Toler recounted the circumstances of that gift:

> Virginia agreed to make a challenge gift which she intended to be a quarter of a million dollars in addition to the million that she had already given earlier. She was not able to be in Columbia to attend the dinner to kick off a fundraising campaign, so she agreed to tape a message to the board, and, bless her heart, she announced a gift of three-quarters of a million. It was not what she had meant to say. Anyway, she didn't rescind it, which was another nice windfall.[33]

The college also benefited in 1980 from two federal sources. Still developing a four-year curriculum, it received a Strengthening Developing Institutions Program Grant (SDIP) from the United States Department of Education to support the Learning Skills Center. Also, a loan of $343,000 from the Department of Housing and Urban Development allowed renovation of the heating plant, dining hall, and dormitories to reduce energy consumption. The work would increase the efficiency of the heating plant by 31 to 50 percent.[34]

Although financial restrictions prevented construction of new buildings on campus, physical plant changes continued. With Merle Hill and Bill Brown gone, their two college-owned homes became available. The house on Vegas Drive, occupied by Hill, was sold in the summer of 1977, and Kelly moved into a recently acquired presidential home on South Country Club Drive. A partial gift, the property was sold to the college by trustee Andy Bass at a greatly reduced price. The former president's home near campus, occupied by Brown when the Hills moved to Vegas Drive, became the Jane Froman Center, the new location for the music department. The new quarters allowed space for twelve practice rooms, a classroom, a chamber room, a recital room, offices, and fifteen pianos. The ground floor of Williams Hall, formerly used by the music department, housed the public relations, alumni, and development offices, as well as a conference room. The business department moved into the second floor of Williams Hall.[35]

In other property transactions, the college sold the off-campus location of the Extended Studies Division offices in October 1978 to KMIZ-TV, the ABC affiliate in Columbia, for $287,500 in cash plus $12,500 in advertising over a five-year period. The college thus integrated the ESD administrators into campus surroundings by housing the program in the newly furnished basement area of the Robnett-Spence Health Center while divesting itself of an unnecessary building. The Hertig, Estes, and Kirkman houses on Christian College Avenue (Tenth Street) adjacent to campus, which had been used to house upper-class students but were no longer needed as residence halls, were rented to local concerns. The Missouri Water Patrol used the Hertig and Estes houses for personnel attending classes at the University of Missouri–Columbia, making use also of Gerard Pool. The Kirkman house on the southeast corner of Rogers and Tenth Streets was later sold. With the drama program no longer part of the curriculum, the administration rented partial use of Launer Auditorium to the Columbia Entertainment Company, sharing the space with college programs. The college also sold a house at 802 North Eighth Street formerly used by the sociology department—a property needing extensive repair. The sociology faculty moved to the second floor of St. Clair Hall, no longer used for student housing. Thus, faculty offices and seminar rooms expanded to include the whole second floor of St. Clair. The use of the building for student housing ended entirely the next year when the third floor also changed from residential space to offices and classrooms for travel administration and fashion.[36]

One of the more significant changes during Kelly's administration came with the May 1980 board meeting when David Rogers became chairman, replacing B. D. Simon. Simon had diligently guided the college through the evolution from a junior college for women and had exercised extreme vigilance as the Extended Studies Division grew. He had been on the board since 1963, acting as chairman since 1972, and would continue as a much respected trustee until 1990. Rogers had come to the board in 1972, proving to be a valuable trustee in the last years of the Hill administration. His wife, Genie Banks Rogers, was the daughter of Hartley Banks, the revered board chairman from 1948 to 1972. Her great-great-uncle was Joseph Kirtley Rogers, third president of Christian College, who guided the college through the Civil War era. David Rogers thus continued the century-old family ties with the college. He would remain as chairman for two years before ending his decade as a trustee in 1982 and passing the chairmanship to Tom Atkins. Remaining as chairman for sixteen years, Atkins would become one of the most successful board chairmen in the college's history.[37]

Some of the more active trustees continuing from the Hill years were Andy Bass, Marvin Owens, Elizabeth Gentry, Leta Spencer, Virginia Singletary, Walter E. Bixby Jr., Peggy Price, and Charles Koelling. The board added a total of twenty-four new members during the Kelly presidency, and those members still active at the end of the twentieth century were Don Schubert, Marvin Owens, Marty Toler, and Daisy Grossnickle. L. V. Mike Angelo served until his death in 1999. Schubert, whose wife, Sandra, taught in the fashion department, became one of the most active additions to development and other committees, including the executive committee. Angelo and Toler, whose son and daughter-in-law, respectively, attended the college, gave important service on the Finance Committee, and Toler also served as vice president of the board. Richard Rathgeb carried on the Hartley Banks tradition as a representative of the First Bank of Commerce, by then called Centerre Bank. Jack Estes, son of alumna and former trustee Evelyn Estes, and James Oglesby performed invaluable service as chairmen of the selection committee for a new president in 1984. Oglesby, assistant provost for administration at the University of Missouri–Columbia, and William Bradshaw, of the university medical school faculty, continued the University of Missouri ties to the college. The Reverend Sam Langley became the traditional Christian Church trustee. Another continuing trustee, Daisy Grossnickle, would send daughters to the college. Especially helpful for his legal advice, Robert Roper had earlier served as the college's lawyer.[38]

As the college ended the 1979–1980 academic year, trustees went on record praising Kelly "for an excellent year": "He has led all constituents of the College through a traumatic period and maintained the spirit of cooperation and loyalty in the staff, faculty, and students." A black budget, a $788,000 turnaround from the previous year, resulted from the Singletary gift and savings in expenditures in all areas.[39]

With conditions apparently improving, the North Central focused visit of November 20–21, 1980, went well. Along with the balanced budget, the Singletary gift and lesser bequests had reduced financial reliance on the Extended Studies Division. In addition, the college expected Title III grant money of $59,000 to finance a long-range planning activity, a learning resources center, and a communication skills center. Also, administrators hoped that removal of the probationary status would lead to increased enrollment despite the sharp reduction in off-campus admissions counselors. Even the North Central team expressed belief that removal of the probationary status would lead to increased enrollment. Impressed by the college's accomplishments, evaluators found "a general sense of community, even while the college is operating on an austerity budget basis. . . . The faculty members at Columbia College display remarkable dedication to the institution." The team's brief report commended the college for the balanced budget, a more productive development effort, administrative reorganization, and improved fiscal management controls. It recommended that the next comprehensive review come in the fall of 1982, giving the college time to implement institutional changes.[40]

Faculty members welcomed a new dean in March 1980 when Jerry Harris, formerly of the English department at Pikeville College, in Pikeville, Kentucky, replaced acting dean Kay Kanger. However, Harris and the faculty would soon wage an impassioned battle on major issues. Harris's decision to take attendance at faculty meetings caused only slight annoyance, and the new policy of requiring all full-time faculty to accept teaching duties in the Evening College "in the best interests of the college" was reasonably well received.[41]

By 1981, however, faculty members found themselves at odds with the chairman of the Board of Trustees. A controversy began in January 1981 when Rogers announced a restructuring of board committees that would prohibit faculty trustees from serving on the board's Educational Policy Committee—a committee on which faculty had considerable expertise to offer and much at stake. Instead, faculty trustees were reassigned to the Alumni-Constituency Coordinating Committee. Rogers argued that faculty trustees might also be serving on the Tenure, Review, and Promotion Council or on the Academic Affairs Committee, giving them dual representation if they also served on an academic committee of the board. Such a justification carried little weight with the faculty, who pointed out their practice of avoiding such situations when choosing the elected faculty trustees. So strong was faculty sentiment that faculty members "overwhelmingly" passed a rare resolution of protest for transmittal to the board: "We recommend the elected faculty trustees be restored to membership on the Educational Policy Committee of the Board of Trustees and be granted membership on one other major committee of the Board. It is further recommended that the elected faculty trustees be included in appropriate executive sessions of the Board of Trustees."[42]

Having received no reply by the fall of 1981, the faculty "passed overwhelmingly a resolution of regret that there was no response by the Chairman of the Board in last week's Board of Trustees meeting to the resolution passed by the faculty last spring." With still no response, faculty on March 30, 1982, unanimously passed a considerably sharper resolution. Referring to the earlier resolution and lack of response, the new resolution pointedly called attention to the fact that "lack of proper attention to faculty governance has been an expressed concern of past North Central Association teams, a concern that should be addressed before the fall, 1982, NCA visitation." It reminded the trustees that the faculty trustees had been assigned to the Educational Policy Committee of the board "from the beginning" and could also "make equally meaningful contributions to the Finance Committee and in executive sessions, which they have previously attended." It concluded, "Be It Therefore Resolved: that this resolution of most urgent concern be transmitted as swiftly as possible to the President of the College and hence to the Chairman of the Board of Trustees requesting the return of faculty trustees to the Educational Policy Committee as of the May, 1982, meeting."[43]

Rogers appeared at the next faculty meeting, on April 21, 1982, standing firm on his decision of January 1981, saying it "has traditionally been the prerogative of the chairman to decide what committees people serve on." He "advised the faculty of his opinion that the resolution might have a divisive impact" if it went to the Board at the May meeting. He asked the faculty to "reconsider sending it." At that point, "Mr. Jack Batterson and Mr. Sidney Larson both announced to the faculty their intention to resign from the Board of Trustees." The faculty then voted "to submit the original resolution [of March 30, 1982] regarding faculty trustees to the Board as a whole at the May Board meeting."[44]

Reporting to the board at the May 14, 1982, meeting, Rogers stated that he had "discussed [his] position with several other members of the Board and agreed to new committee assignments." The two faculty trustees, elected at the April 21 faculty meeting to replace Batterson and Larson, who refused reelection, were Helga Huang, assigned to the Educational Policy Committee, and Gary Maddox, assigned to the Finance Committee. The faculty at their May 19, 1982, meeting passed a resolution "expressing their heartfelt appreciation of the Board of Trustees' sensitivity to faculty concerns and recommendations as evidenced by their reinstatement of a faculty representative on one major committee of the Board of Trustees and the expansion of the faculty's role on two other major committees."[45]

Such action by a faculty, clearly outside the norms of collegial relationships, resulted from an extraordinary situation. Although the college had produced its second black budget by the summer of 1981, decreasing short-term borrowing from $839,000 the previous year to $300,000, Kelly predicted a bleak future. According to the president, the paradox of high inflation and high interest rates, resulting in decreasing profits and a stagnant economy, would combine with a decrease in college-age population to bring a crisis in higher education. He therefore instructed his planning assistant, Roger Fritz, to draft a plan for financial exigency. What had been the administrative council became under Kelly the Executive Management Staff (EMS), a group created to monitor a long-range plan and the institution's progress. Kelly had already formed a Long-Range Planning Committee (LRPC) in November 1979 consisting of some faculty along with administrators, but it would clearly play a lesser role than EMS in the planning process, leaving little opportunity for faculty input.[46]

The final draft of a financial exigency plan, distributed to EMS on June 17, 1981, would allow the president to initiate retrenchment actions to *avoid* a state of financial exigency. It empowered him to eliminate administrative or development programs, reduce courses and part-time or nontenured faculty, modify staff benefits, or eliminate academic programs. Although he would notify the Academic Affairs Committee in writing and consider their recommendation, the faculty would have only a reactive and advisory role.[47]

As dean of faculty, Harris reinforced Kelly's prediction of bad times ahead. Referring to "the best of times and the worst of times," he recognized that the college was in its "best financial condition for a long time" with short-term debt the lowest in five years and two years of a black budget. However, the situation he projected sounded nothing short of desperate. He pointed to diminishing student enrollments, overdependence on tuition, and the population decline of college-age students, concluding that the causes of the college's "impending crisis have been exacerbated by the weak national economy, the present sharp reversal in federal support for higher education, and changes in federal tax laws which have resulted from the election of Ronald Reagan as President of the United States." Working within EMS, Harris reported that a "triple focus plan is by far the best idea we have been able to develop." He made his report to Kelly on December 4, 1981: "We believe that Columbia College can come to consist of three distinct units—each with a sharply focused mission, a separate faculty to carry it out, separate standards and graduation requirements, a separate tuition and fee structure, and to some extent, a separate set of sources of gift and grant support. Nevertheless, these units would share the same central administration and central physical facilities."[48]

The plan proposed three colleges. One would be a career-oriented college (Evening College and the Extended Studies Division), taught in eight-week "minimesters" and consisting of such programs as business administration, computer science, education, fashion, and social work. This "college" would have an "upside down curriculum," in that the students would complete course requirements for their major before taking any general education courses. The second college would be a "no frills" liberal arts and sciences college with "no fancy buildings but a rigorous program for a small elite group of students for whom the college could compete with Ivy League institutions." Finally, there would be a certificate-granting art institute whose students could enroll in the liberal arts college for a B.A. degree. According to Harris, the plan would "divide what is already a small college into three smaller colleges. . . . We believe this is a logical evolution from the institution's history and its historic emphasis on personalized higher education." It would provide "something for virtually everyone." The three separate colleges would take the names of major donors.[49]

Harris developed a detailed schedule of how each "college" would evolve over the next five years, complete with specific figures for projected enrollments, revenues, and expenditures through 1987–1988. Although the original purpose of the exercise had been to deal with possible financial exigency in the coming crisis, both Harris and Kelly acknowledged that the plan would be "costly," requiring a deficit budget. According to Harris, "How these deficits would be financed has not been discussed to any great extent by LRPC." Nevertheless, he anticipated a "total transition related surplus by 1986–1987 of $692,220."[50]

In a related "Confidential Working Paper," Harris elaborated on the fate of the college's various majors: "Major programs which do not fit well with the career orientation of the new mission as well as career-oriented programs which are weak in enrollment must be cut. . . . Our current liberal arts and sciences offerings must be significantly reduced, and our future offerings in these areas must serve primarily as general education, as upper-level electives, or as a specific support for other majors." In this framework, he would continue art, business administration, travel administration, criminal justice administration, education, and fashion as majors. He would abolish majors in English, history/government, music, psychology, public administration, and social work, as well as the bachelor of fine arts degree. He would add diploma programs in art, accounting, and data processing, along with an interdisciplinary, catchall "liberal studies" major to replace history/government, English, and psychology.[51]

The administration reported to the board at a special meeting on February 23, 1982: "[With] the college in probably the best financial situation it has been in many years, the institution is now staring at probably the worst of times based on enrollment probabilities and federal financial aid confusion." The black budget of the last two years had been achieved by cutting programs, decreasing faculty and staff, foregoing salary increases, using part-time personnel, decreasing services, and deferring maintenance. Enrollment in the fall of 1981 had declined to 774 total students in the day program on campus, and further decline was expected. With the economy bordering on depression, gift income would likely go down. Harris's report set forth five options for the college. Option 1 was to go along with business as usual, and option 5 was to close the college, leaving three reasonably serious options. Option 2 would create a career college with new majors and an eight-week format, bringing the day campus in line with the Extended Studies Division and Evening College. The addition of an M.B.A. would appeal to working adults. It would also be possible to add degree programs in computer science, data processing, and accounting. Admittedly, the college would likely lose undecided and liberal arts and fine arts students. Liberal arts courses would be limited to those subjects servicing the general education component, and there would be a decrease in liberal arts faculty. Although there would be no athletic program, recreational and wellness resources would be available. Option 3, a commuter career college, would provide the same curriculum as the career college but with noncredit courses on weekends and some residential provisions, offering child care and emphasizing a placement program. Option 4 was Harris's choice, the triple-focus college already described in his December report to Kelly.[52]

Kelly wrote to the trustees the day after the special meeting to thank them for attending and again pressed home his concerns: "If 80% of the eighteen-year olds finish high school and 38% of those go to college, as is the case today, the net drop in college students on United States campuses over this decade could be as much as one million. That would be like eliminating two hundred colleges of 2,000 each."[53]

While administrators concentrated on the planning options, the Long-Range Planning Committee had been assigned the task of preparing an application for a Title III grant. Finally, at the April 1, 1982, meeting of the LRPC, faculty representatives on the committee began to suspect that an administrative "contingency plan" was being formulated and nearing completion. Those representatives immediately called for a special faculty meeting to be convened as soon as possible so that they and other faculty members might be informed of any such plan. On April 8, faculty representatives of the LRPC were presented with the fully developed sixteen-page "plan," largely the work of Harris, and a similar presentation was made to all faculty at the special meeting five hours later. At that meeting, both Harris and Foster confirmed that no faculty member had been involved in devising the plan.[54]

There followed a plethora of individual and joint communications from various faculty members to Harris, attempting to dissuade him from his intent to eliminate liberal arts majors or any other majors. A plea urging the continuation of the social work program went on to consider the impact of administrative action:

> What frightens us professionally is that there apparently are administrators and will be Board members who believe that a college which they can believe in and sweat for can emerge from this plan. . . . Since we were not privy to the deliberations which resulted in this plan, we cannot comment on professional judgment other than to note that mechanistic methods . . . do not take into account the probable negative impact on the very people who will need to be at peak efficiency physically and emotionally if the solution is to be implemented.

Social work faculty further expressed frustration that no amount of information provided by them had seemed to have any impact: "Throughout the year, the Social Work faculty has provided data to LRPC, Academic Affairs, and EMS in response to every system which has been currently in vogue for evaluation. It is difficult to hit a moving target."[55]

In one of the most thorough responses, Jack Batterson first took Harris to task for intransigence and then argued for the continuation of a liberal arts college:

> You have shown no indication of amending in any way your initial proposal. Nor does the proposal itself show any evidence of the mountain of data, documentation, and recommendations provided to you by faculty members since October 1981. . . . If we are to maintain our collegiate character as an institution, amidst our career emphasis, we must maintain at least a minimum number of liberal arts majors. . . . It would be difficult to call ourselves a *College* if we offered any fewer liberal arts majors than at present. I believe that a collegiate character for the institution is essential if we are to attract students, traditional or non-traditional, to our present and future career programs. They want to attend a *College*.[56]

Batterson noted the high quality of instruction and student achievement in the liberal arts majors and the increasing enrollments, especially in history/government, at the same time that total institutional enrollment was declining rapidly. To indicate that Harris's objection to liberal arts majors was not based on practical considerations, Batterson noted that, in the previous eight semesters, full-time Columbia College enrollments had gone down 32 percent, whereas history/government enrollments had enjoyed a 16 percent increase. Although Harris aimed at increasing the student-faculty ratio to at least 15:1, or maybe 17:1, the history/government ratio was 21:1, whereas the institutional ratio was 14:1. Batterson also noted that removing the last three liberal arts majors (English, history/government, and psychology), which were only three of the fourteen majors currently offered, would save little or no money as the faculty would be needed to teach general education and upper-level elective courses—courses that could also continue to support the major. Arguing for liberal arts, Batterson quoted Peter W. Stanley, dean of Carlton College, from an article in the journal of the Association of Governing Boards of Universities and Colleges:

> The Liberal Arts prepare a kind of person needed by our society, economy, and political culture; and well-meaning attempts to water it down and make it more "relevant" or practical weaken its reason for being. There are all sorts of good vocational schools, graduate schools, and industrial training programs that can develop practical and salable skills in their students, but no other institution in American society that can train balanced, mature, and wise future leaders as effectively as the liberal arts college. Just as liberal arts dare not turn its back on the world of realities, that world ought not to warp this distinctive form of education out of shape, lest in doing so it purchase a modest gain at the cost of a major national resource.[57]

The history/government program presented an especially effective defense. One item in the war of words was a letter from Missouri lieutenant governor Kenneth Rothman to President Kelly on April 13, 1982:

> I have read recently with concern articles in the Columbia *Missourian* and *Tribune* describing contingency plans to eliminate majors in several fields at Columbia College to include History/Government and English. I have had a long-term association with students of your College and have been impressed with their contribution to state government. While I served as Speaker of the House, the legislative assistant program at Columbia College provided a valuable learning experience for your students as well as making a valuable contribution to the legislative process. . . . In my opinion, state and local governments are viable career opportunities that will always be in the market for individuals with degrees in History/Government, English, and other related degree programs. As a matter of fact, we are looking forward to Bill Sword joining our full-time staff upon completion of his degree this May.[58]

Following a request from Penny Braun for more time for faculty to respond to the Harris plan, Kelly received permission from Rogers to delay until April 19 the deadline for mailing materials to the trustees for their May meeting. However, with no possibility for a coherent faculty plan in so little time, the faculty could do little more than argue the weakness of Harris's plan, a work that had been months in the making. Harris acknowledged, "It is highly unlikely that the administration can present [faculty responses] and expect a favorable response from the Board."[59]

What faculty members could and did do was use the faculty meeting of April 21, 1982, to try to convince the board that the traditional role of the faculty had been violated and unwisely so. Statements relayed at that meeting from the American Council of Education and the American Association of University Professors reinforced the faculty's determination to protect its role. The American Council of Education, a prestigious association of colleges and universities, had offered one perspective: "If the faculty has approved degrees and majors in the past, it is a part of the established role. If there are channels through which such decisions may be made and the present policy by-passes established channels, it is indeed extraordinary." According to the American Association of University Professors, "faculty have the primary although not exclusive control over the development of curriculum. To change majors and degrees is not common without meaningful faculty participation before the decision is made, not after. It is not fair to put faculty in the situation of having to react to a plan already developed. It is most unfortunate not to go through established committees."

Following discussion of the problems involved, the faculty passed by separate secret-ballot votes a five-part resolution to be forwarded to the board. The first resolution deplored the absence of any formal participation by teaching faculty in the development of the Harris plan and protested the "de facto usurpation of faculty duties and responsibilities" by a vote of twenty-five to eight with one abstention. The second resolution, seeking to protect the principle that "all curricular content of any proposed contingency plan is subject to its recommendation," passed twenty-eight to five with one abstention. The third, disapproving of the proposed plan itself, especially to "its specific curricular content and attendant consequences," passed twenty-six to nine with one abstention. The fourth deplored the "lack of adequate consideration and/or effective representation of teaching faculty concerns and values," passing twenty-four to ten. Finally, the request that the vote count on each resolution be transmitted to the president as well as to the board through its Educational Policy Committee passed by a vote of twenty-six to six with one abstention.[60]

It was at this same April 21, 1982, faculty meeting that Rogers appeared to express his intention to hold firm on his decision to remove faculty trustees from the Educational Policy Committee of the board and to advise the faculty against sending their strongly written resolution on that subject to the board. As a result of the meeting, both resolutions went to the board, the five-part response to EMS amounting to an overwhelming vote of no confidence in the academic dean. Thus, the faculty tied the resolution concerning board committee membership for faculty trustees to accompanying events, namely, lack of any opportunity for faculty trustees to be present for discussion of the Harris plan at the meeting of the Educational Policy Committee of the board. Yet another statement sent by the faculty to the board on May 12, 1982, illustrated the intensity of faculty distress and the seriousness of the split between the faculty and the administration:

> Despite news articles, announcements, memoranda to the contrary, the faculty representatives on the Long Range Planning Committee re-asserts [*sic*] that

> the role of the corporate faculty in devising contingency plans and recommendations to the Board was usurped, not abdicated. Procedures for faculty governance are clear through tradition, through documents available from AAUP and ACE, and through files on this campus. Those procedures were not followed, nor would the faculty even have seen the contingency plans had not the LRPC faculty representatives insisted. . . . The interpretations presented by sundry are hereby denied.[61]

When Kelly conveyed the numerous communications to Rogers on April 22, 1982, his accompanying memo was the closest he came to showing lack of support for Harris. Trying still to remain above the fray, he took no position on the vital issues but did indicate the dangers of the Harris plan: "If any contingency plan results in the loss of jobs for employees at the College, the Board could be faced with: 1. litigation; 2. demoralization of faculty and staff; 3. potential loss of students; 4. potential loss of income; 5. potential loss of gifts and other revenue; and 6. adverse publicity." Removing himself from any role in the decision-making process, Kelly concluded: "All of us look forward to the guidance of the Board."[62]

Yet another major issue, the adoption of a more career-oriented mission statement, was to go before the board at its May 14, 1982, meeting. Here again, the split between the faculty and the administration became evident. Two administratively sanctioned mission statements went to the faculty for its May 12, 1982, meeting. One was a statement for Columbia College as a "triple-focus" institution, whereas the other envisioned a "more emphatically career oriented institution." Because neither statement included guaranteed protection for any liberal arts major, Polly Batterson offered a third statement, a portion of which included such protection: "Career and pre-professional programs of superior quality and selected liberal arts and sciences majors are offered in a traditional college environment and in other locations across the country."

Faculty first, by a vote of twenty-nine to seven, eliminated the "triple-focus" mission statement from consideration. Voting on the two remaining statements, the faculty voted twenty-five to ten to recommend to the board the faculty-generated mission statement over the administratively sanctioned statement. Board action rejected the faculty version for "selected liberal arts and sciences majors" and adopted a shortened version of the administrative alternative as the college's new mission statement. The contested section read: "By offering career and pre-professional programs based upon and integrated with the liberal arts and sciences, Columbia College seeks to educate as well as train minds both for entry level positions in occupations and for later growth in their chosen fields, including graduate school."[63]

Although the May 14 board meeting resolved the mission-statement controversy, the decision on elimination of specific degree majors was yet to come. A frenzy of faculty meetings after the end of the academic year continued throughout the rest of May. Faculty members of liberal arts majors slated by Harris for possible elimination (B.A. degrees in English, history/government, and social work, and the B.F.A. degree in art) mounted defenses in a series of tense meetings. Meanwhile, other faculty committees continued to meet, including Academic Affairs and Long-Range Planning, an ad hoc committee to convert the college to eight-week sessions, and a committee on changes in general education requirements. In addition, no fewer than nine full faculty meetings took place in May. The ultimate faculty vote on majors came at the last of those meetings, on May 26, 1982. At that meeting, the faculty approved "in principle" a new associate in science degree with a major in data processing, a ninety-hour diploma art program, and an interdisciplinary major in liberal arts in case such individual majors would be eliminated. The faculty also voted to continue majors in English, psychology, and history/government, as well as the B.F.A. in art "at least through 1984–85 so long as they can be offered by the number of faculty allotted to the discipline by the administration and/or if prospects for a consortium music department seem good." The major in public administration was eliminated for lack of adequate student interest. The faculty rejected adoption of the eight-week format for the on-campus day program.[64]

The May 26, 1982, faculty meeting also passed more rigorous general education requirements, effective August 1, 1983, stipulating course work in four categories: basic skills, including six credit hours of English composition and six in computer skills; eighteen hours in humanities, including six hours of Western Civilization and twelve in at least four other disciplines of the humanities; nine hours in the social perspective in at least three separate disciplines; and eight hours in science and mathematics.

Events of May and early summer resulted in strained relations at all levels of the college. Trustees, faced with such blatant strife, had a wide range of options, from the rejection of administrative leadership to giving the administration free rein.

Into this emotionally charged environment came one of the most startling events of a wholly extraordinary period, as described in a letter from Kelly, Harris, Foster, Kanger, and Dunathan to Rogers on June 4, 1982: "It was obvious this morning that several Board members expressed lack of confidence in the administration. Therefore, as a group, we offer our resignations so you and they may supply the institution with the kind of administrative leadership you feel is necessary." Administrators had requested approval for specific administrative actions and for the board to "empower the administration to use its best judgment in acting upon these matters without having to come back for Board approval. . . . The Executive Committee referred these recommendations to two other Board committees. By this action you indicated your lack of faith in the administration's ability to make critical decisions." The trustees, "astonished by the turn of events," refused to make concessions, considering the action a "very inappropriate power play." The mass resignation was tendered to a joint meeting of the Finance Committee and the Executive Committee of the board, and the members of those committees chose not to take the matter to the full board. Instead, the trustees involved kept the situation confidential, allowing the administrators to back away from their position so that all concerned could give their attention to important concerns at hand. As Foster, who was to remain a valuable part of the college administration for years to come, later put it, "It was not our finest hour."[65]

When board action on degree majors took place on July 2, 1982, the trustees had moved well beyond consideration of so drastic a revision as Harris's triple-focus plan. Kelly correctly commented that "these were difficult decisions to make and ones which could strain and break friendships." In something of a compromise, the trustees approved the new associate in science degree with a major in data processing, though eliminating the English and music majors, leaving the history/government, psychology, and social work majors in place. Asked seventeen years later about the elimination of the English major, trustee Don Schubert reflected on the board's agony: "The realization then began to set in. It seemed to be a real challenge between the business side of the college and the academic side of the college. . . . I think there are those people who want to major in English. I don't think it really served a good purpose. No, I don't."[66]

According to the board minutes of August 11, 1982, "Dr. Harris has left for Alaska, and Dr. John Henricks is doing a very good job as the Acting Vice President for Academic Affairs." As one of his final acts, however, Harris put in place a "new configuration for the 1982–83 academic year." The new academic structure, which proved highly divisive, created a Career Division and a General Education Division. The General Education Division was divided into Area A and Area B rather than into traditional departments. Thus, history/government, psychology, and social work, though still majors, were eliminated as departments, partially accomplishing structurally what the board refused to do in ending majors. Two area coordinators replaced former department heads. With the exception of Larson, who was the natural choice to head the art program, department chairs were untenured and relatively short-term faculty members who had supported Harris the previous spring. Henricks, who had been director of the Evening College, presided over his first faculty meeting on August 20, 1982. At that time, plans began for restructuring the divisions, and a search committee was already under way for a new dean.[67]

A major change occurred on the board when Rogers sent a letter to the trustees assembled for their September 17, 1982, meeting resigning both as chairman and as a trustee. Rogers had prevailed over crises and hardships equal to any in the history of the college and "took the opportunity of better times" to leave the board, having "directed his interests toward his alma mater [the University of Missouri–Columbia] in the last few months." When Tom Atkins replaced Rogers as "interim" chairman, the "interim" designation was soon removed, beginning sixteen years of outstanding leadership during which the college reached new heights under the guidance of a strong board.[68]

After the tumultuous spring and summer, preparations intensified for the comprehensive North Central review to come November 29–December 2. The three-member team evaluated the Columbia campus, after which two team members visited the Fort Leonard Wood and St. Louis sites while the third member went to the Aurora, Colorado, site.

The North Central team report, the most positive of the Kelly presidency, reflected a significant new attitude toward the Extended Studies Division. Whereas earlier reports had stressed the need for the college to become independent of Extended Studies revenues, the 1982 report concluded that "the ESD program is in excellent condition and may provide needed revenue in the future"—the first acceptance by a North Central team of the permanence of the program. The team praised increased faculty involvement and encouraged a strong on-campus faculty role: "The fine administrative work which has enabled the college to improve the organization and implementation of its external sites now needs to be supplemented by the initiative and responsibility of the faculty for maintaining the quality of the educational programs at these same sites." The team called the program "well organized, capably administered, and adequately supported with necessary personnel and other resources," proclaiming its satisfaction with "the quality of the organization and administration, faculty, and students, and academic progress of the Extended Studies Division." Therefore, the report concluded, it was unnecessary to impose any restrictions on site development or to require reports. The program from that time forward operated under only the college's own self-imposed restrictions.[69]

Financial conditions and fiscal management also fared well in the report, a result of the college's third year with a black budget. According to the team, "The College has an excellent financial reporting system that is both accurate and timely."[70]

In the academic area, problems related largely to structure and morale. Team members praised the 130 percent increase in the library's holdings since 1977 and the significantly increased library usage. They also noted the improved faculty evaluation system that would soon provide for an annual evaluation by the immediate faculty supervisor and by the dean, with new provisions for evaluation of advising. On the negative side, the team found a lack of cohesion in the academic structure, which it called "duplicative and cumbersome for the size and traditions of the institution." Noting that the two divisions were supposedly coequal, the team suggested that "area coordinators" in the two areas of the liberal arts and sciences "seem less in status and authority than the Department Chairs in the Career Division." The report continued:

> Budget responsibilities in the Liberal Arts Division are vested in the Division Head without formal participation by Area Coordinators compared to the budget responsibilities of Department Chairs in the Career Division. . . . The differentiation in discipline organization and authority between the two divisions has apparently resulted in considerable frustration within the Liberal Arts and Sciences Division. This situation needs early resolution.[71]

The report criticized the administration for inadequate faculty benefits, especially the lack of a retirement plan. It pointed to the lack of an endowment fund as the most rudimentary problem, one that had been deplored by every president in the college's history. Nonetheless, the overall conclusion was positive: "The future is not yet secure for Columbia College, but this is also true for many other colleges. The team believes that Columbia has made significant advances in recent years and has reached a level of stability and maturity that will enable it to face the future with increased confidence."[72]

The recommendation by the team, adopted formally in July, continued accreditation for all components of the college with no reports or focused evaluation and no restrictions placed on the Extended Studies sites. The college would have the next comprehensive evaluation in the 1986–1987 academic year.

Going into 1983, the college had regained some stability, moving on several fronts. In an important step forward, the administration formed articulation agreements with community colleges to facilitate transfer of students to Columbia College. Beginning first with arrangements with Jefferson and Mineral Area Community Colleges, the concept soon expanded to include Penn Valley, Meramec, and Florissant Valley Community Colleges. Henricks, in reporting the success to the board, shared the credit: "Through the enormous efforts of one faculty member, Dr. Mary Miller, the on-campus program has developed a number of articulation agreements with community colleges throughout the state." Also in the spring of 1983, Novelle Dunathan reported dramatic increases in the use of the college's Career Planning and Placement, Communications Skills, and Counseling Centers. In other positive activities, faculty-sponsored field trips included not only ones by on-campus faculty (fashion to Paris, government to Washington, D.C., and travel to Cancun), but also a history tour to Europe led by faculty of the Aurora, Colorado, site. Students also participated in the college's exchange program with Bradford University in Bradford, England, in the summer of 1983. In addition, the Jane Froman Singers continued the college's tradition in music performance. Begun in 1920 by Anna Froman Hetzler as the Christian College Sextet, the group adopted Double Sextette as its name under Geneva Youngs, director from 1936 to 1956. With the coming of coeducation, the group became Double Sextet and finally the Jane Froman Singers in 1982.[73]

The summer of 1983 brought further stability. The fourth year of a black budget ended in June, and by July 18, 1983, a new academic dean took office. The black budget, partly the result of a capital campaign, led to significant scholarship offerings for returning and transfer students. Under the Achieving Curricula Excellence (ACE) plan, tuition reduction based on grade point average and years at the college ranged from a 50 to 100 percent tuition reduction. An increase in tuition from $3,975 to $4,425 also helped finance the plan. The new vice president for academic affairs and dean of faculties, Bob Evans, restructured the academic area into three divisions, each division including both liberal arts and career programs, thus relieving tensions resulting from the Harris structure. Evans's coming to the deanship brought hope to the faculty of new competence in the position only to lead to disappointment at his resignation for health reasons just seven months later.[74]

A real success story for the college, the Evening College, continued its growth. Although 85 percent of evening students lived in Boone County, some drove for an hour or more to take classes. Of them, 88 percent were employed, and 45 percent were female. Their average age was twenty-seven. The Extended Studies site in Jefferson City became a satellite Evening College in 1983, quickly increasing enrollments there from 18 to 76. The home campus Evening College, under the capable leadership of its acting director, Bob McDaniels, boasted 320 students by March 1983 and 540 course enrollments. As ties between the college and the community grew ever stronger, the concept of "Columbia's College" grew steadily, as indicated by trustee Don Schubert in 1999:

> [The Evening College] has done more for this school than any other single thing I can think of. . . . Fifteen years ago, if we had a college graduate here [Boone County Bank], it probably was from the University of Missouri. Today, if we count noses, there are more Columbia College graduates employed by this bank by far than from any other institution. Person, after person, after person, it has allowed them to go back and finish their degree. You know that same story is told all over Columbia. That has provided a phenomenal service to this community.[75]

Mary Miller, who had led the effort to acquire articulation agreements with community colleges, came to the fore again in heading a faculty task force on teaching effectiveness, a move encouraged by Evans. Faculty members met in December and into January 1984, dividing into subgroups and proposing in their report a variety of improvements. In contrast to the action of the spring of 1982, they recommended that "careful monitoring of the courses in each major . . . should be on-going by faculty members in each major" to ensure a "more reasoned decision." The report recommended various combinations of majors and minors, complete with sample programs. It urged strengthening and expanding existing majors rather than creating totally new programs and urged more interchange among majors and programs and more internships involving the community.[76]

The Miller report also suggested improvements for the instructional delivery system: a mentor system for new faculty, funded in-service workshops, creation of the Effective Teaching Resource Committee, use of a variety of teaching strategies, information on how to teach minority students, an active program of self-evaluation, and institutional recognition of teaching excellence. Task force members criticized the twenty-seven-hour teaching load as detrimental to effective teaching, suggesting that the policy be reviewed. They supported a system of second-year review of new faculty to make them more aware of expectations and to provide an early full evaluation. They also proposed that "monitoring by directors of all academic information printed in such materials as the college catalog and admissions materials be a standard procedure."[77]

Miller was one of several new faculty members during the Kelly years who would have a long-range impact on the college. Joining the faculty in 1982 with extensive experience, she taught education and mathematics, acting as division chair for five years. In addition to strengthening the education department, she worked with Glenna Mae Kubach and Sally Wells to revise the curriculum of the business department. She was executive secretary and a past president of the Missouri Unit of the Association of Teacher Educators and a member of the national board of that group. In July 1987, she replaced Walter Williams, first as acting dean of faculties and then as permanent dean in December, a position in which she served with distinction until her retirement in 1993. Miller would do much to enhance the professionalism of the faculty, especially in increasing the number of faculty members with terminal degrees.[78]

Other valuable faculty members coming in the early 1980s and giving long and effective service to the college included Anthony Alioto, Carolyn Dickinson, and Sally Wells. Alioto, in European history, came in 1981 and became not only an exciting and popular classroom teacher but also a prolific author. His *History of Western Science* and *Christianity in Context* experienced success as college textbooks, and his colleagues and students rewarded his teaching, twice choosing him as teacher of the year and in 1996–1997 naming him as the college's selection for the Missouri Governor's Award for Excellence in Teaching. Alioto also served as a faculty advisor for Alpha Chi, the scholastic honor society. Carolyn Dickinson became a full-time faculty member in English in 1983 after several years of part-time teaching. In addition to being an active committee member and editor, she conducted student tours to England, Ireland, and Scotland. She also served as chair of the humanities department from 1993 to 1998. Sally Wells, coming to the college in 1983 in the business department, had experience in real estate and banking and incorporated her experience as a certified financial planner into her teaching.[79]

Despite constructive academic activity, administrative roles remained unsettled, climaxing with a letter from Kelly to the trustees on September 9, 1983, tendering his resignation effective June 30, 1984: "I've accomplished what I set out to accomplish here. It's time for something new." Kelly moved to St. Louis, where he embarked on a new career in insurance. A special faculty meeting in November 1983 resulted in the election of a faculty representative to a search committee, and the screening process began in February with names of finalists sent by the committee to the board in March. Just as the presidential search committee got under way, Evans resigned as dean of faculty, and Kelly declined to form a dean's search committee, preferring to leave the action to a new president. By March, with Kelly already off-campus, Foster had taken the role of "chief operating officer," making monthly reports to board chairman Atkins. Henricks again became acting dean of faculty "for as long as is necessary." In April, Henricks reported a "deep-rooted malaise which has affected the faculty," blaming in part the odious twenty-seven-hour teaching load. Henricks also noted that "a full fifty percent of faculty salaries are in the bottom ten percent of total faculty salaries."[80]

In March, Foster appointed a small committee consisting of two faculty and three administrators as the Future Focus Committee to produce a report on the future student body "in time for faculty debate and input at its last faculty meeting of the year." Faculty response to the committee and to the limited faculty input was both wary and weary, a form of battle fatigue taken by Foster in his June report to Atkins as indifference: "I take no pleasure in telling you that my prediction of almost total faculty disinterest in the Future Focus Committee's report was correct."[81]

In seeking a new president, the search committee ranked strong leadership and fund-raising ability high on its list of criteria. From the 105 applicants, the committee chose 8 names to be sent to Atkins, all of whom were brought to campus for interviews. Three returned for more intensive talks, and clearly one stood head and shoulders above the rest. Donald B. Ruthenberg told the trustees, "I'm the only man for the job." He had taken the time to learn as much about the college as he could. Undaunted by remaining problems, he was highly enthusiastic about the challenge. As trustee Marty Toler later expressed it, "He just sort of took the job from us."[82]

Ruthenberg possessed qualifications and personal characteristics uniquely fitted to the needs of the college at that time. In addition to twenty-eight years of teaching and administrative experience, he held degrees from Baldwin-Wallace, Iliff School of Theology in Denver, the University of Southern California School of Theology, and the University of Denver, encompassing the fields of religion, psychology, and education. He was also an ordained Methodist minister. Formerly president of Southwestern College in Winfield, Kansas, he had served since 1980 as president of the Iowa Association of Independent Colleges and Universities. His aggressive, enthusiastic style allowed him to ask anything of anybody, a request frequently meeting with success. The faculty representative on the search committee, Jack Batterson, summed up the mood on campus: "I was pleased with the smooth conduct of the search process and especially delighted with the selection of Dr. Ruthenberg. He will be taking his post with the overwhelming support of faculty, trustees, and students. There is general excitement on campus in anticipation of his arrival and leadership."[83]

By fall 1984, the college's bleak financial period had ended, and Ruthenberg's leadership would bring the economic stability long needed, though not the elusive endowment fund. Kelly had, in his early years, provided a more stable relationship with the board, a board that grew in stature. The trustees, who once may have considered board membership a social nicety, met the challenges, took hold, and pulled the college through the Hill and Kelly years until major transitions could be completed and stability reinstated. Local board members, often the salvation of the college, met frequently at crucial periods, displaying dedication and cementing their relationship to the college and to one another. Don Schubert remembered the trying times and what made it all worthwhile: "The board has done a lot of growing up, and we have had a lot of continuity on the board. That college is bigger than any one of us or any group of us. . . . We meet the needs of the student—we have had both faculty and administration who have been responsive to that. Now we are swinging back to liberal arts."[84]

Significant as the board role proved, it was trustee Charles Koelling who recognized the role of the faculty in the critical years under Hill and Kelly: "All the way through, the faculty was a stabilizing influence in every transition of the college."[85] Cognizant of the need for change, the faculty had at the same time experienced the transient nature of some vocational majors in contrast to the enduring strength of the liberal arts. A changing society was demanding a variety of offerings, and a changing curriculum continued to recognize those needs. Society also demanded an education that would go beyond mere training to provide the adaptability and personal growth possible only through those standards and values found especially in a liberal arts base and in appropriate liberal arts majors. In this need, society had not changed, nor had the college.

12

Securing the Heritage, Part 1

DONALD B. RUTHENBERG: 1984–1995

The establishment of this institution 140 years ago did not close the books on its founding. . . . The founding of any great and viable institution is an ongoing matter. . . . We honor [the founders] by going forth unafraid to stand for what is right more than we stand for what is comfortable . . . caring enough about each other—and those we will never know—to want their opportunities to be better tomorrow than they are today—knowing we have the capacity to make it happen and dedicating ourselves to doing it.

Bob Priddy, Missouri journalist and historian,
at Charter Day address, January 18, 1991

UNDER DONALD RUTHENBERG'S LEADERSHIP, Columbia College, virtually overnight, moved from a reactive to a proactive stance. On May 4, 1984, two weeks before his official election by the trustees, Ruthenberg wrote to Marvin Owens that "there are several matters which can be handled prior to my physical relocation. Therefore, I am assuming direct responsibility for administrative leadership and will guide the direction of the institution as much as possible through the mail and by telephone." At his election at the May 18 board meeting, Ruthenberg explained his actions: "It may have been presumptuous on my part to assume responsibilities as president prior to being with you all in a formal setting. My haste and concern to get into important movement and capture the enthusiastic response I felt at the trustee committee's invitation makes my bold actions seem lethargic."[1]

When Patricia Thrash of the North Central Association (whom Ruthenberg had known in the past) asked why he would leave his comfortably successful position with the twenty-seven private institutions of Iowa, Ruthenberg replied, "I look forward to working with you on an institution which . . . is now ready not only to walk in out of the woods but stand in the sunlight of a hopefully bright future." Convinced of that future, Ruthenberg wanted to be the one to "turn the institution around," proving that his previous successes were not "just a fluke." Ruthenberg continued, "I've ten or eleven years left before I'm sixty-five, and I'd like to have something for people to remember me by. I want to build a monument to myself." Having observed dozens of academic presidencies in his previous pursuits, he concluded that successful leaders had "made the institution an extension of their lives. They functioned as proprietors, not as administrative managers and not as functionaries of the board of trustees."[2]

Ruthenberg, in his relationships with the various constituencies of the college, was avowedly proprietary, impulsive, irrepressible, candid, authoritative, and sometimes brash. He was proud to say that he made the college central to his life, and his activist leadership demanded much of him and of all around him. According to Bob Burchard, the college's highly successful basketball coach and athletic director, Ruthenberg had a way of "pushing you beyond where you felt comfortable" and of "saying outrageous things and then making them happen." The result was a spectacular record of accomplishment.

Ruthenberg learned quickly from the college's recent past, as seen in a report of his first news conference:

> The era of increasing emphasis on vocational training at Columbia College could come to an end this summer when Donald Ruthenberg assumes the school's presidency. With a mandate from the college Board of Trustees and support he senses from the faculty, Ruthenberg told reporters this morning he is going to shore up liberal arts at the college. "I'm going to halt that in its tracks," said Ruthenberg of the trend that led to scrapping three liberal arts degree programs in May 1982. "We can't train people for jobs in 2012 or 2020, but we can educate them to live in that framework."[3]

The president's remarks to the faculty fall conference expressed similar insights:

> The trustees have asked me to center on the [previous administration's] 'future focus document' which was given to me when I was here to be interviewed. I have found some flaws in that document. . . . I assume nothing from the past except the heritage upon which we build. . . . I do not pretend we can continually live together without difficulty and some strife. I *do* contend that if we indeed have at the center of our existence a desire to see Columbia College

thrive, she not only will continue to exist but will thrive beyond anyone's expectations.[4]

The same positive tone carried over to the installation of the college's sixteenth president, "a dignified yet simple ceremony" held on the Saturday morning of Parents Weekend. Ruthenberg included a very limited number of presidents and representatives from other institutions, preferring to avoid the expenditure of time and money necessary for a full-blown inauguration. His address embraced all constituencies of the college: "There are gathered here strong and bright colleagues, a church body, an international community, an interesting and eager student body, a willing civic group, an affectionate and true alumni association, and trusting trustees. All have voiced support for the potential dreams and visions. All are willing to give breath to the ideas and ideals of the future."[5]

The administrative team upon which Ruthenberg depended evolved gradually into an effective group. In one of his early acts, the president appointed Marilyn Dimond as dean of admissions and records in January 1985 upon the departure of John Bart, who had worked closely with the former academic dean, Jerry Harris. Dimond remained at the college until 1991 and was followed in 1993 by Ron Cronacher for the next three years. Don Foster, who had served the college in a variety of positions for twenty-two years, remained as vice president for administrative services until he left in February 1986 to become business manager and treasurer of Huntington College in Montgomery, Alabama. Ruthenberg deplored Foster's departure: "Don has been invaluable to me. . . . His loyalty and support of this institution have been exemplary. He has given excellent leadership to the College and he will be missed." Chuck Bobbitt, appointed as manager of administrative services to replace Foster, became one of Ruthenberg's closest associates, managing, on the side, to put in place and coach a winning women's fast-pitch softball team. The search for an academic dean to replace John Henricks as acting dean resulted in the selection of Walter Williams, who remained for two years. Following Williams as dean, Mary Miller served for five years until her retirement in 1992, bringing the most stable and productive leadership to that position since 1976. When Miller retired, Frank Vivelo followed for a two-year period, after which Michael Polley served as acting dean for the remainder of the Ruthenberg presidency.[6]

Others carrying over from the Kelly years included Diane O'Hagan as director of alumni activities, Kay Kanger as vice president for business affairs, Novelle Dunathan as vice president for student life, Frazier Moon as director of administrative services for the Extended Studies Division, and Frank Westling as associate dean in ESD. When Diane O'Hagan left (returning, however, to teach part-time), she was replaced by Bruce Bynum. Lindi Overton followed Kanger, bringing exceptional professionalism and expertise to financial management. She remained a trusted and effective advisor to the administration and the board until her relocation to Oregon in 1997. Dunathan, who returned to teaching as chair of the education department in 1986, was followed by Robert Harris from 1987 to 1989. Faye Burchard, replacing Harris in 1989, remained throughout the Ruthenberg presidency to serve in the next administration, while her husband, Bob Burchard, set new heights for sports at the college as coach and athletic director.

In a major step forward (after Kelly had functioned without a director of development), Ruthenberg turned his attention to the expansion of the development staff. Ralph Glenn became vice president for development in 1985, followed in 1987 by Howard Maxwell and, in 1990, by Dona Sue Cool. Aiding in the development area, former Christian College president Kenneth Freeman, who had returned to Columbia to retire, agreed to act as director of estate planning. Ruthenberg expressed his admiration for Freeman: "Twenty-five years ago a predecessor of mine suggested that the institution was in a renaissance. Some have suggested he did not achieve his goals. . . . With the exception of a building plan . . . the goals of the institution have not only been met but surpassed in many ways." When Freeman relinquished the position in 1986, Ruthenberg and the trustees demonstrated their appreciation of his career by naming him president emeritus. Freeman continued to make his home in Columbia as an active friend of the college until his death in 1998.[7]

Ruthenberg also appreciated the role of his wife, Dee, "my best friend and my best supporter," whom he called "a part of all that I do." With a background in speech pathology and elementary education and graduate study at the University of Southern California and at Illinois State University, she had become an "understanding helpmate" in her husband's career. In Columbia, she launched into community work in civic organizations and activities in addition to the typical first lady duties, also traveling extensively with the president. She served a three-year stint as a part-time volunteer in the college's Stafford Library, helping to bridge the gap to the new automation system and allowing the library to extend its hours devoted to student service.[8]

No other issue illustrated Ruthenberg's ability to "make things happen" more clearly than his immediate attention to financial matters. The college ended the July 1984 fiscal year again in the black and made a sizable repayment to the building fund. Short-term borrowing stood at zero for the first time since 1976, and current funds also paid for increased financial aid. Auditor Stephen C. Smith pronounced the college "operating within its means, a vast improvement over some of the past years." The president noted, however, that this accomplishment had been at the expense of "low salaries for the committed faculty and staff." He launched into a salary study, comparing Columbia College salaries with those of forty-five similar (category IIB) colleges, largely in Missouri, intending to make Columbia College salaries comparable to the mean of those institutions.[9]

Never far from the president's attention, the need for an endowment became a subject of many of his public addresses. He also preached to the trustees:

> In her inaugural speech, President St. Clair said, "Christian must be endowed." She used this in every speech she made, but somehow the message did not register. I must say the same thing to you today. . . . If the institution had been endowed from her administration, the College would not have problems today. Each of you can help by adding this little sentence to your wills, after you have taken care of all your desires: "The residue of my estate is left to Columbia College."[10]

The last sentence of his remarks became a hallmark of his presidency, causing genial laughter on many college occasions but penetrating adequately to make its point in the form of a number of bequests.

In perhaps the best example of "saying outrageous things and then making them happen," Ruthenberg proposed at the September 21, 1984, board meeting that the college eliminate its entire federal debt of $1,841,184.25 with a payment of $586,247.73, an amount that must be raised within one week. In a new program announced on August 1, 1984, with a deadline of September 28, the government encouraged debt prepayment based on a formula involving current treasury note rates, remaining balance, and time of amortization, granting substantial forgiveness of the remaining debt. For Columbia College, this meant the opportunity to eliminate its federal debt at thirty-seven cents on the dollar, including both principal and interest. Loans involved included: Dulany food service and counseling center, built in 1959 with a loan lasting until 1999: Miller Hall, built in 1963, with a loan to 2003; and a federal energy renewal loan granted in 1979, with payment until 2020. The only capital expense remaining for the college would be a private loan for Banks Hall. Ruthenberg argued that such an opportunity "would not be available again in this century" and would enable the college to put $50,000 a year into endowment instead of into payments. Columbia College would be one of the few academic institutions in the United States with no major capital debt service, and the relatively small debt on Banks Hall would end in 2003. With potential donors waiting to see what the trustees would do, the board voted unanimously to support the repayment of the federal loans by September 28, taking personal responsibility for $150,000 of the total amount needed. On January 18, 1985, the president wrote his report to the board: "As I speak today, we have no long-term federal indebtedness, one of only five schools in the United States who can suggest that. . . . I am pleased to be able to report that, as of this moment, the institution is in the best financial condition it has enjoyed probably in its One Hundred and Thirty-four Year History."[11]

By May 1985, Ruthenberg marked his first anniversary, writing in his report to the board, "CONGRATULATIONS! You have survived the first year of the Ruthenberg era." Certainly, the college had reason to celebrate its position, and Ruthenberg showed no lessening of his efforts in 1985–1986. Particularly good news came in the form of enrollment numbers. The *Columbia Missourian* reported the steady climb: "While other colleges in Columbia reflect the nationwide trend of declining enrollment, Columbia College is providing a bright spot with a two percent increase in registered students. The figures reflect a higher quality student body as well as a larger one." According to the article, the University of Missouri–Columbia began its year down by some four hundred students, and Stephens College, down 18 percent in 1984, experienced another 3 percent decrease in the fall of 1985. The *Missourian* reported again the next February on a 4 percent increase at Columbia College: "The figures are in contrast to the nationwide trend of declining enrollment that has affected UMC and Stephens College."[12]

A variety of activities enhanced the sense of progress. The administration reported its seventh consecutive year of a balanced budget, the addition of $110,000 to its endowment fund, acquisition of neighborhood property, and the lack of any short-term borrowing. As a sign of good times, the trustees decided to dispense with full board meetings each January and authorized the Executive Committee and the Finance Committee to conduct necessary business each January.

In another development, the college strengthened its ties to the Christian Church. As part of a "reaffirmation" of the long-standing relationship, Ruthenberg announced a $60,000 yearlong venture, jointly sponsored by the college and the church, to explore the establishment of a religious studies program for 1986–1987. Attending the church's national conference, he created quite a sensation: "Ruthenberg hauled his seven-story-tall hot air balloon to the meeting and kicked off the weeklong conference by ascending over central Des Moines." The college routinely received about $50,000 a year from the church as a share of money distributed to fifteen affiliated institutions, and the relationship was further strengthened by the hiring of Ralph Glenn, an ordained Christian Church minister, as the Columbia College director of development.[13]

Another example of the Ruthenberg style occurred when the president stunned a meeting on campus of the United Farmers and Rancher Conference in October 1986 by announcing that Missouri farmers, forced into bankruptcy by the three-year agricultural crisis, could attend Columbia College under a tuition waiver policy. Roger Allison, director of the Missouri Rural Crisis Center, led a standing ovation, and the next semester saw the registration of ten beneficiaries of the program, with fifteen enrolling in all.

Ruthenberg stated that he had come up with the idea the day before the announcement: "It's one way we can stand and be counted and say we believe in rural America."[14]

In more long-range activities, Ruthenberg began to set forth his goals for the college. His plans for a $10 million endowment program would fund ten chairs for professorships at $500,000 each and 120 full scholarships at $300,000, leaving $2 million for general endowment. Although the goals never fully materialized, attention gained by the announcement encouraged giving. A more elaborate ten-point plan followed in 1986. It called for construction of a multipurpose building in time for the next year's basketball season as well as a library building and an academic–cultural arts center. Land acquisition for peripheral parking would provide an all-pedestrian campus. The plan proposed funding of faculty salaries at the 60 percent level of the category IIB colleges and establishment of a pension plan. Ruthenberg hoped to add faculty for early childhood development, religious studies, and choral music and to form advisory boards to help guide appropriate academic departments. Another goal was to create Asian locations similar to ESD sites. Finally, he planned to develop an alcohol and chemical dependency program on campus.[15]

The planning processes of 1985 and 1986 evolved naturally into preparation for the North Central Association visitation scheduled for October 27–29, 1986. The introduction to the college's *Self-Study* reflected the new attitude since the last evaluation:

> Academic planning and changes have resulted not so much from necessity as from the determination to upgrade quality and to respond positively to challenges emerging under new leadership in a period of anticipated growth. . . . While career programs have been further strengthened, liberal arts programs, both as majors and in support of general education, have reemerged with renewed vigor and popularity, perhaps reflecting national trends in education as well as internal strengths of the liberal arts at Columbia College.[16]

With tensions from past conflicts defused, the academic structure had reverted to two divisions. The Division of Arts and Sciences included art, history/government, English literature, language, speech, religious studies, journalism, sciences, and mathematics. The Division of Professional Studies included business administration, computer information systems, criminal justice, education, fashion, psychology, social work, sociology, and travel administration. More positive attitudes and the cordial relationship between the two division heads, Jack Batterson and Mary Miller, relegated interdivision hostility to the past.[17]

The North Central report weighed far more heavily on strengths than on concerns. Praising "supportive and committed trustees," the "strong administrative leadership," and a faculty and staff "dedicated to student welfare," it noted especially the "capably managed" financial affairs: "The College's budget preparation, information and control seem to be excellent." It called the Center for Academic Enrichment "a source of innovative enhancement of the curriculum" benefiting the entire academic community and called the computer resources "used creatively to meet both academic and administrative needs." The team cited "noticeable improvements in the physical plant" and saw potential for alumni contributions that "should provide future support." The Extended Studies Division and Evening College, according to the report, constituted "a unique and successful system of delivery of selected associate and baccalaureate degree programs to working adults."[18]

Concerns noted in the report included several needs: more library space and holdings, greater cooperation and interaction between on-campus and ESD faculty, and more attention to Evening College advising, counseling, career planning, and placement. The team found faculty salaries and fringe benefits comparatively low and faulted the lack of a retirement program, also noting that the faculty was spread too thin. Of particular concern was the lack of adequate faculty governance: "Despite the organizational structure and extensive array of committees, the faculty do not have an effective voice in campus governance. Leadership tends to be from the top down rather than shared. . . . If this situation is to improve, both the administration and the faculty will have to define more precisely the role of each and find ways to affect a meaningful partnership for the governance of the College."[19]

The team's wholly positive recommendations called for no further evaluations for six years, no stipulations, no reports, and no focused evaluations. After the exit interview, Ruthenberg called an all-campus assembly in Launer Auditorium at eleven in the morning on October 30, 1986, to share the good news. Jack Batterson's reaction in a memorandum to the president typified faculty sentiment: "I thought you would never get to the bottom line, and when you did, my stored-up emotions let go. . . . I was confident that the College is stronger than it has ever been, but it is good to know that outside observers agree."[20]

In another positive area, Ruthenberg entered his presidency with a good relationship with the faculty. Slightly more than one-fifth of the faculty were new in the fall of 1984, but for the large number staying, the selection of a new president brought hope for "revitalization and the realization of the faculty's rightful role in curricular and institutional development." As acting dean in 1984, Henricks reported to the board: "The level of involvement and participation . . . is higher than it has been in the past five years," and faculty members welcomed Ruthenberg's statement at their fall conference that he would leave academic matters to them. The president announced that he would lay the plans for "the size of the institution, the amount of endowment, and the positions of financial support, and you will have to structure the business of the academic program. In this sense we are partners in the future of this institution."[21]

Those faculty members staying with the college included such active stalwarts as Sid Larson, the Battersons, the Grevs, the O'Hagans, Novelle Dunathan, and Christine Cotton. By May 1986, the dean reported no vacancies to be filled other than for retirements. Some notable retirements did take place, including that of Norman Reves. After twenty-five years as a full-time faculty member in English, Reves retired in 1989, still teaching part-time in the Evening College. May 1990 brought the retirement of Burnett Ellis after forty years in geology and audiovisual support and of his wife, Jessie, after thirty-six years in geology and geography, a total of seventy-six years of service. The Ellises divided their time between Columbia and the cabin they built in Wyoming. Glenna Mae Kubach, who also retired in 1990, had served the college for thirty years in accounting. The college family was distressed by the forced retirement for health reasons in January 1986 of Dan Hoagland after twenty-seven years of teaching mathematics and astronomy. When Ruthenberg notified faculty and staff of the resignation in a memorandum of November 12, 1985, he praised Hoagland's service to the college, teaching, creation of the honors program, and contributions toward planning the four-year degree. He also praised him as a human being: "It is evident in the concern expressed by colleagues that his humanness and personality are living testaments to his ability to achieve. We honor him with the designation as 'Distinguished Professor of Columbia College.' He is a man who asks for no recognition but deserves and achieves it by the integrity he has demonstrated as a teaching faculty member of Columbia College for twenty-seven years."[22]

Honor went as well to Sidney Larson, who, in 1987, became the Professor of the Year for Missouri and the bronze medalist in a national competition sponsored by the Council for the Advancement and Support of Higher Education. Larson's accomplishments were best noted in a plaque presented to him on April 24, 1992, by Ruthenberg and board chairman Tom Atkins in recognition of forty years of "dedicated and loyal service." It praised him as "artist, conservator, curator, scholar, public servant, designer, builder, mentor, teacher, lecturer, humorist, and loyal friend." It also noted that he was "distinguished nationally as a master teacher, honored by the State of Missouri as a cultural treasure, and respected as a skilled technician in art conservation and restoration."[23]

Among the faculty new at the beginning of the Ruthenberg presidency, some stood out through their years of service and leadership roles. In business management, Anthony Marshall joined the college as head of the business department and director of the Small Business Institute. Coming from a background in banking and private management as well as teaching, Marshall worked to strengthen the business curriculum, upgrading the core requirements for the B.A. degree in business administration to be the same as for the B.S. degree. He also established a community advisory group and, in 1995, led the department's creation of a master of arts in business administration degree. The faculty elected Marshall to represent them as a faculty trustee and as president of the Faculty Association.[24]

Also new to the business program, coming in 1987 and retiring in 1999, Ellen Atkins brought experience as a certified public accountant and teacher, specializing in the use of software in teaching accounting. Timothy Ireland joined the faculty in 1990 in marketing and accounting, taking responsibility for coordinating the internship program of fifty to seventy-five students per year assigned to local businesses. He helped develop the international emphasis within the business program, a field that became his specialty. Ireland was also active in committee work dealing with faculty development.[25]

Hoyt Hayes, in management and marketing, brought experience as a private consultant to the business administration department. Hayes organized a Columbia College chapter of Students in Free Enterprise (SIFE) in 1993, just one year after coming to the college. The group won the Rookie of the Year award its first year for its activities in promotion of free enterprise, frequently winning the regional competition and advancing to the international competition. In 1997, the club won acclaim as one of the top ten chapters in the world. Hayes, a member of the SIFE Academic Council and a regional director, worked regularly with "rookie teams" in Missouri and Iowa and appeared in internationally distributed SIFE training videos.[26]

New strength in teaching and leadership in psychology came in 1988 with the hiring of Ronald D. Taylor in 1988 and Cheryl Hardy in 1989, each becoming a recipient of the Missouri Governor's Award for Excellence in Teaching. Taylor's background in teaching and as a counselor and administrator of correctional rehabilitation combined theoretic and practical experience. In addition to his prolific publication of books and articles in numerous specialties within the field of psychology, Taylor performed significant service in committee work. He was a member of the Faculty Handbook Committee and the Faculty Governance Committee to write the constitution for the Faculty Association, chaired the Curriculum and Academic Policies Committee, and served on other major committees, particularly ones involving academic assessment and general education requirements. In addition, Taylor worked toward the establishment of both education and psychology graduate programs. His accomplishments led to his inclusion in *Who's Who in the World*.[27]

Cheryl Hardy became one of the first faculty members at the college to introduce computers into the classroom. She was also heavily involved in working with campus student groups. In addition to serving as a sponsor for Alpha Chi for three years, she sponsored Psi Chi, the psychology honor society, as well as the Psychology Club, open to all majors. Deeply involved in the problem of student alcohol abuse, she created the Bacchus Group, dedicated to the promotion of responsible drinking, and led SOS, Students Supporting Other Students. She also joined with Tom Sawyer in social work to lead student groups on four spring break trips to Louisiana, Virginia, and South Carolina to work with Habitat for Humanity. As president of the local Habitat for Humanity group from 1997 to 1999, she helped build fourteen houses and brought heightened awareness to the program and its work.[28]

In the area of criminal justice administration, Michael Lyman became the new program director in 1989 and built the program from a one-man major to a department of four full-time faculty members assisted by five adjunct faculty members. Lyman brought experience as a program coordinator of the Law Enforcement Training Institute of the University of Missouri–Columbia School of Law and as an agent for the Kansas Bureau of Investigation and the Oklahoma Bureau of Narcotics and Dangerous Drugs Control. Hired to "build a program," he found no student association, no advisory board, and a total of 23 majors in the day and evening programs. By 1999, the program boasted 208 majors in day and evening classes and 54 graduate students in the master of science in criminal justice program created by Lyman. Through the addition of courses in all three areas of criminal justice—policing, courts, and corrections—and the use of innovative field trips, Lyman overhauled and upgraded the program far beyond expectations. Also a prolific author, he published on such subjects as introduction to policing, criminal investigation, drug trafficking, and organized crime, writing eight textbooks as well as numerous articles and other works. Lyman appeared on local and national radio and television shows and as a speaker and consultant.[29]

The history/government department expanded in 1990 by hiring Michael Polley, author of a biography of George F. Kennan and of numerous encyclopedia articles during his years at the college. Polley chaired the Freshman Experience Committee that created a freshman orientation course and taught in the program. He served as department chair when Jack Batterson stepped down in 1992, serving until 1994 when he became the acting academic dean upon the resignation of Frank Vivelo. He remained in that position until 1996 when Terry Smith became dean. When Batterson retired in 1996, Polley again chaired the department until 1999 when David Roebuck in political science replaced him.[30]

Moving from part-time to full-time in the English department in 1986, Terry Lass, despite his love of teaching as his foremost effort, became a campus leader of the drive to improve the college's retention effort. He chaired the Retention Council in 1997–1998, a body representing collegewide constituencies. He participated in the evolution of the Freshman Experience class into a newer version, Introduction to Columbia College. Combining his love of baseball with his love of literature, Lass in 1986 made the keynote address at the annual conference of Baseball in American Culture, an organization sponsored by the Baseball Hall of Fame.[31]

In the sciences, Kenneth Torke became the college's biologist in 1986 upon the retirement of Grace Baker. The holder of three research grants from the National Science Foundation, Torke helped shape the needs of the college in planning and implementing updated laboratories and with the addition of eight new courses to the curriculum. In 1988, he worked with Dennis Grev to create the college's nursing program. In addition, he helped establish Alpha Lambda Delta, a scholastic honorary society for freshmen, and served as its charter sponsor.[32]

In 1990, the coming of both Peter Meserve in geology and geography and of Soumitra Chattopadhyay in physics and mathematics rounded out a new science department, with Dennis Grev continuing in chemistry. Meserve had been involved in research and consulting as well as publishing widely both before and after coming to Columbia College. He contributed most of the copy, including all of the physical and cultural geography, for the *Desk Reference for the "National Geographic."* In collaboration with Robert Boon of the English department, he also helped create the first interdisciplinary minor at the college, a program in environmental studies. Active in professional organizations, he chaired the Canadian Studies Specialty Group in the Association of American Geography and the geography section of the Missouri Academy of Sciences. On campus, he chaired the Curriculum and Academic Policies Committee as well as serving on other major committees. Chattopadhyay published widely and was active in acquisition of grant money and committee work. As department chair, he led the development of the college's first separate science majors in biology, chemistry, and health-related sciences.[33]

Michael Sleadd, coming to the art department in 1989 in graphic design and illustration, had served on the board of directors of the University and College Designers Association, in which he remained active. He received regional and national awards, including a national award from the association. He exhibited regionally and nationally in group shows and produced one-man shows throughout the Midwest. Active in commercial illustrating, he contributed to advertising campaigns for local concerns and for such national corporations as IBM and McDonald's.[34]

In addition to new faculty, academic changes brought a more demanding and varied environment. New honors designations in 1986 adopted the traditional titles summa cum laude, magna cum laude, and cum laude for graduates with high grade point averages in addition to the ongoing program for graduation with distinction upon completion of an honors project. Also in 1986, new general education requirements for the A.A. degree included English composition, computer literacy, and fifteen hours of credit distributed over the humanities, mathematics and science, and social studies in addition to requirements related to an area of concentration. By 1990, at least one three-credit-hour course designated as "World or Eastern Culture" became a requirement for candidates for a baccalaureate degree. The college also offered its first summer Elderhostel program in 1990 and, with the expansion of regular summer classes, held its first summer graduation exercises in 1992.[35]

New areas of study included computer information systems, early childhood education, meeting and convention planning, and religious studies. Students majoring in business administration received greater ability to specialize with the adoption of areas of emphasis within the major available in accounting, marketing, management, finance, and shopping centers. In 1990, the United States Small Business Administration named the college as a Small Business Institute, allowing the business administration department to counsel small businesses upon request in any of twenty different aspects of business management. Three teams of students, five to a team, received credit in directed study for working with faculty to respond to requests for aid.[36]

In the renewal of support for liberal arts, a move began as early as 1986, four years after its elimination, to reinstate the major in English, but numerous obstacles slowed the process. With an administrative edict of "no new majors," advocates of the major presented it as the retrieval of an old major. Further delay came when Mary Miller, as academic dean, required that the proposal for the major be approved by the Missouri State Coordinating Board for Higher Education. Christine Cotton, chairing the English department and coordinating the humanities area, carried the brunt of the work in organizing and writing the proposal, which received immediate and unconditional approval from the Coordinating Board in August 1989. In September, trustees voted unanimously that "the reorganized and revised English major be reinstated to better serve the needs of our students."[37]

Demands of the time did lead to the addition of new majors, as seen in the expansion of the education program, originally offered only in elementary education. Department chair Novelle Dunathan led the move to provide a full teacher education program, which required the approval of the Missouri Board of Education. The evaluation on October 17–20, 1989, included sixteen categories of inspection in such areas as library facilities, faculty, administration, science laboratories, and handicap facilities, in addition to specific education topics. The program not only passed in all categories, but also was declared outstanding in four. The director of teacher education for the Missouri Department of Elementary and Secondary Education called the program "one of the strongest in the state," and the *St. Louis Post-Dispatch* proclaimed it "a benchmark for other colleges to be examined." The program was further strengthened the next fall with the addition to the faculty of Owen Jackson, bringing thirty-four years of experience in the public school system, eleven of them in the Columbia public schools. Jackson coordinated and supervised student teaching.[38]

In another program upgrade, a long, arduous process began in 1988 to establish a nationally accredited social work program. The effort was led by Tom Sawyer, who came to the college in 1983 with practical experience in both social work and counseling and a reputation as a presenter in workshops on social problems. After more than one year of work, Sawyer received permission from the accreditation board of the National Council on Social Work Education for the program to become a candidate for accreditation. A representative of the council examined the program in September 1990 to ensure that it was proceeding appropriately, and the final on-site visit took place in the spring of 1991, concluding with a positive report. In June 1992, the council granted full accreditation, making Columbia College one of only fifty-three colleges with a social work program accredited at the national level. Enthusiastic that "this college is moving forward," Sawyer stated that "social work requires a solid liberal arts basis. Columbia has always offered that in its social work program. Now we offer accreditation to complement that." Sawyer, an ordained minister, left teaching to serve in the ministry in St. Louis. Through the efforts of Helga Huang, the college also added a major in sociology, approved at the faculty meeting in November 1994 and by the trustees in January 1995. The major's combination of traditional liberal arts courses with social science research skills prepared its graduates for both public- and private-sector careers.[39]

Also new, a nursing program began in 1988 as a cooperative venture with the Columbia Public Schools' Health-Occupations Center. Because applicants for the program must already be licensed as practical nurses, the public school system offered a one-year program to prepare students to take the licensing test, providing eligibility for entrance into the A.A. in nursing program at Columbia College. The college could receive accreditation from the Missouri State Board of Nursing only after the graduation of the first class and receipt of the scores from tests given by the State Board of Examinations. The first class, graduating in December 1989, achieved an average score of 89 percent on the examinations, three points higher than the national average. After accreditation, the next class improved the test scores, producing a 94 percent average.[40]

Much of the positive activity in the academic area came under the leadership of Mary Miller, who came to the deanship in 1987 at the departure of Walter Williams. Preferring to work closely with faculty, Miller discontinued use of the two-division structure (although faculty still elected representatives to the Academic Affairs Committee and to the Tenure, Review, and Promotion Council by divisions) and kept in close touch with "program directors" and "area coordinators" at the department level. Within her first few months as dean, she organized a High-Risk Student Task Force to track performance of students admitted on a provisional basis and then to provide institutional support. In another reflection of her concern for serving students, she supported the work of the Student Retention Committee in creating the college's first *Advising Handbook*, working closely with Polly Batterson, who chaired the committee and wrote the handbook.[41]

One of the hardest-working academic deans ever to hold that office, Miller had great respect for teaching and for good faculty leadership but never hesitated to step in personally if that leadership faltered. Active in evaluation of the faculty, she visited classes, conferring with the instructor after each visit, and discussed the annual review performance with each faculty member. Her open-door policy provided easy access for the faculty and others, and her five years of dedicated leadership brought the first real stability to the deanship since 1976. Under Miller, faculty retention showed marked improvement, and curricular revision became a major priority.

Another primary concern for Miller was the professionalization of the faculty. Careful hiring brought faculty members who were appropriate not only on the basis of qualifications but also because of their "fit" for Columbia College. Through hiring and various tactics used to persuade faculty members to return to graduate study to complete terminal degrees, she raised the percentage of faculty members with such degrees from 41 percent to 73 percent in her years as dean. This figure would increase to 77 percent by 1994.[42]

Miller, as part of her campaign to lure faculty back to graduate school, made sabbatical leaves a tool toward that end. The trustees had established a policy of allowing faculty members only three-fourths pay for a one-semester sabbatical and one-half pay for two semesters. A faculty recommendation reflecting discontent with that policy passed at the May 1986 faculty meeting, proposing full pay for the one-semester sabbatical. However, that recommendation had not been presented to the board. At a specially called meeting on August 27, the faculty voted to raise the question again, despite some trustee sentiment questioning the need for sabbaticals. With Miller's support, the trustees at the September 18, 1987, meeting moved to restore the policy of providing full pay for a one-semester sabbatical.[43]

In another sabbatical-related issue, however, Miller ran afoul of faculty sentiment—causing a reemergence of other latent faculty concerns—when she revised a policy over the summer without faculty input or knowledge. The policy, passed by the board on September 30, 1988, stated that until 80 percent of full-time faculty held doctoral or M.F.A. degrees, the college would consider sabbatical projects only for those faculty who already held such terminal degrees or intended to use the sabbatical to complete a terminal degree. Offended by both the content and the procedure by which the policy came about, the faculty complained that it was "initiated and implemented without notice to the general faculty or opportunity for faculty input into the policy before submission to the Educational Policy Committee of the Board." Many faculty, apprehensive that the policy made non-Ph.D.'s second-class citizens, saw the policy as potentially divisive, negatively impacting collegiality, and perverting the purpose of sabbaticals. According to a formal faculty statement, "this distinction creates an arbitrary discrimination not justified by merit, service to the college, or the purposes for which sabbaticals are historically intended." The faculty urged the dean to achieve her goals through hiring practices rather than by resorting to a policy "outside the mainstream of higher education." A faculty resolution regretted the adoption of the policy and requested that it be set aside but to no avail.[44]

Miller's unilateral determination of the sabbatical policy renewed faculty frustration at the lack of administrative recognition of the traditional role of faculty. The faculty strongly desired a clear and definitive statement on their role as put forth in the "Joint Statement on the Role of the Faculty" in documents from AAUP publications—a statement adopted by national bodies representing trustees and administrators as well as by the AAUP. When Ruthenberg, puzzled at such a strong desire for adoption of the statement, asked why it was important, faculty members replied that they and the administration would continue to suffer repeated quarrels about prerogatives and jurisdiction until such a defining statement in the legally binding *Faculty Handbook* provided a mutually accepted model for reference. To some administrators and trustees, distrustful of the AAUP, the statement remained suspect, despite its adoption by national administrative and trustee bodies. Resolution of the issue finally came with the agreement to paraphrase the AAUP wording in terms acceptable to both the administration and the faculty. Thirteen faculty members met with Dean Miller to work out such a version from a text prepared by Miller and Christine Cotton. The statement became the benchmark for future questions relating to the role of the faculty, appearing in all subsequent editions of the *Faculty Handbook*. Despite administrative reluctance, the addition of the document to the *Faculty Handbook* proved a major advance in the professionalism of the faculty and facilitated resolution of future disagreements on jurisdictional matters.[45]

Gradual improvement in faculty salaries and the addition of a salary increment toward a retirement plan also furthered professionalism. At a special faculty meeting called to discuss salaries, Ruthenberg expressed shock at the low pay, especially of full professors, the rank lowest in its percentile of the mean used as a goal. Ruthenberg's plan intended to establish the Columbia College mean faculty salary for each rank to exceed 90 percent of the mean salaries for the control group. It also anticipated having its mean salary for each rank attain at least the fiftieth percentile of the mean salary paid at other institutions of the comparison group. Although faculty testily commented that they considered their work to be "better than ninety percent of average," such adjustments did represent a major improvement.

Miller reported the achievement of 90 percent of the mean in each rank in her April 1991 statement to the board, and, by 1992, salaries over the previous six years had increased more than 50 percent for professors, 34 percent for associate professors, 34 percent for assistant professors, and 25 percent for instructors.[46]

Faculty ranks also benefited from a retirement plan, begun in 1989, granting a 2 percent contribution by the college toward a tax-deferred annuity plan for each eligible faculty member, a contribution eventually rising to 7 percent by 1996. The faculty, still concerned that Ruthenberg based raises entirely on merit despite the absence of any clear evaluative measurement, established evaluative criteria by assigning relative weight to various faculty duties. According to the plan, individual merit raises would be based 55 percent on the quality of teaching, 10–25 percent on advising, 10–25 percent on scholarship and professional development, and 10–25 percent on service to the college and the community. The fact that teaching and advising together could count 80 percent of the evaluation demonstrated the importance faculty attached to those roles.[47]

By the time of the 1992 North Central visitation, the college *Self-Study* demonstrated impressive gains since the 1986 evaluation, and the team report reflected that progress. Miller, who wrote the *Self-Study,* retired as dean in the summer of 1992 but stayed on until December with the title of provost to guide the reaccreditation effort. The college's *Self-Study* reported a 68 percent increase in enrollment since 1986, a nearly 72 percent level of full-time faculty with terminal degrees, and an impressive start toward successful applications for grants. The college had received ten thousand dollars from the Missouri Coordinating Board of Higher Education to improve instruction in mathematics, fifty thousand dollars from the United States Department of Education to help area elementary schools increase mathematics literacy, fifty thousand dollars from the 3M Corporation to foster cultural diversity and increase intercultural communications, ninety-one thousand dollars from the Fund for the Improvement of Post-Secondary Education for a drug and alcohol awareness and wellness program, and four thousand dollars from a state grant for Literacy Investment for Tomorrow.[48]

The *Self-Study* noted four major academic publications since 1986: the revised *Academic Policies and Procedures Handbook;* the *Curriculum Guidelines,* a publication stating the expected outcomes for each major and for general education; the *Advising Handbook,* coordinating advising procedures with institutional goals; and the newly updated *Faculty Handbook.* Working together, Miller and faculty leaders had also created a new procedure for faculty evaluation, including self-evaluation, annual evaluation by program directors, classroom observations, student evaluations of all classes and of advisors, a second-year review of all new faculty as a pretenure assessment, and the evaluation for tenure. Also, departments developed an extensive "culminating experience" as a capstone course for each major program of the college.[49]

Other areas of improvement included creation of a long-range plan, and improved faculty development. A Faculty Development Committee began allocation of ten $500 grants for faculty projects, and every full-time faculty member received an annual $325 grant for professional expenses. In addition, the college agreed to pay for three courses per year for any faculty member working toward a terminal degree. In physical improvements, a major building program was under way, including the construction of a Chinese pavilion, cultural center, soccer field, gymnasium, and library as well as massive renovations of older facilities. Improvements also included an increase in college acreage from 20 acres in 1986 to 27.5 acres in 1992.[50]

A team of five evaluators conducted an intensive review of on-campus day and evening programs on November 16–19, 1992, drawing upon one evaluator from the Southern Association and one from the Western Association for on-site visits at Orlando, Florida, and Treasure Island, California. In the North Central area of jurisdiction, the team visited Lake of the Ozarks and Fort Leonard Wood, Missouri.[51]

The exit interview on November 19, 1992, during which the team stated its intended recommendations, included administrators and the subcommittee chairs for the *Self-Study*. A faculty meeting, scheduled later in the day, turned into a celebration. The team's recommendation for a ten-year accreditation cycle, the maximum possible by North Central, with no stipulations and no focused visits, though not totally unexpected, brought rejoicing. President Ruthenberg presided over a brief ceremony at the meeting, presenting Miller with a bouquet and a silver plate engraved "Happy North Central Review for Ten Years." When Miller then thanked the faculty for its support and cooperation, she received a standing ovation in response.[52]

The team's written report, received on December 22, repeatedly stressed improvements. It complimented the well-defined tenure and promotion system and the grievance procedures in the *Faculty Handbook,* a matter given great attention by Miller and the active Handbook Committee. Noting the high level of faculty energy and morale, the report concluded that the faculty "appear to understand the Mission of the Institution and have an extraordinary understanding of their responsibility to serve their students." It praised in particular the reinstatement of the English major.[53]

In the area of student life, the team reported an active student body "genuinely responsive to the faculty as teachers and advisors," who "find the faculty not only well prepared but also readily available and often involved in common social activities." Calling the number of student activities "notable," the report praised the comprehensive drug-abuse counseling services, international student services, career services, health services, the full range of athletics, residence hall programs, and college-sponsored trips.[54]

In the financial area, evaluators, impressed with the absence of any debt for the past six years, recommended that the college adopt an investment policy for the $1.5 million in the endowment and quasi-endowment funds.[55]

In conclusion, the report listed eight areas of strengths and an equal number of concerns. Strengths included the "leadership of an experienced, capable, imaginative, and energetic president," a responsively active and "unusually knowledgeable Board of Trustees," and a "professionally-qualified full-time faculty" dedicated to the college mission and to student academic development, along with an improved faculty profile. The team also cited "comprehensive and diverse" student-life programs and a student-oriented staff. Finally, the team praised the valuable educational service to the Columbia community and the "seriousness of academic purpose and integrity" of administrative leadership of the Extended Studies Division. In its concerns, the team faulted the long-range plan for relating more to day-to-day issues rather than tying academic and physical objectives to fiscal resources. The report cited the lack of an admissions strategy capable of preventing future enrollment fluctuations. It also found insufficient ESD-documented guidelines, library and computer resources at ESD sites, computer resources on the home campus, and library automation. Faculty salaries still needed upgrading, as did the level of congeniality and participation for evening and ESD faculty.[56]

The team's recommendations were all the college could have hoped. The recommendation for a ten-year cycle put the next visitation at 2002–2003—at a time when ten-year accreditations were not common. Although there were no stipulations and no focused visits, the team did require that the college report on enrollment patterns until the "optimum full-time enrollment of 850" for the on-campus day program was achieved or until that goal might be modified. The college was also to report on a comprehensive assessment plan and long-range plan in 1994. Commission action upheld the recommendations in February 1993, leading to final action at the North Central meeting of April 5, 1993.[57]

The ten-year reaccreditation represented a high point in the college's resolution of its problems. Trustee Marty Toler called the result "an affirmation of what we were trying to do and thought was being done. It really did lift our spirits." The next issue of *Friends* carried the president's remarks: "We are immensely pleased and very excited about our continued accreditation. It reflects our continuing work to provide our students, those in Columbia and those throughout the nation, with the best education possible. . . . The report and the length of the accreditation provide us with the assurance that we are not only meeting the needs of those seeking a college education, but we are providing the utmost in flexibility and quality in that education."[58]

Having accomplished much in her years as dean, Miller prepared to retire in the summer of 1992, although remaining on campus until the North

Central visitation. Meanwhile, a dean's search committee began its work in January 1992, selecting Frank Vivelo as the new academic dean, slated to take office on July 1, 1992. Vivelo, an anthropologist, had been dean of the School of Arts and Sciences at Harrisburg Community College in Pennsylvania and liked what he saw in Columbia, particularly the linkage between college and community that, he believed, "would keep Columbia College on the cutting edge of education."[59] However, it soon became apparent that Vivelo's style was significantly different from that experienced in the past. Valuing efficiency, speed, and decision making by formal and uniform rules and procedures, Vivelo hoped to eliminate personal judgment and subjective factors, relying as much as possible on quantitative information and impersonal guidelines. He preferred centralized leadership, dealing with a small group of faculty and delegating to them the relationship with the bulk of the faculty.

Vivelo's top-down leadership almost immediately caused friction. In one of his earliest actions, he put forth a revised evaluation form for students to use in their review of faculty, a matter previously falling under faculty jurisdiction. He caused much more consternation when he unilaterally wrote and sent to department chairs a full set of class schedules, normally prepared within departments and sent to the dean for approval. Department chairs found the schedules unworkable and revised them with much attendant frustration.[60]

In a more positive vein, Vivelo's desire for a structured faculty governance body resulted in an important advance for the faculty. A memorandum to six faculty members, written on October 5, 1992, proposed that the faculty create a faculty governance structure. Typically, the memo included the dean's own eighteen-page proposal for a faculty constitution in which the governing body would be a Faculty Council consisting of a president, vice president, secretary, and one elected representative from each of the three divisions to "act on behalf of and represent the faculty." A Faculty Organization, composed of all holding academic rank, would meet once a semester, but the Faculty Council would be all-important:

> Faculty Council serves as the formally recognized "voice of the faculty of Columbia College," transmitting the will of the faculty to the Dean of Academic Affairs, . . . EMS, and the President of the College. Faculty Council, as the recognized representative body for faculty joint governance, reacts to proposed or completed policies, procedures, practices, and other actions; recommends policies, procedures, practices, and other actions on behalf of the faculty; and initiates proposals on behalf of the faculty.[61]

The Faculty Governance Committee named by the dean chose Christine Cotton as its coordinator and launched into the work of writing a constitution. With a faculty numbering only in the forties, the committee rejected the dean's idea of faculty representation by a small council. In careful and deliberate fashion, the committee gathered examples of governing bodies and their structures and powers from numerous similar colleges. The committee provided for the election by the faculty of an interim council to operate only until the committee could produce an all-inclusive body in a final faculty-approved constitution. The constitution, adopted by the full faculty at its September 9, 1993, meeting, became part of the 1993 *Faculty Handbook*, as approved by the board. The council was limited in its role to that of facilitator for the full faculty body and in November was eliminated altogether.[62]

The Faculty Association became the framework through which the faculty acted to govern itself, participate in the governance of the college, and communicate and coordinate with the various constituencies of the college. The constitution defined membership as all employees in academic divisions of the college whose primary responsibility was teaching, including professional librarians. Others, including the academic dean and the president, would attend meetings at the invitation of the association. The practice evolved of opening meetings with remarks from the president and the dean, who would, unless invited to stay, leave while the faculty conducted its business. A network of eleven faculty-elected committees became the workhorses of the governance system, along with joint committees of the college to which the faculty were appointed by the dean to act along with members from other constituencies.

One of the more important of the Faculty Association committees, the Welfare and Personnel Policies Committee, took charge of establishing a thorough evaluation system for academic affairs, creating forms and procedures for student evaluation of faculty, including space for open-ended comments. The system also included evaluation of faculty by peers, by department heads, by the dean, and self-evaluation, as well as faculty evaluation of relevant administrators. The committee, like the Governance Committee, solicited ideas from other colleges, rejecting the position of the dean that evaluations at all levels be exclusively quantitative. Thus, Vivelo had motivated the faculty to create its own professional body, bringing the faculty into modern means of self-governance, although in a system greatly different from what he had envisioned. Vivelo had hoped to bring about the formation of a staff council and a student council, making them, along with the faculty council, the governance system of the whole college, all reporting to the appropriate authorities at the top. However, only the faculty acted to create a governing body, claiming as its jurisdiction those matters set forth in the *Faculty Handbook* statement on the role of the faculty.[63]

Although Vivelo's version of a governance system failed to be accepted by the faculty, he did devise a new academic administrative structure reducing the number of faculty with whom he must routinely deal. He reorganized departments into three divisions: Art, Humanities, and Communications Division (AHC); Behavioral, Applied, and Natural Sciences Division (BANS); and Business and Management (BM). He relied on division chairs to deal with department heads and on department heads to deal with "their faculty members." Also, his communications to division chairs "to share with your faculty" reflected the centralization of the system. A note of appreciation for the extra work his system required of faculty administrators concluded with the request that they "please pass my appreciation on to the rest of the faculty." With faculty administrators accepting duties previously performed by the academic dean, and with a system of strict and detailed procedural guidelines, meetings and paperwork proliferated. Sufficient time available for the large number of meetings became such a problem that Vivelo at one point suggested eliminating a class hour on the schedule to allow more opportunity for meetings. The faculty chose not to adopt his suggestion.[64]

Despite differences between Vivelo and the faculty, positive changes occurred. A modified *Faculty Handbook* approved by the board in September 1993 removed the denial of a sabbatical to those faculty members not holding the terminal degree and not using a sabbatical toward completing a terminal degree. In addition, Vivelo recognized the inadequacy of faculty pay levels and brought about a 12 percent average salary increase in 1994. Also at this time, the faculty reorganized committee structures, replacing the Academic Affairs Committee with a restructured Curriculum and Academic Policies Committee. The new structure had the virtue of adding representation for ESD, the Evening College, and other constituencies. Although the move diluted faculty control by increasing administrative representation on the committee, only faculty members of the committee could vote.[65]

Vivelo's zeal for more formalized and uniform structures and procedures and for the use of written forms was intended to bring order where he viewed previous methods to be too casual. He devised a master course syllabus to be used as a model by all faculty in every course taught, a system welcomed by ESD administrators to bring uniformity to syllabi coming from campus to adjunct faculty at the sites. Hoping to rule out personal considerations, the dean devised a system of Academic Affairs Regulations (AARs) to cover in great detail any possible contingency in academic activities, leaving as little room as possible for discretion. A large binder soon grew with entries as multipaged AARs were added for such matters as public relations, use of the college logo, committee work, key control security, parking, art displays and artistic expression, budgets, travel, admissions, registration, curriculum development, advising, class activities, student status, and more. There was even an AAR on how to write AARs. They replaced the less rigid manual Miller had produced and covered areas not previously included. Vivelo's goal of devising AARs for all areas of the college never materialized, and the difficulty of adhering to the detailed stipulations of each AAR resulted in faculty resistance to their use and even ridicule.[66]

The major problem Vivelo faced in relating to the Columbia College faculty was the college's tradition of fitting solutions to individual needs within the bounds of existing rules. To the faculty, this tradition, now threatened by such tightly structured regulations, had constituted a central value of Columbia College in contrast to a large university. Also, the massive amount of paperwork and the heavy workload of faculty administrators "nearly paralyzed the educational system and faculty governance." In what turned out to be Vivelo's last faculty meeting, on May 5, 1994, the faculty complained about the paperwork. Vivelo replied that he "could administer with less [faculty] input if the faculty wished." He charged faculty members with thinking about which option they wanted, making a decision by the next fall.[67]

By the time of the fall conference, Vivelo had accepted the presidency of Wharton County Junior College in Wharton, Texas, leaving "for an opportunity and challenge I can't pass up." Faced with a sudden vacancy in the academic dean's position, Ruthenberg offered a creative solution. After announcing Vivelo's expected departure at the end of September, the president asked for volunteers from the faculty to be considered on the spot as acting dean. He then instructed faculty members to vote their preference at that time, although he did not pledge that he would necessarily follow the faculty vote. Ruthenberg interviewed the four volunteers that afternoon, a Friday, and called Michael Polley that evening, informing him that he was the faculty's and his own choice. On Monday afternoon, he announced Polley's appointment as acting dean beginning in October.[68]

Polley, who had joined the history/government faculty in 1990, continued to serve as acting dean from October 1, 1994, until a search was completed to install a permanent dean in May 1996. Congenial, able, and accessible, he worked well with the faculty and respected their role in governance. Following the practice that the dean usually appeared briefly at the beginning of faculty meetings, he attended the September meeting before officially becoming dean. At that time, he accepted the will of the faculty to "look into the possibility of revision of the committee structure to be less bureaucratic," a sentiment expressed unanimously in a resolution at the October 1994 faculty meeting. Also as acting dean, Polley presided over the early stages of the college's creation of its first graduate programs, supervising the effort to comply with the North Central Association's demands. His service as acting dean provided continuity in academic matters after Ruthenberg retired in 1995 until a national search resulted in the installation of a new president and, later, a new dean.[69]

The Ruthenberg presidency had seen the academic quality of the college, both on and off campus, validated by the North Central Association's actions with program expansion, improved conditions for faculty, growth of a more professional faculty, and the coming of age of a governance process to guide future relationships. These successes proved not isolated instances, but part of a pattern of progress evident in all areas of the college during the Ruthenberg years.

13

Securing the Heritage, Part 2

DONALD B. RUTHENBERG: 1984–1995

Vision is fine, but without action it is only a dream.

Helen Walton, speech on January 26, 1995

DONALD RUTHENBERG'S "pattern of progress" manifested itself in a number of ways beyond the academic area, impacting every facet of campus life, including a building program like no other since the presidency of Luella St. Clair Moss.

Trustees held the first board meeting of 1985 in an elegantly refurbished boardroom in Dulany Hall, the result of a $20,000 gift from Desmond Lee in honor of his father, Edgar D. Lee, president of Christian College from 1920 to 1935. Discussion turned to the purchase of the Advent Enterprise Building, a sheltered workshop across Rangeline at the eastern edge of the campus. The building became the new home for the art department when the lease on the Allton Building on Broadway expired. With rent and utilities skyrocketing at the old location, trustees saw the purchase as fiscally sound in addition to the benefit of returning the art program to campus. The move to the extensively renovated building on Rangeline took place in August, celebrated by an open house on October 1, 1985. Faculty and students welcomed the move; although smaller, the 8,700-square-foot building had the advantages of accessibility, better organization of space, and improved lighting.[1]

Ruthenberg next fulfilled a promise made to Columbia College basketball players, who had been using the National Guard Armory for four years. He convinced the trustees to buy Howard's Garage, a metal building facing Rangeline in front of the art center, as a gymnasium site. B. D. Simon agreed to erect the building at cost, and another trustee, William Eckhoff, made the same offer for the concrete work, resulting in the acquisition of a 13,500-square-foot facility at a cost of $680,000. The project created the Southwell Complex, incorporating the Southy Building to the north to house the athletic department office and a weight room. Basketball and volleyball teams began using the new gymnasium in the fall of 1988.[2]

The soccer team, also athletes without an on-campus home, had been playing their home matches in the city parks. Ruthenberg introduced the idea of building a soccer field in 1989, although no space on campus could accommodate it. In response, the college purchased virtually an entire block of property to the north bounded by Wilkes Boulevard on the north, Alton on the south, and Rangeline on the east. Ruthenberg then convinced the city to close Alton Street, allowing unbroken green space all the way from back campus to Wilkes Boulevard. The college acquired much of the property below market value through the influence of former trustee Evelyn Estes, whose family owned a large part of the area involved. The soccer field, built on the northeast corner of Wilkes and Rangeline, was dedicated on Friday, October 18, 1991, as the R. Marvin Owens Field. It honored the trustee who had come to the board in January 1975 and, as head of the Finance Committee since 1976, had brought skillful and faithful leadership to see the college through its difficult times.[3]

In further construction, a separate library building in 1989 brought fulfillment of plans and dreams of several past presidents. The donation by Stan and Lois Stafford of stock realizing a price of $238,000, a contribution of $50,000 by Helen Walton, and the use of other smaller gifts made possible the completion of the J. W. and Lois Stafford Library, dedicated as a highlight of Parents Weekend on October 21, 1989. The library soon included tables and carrels for 150 patrons, a classroom for bibliographic instruction, a listening area, a curriculum resource center, and five microfilm readers. Technology included a computerized periodical index, on-line computer access to the holdings of Ellis Library at the University of Missouri, and a statewide database to all Online Computer Library Center (OCLC) libraries in Missouri. By the end of the Ruthenberg administration, librarians were preparing for automation.[4]

Carolyn Jones, hired as librarian in 1984, became director of Stafford Library in 1990 and welcomed automation as a long-needed improvement. Jones continued the tradition of service, staffing the circulation and reference desk eighty-seven hours a week, in addition to providing for heavy student computer use. She interacted with other constituencies of the college through participation in the Library and Audio-Visual Committee and through service on such other major committees as the NCA Self-Study Committee. She represented the college and the library on the Missouri Library Association Executive Board and the Mid-Missouri Library Network. The library served also as a valuable source of learning for the University of

Missouri–Columbia School of Library and Information Science as a student practicum site.[5]

The "capstone facility of the physical plant," an arts and humanities building, became possible with the bequest of more than $1 million from Emma Jean Brown Ballew, a 1923 graduate of the college. Brown Hall, planned since 1993, was dedicated in September 1995, just months after Ruthenberg's retirement. Other gifts allowing the completion of the building included a $150,000 challenge grant from Desmond Lee, which the college was required to match two-to-one at $300,000, and a 100 percent record of trustee giving. A special feature of Brown Hall, the handsome and spacious art gallery, became the Sidney Larson Gallery in tribute to his career.[6]

In addition to new construction, the college badly needed major renovation of St. Clair, Dorsey, and Williams Halls, Launer Auditorium, the Robnett-Spence Building, the Gerard swimming pool, and the old gymnasium in Dorsey Hall. As part of a $1.8 million campaign, the college acquired a $360,000 grant from the J. E. and L. E. Maybee Foundation of Tulsa, a foundation aiding religious and charitable institutions of higher learning from Missouri to New Mexico. The balance of $1.4 million needed to meet the goal included a $150,000 gift of stock from James L. "Bud" Walton, senior vice president and cofounder of Wal-Mart with his brother Sam. The Walton gift reflected the influence of his daughter Ann Kroenke, wife of Stan Kroenke of the Columbia-based Kroenke Group. Ann Kroenke, a trustee of the college, had attended Christian College in 1968. A registered nurse, she took special interest in the college's nursing program, and the gift, earmarked for upgrading the science laboratories, established the James L. Walton Laboratories. The sciences then moved from the basement level of Dorsey Hall into a space in Robnett-Spence four times as large. Meanwhile, in Dorsey Hall classrooms, plaques recognized donors contributing toward each room's renovation. Along with the remodeling, Williams Hall received a special marker from the Daughters of American Colonists recognizing its historic importance.[7]

Other gifts aided renovation. The former New Classroom Building became the Genevieve Koontz Buchanan Classroom Building with the gift of $148,000, and a contribution from Dora M. Johnson, dean of students from 1951 to 1957, provided for renewal of St. Clair Hall parlors in a period style. The Charter Day celebration of January 1993 included the college rededication of a refurbished Launer Auditorium in ceremonies including a speech by trustee Desmond Lee. Lee's gift of $10,000 for new stage curtains was reminiscent of his father's 1944 gift of $500 for precisely the same item a decade after he had left the presidency. Alumni financed another project, the complete refurbishing of the chapel, completed in the spring of 1995. Results of the campuswide overhaul were impressive, preserving the old charm while bringing the college up-to-date.[8]

The Ruthenberg administration also tended to technological needs. An upgraded and expanded computer system and installation of IBM personal computers, both on campus and at ESD sites, provided a 480 percent increase in computer availability. By 1991, the Instructional Technology Services Center with a new computer system provided expanded terminals for student use and the ability to coordinate with specific academic classes. In 1992, a new Hewlett-Packard HP9000 replaced the old mainframe, providing increased storage ability at twelve times the speed of the earlier system. In the area of energy technology, a new ground-source heat-pump system for the entire campus replaced the antiquated radiators and window air conditioners with a state-of-the-art system. Causing massive upheaval and deafening noise during completion, the project proved its worth. In addition to the comfort of year-round temperature control for each room on campus, the system, available on few campuses at that time, brought a drastic reduction in costs.[9]

With the addition of surrounding property on Eighth Street and Rangeline, the college added substantial space for parking, especially crucial for accommodating the needs of the Evening College. Reluctant to destroy still usable property, administrators turned one problem into an opportunity. The *Columbia Daily Tribune* described the solution: "There are three two-story houses advertised in the 'Free for Free' classifieds under an ad for Great Pyrenees crossguard puppies." The college received fifteen calls for the houses at 605 and 806 Eighth Street and at 813 Rangeline, conducting tours of the properties on December 15 and 16, 1992. The *Tribune* article called the proposition a "perfect present for that hard-to-shop-for someone on your Christmas list." Recipients bore the cost of moving the houses, and the college, wanting "to give the homes to someone who will use them," got what it wanted with the empty lots.[10]

Ruthenberg's love of Chinese culture and his long-developed close ties to Taiwan resulted in another acquisition. A gift of $500,000 for the "advancement of Chinese culture in mid-America" came from David T. Lee, a restauranteur in Washington, D.C., and director of the National Center for Asian Cultural Arts in Washington. This gift subsidized a fund bringing the college $40,000 to $60,000 per year in payments, allowing the purchase of a former church building on the southwest corner of Eighth and Alton Streets. The college used the site, beginning in July 1987, for a three-year Cultural Center pilot project. Ruthenberg hired Patrick Overton, an ordained minister who had worked in the area of cultural diversity and intercultural communications, to head the project while teaching religious studies and communications. The Center for Community and Cultural Studies not only served the Columbia College community but also offered outreach programs for rural and small-town settings. Through Overton's efforts, the center entered into partnerships with the Columbia Arts Resource Council, the Missouri Association of Community Arts Agencies, the Missouri Alliance for

Arts Education, the Asian Pacific Council for Arts Education, the Missouri School of Religion, the Middle States Consortium of Statewide Assemblies, and the Mid-American Academy of the Christian Church.[11]

In addition to taking workshops, seminars, and training sessions to rural and small-town areas, the center and its partners brought to the Columbia College campus the 1989 meeting of the Asian Pacific Conference of Arts Education. Columbia College representatives attended the organization's 1987 biennial conference in Kanasawa, Japan, in preparation for hosting the conference, and at that conference, Ruthenberg was named president of the Asian Pacific Confederation of Arts Educators, the first non-Asian to hold the position. The organization, representing more than seventy Asian and Pacific nations, including Canada, the United States, and Mexico, had held previous conferences in Singapore, Indonesia, the Philippines, Taiwan, and Japan. Ruthenberg acted as host of the 1989 conference in Columbia, held July 29–August 2, with Overton serving as conference director. Attendees included 315 arts educators, artists, and arts leaders from twelve countries with keynote speakers from the National Endowment for the Arts, Smithsonian Institution, ASIA Society, and Getty Center for Education through the Arts. Of seven languages used throughout the conference, the opening session was translated into Japanese, Korean, and Mandarin.[12]

The center became the Wang Cultural Arts Center at a dedication in May 1993 in honor of Wang Yu Fa, whose two sons attended Columbia College. Wang published the *Times* (Taiwan) and headed a copper and steel company there. As part of the ceremonies, another benefactor, Hau Pei-tsun, former premier of the Republic of China, received an honorary degree given on behalf of the American League of Colleges and Universities (ALOCU), a voluntary association of more than twenty colleges and universities organized by Ruthenberg in January 1984 as an agency for recruitment and facilitation of international students wishing to attend colleges and universities in the United States. The league established sister-institution relationships and other academic and economic ties, also aiding educational programs overseas for Asian students to study English before attending institutions of higher education in the United States.[13]

Another offshoot of Ruthenberg's ties to high government and academic officials in Taiwan was the gift to the college in 1990 of a Chinese pavilion, erected on back campus. Ruthenberg had envisioned a "cultural park," complete with five hundred plum lotus trees from Taiwan, as the site of an annual festival. Although the plum trees, victims of bureaucratic restrictions, never arrived, the venture eventually led to construction of the pavilion, the result of a 1984 visit to Taiwan during which Ruthenberg discussed the idea with T. L. Chang, president of the National Taiwan Academy of Arts. The academy became a sister institution to Columbia College, sending students to campus during the next two summers. In the fall of 1986,

Ruthenberg led a group called the American Association of College and University Presidents on a trip to Taiwan, after which Columbia College became the only institution in the United States allowed to offer courses to faculty members of Taiwan institutions in Taiwan. As these and other numerous relationships developed, the pavilion became a reality, a gift of the Taiwanese government.[14]

The construction in Taiwan of the pavilion, with its ornate and intricate tiles, took six months, after which it was dismantled and shipped to Columbia College to be reconstructed, piece by piece into a twenty-six-ton structure thirty-one feet high and seventy-two feet long. Six Chinese workers from the Tradition Sculpture and Relief Construction Company and one from the National Taiwan Academy of Arts put the pavilion in place between July 16 and August 5. The college dedicated the pavilion on October 28, 1990, in the presence of high-ranking officials from Taiwan: Gen. Wego W. K. Chiang, second son of Gen. Chiang Kai-shek and secretary general of the National Security Council of the Republic of China; Raymond Pai, director general of the Coordinating Council of North American Affairs for the Republic of China; and T. L. Chang. Calling the pavilion "an acknowledgment of the friendship and support of our peoples," Ruthenberg built upon that friendship throughout his presidency.[15]

As a president who "made things happen," Ruthenberg, according to Atkins, "saw opportunities in the Pacific Rim that a lot of people might not have seen." Not content with bringing Asian students to campus, he organized sister-city and sister-institution relationships, involved the college in class work in Taiwan and Japan, and even set up a pilot program as a potential overseas Extended Studies site.[16]

Ruthenberg announced in September 1986 that Columbia College could accept 30 to 35 Asian students and that he would "broker" for other colleges who were interested in accepting students. When 276 students applied to come to the United States in 1987, he accepted the first 19 from Taiwan, placing them in a degree-completion program at Columbia College with a concentration in American studies, and arranged for others to attend colleges elsewhere in the Midwest. He facilitated the process not only by making sister-institution arrangements but also by hiring an international studies director on campus to manage all international student admissions and preregistration activities. By the fall of 1989, the college had sixteen sister-institution agreements, particularly in Taiwan, Japan, Korea, and Malaysia, and a sister-city agreement between the City of Columbia and Matto City, Japan. By 1991, 189 international students constituted 23 percent of the student body, and students on campus represented such diverse countries as Taiwan, Korea, China, Japan, Thailand, Indonesia, Malaysia, Zaire, Kenya, Qatar, Egypt, Spain, Finland, Cyprus, Greece, Peru, and Switzerland.[17]

The college developed a variety of programs to meet the needs of international students, programs based on student preferences and language skills. A Language Certification Program, a ten-day program for high school students, combined intensive study of English as a Second Language (ESL) with field trips in the Columbia area, granting a Certificate of Achievement upon completion. Another, the American Experience Program, required enrollment in five courses with a heavy concentration on ESL and featured weekend field trips. A third program, the Senior Year Completion Program, actually a degree-completion program for adults, allowed the transfer of courses from the native country, giving special attention to language needs. Graduates received bachelor of arts in individual studies degrees. In the Traditional Student On-Campus Program, international students attended regular classes, including English composition, and participated in forums and special activities targeting their needs. These programs, offered under the auspices of the American League of Colleges and Universities, facilitated movement of international students into American institutions. Because of the enormous demand, especially in Japan and Taiwan, for American degrees, potential full-time international students sought ways to ensure entrance while maximizing their chances for success through programs emphasizing language skills. These courses could be taught overseas before the students came to the United States, preparing the student to sit in the American classrooms of participating ALOCU institutions.[18]

One such preparatory program played a particularly innovative role. The Transitional Academic Program (TAP) was taught in Japan at the Shin-Yokahama campus under an agreement between Columbia College and a corporation, the American Universities League, Japan Campus (AULJC). Students in the program received thirty-six hours of credit from Columbia College for completion of the courses with at least a C average, automatically making them eligible for entrance into any ALOCU institution. Students were to improve their English language skills while studying college-level general education courses. With American instructors hired by Columbia College, students could also become familiar with the American teaching style. The program included classes in English composition, algebra, Western civilization, geography, and biology, using laboratory facilities of a local high school. Faculty members used Columbia College–recommended textbooks and syllabi and were approved for hiring by Columbia College faculty, as at the college's ESD sites. The college also hired a director to oversee the academic program and administrative affairs. It was, in fact, a pilot program for an overseas ESD location.[19]

Shin-Yokahama (meaning "New Yokahama") was a bold experiment, the first American college venture in Japan to be examined by the North Central Association. Dean Miller reported to the board on September 1988: "The Transitional Academic Program (TAP), which is taught at the American

University League in Shin-Yokahama, was approved by the NCA Accrediting Association in late August 1988. A focused visit by an NCA team . . . in early February 1989 will complete the process."[20] However, the TAP management structure varied greatly from the college's usual ESD sites. The campus was run by the American Universities League, Japan Campus, headed by Kan Terada, a Japanese businessman, who provided the site, paid the instructors, and collected tuition from the students, sharing a portion of the fees with Columbia College. The college controlled the curriculum and teaching, entering into a contract with the AULJC for physical facilities and administration of the site, including marketing of the program. The major problem of the agreement, as it turned out, was the inability of Columbia College to control the site, and the corporation's relationship with faculty became particularly strained. The focused visit by the North Central Association began when the team came to the Columbia College campus on January 30–31, 1989, continuing with a visit to the Shin-Yokahama campus on March 12–14, 1989. Dean Miller preceded the team to Japan by a few days and discovered, to her total dismay, that faculty members were "in the middle of a virtual strike situation." The director of the program had not notified her of existing conditions, and the team walked into the middle of a battle between the corporation and the faculty over pay and academic freedom.[21]

According to the NCA team report, the faculty, shortly before the site visit, had received unexpected termination notices from the AULJC. The corporation had told instructors that they could expect to be rehired, but that there would be an evaluation process, including a classroom observation. Further, faculty members were dismayed by AULJC curricular changes made over the holiday without their consultation. The team reported:

> It was apparent that acceptable guarantees of academic freedom were totally absent. . . . The Shin-Yokahama on-site visit provided clear evidence that Columbia College could assure neither quality control nor normal standards of academic freedom. . . . The management of AULJC activities was frequently subject to the prerogative of a single individual, with no check or balance from either AULJC management . . . or Columbia and/or ALOCU oversight.[22]

The recommendation and final action by the NCA was that "the TAP program be terminated." The team did consider the concept "an educational experiment which shows great promise," but conditions mitigated against success. Adding to North Central's pique may have been an apparent lack of sufficient formal communication by Columbia College at the start of the program, despite Miller's assumption to the contrary. A commission policy required that an institution gain approval for a change in status before initiating any change, such as adding an overseas site. The college did request a change in status to add a statement that "some courses are also offered in

Shin-Yokahama, Japan," but apparently signed the contract with AULJC and began the program before receiving commission approval. The NCA issued a "Memorandum for the Record," meaning that the institution had initiated a change without the required approval and had thus "violated its institutional obligations of affiliation."[23]

The final commission report of May 23, 1989, gave the college until April 1990 to close the Shin-Yokahama location, and the college withdrew from the arrangement with the Japanese management firm. The experiment paved the way for later overseas programs by other institutions to be accredited, although none was offered again by Ruthenberg, who turned his efforts to other channels and relationships in the Pacific Rim. He was named Ambassador at Large by the Territorial Government of Guam in 1992 and received a Friendship Peace Prize from the Japanese Government, Ishikawa Prefecture.[24]

Although the potential overseas ESD site was aborted, those ongoing locations across the United States flourished under a well-administered program. Frank Westling, dean of the ESD program since 1975, worked with Frazier Moon, director of administrative services, until Westling's death in 1987. Moon then became dean of ESD, aided by Rene Nichols, former administrative assistant who became director of administration. Site directors, as chief administrative officers, reported to both the dean and the administrative head on campus, who supervised the budget and physical resources. The sites, both military and civilian, served a variety of students, 95 percent of whom were fully employed; 80 percent were under forty years old, 67 percent were male, and 66 percent were married.[25]

One of the fastest-growing sites, Jefferson City, moved back and forth from Evening College to ESD status, becoming finally an ESD site in 1987. The program, increasing 142 percent in 1984–1985, moved in 1985 to the former Richmond Hill grocery store at 630 Main Street, a structure placed on the Federal Register of Historic Places for its period architecture. The building was sold to the state in 1988, and the program continued to move frequently until, by the fall of 1994, it was in its sixth location, with the college finally occupying a building of its own in 2000. Of the military sites, Fort Leonard Wood, in southern Missouri, expanded regularly. When federal action in 1984 led to the closure of eighty-six military bases, five Columbia College sites were either closed or relocated, but expansion of Fort Leonard Wood as a base merely enlarged the Columbia College program at that location. By 1993, the site numbered roughly 760 students in each eight-week session, graduating around 1,000 students per year.[26]

The on-campus role of ESD also expanded. An elected representative of the program's directors served regularly on the Academic Affairs Committee, and directors attended weeklong conferences on campus each April and September. A special luncheon on March 15, 1993, celebrated the program's twentieth anniversary, highlighted by the presentation of a plaque to Don Foster for his nineteen years of service. Foster, who would retire in May 1993, had come to the college as assistant to the dean of faculty and registrar, moving on to be dean of ESD, acting president, dean of faculty, and vice president for administrative services. He later became a site director of the Blue Springs, Missouri, location. By 1994, the twentieth ESD site, Phoenix, opened, and enrollments at all locations exceeded 7,000 in the January 1994 session. Much refining of the program had also been the work of Frazier Moon, a decorated Vietnam War veteran and Columbia College graduate, who had served ESD for almost twenty years. The college recognized his contributions at the honors and awards convocation on April 22, 1994, with an honorary degree from Tiffen University. An article in *Friends* described the man and the event:

> It is easily understood why Moon received such an honor. . . . He served three tours in Vietnam and earned a bronze star with five clusters, the Vietnam cross of gallantry with palm and bronze star, and the army commendation medal, among many other awards. Cited as a "renaissance man," Moon has dedicated his life to . . . learning for himself and thousands of others. . . . Frazier Moon is just one more shining example of the driving forces leading Columbia College to be the best it can be.[27]

The most unusual opening of an ESD location resulted from Ruthenberg's personal initiative, acting outside board instructions. Quick to see opportunities where others might not, Ruthenberg recognized the need for availability of higher education in the area of the Lake of the Ozarks, where only 26 percent of high school graduates went on to college. The property he chose for a civilian ESD site and retirement center had a checkered past. In the 1970s, the Worldwide Church of God had developed 160 acres along Osage Beach D Road and near the junction of Highways 54 and 42, but had withdrawn a few years later. H&W Company, owners of Factory Merchants Outlet Mall, bought the property as the site for a mall but ultimately located a few miles away and offered the former church property for sale. A horse-racing enthusiast next had an option to buy the land but, unable to obtain a state license for his plans, abandoned the idea. Ruthenberg then decided to make his move, despite the trustees' refusal to make the purchase, and formed a private corporation that he funded personally to purchase the 154-acre property for $1.6 million. With the president as chairman of the not-for-profit board, his entire administrative staff—Mary Miller, Chuck Bobbitt, Frazier Moon, Lindi Overton, Dona Sue Cool, and Faye Burchard—constituted the board of Lake University Corporation. Although the Columbia College Board of Trustees was not directly involved, plans called for 34 acres to be used for college purposes and the rest to be sold to developers or kept for development. Once the mortgage was retired, the property would revert to the college, and Lake University would be dissolved. The college had the right of first refusal for any land sold.[28]

With classes to begin in October 1990 at the lake site, Ruthenberg reported to trustees in September that 60 students had already enrolled. That number increased to 211 by September 1991, and students reportedly thought it was "one of the greatest things that has happened to that area." The Missouri Coordinating Board for Higher Education had denied a request for a state-supported community college before Lake University had come about, and Moon reported that "expressions of support have been overwhelming."[29]

Despite local enthusiasm, financial arrangements proved problematic. Combined loans of $1.6 million had been reduced by the sale of 42-plus acres to Ozark Meadows for $253,000 in December 1992 and by lease payments made by the college, but Ruthenberg's plans to sell acreage to developers did not materialize. Since the college was providing virtually all of the proceeds toward paying off the loan anyway, trustees decided to buy the property, concluding that it was better to acquire the title and pay off the loans than to make payments. Thus, in January 1993, the college became the owner of significant lake property and a successful civilian site.[30]

In addition to the success of the Extended Studies Division, the college enjoyed an equally prosperous Evening College, established in March 1975. By its tenth anniversary, student numbers had increased from 60 to 415, with 714 course enrollments, and the college was renting classroom space from the neighboring junior high school until a new classroom building could be completed. On November 3, 1988, Southwestern Bell Telephone Company awarded the program its first Continuing Education Achievement Award and praised its work: "Programs like this are vital to the state's efforts to develop a literate work force, an important ingredient for Missouri's economic future." By May 1989, Virginia Ponder, the program's director, for the first time reported 1,000 course enrollments for the eight-week session. By April 1990, the Evening College boasted 903 graduates and released a study of its student body: 56 percent were between the ages of twenty-six and forty; 60 percent were female; 51 percent were married; 90 percent were employed; 78 percent were from Boone County; and 54 percent were on financial aid. Appreciative of the opportunity for a well-educated workforce, 111 Boone County businesses paid toward employee education. In the fall of 1992, the Evening Program officially became the Evening and Continuing Education Division as a more descriptive title. It had developed a coterie of long-serving adjunct faculty members, including such popular instructors as Lloyd Miller in business, Jim Metscher in sociology, Jack Barnhouse and Jim and Liz Brydges Metscher in English, and Lisa Isaacson in philosophy.[31]

Of all the programs impacted by Ruthenberg's presidency, none showed more startling results than the sports area. The more aggressive cougar replaced the centaur as mascot, and an Athletic Review Committee formed in 1985 carried out recommendations to improve the athletic program. By 1986, the college fielded varsity teams in men's basketball and in women's softball and volleyball under the direction of Athletic Director Art Siebels. With the addition of soccer in 1987, the college hired Jon Leamy as coach, boasting seven intramural sports and four intercollegiate teams.[32]

The most decisive change in athletics, however, came with the hiring of Robert Burchard in 1988 as director of athletics and head basketball coach. The college also hired his wife, Faye, as director of student activities. Bob Burchard came to the college after seven years at Missouri Western State College. He was well known in Missouri athletic circles as secretary-treasurer of the Missouri Basketball Hall of Fame and of the Missouri Basketball Coaches' Association and as a member of the executive committee of the Missouri Show-Me Collegiate Committee. Also respected for his awards and accomplishments, he received the Show-Me State Collegiate Conference Award in 1989, the first of four such awards. In 1990, he won the District 16 coach of the year title. Asked whether he believed he had reached his potential, Burchard's response revealed much about his philosophy: "Oh, gosh no! If I reached my potential I'd quit; there wouldn't be anything else for me to do. I hope I never do reach my potential because then I wouldn't be able to live my dream anymore. Today I read a quote that said 'never let a day go by without a dream,' and I won't."[33]

Named National Association of Intercollegiate Athletics (NAIA) administrator of the year for 1991–1992, Burchard could have made his years at Columbia College a stepping-stone to other positions. The intangible sense of identifying with the college that had kept outstanding faculty from leaving affected Burchard as well. Praising the college's flexibility and willingness to change, he valued having a role in an "ever-changing situation" where there was abundant opportunity to be successful. His appreciation of Ruthenberg's management style added to that growing loyalty. When Burchard arrived as coach, the basketball team was traveling in old, "basically dangerous" vans. Ruthenberg promised buses for the next year, seemingly impossible, but they had buses the next year. Other rash predictions by Ruthenberg, such as having a nationally ranked team and hosting the national softball championship tournament, also came about. Ruthenberg pointed to an unattractive property near campus, promising that within two years the college would have a soccer field right there, and the program "wound up with a gorgeous soccer field." Burchard liked the fact that Ruthenberg was also a dreamer, a risk taker, and a passionate promoter of the college. Both men understood the value of the athletic program and had much the same goals and philosophy, according to Burchard: "He would take you beyond where you thought your comfort zone was. He had a great way of getting the most from the least."[34]

The athletic program began to take off as soon as Burchard took charge. By January 1989, the men's basketball team finished second in Show-Me Collegiate Conference play. The women's softball team, with a 38–10 record, was ranked sixth in the NAIA top twenty. The women's volleyball team (41–11) went to the district playoffs, as did the men's soccer team (10–4–3) after not having won a game the year before. Equally important, the fifty-four Columbia College student athletes had a combined 2.8 grade point average, and twenty-four of them (44 percent) had 3.0 or better.[35]

The Columbia College basketball team went to the NAIA national tournament in 1990, even making the "Sweet Sixteen" round before losing to Oral Roberts University. Perhaps the team's biggest fan was Ruthenberg himself, an inveterate traveler to out-of-town games, relating easily to players and fans. When the team met Drury College at Springfield in the district finals in 1990, Ruthenberg and the Drury College president sat together. Columbia College was down twelve points at halftime, which was no surprise to the Drury president, who had already reserved a special suite in the Kansas City Kemper Arena for the nationals. When Columbia College came back in the second half to win with a last-second shot, not only did the victory keep Drury from the nationals, but also the Drury president presented Ruthenberg with his tickets. This win marked the first time a Columbia College team had gone to any national play, and, according to Burchard, "I don't think we've looked back since." The team returned to national competition in 1995 when, ranked ninth nationally, it received an at-large bid but subsequently lost to Fresno Pacific College.[36]

The college won still greater recognition through its women's fast-pitch softball team. The Columbia College High School Invitational Tournament, begun in 1989, and the National Junior College Athletic Association Regional Tournament, added in 1994, brought attention to the college and the team. Coach Chuck Bobbitt, manager of administrative services under Ruthenberg, was conference coach of the year every year from 1988 to 1993. District coach of the year in 1990, 1991, and 1992, Bobbitt became National NAIA softball coach of the year in 1990. He believed strongly in the "student athlete" concept, and several of his team members made the academic all-conference team each year. The team ranked in the NAIA top twenty-five each year from 1987 to 1995 and rose to number seven in the national rankings in 1990. It became district champion in 1990, 1991, and 1992 and went to the national tournament each year from 1990 to 1995.[37]

One outstanding team member, pitcher Wendy Mertz, was honored by *USA Today* as its "Missouri 1989 amateur achiever of the year" with a 34–2 record. Named NAIA district pitcher of the week four times and national pitcher of the week, she was a second-team All-American. Between graduate degrees, she went back to work for Bobbitt briefly before becoming championship coordinator for the NAIA in Tulsa. She eventually went to Knoxville, Tennessee, as the assistant director of the Women's Basketball Hall of Fame, the only facility dedicated solely to women's sports. A teammate of Mertz, Wendy Spratt, also an All-American, replaced Bobbitt as softball coach in 1994. As a student, she combined scholarship with sports, achieving a 3.98 grade point average. Playing at Columbia College from 1987 to 1990, she was an all-district player four times and an NAIA All-American scholar athlete. Before replacing Bobbitt, she served as assistant women's softball coach at Yale.[38]

The college brought national tournament excitement to Columbia by hosting the NAIA National Women's Fast-Pitch Softball Tournament at the Rainbow Softball Center in Columbia in 1991 and for the next three years. The Columbia College softball team ranked second nationally in May 1991.[39]

The women's volleyball team made headlines in 1989 when it accepted an invitation to open the Japan Sports Complex in Matto City, Japan, sister city to Columbia. The college took seven team members, six to play and one substitute, to face a Kinjo College team of thirty or so players. The event was held with much fanfare, including a celebratory dinner following play. With matches traditionally won by the team taking any two of three games, the Columbia College team won the first two games, but the mayor of Matto City rose to announce that there would be a third game. The match then continued, the Kinjo players won the third game, and all involved, satisfied, went to dinner.[40]

The Columbia College volleyball team excelled, becoming conference champions seven of the eight years from 1987 to 1995 and appearing in the NAIA National Volleyball Championship Tournament in 1994 and 1995. Chris Viers, coach from 1985 to 1989, was replaced in 1990 by Susan Kreklow, who also served as a volleyball camp clinician throughout the Midwest and as the NAIA representative on the Board of Directors of USA Volleyball. In 1994, her husband, Wayne, joined her as coach. Wayne Kreklow, a former NBA Boston Celtic and a member of that club's world championship team, had been an assistant to the head volleyball coach at the University of Missouri–Columbia. In the later 1990s, the Kreklows would make the Columbia College women's volleyball team a powerhouse in its sport as the top NAIA team in the United States.[41]

Men's soccer progressed, winning the conference title in 1989, 1990, and 1994. Columbia College coaches who won conference coach of the year titles included Robert Godsey in 1989, Bill Chapman in 1990, and Dan Hogan in 1991, 1992, and 1994. Under Hogan's guidance, the team continued to excel in the later 1990s. Hogan, coming to Columbia College from Northeast Missouri State University at Kirksville, where he was assistant soccer coach, and from Ottawa University in Kansas, had won All-American honors as an undergraduate and played internationally. He served as NAIA regional soccer representative and as chairman of the American Midwest Conference's Men's Soccer Committee.[42]

The Show-Me Collegiate Conference, founded in 1987, included Columbia College, Hannibal La-Grange College, Harris-Stowe State College, Lindenwood College, McKendree College in Illinois, and Missouri Baptist College. In 1993 it added Iowa Wesleyan College, Park College, and William Woods University. Faced with the presence of two non-Missouri institutions as members, the group became the American Midwest Conference (AMC). Conference champions advanced to district tournaments and then to the national NAIA tournaments. In 1991, President Ruthenberg accepted a three-year term on the NAIA Council of Presidents of the eighteen NAIA schools in District 16. Columbia College's major coaches—Burchard, the Kreklows, Hogan, and Spratt—remaining with the college into the next administration, showed amazing longevity that, according to Burchard, "says a lot for the college."[43]

In addition to a more active and successful sports program, the college enjoyed a more vigorous student-life program in the Ruthenberg years. The term *cocurriculum* came into early use at Columbia College, intended to indicate that student services, just as in the academic area, were planned, implemented, and evaluated. In addition to athletics, these services included physical recreation, career planning and placement, counseling services, a health center, residential life management, and student activities.[44]

The dominant figure in student life, Faye Burchard, came to the college with her husband, Bob, in 1988 as director of student activities. Formerly coordinator of intramural sports and student recreation and facility manager at Missouri Western College, her move to the deanship of student life occurred almost without her knowing it. When Robert Harris resigned from that position in 1989, a question about his replacement was raised in a staff meeting. Ruthenberg replied that "Faye is going to be my new dean of students." She laughed it off as a joke until, following repeated comments by colleagues that she was, indeed, dean of students, she paid a call to the president, who confirmed his intent. Somewhat reluctant to take the assignment, she made a pact with the president that she would accept if he would be supportive of her efforts. From such a beginning came a productive and mutually supportive relationship.[45]

A major feature of Burchard's impact on student life was the expansion of the role of student leaders. Student resident assistants (RAs) maintained close contact with students not only in problem solving but also in encouraging participation in campus activities, providing programs of interest, explaining policies and rules, and recording violations. Orientation leaders (OLs) helped student-life staff conduct intensive orientation of students new to the college each fall and also participated in "Summer Connections," a series of preregistration days each summer for students coming the next fall. Burchard made retention a focus of her attention, helping form the Retention Council as a campuswide body for problem solving. She stressed as well the role of the Freshman Experience class, contributing to its refinement into the Introduction to Columbia College class that replaced it. Burchard would continue such interests into the next administration, providing still more opportunities for student leadership in both student-life and academic areas.

Increased enrollments rewarded the college's efforts, reaching 783 in 1990. Ron Cronacker became director of admissions in 1992, and, by 1994, the admissions office reported 34 percent more applications than the fall of 1993 with 30 percent more acceptances and 22 percent more students committed to attend. Retention efforts increased with the creation of the first *Advising Handbook* and the use of Noel/Levitz Retention Management System Inventories to measure student attitudes. In the spring of 1991, Elliot Battle, a retired and well-experienced local high school counselor, became a special assistant to the president as "unofficial counselor" to minority students and chaired the Cultural Diversity Task Force. Retiring from that position in 1997, Battle became a trustee in 2000.[46]

Student clubs increased along with other student activities. New honorary societies included Alpha Lambda Delta, the freshman scholastic honorary, and an international English honor society, Sigma Tau Delta, which held its charter initiation on April 29, 1991. With the influx of international students, the International Students Fellowship provided social interaction, academic assistance, field trips, and general information and adjustment measures, and Cathie M. Muschany became director of international programs. A history society began for any interested students, the Arts Club reemerged, and a highly successful chapter of Students in Free Enterprise began, all adding to opportunities already present on campus.[47]

Meanwhile, the college's alumni office expanded its activities as the number of living alumni increased. Records in April 1988 disclosed 16,962 alumni with mailing addresses: 9,799 were from the day program, 646 from the Evening College, and 6,517 from ESD sites. With the rapid growth of adult graduates, the alumni office, under Diane O'Hagan, concentrated on integrating Evening College and ESD alumni into college activities. It also cosponsored campus ambassadors (students helping in the admissions effort), published an alumni directory, and, in 1988, expanded the awards given by the college at the spring homecoming ceremonies. In addition to the Distinguished Alumni Award, other honors included the Young Alumni Award, Community Service Award, Columbia College Service Award, and Professional Achievement Award. By September 1988, alumni numbered 21,376, 60 percent of whom had graduated in the preceding twenty-nine years. The number swelled to 27,000 in 1994 with 19,000 graduated at sites outside Columbia.[48]

By the end of the Ruthenberg administration, the alumni office staff was engaging in more activities than ever. In addition to working with the National Alumni Association and local clubs and organizing the annual alumni weekend and the granting of awards, it gave support to an active Alumni-Admissions Volunteer Program, sent out direct-mail solicitations for the Alumni Fund, held receptions for the three graduation ceremonies held each year, and published four issues of *Friends* a year. *Friends,* mailed to supporters of the college as well as to alumni, went to 29,000 addresses by 1995.[49]

The alumni office lost a longtime loyal member in 1994 when Jane Crow retired after thirty-two years of service. A 1957 graduate of the college, she had served as director of alumni services from 1963 to 1984 and as associate director for ten years. She contributed to making alumni the single largest source of gift support for the college, carrying out her duties "with grace and dignity," appreciated and "universally respected by faculty, staff, students, and alumni alike."[50]

The financial strength of the college depended on a successful development office under the leadership of Ralph Glenn and later of Dona Sue Cool, as well as on the president's influence. An increase in gifts in 1986 included a bequest from Louis Blosser, trustee from 1937 to 1965, who had died in 1974 and left the college proceeds from the sale of his 733-acre Saline County farm. Another former trustee and 1941 graduate, Althea Whitcraft Schiffman, contributed $250,000 to the endowment fund in memory of her mother, Althea Whitcraft. Schiffman, a trustee from 1983 until her death in 1987, was the mother of a 1965 graduate, Joy Schiffman. She was also a director of the National Alumni Association and recipient of the college's Distinguished Alumni Award in 1985. Another major gift, the 1986 contribution of $500,000 for the promotion of Chinese culture, came from David Lee. That same year, James Silvey, trustee from 1958 to 1964, gave $136,000 toward endowing a chair in philosophy and religion, leaving also a bequest of $96,000 to the college upon his death in 1988. Silvey's daughter, Marilyn, a 1960 graduate, served as a trustee from 1988 to 1993.[51]

Later gifts included, among others, significant funds from Dorothy Heinkel, a trustee from 1959 to 1990, and from the 3M Corporation to foster cultural diversity. By September 1993, the college had received gifts of more than $1 million for the year, and revenues had exceeded budget projections by $3,091,425. Trustees then proclaimed that funds from planned giving not otherwise designated would be placed in the permanent endowment fund. In 1994, the president, continuing to remind audiences that "the residue of your estate belongs to Columbia College," established the St. Clair Society for those who complied. In the later years of the Ruthenberg administration, a bequest of $325,858 from the estate of Gen. Ralph Richards of Washington, D.C., and a $200,000 contribution from Desmond

Lee for an indoor tennis facility, brought restricted and unrestricted gifts for 1994 to nearly $2 million. In addition, Lee donated $150,000 in matching funds toward the arts and humanities building to be named Brown Hall in appreciation of the million-dollar bequest from the Emma Jean Brown Ballew estate. Funds to renovate the college chapel, at a cost of $80,000, took the form of gifts in memory of Virginia Southwell Singletary. By the time of Ruthenberg's retirement in 1995, renovations and construction had been virtually completed with the help of gifts and bequests far exceeding the imagination of trustees before 1984.[52]

As president, Ruthenberg enjoyed the support of a strong and active board, tempered by past adversities and enthusiastic about the future. An especially able body carrying over from the Kelly years, most of whom remained as trustees after Ruthenberg's retirement, included B. D. Simon, Tom Atkins, Marvin Owens, Andy Bass, Marty Toler, Don Schubert, Mike Angelo, Peggy Price, and Daisy Grossnickle. However, a number of effective and faithful trustees continuing from previous administrations were lost to the board through death. Virginia Singletary of the class of 1939, one of the most significant benefactors of the college, died in 1995 after serving as a trustee for twenty-seven years. Her death came just one year after making her last gift to the college, a donation for the construction of the arts and humanities center. A twenty-nine-year trustee, Elizabeth Gentry, of the class of 1920, died in 1993. Founder of the St. Louis alumni club and a president of the National Alumnae Association, she, like Singletary, had received the college's Distinguished Alumni Award. Both Dorothy Heinkel and Leta Spencer died in 1990, having been active and valuable board members for thirty and twenty-five years, respectively. Althea Schiffman, who died in 1987, had also been active in gifts and work for the college. Other valued members lost to the board through death included Isabel Browning, Estelle Bradford, Mary Banks Perry, and Jack Estes.

More than fifty trustees served at some point during the Ruthenberg presidency, most coming onto the board as new members during those years. Desmond Lee, son of former president Edgar Lee, was a frequent benefactor, as was J. W. Stafford, whose name graced the new library built from his generosity. Sally Six Landon, graduate of the class of 1938, distinguished herself and the college by producing a comprehensive *Trustees' Handbook* of such excellence that Ruthenberg declared it "the case study that every college has been looking for." Upon nomination by Chairman Atkins, Landon received the Distinguished Service Award in Trusteeship from the Association of Governing Boards for her work. Walter E. "Web" Bixby III, whose father had served before him, joined the board, as did John A. Schiffman, husband of the late trustee. Bixby was responsible for maintaining the Reynolds Foundation established by his grandmother. The Reverend John Yonker Sr. continued the tie between the Christian Church and the board. William H. Stewart and William Eckhoff became valuable members of the Finance Committee, with Eckhoff contributing significantly in the area of construction. Other active and effective members included Robert Maupin, Justin Perry, Richard Pryor, and William Toalson, whose mother was an alumna. Richard Montgomery, coming to the board in 1994, became its vice president in 1999. One of the most important recruits, brought to the board by Ruthenberg through their mutual interest in community service, was Daniel L. Scotten, former president of the Columbia Chamber of Commerce and a worker in the college's community campaigns. Inspired by the quality of the board and the harmonious mesh of affection for the old Christian College with progressive changes as Columbia College, Scotten so impressed his colleagues that they named him chairman of the board when Atkins retired from that position in 1999.[53]

The last five years before President Ruthenberg's retirement in 1995 saw continued innovation and financial stabilization. The college had completed its tenth consecutive year in the black with revenues exceeding budget projections by $800,000. Academic priorities included increasing minority enrollments, continuing self-evaluation of the curriculum and instruction, and completing accreditation activities for teacher education, social work, and business administration. In admissions, emphasis on preenrollment activities included involvement of faculty through telephone calls and letters sent by the admissions office. Student life stressed improvements in the grievance system, cultural awareness, counseling, alcohol and drug prevention, and career services. The planning process produced a long-range plan for 1990–1995 emphasizing synchronization of academic instructional standards and delivery among day, evening, and ESD programs. It also stressed the need for a sustaining endowment fund and funding by federal, state, and private sources. The plan sought to upgrade employee compensation and stability, attain retention and enrollment stability, and continue property development. Finally, preparation for a successful accreditation review rounded out the agenda.[54]

Although all of the plan met with varying degrees of success, it was the 1992 North Central Association accreditation review, resulting in the awarding of the maximum ten-year reaccreditation, that typified the successes of the period.

With a greatly changed environment, the old 1982 mission statement seemed out of date, and the board approved a new version on May 14, 1993, calling attention particularly to the preparation of "students who vary in age, background, and ability for entry-level positions, for advancement in various occupations and professions, for a broad understanding of the liberal arts and sciences, and for graduate study."[55]

In a major program expansion, the college moved ahead quickly in 1994–1995 with the introduction of graduate study. A proposal for a master of arts in business (M.B.A.), presented by the business department, received faculty approval and support of the Educational Policies Committee of the board by the end of 1994. By January 1995, it was under review by the Missouri Coordinating Board of Higher Education in Jefferson City and gained the approval of the Columbia College Board of Trustees at its January 13, 1995, meeting. Proposals from the education and psychology department followed the same course for a master of arts in teaching (M.A.T.), completed with the aid of a Teacher Education Advisory Board. Graduate courses, career-oriented and designed for adult learners, would be offered in the evening for part-time students utilizing regular full-time day faculty members as well as adjunct faculty. Completion of plans and North Central Association action awaited the coming of a new administration.[56]

Looking back on his decade of leadership, Ruthenberg announced on September 23, 1994, that he would leave office the next May. He had promised the college ten years and stayed eleven, completing the college's fifteenth consecutive year in the black and its ninth year with no short-term borrowing. He had spent more than $8 million in renovations in addition to expanding the college acreage and engaging in the construction of the Southwell Sports Complex and Stafford Library, the near completion of Brown Hall, and the purchase of the Wang Cultural Arts Center. The college also had new science laboratories, an Instructional Technology Services Center, new soccer and softball fields, and increased parking areas. Ruthenberg reduced the college debt from $1.8 million to zero and increased the endowment from $350,000 to nearly $2 million. He saw the college receive a ten-year accreditation and the percentage of full-time faculty with terminal degrees increase from 48 percent to 77 percent. The day program enrollment had risen from 652 in 1984 to 817 in 1994, with 1,148 class enrollments in the Evening College. The college prospered in an environment that had caused sixty-two colleges in Missouri to fail since 1851.[57]

As early as January 1994, Ruthenberg had cautioned trustees that it was time "to think about a transition in leadership." Trustee Marty Toler headed a search committee to select a new president by January or February 1995 to allow transition time. The college accepted applications until November 10, 1994, after which a selection committee of six trustees, one faculty member, one staff member, and the president of the Campus Community Government narrowed the field to five candidates. Two finalists visited campus the week of January 16, and, ten days later, Atkins introduced Gerald T. Brouder to an all-campus assembly as the next president, effective May 15, 1995. Brouder paid homage to Ruthenberg as a "tough, tough act to follow," noting that "the college is really poised to do great things, and the credit goes directly to

Dr. Ruthenberg." That evening, Brouder attended a special dinner honoring Ruthenberg.[58]

The honor given Ruthenberg at the January 26 dinner, the Distinguished Eagle Scout Award, was granted by the National Eagle Scout Association after receiving a nomination from the local council. The award, begun in 1969 and given to such disparate recipients as Samuel Walton, Gerald Ford, H. Ross Perot, Bill Bradley, and Stephen Spielberg, was intended for those people who had received the Eagle Scout Award twenty-five or more years earlier and had achieved success in life's work along with active volunteering in the community. The keynote speaker at the dinner given for Ruthenberg was Helen Robson Walton of the class of 1939 and widow of recipient Sam Walton. She said of Ruthenberg: "Vision is fine, but without action it is only a dream. . . . He finds the things that need to be done and he does them."[59]

The college bid farewell to Ruthenberg on Friday, May 12, 1995, with daylong festivities. A board meeting in the morning, followed by a luncheon for the entire college family, preceded a reception in the afternoon. Recognition and gifts came from the National Alumni Association, staff, faculty, and students. Threatening weather grounded a balloon ride, but memories for the outgoing president included a magnificent Waterford bowl, a collection of letters from well-wishers, and a collage of pictures. Perhaps one of the most unusual gifts was "An Ode to Dr. Donald B. Ruthenberg," composed and presented by board chairman Tom Atkins.[60]

The transition from Ruthenberg to Brouder came with commencement ceremonies at Columbia College and at the University of Missouri–Columbia on May 14, 1995, with Brouder taking office on May 15. A *Columbia Daily Tribune* editorial marked the event:

> As he presided over graduation exercises Sunday, Don Ruthenberg did his last official act as president of Columbia College. Standing nearby, ready to take over, was Gerald Brouder, former provost and interim chancellor at MU. The moment is right for both men. Along with the tireless efforts of board members Marvin Owens, perennial chairman Tom Atkins, and others, Ruthenberg made Columbia College one of the surviving private educational institutions among many that inevitably will fail. In a real sense, he and his institution have been at the front of the higher education curve. The most prestigious institutions today are discussing among themselves how they can become more customer oriented. Columbia College . . . had to become customer friendly, and in the process it became an institution of eminent value. In making this transition, Don Ruthenberg not only helped save the college, he put it on good ground for the indefinite future. Gerald Brouder is the right person to carry the baton on the next leg.[61]

What the *Tribune* article did not mention was that Ruthenberg's "last official act" was to present his daughter, Janet, the last degree he would ever grant as president. Brouder's ascension to the presidency of Columbia College on May 15 came the day after he had seen his son be graduated from the University of Missouri–Columbia.

Although he had left the college, Ruthenberg's activities hardly slackened. He served as a consultant for many of the private colleges in mid-Missouri and became a trustee of Kemper Military School and College in Boonville from 1996 to 1999. He served as acting dean at Kemper for six weeks just before that institution's North Central Association visitation in January 1997. Continuing his frequent travels to Asia, he spent twenty-two weeks in mainland China in 1997 in a variety of educational ventures as well as concentrating on establishing an English language school in Thailand. From his residence in the Lake of the Ozarks area, he continued to orchestrate events ranging from local activities to the international arena, showing no sign of truly "retiring" as of the end of the century.[62]

The selection of Gerald Brouder in January 1995 caused excitement not only on campus but also throughout the community. An editorial by H. J. Waters III in the *Columbia Daily Tribune* as early as January 16 called him "one of the best-liked MU top administrators . . . [who] would bring an aura of elevated academic emphasis." Brouder had lived in the Columbia area for eighteen years. He had not only served as director of clinical services and in other positions at the University Health Sciences Center, but also held such campuswide positions at the University of Missouri–Columbia as provost, deputy chancellor, and interim chancellor. His degrees in nursing included a Ph.D. degree from the University of Texas–Austin, an M.S. degree from Northern Illinois University, and a B.A. degree from the University of Illinois. He was also active in community service, especially as an advocate of the United Way and the Rusk Rehabilitation Center, activities he would not only continue but also expand as president of Columbia College.[63]

Brouder's official election as president by the trustees at the May 12, 1999, board meeting brought the college even more in touch with its roots. It reinforced the historic tie between the college and the university, recognizing a community of interest to both institutions. It also reemphasized the early practice that the president's wife be fully and intimately involved in college affairs. Bonnie Brouder, a registered nurse at the University Health Sciences Center, resigned her position to become a full-time supporter of the college and its interests as well as a worker for the preservation of its history. Brouder's election also continued the process of opening new doors in education, of placing a high value on quality and integrity in education, and of supporting the college's traditional emphasis on the teaching role. Before taking office, Brouder made clear his priorities: "There are few things more noble in life than to be a teacher, an educator. I am extremely proud to be the next president of this fine college. I look forward to taking on the responsibility of acquiring fine students for this college and its outstanding faculty and programs."[64]

By the end of the century, as Columbia College approached its sesquicentennial in 2001, the college not only had regained financial stability and proved its viability but also, under Brouder's leadership, would come full circle in renewing the values and fulfilling the promise of its founders.

14

Full Circle

GERALD T. BROUDER: 1995–PRESENT

The choice in this closing decade of the 20th Century is not between innovation and tradition but between adaptation and stagnation.

—Michael G. Dolence and Donald M. Norris,
Transforming Higher Education

COLUMBIA COLLEGE HAD FOUND its president to lead it into the sesquicentennial year of 2001. As Gerald Brouder addressed his inauguration audience, his remarks could have been written by John Augustus Williams for his own inauguration in 1851.

Brouder, progressive in administrative matters, realistic in assessment of the college's needs, and an ardent advocate of auspicious adaptation, nevertheless held some values to be timeless. Words such as *commitment*, *civility*, and *respect* appeared routinely in his speeches. His inaugural remarks urged the faculty to appreciate teaching "for the moral act that it is." He referred to "developing intellects, shaping reason, inspiring to learn" as "not some job" but "a privilege assigned by God or the fates to a few. . . . I stand before you with no greater passion than to be called teacher, even more so than president."

To Brouder, Columbia College was the place to practice outstanding teaching. Determined that "we will stimulate, not indoctrinate," he took seriously the obligation to provide the kind of education worthy of students' trust:

> We must evaluate continually our programs for relevance by methodically scanning the external environment. . . . What Columbia College does best

> is adapt while retaining relevance and quality. . . . We will take calculated pedagogical risks in order to lead in innovative ways in making learning more accessible to all while being good stewards of our human, capital, and financial resources. Of one thing you can be sure, in the administration now beginning, the basics will be taught *very* well. Rigor will be rewarded. Respect and civility will be expected and honored whether the area of activity is the classroom, the hallway, or the athletic venue.[1]

Such values had already molded Brouder's management style. H. J. Waters III wrote of that style in the *Columbia Daily Tribune* on January 16, 1995, when Brouder was a candidate for the college's presidency: "One of the best-liked MU top administrators . . . Brouder would bring an aura of elevated academic emphasis, and he is a proven consensus builder. He has a nice personal management touch; he is able to exert discipline among his troops while retaining their respect, even affection. His integrity and honesty are well established. He is down-to-earth and straightforward and smart."

The celebration of Brouder's inauguration on Friday, September 16, 1995, featured an address by Haskell M. Monroe Jr., former chancellor and still active professor of history at the University of Missouri–Columbia, a fitting continuation of shared institutional history. Former Columbia College presidents Kenneth Freeman and Donald Ruthenberg attended the festivities that included a postinaugural luncheon held on Bass Commons under a giant white tent.[2]

Trustees, happy with their success in acquiring an educator of such stature, uniformly referred to their new president as "the right man for the time." Their confidence in him became evident within the first year. When Brouder informed the trustees that he would ask for authority to act in place of the board on certain matters, they complied. Allowing the president merely to report some actions to the board could eliminate bureaucracy and "bring decisions close to the person that deals with these policies on a daily basis." The May 1996 board meeting, marking the close of Brouder's first academic year, witnessed a number of firsts. The college had begun offering its first graduate degree, a master of arts in teaching (M.A.T.), in January, and the nursing program had received its initial accreditation from the National League of Nursing, granting the maximum term possible. Brouder had also begun the first series of formal program reviews by outside evaluators, and trustees, viewing the high activity level at the college, decided to revert to full board meetings in January for three full meetings a year. Brouder marked the first anniversary by recognizing trustees for their service with the gift of windbreaker jackets carrying the college's new logo and "Trustee, Columbia College" on the front.[3]

Board membership varied little from the previous administration. New bylaws set the size of the board within a range of fifteen to twenty-seven, and twenty-six members held office in 2000. Three trustees, unable to attend as frequently as desired, left the board, and the college lost the services through death of Mike Angelo, Andrew Bass, and Walter E. Bixby Jr. Don Landers, one of only two new trustees, joined the board in 1996 and began working with Marvin Owens as vice chairman of the Finance Committee of the board, capping thirty years of involvement and interest in the college. Landers had served as the college's business manager under Merle Hill before leaving to form his own tax consulting firm, but he had never lost touch with college affairs. Also new to the board, Elliott Battle became a trustee in 2000. A veteran of thirty years of experience as counselor and guidance director in the Columbia public schools until 1991, Battle came to the college as assistant to the president, specializing in minority recruitment and counseling. After retiring from that position in 1997, he joined his wife, Muriel, also a retired public school administrator, in forming a consulting firm. An author and lecturer as well as active civic leader, he shared honors with his wife as Chamber of Commerce "citizen of the year" before joining the board.[4]

A major change on the board came with the retirement of Tom Atkins as chairman in 1999, a position he had held since 1982, having come to the board in 1976. In recognition of a chairmanship unsurpassed in both demands and excellence of leadership, the board presented Atkins with a plaque commemorating his outstanding service, and the faculty awarded him an unusual certificate of appreciation. Dan Scotten, new to the board in 1994, became chairman at the May 1999 meeting, and Richard Montgomery replaced Marty Toler as vice chairman. Both Atkins and Toler remained on the board.[5]

Congeniality also marked Brouder's relationship with his top administrators. According to Bob Hutton, director of plant and facilities, Brouder's demonstrated leadership at a major university lent a distinction to his role, and, beyond reputation, his personal dignity and grace of style inspired deference. With a respect bordering on reverence, those people who worked most closely with the president found him to be approachable, genial, and accessible, practicing his belief in "civility and respect" in all relationships. Mike Randerson, dean for the Extended Studies Division, expressed such admiration: "We have an all-American, world-class educator as head of our institution. You would not anticipate that a college of our size and location would have a president of his stature." The new academic dean, Terry Smith, described Brouder's management style as "empowering, positive, optimistic, focused, and supportive." Deliberate in selecting his people, Brouder then gave them freedom to act. Cautious but willing to take calculated risks, he emphasized quality as the "key to everything." Smith further described the president: "He is a very centered man with a good sense of who he is. He has a very solid set of values that guide his life and work. He has his priorities straight; he knows what shield he wants to be carried out on."[6]

What had been the Executive Management Staff under Presidents Kelly and Ruthenberg became the Academic Council of the Brouder administration. Titles of positions changed as well. With Brouder, there was only one vice president—the vice president and dean for academic affairs—a position second in command to the president. A search began October 1, 1995, for a permanent academic dean, the most important appointment the president would make. After a thorough and broadly based process, Brouder named Terry Smith to begin his duties on May 13, 1996. A dean and faculty member at Northeast Missouri State University in Kirksville for eighteen years, Smith had spent the previous three years as vice president for academic affairs and professor of political science at Peru State College in Peru, Nebraska. A Fulbright scholar, he held a Ph.D. degree in political science from Michigan State University. He had also served as a consultant and evaluator for the North Central Association of Schools and Colleges' Commission on Institutions of Higher Education. Brouder gave him not only a preeminent position but also an exceptionally broad span of control encompassing admissions, registration, and financial aid, as well as the library and academic programs. However, a later reorganization placed financial aid under the jurisdiction of the business office.[7]

Replacing Frazier Moon in Extended Studies, Mike Randerson took the title of assistant vice president and dean for the Extended Studies Division, becoming full-time in his role in April 1996 after serving part-time at the college. A retired colonel with twenty-five years in the air force as an intelligence officer, he came to the college from the air force ROTC program at the University of Missouri–Columbia.[8]

Following Chuck Bobbitt as director of plant and facilities in January 1996, Bob Hutton had been a self-employed contractor and former director of facilities and general services at Stephens College and had served as a member of the Columbia City Council. In another area, when Lindi Overton left after thirteen years as controller and chief financial officer, the board recognized her for outstanding service, and Bruce Boyer, who had performed the college audits as a CPA, became chief financial officer in February 1999. In development, Bryan Van Deun replaced retiring director Dona Sue Cool in 1996, assuming the newly created position of director of development and alumni services. He left in May 1999 to become president of a Catholic high school in Waukesha, Wisconsin, and John P. Schirmer, in capital giving, became director. Joining the college in January 1999, Schirmer had been a problem-solving consultant and curriculum writer for corporate training. Working with Schirmer as associate director of alumni services, Susan Davis joined the staff the same year after thirteen years as associate director of admissions at Central Methodist College. Another newcomer, Regina Morin, began her duties as director of admissions on May 27, 1997, coming from a background at Northeast Missouri State University and Simpson College in Iowa. A new public relations director, Barbara Payne, began her duties in 1999, bringing fifteen years of experience in her field. Faye and Bob Burchard remained in their positions in student life and in athletics.[9]

Brouder's emphasis on academic quality added greater than usual weight to Smith's role. Admitting that the deanship "turned out to be more complex than I had thought," Smith expressed his unabashed love for his position and the college: "This is the job I truly hoped I would have at the culmination of my career. I love this job, I love this school, and I gladly give full measure of my devotion to this work." Citing the leadership, the "really good faculty," and the college's "promise," Smith explained why he called the private liberal arts college his roots: "It is so many things—high risk, high gain—you start every year with zero budget guaranteed. The trade-off is that we can do pretty much what we want. That's a good thing. What I want to focus on is quality. How do we measure it and how do we get it? Where will I be ten years from now? Right here being a member of a faculty and staff that have made this an outstanding institution."[10]

Because quality, to both Brouder and Smith, must be tested and proved, Brouder in his inaugural address introduced the subject of program review to answer the question "How good are we?" and to "rethink whether programs are still relevant." Brouder and Smith embarked upon program reviews of all departments and offices, a task to be undertaken on a regular basis with reviews of each area every five years. Guidelines for selecting visiting teams included faculty input and brought recognized scholars to campus, coming largely from other Missouri colleges and universities. Program reviews proved valuable in a number of ways. The departmental self-studies preceding each review brought productive self-examination and self-revelation, and the resultant body of knowledge gave the president a thorough view of each area of the institution. The diagnostic nature of the reviews in identifying strengths and weaknesses provided an objective base upon which to evaluate quality. Results varied from encouragement to "keep up the good work" to calls for major curricular revision or even program discontinuance, all in continual pursuit of "finding better ways."[11]

A "better way" for the natural sciences and mathematics department was "to deepen the sciences." The college began in the fall of 1996 to offer both B.A. and B.S. degrees in natural sciences. The new B.S. degree allowed an emphasis in chemistry or biology, whereas the B.A. degree offered an emphasis in a health-related field as well as in chemistry or biology. A grant of thirty thousand dollars from the Fred V. Heinkel and Dorothy H. Heinkel Foundation helped fund new equipment for biology, chemistry, and physics laboratories in Robnett-Spence Hall. In a related field, the nursing program had already been accredited by the Missouri State Board of Nursing and by the North Central Association, but the college went beyond these agencies to acquire accreditation from the National League of Nursing (NLN). The NLN accreditation, strictly voluntary for nursing programs, "shows the public and the education community that a nursing program has clear, appropriate educational goals and is providing the conditions needed to achieve them."[12]

In a new academic venture in 1996, Columbia College entered a law enforcement partnership with the University of Missouri–Columbia Law Enforcement Training Institute (LETI) in "the only program of its kind in Missouri." In August 1996, most Missouri law enforcement agencies began to require job applicants to be "recertified" as having attended a police academy. An increase from 120 to 470 hours of minimum training to meet academy requirements proved a problem for baccalaureate degree holders wanting a career in law enforcement. Because the university did not offer a degree in criminal justice, a cooperative program between the criminal justice program of Columbia College and LETI permitted students who had attended the UMC-LETI or one of fifteen other academies in Missouri to attend any Columbia College site offering criminal justice classes. Students could obtain class work in criminal law, police, constitutional law, laws of evidence, and criminal justice practicums I and II, completing both the bachelor of science in criminal justice (B.S.C.J.) degree and the law enforcement academy requirement within a four-year period.[13]

Further collaboration occurred when the university Engineering College listed Columbia College as an institution where students could obtain their general education requirements and transfer them back to the university. Also, the University of Missouri–Columbia Independent Study Catalog listed Columbia College as one of four institutions allowing students to take independent study credit at the university and transfer the credit hours to a Columbia College site or to the main campus.[14]

In other academic changes, the faculty adopted a new undergraduate major in computer science and separated history and political science (formerly government) into two majors within the department. They also approved minors in philosophy, religion, ethics, environmental studies, and geography. Opportunities for internships resulted in placing 131 interns during the 1998–1999 academic year, positions carefully arranged by faculty with on-site supervision. Also, in a general tightening of procedures, the Faculty Association in 1997 ended credit by experiential learning, a practice little used by that time.[15]

With increased emphasis on student quality, Smith encouraged the faculty to create an honors program. A task force produced a plan approved by the Faculty Association for a program open to high school graduates with a 3.5 grade point average or better or a Columbia College grade point average of 3.5 with thirty hours of credit. Completion of the program required enrollment in special honors courses for twenty-one credit hours, nine hours of which could count toward general education. In addition to this option, the baccalaureate degree with distinction opportunity remained in place for those students who qualified for the two-semester research or performance project.[16]

As program reviews progressed, the process did in one instance contribute to the elimination of a department and its major when the college phased out the fashion program after 1997. Although the program review of 1996 was positive overall, a study of syllabi and directed studies contracts led to questions about the academic rigor and the seventy-five credit hours required for the major, which left little time for general education. Also, the cost-per-student credit hour compared unfavorably with other departments, most of which produced more graduates. Although the faculty Curriculum and Academic Policies Committee supported elimination of the program, the Faculty Association meeting resulted in a vote against the recommended termination. The recommendation did, however, win board approval with the "recognition that a reassignment of funds from fashion costs could fill four new faculty positions needed in other programs," all of which were seeing an increase in enrollments. Another consideration, according to the *Columbia Daily Tribune,* was the fashion program's lack of "fit" within the college's overall goals, an indication of how greatly the curriculum had altered in response to shifting social patterns. Brouder later commented on the decision: "Our bright future is dependent upon adaptability. Sometimes that adaptability can be painful." Travel management, eliminated earlier in 1997 due to lack of student demand, was discontinued on the recommendation of its director and with the approval of the Faculty Association.[17]

Academic changes also included a structural reorganization of departments to achieve more equity in department sizes, thus equalizing the burden of department chairs. The number of departments was reduced from twelve to eight, and Smith increased time spent with department chairs, conducting workshops and sending faculty to national management conferences. His emphasis on personnel management stressed the need for new skills in this crucial area, one in which most department chairs were least prepared. Still not losing sight of the dominance of the classroom role, Smith insisted: "You all will be teachers with administrative assignments. I do not want administrators who teach." In line with other streamlining, the Faculty Governance Committee and Faculty Handbook Committee reduced the number of Faculty Association governance committees from ten to seven; Smith responded in kind by reducing faculty standing committees from ten to seven and faculty joint committees from five to three.[18]

The most significant academic change, implementation of graduate programs and their accreditation by the North Central Association, proceeded well. The college proposed three graduate programs when a North Central team visited campus on September 21–22, 1995. The team recommended that only one be introduced at a time, allowing its success to determine when to begin a second program. Thus, the master of arts in teaching (M.A.T.) received approval and began class work in January 1996, putting the master of arts in business administration (M.B.A.) and the master of arts in counseling on hold. When the master of arts in counseling failed to materialize, trustees approved a proposal to offer a Graduate Certificate Program in Professional Counseling. The certificate program, not requiring North Central approval, became an appendage to the M.A.T. program, intended for students who had or were pursuing the M.A.T. or a graduate degree in psychology or in another closely related field. It required that students pass the National Counselor Exam, making them eligible for supervised practice as "board-eligible national certified counselors." Due to complications with state certification and other issues, however, the education and psychology department phased out the certification program and replaced it with emphases in gifted education, special education, and reading.[19]

Brouder received notice from the North Central Association on November 25, 1996, that the M.B.A. was "approved by unanimous vote" with no site visit necessary, and offerings began in the fall of 1997. Another graduate program, the master of science in criminal justice (M.S.C.J.), gained approval in February 1998 to begin in the fall of 1998, making it the only criminal justice graduate degree program in mid-Missouri. In addition, the college requested a change of status from the North Central Association to export the M.B.A. and M.A.T. to Extended Studies sites, and approval was granted for the M.B.A. to be offered at Marysville, Washington, and for the M.A.T. to be offered at Lake Ozark, Missouri. On campus, the graduate degrees, tailored to serve working professionals, were taught in the Evening College, with most of the courses taught by full-time faculty of the day program.[20]

The addition of graduate programs brought alterations in other areas. As an expansion of the tuition waiver benefit for full-time faculty and staff and their spouses and children for undergraduate courses, the Employee Graduate Educational Grant provided a 75 percent tuition waiver for graduate courses. Also, the Faculty Association created a Graduate Council, providing a formal voice for graduate faculty to make recommendations to the Faculty Association and to the vice president and dean of academic affairs. The council included two full-time faculty members appointed by the chair from each department having a graduate program. In addition, the Faculty Association elected two members from departments having no graduate program, and the assistant dean for graduate studies was an ex-officio member.[21]

In response to academic changes, Brouder pressed for a new mission statement and reconsideration of the general education requirements to "ensure that our core is well-rounded." In place of the 1993 statement, a new version, approved by the board on May 17, 1996, consisted of two parts, a Statement of Mission and a Description. The Statement of Mission retained the traditional emphasis on the liberal arts, the role of "exemplary teaching," and preparation for "life-long learning." The Description defined degrees, the multicampus structure, accrediting agencies, and a brief historical statement.[22]

It was the president's call for reconsideration of the general education requirements that resulted in an intensive study. In December 1997, the faculty elected representatives to a committee including also faculty from the Evening College, graduate programs, and the Extended Studies Division. A laborious process of consultation and deliberation resulted in the realization that the traditional curriculum failed to meet the needs of adult learners in the Evening College and ESD sites. Thus, the committee devised a two-track program. The Preferred Program of Study applied to students who began their studies at Columbia College or who transferred to the college with thirty-six or fewer hours of credit. The program included basic studies, to be completed in the first sixty hours of course work, consisting of computer studies, speech, English composition, and a mathematics course at the level of algebra or higher. Requirements also included introductory courses of six credit hours in American History or Western Civilization, arts and humanities, natural science and mathematics, and social and behavioral studies. However, students who transferred to the college with more than thirty-six hours had the option of following the alternative program of study, allowing the option of upper-level courses in arts and humanities and in social and behavioral studies. One requirement was not optional: "Every student who graduates from Columbia College must complete an ethics course."[23]

In another area of activity, the college reexamined a tradition jealously guarded by many faculties, the tradition of tenure. At a faculty meeting on October 5, 1995, just months into his presidency, Brouder surprised the faculty with a request that they "reconsider that portion of the *Faculty Handbook* on non-tenure track faculty requiring the six-year-and-out provision," requesting "the flexibility of using renewable period contracts with no time limit, ensuring a sufficient amount of turn-over." As the handbook stood, all full-time faculty contracts were either probationary appointments or appointments for continuous tenure. Any probationary faculty member who was denied tenure after the three-year or six-year probationary period would receive a terminal contract the next year.

The Faculty Association assigned the study of a possible policy revision to the Welfare and Personnel Policy Committee with instructions to bring a recommendation to the Faculty Association. Weighing the greater flexibility of nontenure track appointments against the continuing importance of the tenure system, the committee addressed the question of "whether the two modes are compatible" and determined that they could be. The option of a system of "parallel track" appointments seemed to be the answer. The solution adopted by the committee accepted the concurrent use of tenure-track appointments along with renewable nontenure-track appointments in which reappointment could be granted indefinitely and for a varied number of years after the initial one-year term. Research had shown that although 90 percent of faculty nationwide taught at tenure-granting institutions, 11 percent of full-time faculty in liberal arts and sciences colleges operated under a nontenure-track appointment—and the practice was growing. At Columbia College, 62 percent of the fifty-two full-time faculty members were tenured compared with 63 percent in all independent four-year Missouri colleges and 66 percent in all Missouri colleges and universities.

The committee's recommendation for the use of a limited number of renewable nontenure-track appointments set conditions that recognized and secured the continued presence of a tenure policy: no more than 15 percent of the total tenured and tenure-track faculty could be on nontenure-track appointments at any time, such appointments could be used only when agreed to by the academic dean and the department head after full consultation with full-time department faculty, and wording in the *Faculty Handbook* regarding tenure would remain in place as written, with renewable nontenure-track appointments cited as "exceptions to the normal tenure track appointments." After Faculty Association approval by secret ballot, unanimous board acceptance of the recommendation followed a week later. Faculty members had shown themselves to be amenable to change but firm in their support of the concept of tenure, an outcome Brouder later called "as good as anyone could have predicted."[24]

Another area of change, the improvement of campus technology, received early and continuing attention in the Brouder presidency. The administration placed computers on desks in all faculty offices where desired and by 1997 had established a thirty-station Internet laboratory for student and faculty use, along with computer laboratories in every residence hall. Instructional Technology Services expanded to the use of ninety personal computers, upgraded to be three times as fast as previous models. Also, library automation proceeded with the purchase of the Dynix System, installed in August 1995, and an on-line catalog soon replaced the card catalog. Internet connections provided access to First Search, EbscoHost, the on-line catalogs of the University of Missouri libraries, and the World Wide Web.[25]

Connection of Stafford Library to ESD sites opened unprecedented opportunities for library use, and Missouri ESD sites also had access to databases as the result of Columbia College membership in the statewide MORENET consortium. Sites in other states gained access to area libraries and databases through other consortiums. A college task force, established in October 1998, surveyed site directors for needs and compiled a long-range plan for extending library services on-line to the Extended Studies Division. The 1999 report included suggestions for negotiating agreements with area libraries near ESD sites, recommending that all ESD sites have Internet access provided by the home campus or local Internet service providers. As the result of continuing library needs, the college became a member of MOBIUS, a statewide consortium of some fifty academic libraries allowing access to students and faculty of the Columbia and ESD campuses.[26]

The Brouder years brought changes in faculty ranks as well, especially in the retirement of key older faculty. Jack and Polly Batterson announced their retirement effective May 1996 after a combined total of sixty-nine years the two had devoted to the college. A *Friends* article explained their long-standing ties to the college after Polly Batterson left temporarily in 1959 to spend time with their expected child: "[Jack] stepped in and took her place: 'I came here as a matter of expediency. I was finished with my graduate work and my wife was pregnant, and her job was the only opening I knew about. My intent was to stay a year or two, but then I just fell in love with the place.' " Lynne Stuver Baker, president of the National Alumni Association and a future trustee, arranged to commemorate the Battersons' contributions to the college by establishing the Jack and Polly Batterson Scholarship Fund. She also welcomed them as honorary members of the alumni association, calling Jack Batterson's influence on her as a student "tremendous and life impacting." Trustees granted the Battersons emeritus and emerita status.[27]

Elaine Grev retired in May 1998 after serving thirty-three years at the college. She had directed the Jane Froman Singers from 1984 to 1992, moving then to the Evening College staff as an academic advisor. Trustees conferred emerita status on her at the May 1, 1998, meeting, and when Grev performed her farewell faculty recital in Dorsey Chapel on April 17, 1998, she exited to a standing ovation. Dennis Grev joined his wife in retirement with emeritus status in May 2000, having served the college for thirty-seven years, a combined service for the Grevs of seventy years. Another long-standing professor, David O'Hagan, retired in May 2000 after thirty-five years of teaching, leaving only Sidney Larson of the pre-1970 faculty. O'Hagan had lent distinction to the music program since 1965 and also received the emeritus designation. Retiring at the same time, Diane O'Hagan had been teaching part-time in the Evening College since leaving her position as director of alumni affairs, a position she accepted after having served for fourteen years as a full-time member of the history/government department.[28]

With Larson due to retire in May 2001 after fifty years of exemplary service, the board, upon the request of the Faculty Association, formally established the title of "distinguished professor" with the intent that it be incorporated into Larson's last contract. The title had been used at the retirement of Dan Hoagland but had not been incorporated into the *Faculty Handbook*. As established in 2000, the distinction would be reserved for faculty serving at least twenty-five years with a record of outstanding teaching who had achieved national prominence "through scholarship, creative work, or distinction of service to the profession." Larson's career would be marked by special events in his last semester of teaching as part of the college's sesquicentennial celebration. The alumni reunion weekend in April 2001 would recognize his fifty years with an exhibit of his work in the Larson Gallery and a special reception, and a poster of a Larson mural became available for purchase though the efforts of the sesquicentennial committee.[29] Other faculty soon to retire also included Helga Huang, who would leave in May 2001 after twenty-eight years, having created the college's sociology major. Novelle Dunathan, a former director of the teacher education department, anticipated retirement in the spring of 2002 after twenty-eight years at the college.

Another new crop of "old hands" emerged. Leaders of the generation coming since 1970 not only made the college the mainstay of their careers but also contributed heavily to its progress and well-being. These faculty included Anthony Alioto, Christine Cotton, Carolyn Dickinson, Novelle Dunathan, Cheryl-Ann Hardy, Hoyt Hayes, Timothy Ireland, Michael Lyman, Anthony Marshall, Peter Meserve, Michael Polley, Ronald Taylor, Kenneth Torke, Thomas Watson, Joann Wayman, and Sally Wells. Newcomers were not wanting. The forty-eight full-time faculty members in 1995 had expanded to fifty-six by the fall of 2000.

The college also mourned the death of some faculty members already retired. Hazel Kennedy, who had taught for twenty-two years in the English department, died on September 11, 1995, and Burnett Ellis, retired after forty years at the college, died on December 1, 1996. Norman Reves, who had taught full-time for thirty years and continued on a part-time basis in the Evening College, died in 1999. The death of Jack Batterson on September 28, 1997, "brought a great sadness to the College Community." The college flag flew at half mast for one week, and Brouder remembered Batterson at a memorial service in Dorsey Chapel:

> Jack was a true renaissance man. He administered, he counseled, he mentored, and, most importantly, he positively changed countless lives through his teaching. The volume of knowledge he imparted is incalculable. The nature of his friendship was genuine and warm, his smile disarming. . . . It is not an overstatement to say that were it not for Jack's steady hand on the tiller of this venerable, old, academic ship during that transition [to a four-year college], we may not have made it. . . . To no more humble, yet noble, a man could there have been awarded the title of Professor Emeritus.[30]

Change came to the college in other ways. One aspect involved acquisition of property with the college eventually adding all lots on Eighth Street directly west of the campus. On its east side, the college purchased part of the Hinshaw property on Rangeline Street in 1995 and the Henderson

Oil property on Fay Street adjoining the Wightman Building parking lot. A lease for a lot at the corner of Rogers and Rangeline Streets expanded the parking area.[31]

Renovations also provided added space. Nine badly needed classrooms were created on the lower level of St. Clair Hall and in Brown Hall, the art and humanities building. October 1995 brought the dedication of Brown Hall and of the renovated Dorsey Hall Memorial Chapel. Adjoining the chapel, the Jane Froman Studio had seen a rich history as a study hall, the college library, a dance studio, a practice room for the Jane Froman Singers, and a location for receptions and conferences. A major renovation came in the summer of 1999 when the college converted the former fashion studios on the third floor of St. Clair Hall into seminar rooms and classrooms for the graduate program. The off-campus house formerly used as the president's home by Kelly and Ruthenberg, renovated in 1995, was sold when Brouder chose to remain in his own home. Following a plan to move maintenance quarters to the former art building once the art program moved into Brown Hall, the college razed the old Wightman Building, requiring maintenance services to operate from trailers until the art department could complete its move to Brown Hall.[32]

Renovation failed to be an option for one structure, the Chinese pavilion, literally falling apart as the result of the Missouri climate. Brouder worked with the Chinese/American Association of Columbia to consider options, and discussions led to the decision that the college should dismantle the pavilion to preserve its parts inside the Cultural Arts Center. The Taiwanese counsel general from Kansas City and the Washington, D.C., counsel to Taiwan also visited campus to study the need to preserve as much as possible. Pieces of the pavilion were displayed in Brown Hall and in the Cultural Arts Center and later deposited at the center for safekeeping.[33]

Improvements in the physical plant went beyond structure. Concerned with increasing pride and improving aesthetic aspects of the campus, Brouder and Hutton launched a massive beautification effort, replacing chain-link fences with landscaping, improving signage, and engaging in plantings in consultation with landscape artists. In less glamorous duties, they maintained the integrity of the buildings, shifting the emphasis to long-range quality in repairs where expediency had once dictated economy. Increased professionalism and reorganization of the maintenance staff brought a sense of pride to the entire maintenance effort.[34]

By the fall of 1996, the college began the process of developing a twenty-five-year master plan with updates to be considered periodically in response to changes in educational delivery, curricula, and student needs. The college selected Mackey, Mitchell, Zahner Associates, an architectural firm from Kansas City, in conjunction with Simon Walther, Inc., of Columbia to develop a comprehensive plan. Input from focus groups included representation of trustees; the administrative council; alumni; day, evening, and graduate faculty; staff; athletic personnel; students; and neighboring community groups. Planning activities resulted in campuswide recommendations by the next fall with top priority given to renovation of Missouri Hall, creation of a new student commons, addition of more parking facilities, centralization of campus security, and renovation of residence halls.[35]

The most immediate action called for expansion of Southwell Gymnasium by fifteen thousand square feet to provide a fifteen-hundred-seat arena, an indoor tennis facility, and additional space for basketball courts and other student recreational events. Announcement of the plan at a July 2000 reception included the unveiling by Larson of a portrait of Edgar Lee, Christian College president from 1920 to 1935, to be placed in the new gymnasium. Lee's son, Desmond, present for the unveiling, had donated the lead gift for the project. With $650,000 in hand, the college planned to raise another $850,000. The same reception featured the announcement of the college's reinstatement of women's basketball, a sport introduced at the college by St. Clair Moss in 1900 but discontinued in the 1970s. With one year allotted for hiring a coach and recruitment of players, the college set the first season to begin in the 2001–2002 academic year.[36]

Planning relied heavily on financial stability, a condition illustrated by continued black budgets in the 1990s. The endowment, approaching $2 million in 1995, increased to $5 million by the end of the decade but remained a constant source of concern. In his State of the College address on September 4, 1997, Brouder reviewed accomplishments, noting the nearly $2 million given in financial aid in the past year. The president tied the importance of being competitive in financial aid offerings to the intent to build a strong student body, heavily dependent on income from a growing endowment. The college had, in the two preceding years, spent $1.3 million in physical improvements and $1.5 million for better computers. It had added nine new faculty members and nineteen new staff positions, created nine new classrooms, and graduated more than three thousand students in two years from all its locations. It was in its eighteenth consecutive year with a black budget, with no short-term borrowing for operations since 1986. The retirement contribution had risen from 5 percent in 1995 to 7 percent in the 1996–1997 budget. By the time of the president's 1999 biennial State of the College address, he could make an even stronger statement:

> We close the budget year in the black for the 20th consecutive year. That is an incredible statistic given the rather precarious status of many private liberal arts based colleges today. . . . It is my goal to close every year with a functional, corporate operating reserve to allow for contingencies in cash flow and to fund long desired capital improvements such as renovating Missouri Hall, our

> addition of a multipurpose and tennis facility at Southwell Gymnasium, and the critical need for a student commons.[37]

Grants and gifts helped in the transition. More than $100,000 came from the National Science Foundation for computer technology improvements, and the Heinkel Foundation contributed $30,000 for science laboratories and another $45,000 for improvements to Launer Auditorium. The college received a grant of $25,000 from the Kemper Foundation for training faculty to offer the first Web-based courses in October 2000. Trustee Web Bixby secured $25,000 from the Reynolds Foundation toward the tennis and multipurpose facility. In addition to his generous contribution for the indoor tennis building, Desmond Lee made a $50,000 scholarship gift in the name of his father. The college received $219,000 from the estate of Marion R. Lincoln, a 1925 graduate, to be used for the Marion Lincoln Scholarship for financial aid. With a $100,000 gift from Sarah Botts of the class of 1941 and $20,000 from Florence Lash of the class of 1949, gifts from 1,681 donors reported in May 1999 totaled $665,516 with a total of $831,000 for the whole of 1999.[38]

Facing outstanding needs ahead, the college in 1998 employed Clyde Watkins, a fund-raising consultant, to help determine the feasibility of a capital campaign. A favorable report led to a decision for a two-year preparation phase and then announcement in 2001 of a three-year campaign to raise $12.5 million. Goals projected $5 million for the renovation of Missouri Hall, $5 million for endowment, and $2.5 million for expendable funds. Endowment money would provide for an expanded scholarship program, including special category scholarships, a fund for the arts, an enhanced honors program, and general endowment. The first gift, that of $100,000 from trustee Peggy Price and her husband, Jim, provided a fitting kickoff. Reports showed a 39 percent increase in individual donors in the first half of 1998–1999 and a 36 percent increase in nonbequest gifts.[39]

In another area, enrollments grew despite tightened admissions standards. The September 1995 figure of 616 full-time students included a 29 percent increase in freshman students. An 8 percent increase in enrollments in the fall of 1996 saw 689 full-time students and 160 part-time students on campus, creating a waiting list for rooms in residence halls. The Evening College, with 1,380 course enrollments for the session, was up 15 percent, whereas the Extended Studies Division's eight-week fall session increased by 7 percent to 4,484 enrollments. Fall 1997 figures showed a 5 percent increase of day students, for a total of 902, and a 6 percent Evening College increase to 1,474 course enrollments. A 10 percent rise in ESD to 5,010 course enrollments for the eight-week session amounted to 42,600 ESD total class enrollments for the year. The ESD unduplicated student count for the academic year stood at 10,090. By 1998–1999, that figure had risen to a five-session annual unduplicated count of 10,805 part-time students. The fall of 1999 placed the day program at 852 students and the Evening College at 1,492, including 113 graduate students.[40]

Stabilization of enrollments coincided with greater attention to the admission of better-qualified students. Smith began to chair the admissions committee in 1996, helping to screen those applicants falling into the "contingent" category, that is, having a grade point average below the required 2.00. Automatic admission was possible only for applicants in the top half of their class who had a 2.00 grade point average or who ranked in the fiftieth percentile or higher in such standard college aptitude examinations as the ACT, SAT, or GED and had a 2.00 grade point average. Admissions standards adopted by the faculty in March 1997 applied for the first time to the Evening College and to international students as well as to the students in the day program, and international students were required to have a Test of English as a Foreign Language (TOEFL) score of 500 or better. The college recommended that applicants show in their high school transcripts a minimum of four units of English, three of mathematics (two years of algebra and one of geometry), two units of natural science, and two units of social science. Studies of entering classes of 1998 and 1999 indicated that the average high school grade point average was 3.1. After the admissions committee in 1998 and 1999 rejected roughly half of the contingent applicants coming before the committee, the college began to receive fewer applicants not meeting the automatic admission category. However, the denials came at a financial cost; the college turned away 125 day student applicants and 137 Evening College applicants between the summer of 1997 and April 1999. Nevertheless, the search for quality looked to the "long-term pay-off" of admitting only those stronger applicants.[41]

Although the on-campus day program remained the core of the academic program, overbalancing numbers in the Evening and Graduate Division and in the Extended Studies Division illustrated how far the college had come, as indicated by Brouder:

> As the College appropriately repositions itself . . . its core curriculum requirements have changed. Some would even argue that the mission of the College shifted away from education for its own sake to one of preparation for the world of work. . . . We do well in liberally educating our students while at the same time preparing the majority of them for the world of work. . . . Heading further down that path will enhance both our uniqueness and our reputation. More importantly, it will improve our quality and responsiveness to those who believe that combination to be among the fundamental purposes of a college education.[42]

Brouder explained change at Columbia College as a reflection of trends in higher education. By 1997, more than sixteen hundred corporate "universities" were offering degrees, as opposed to thirty-seven hundred traditional colleges: "40% of post-secondary students today are studying at nontraditional schools. Nearly ½ of college and university students pursuing degrees today attend on a part-time basis—nearly 7 million today—up from fewer than 3 million in 1970. The number of full-time students grew by 38% over the same period." Looking to the future, Brouder suggested a "full-blown, heavily marketed weekend program to complement day, evening, and ESD as a 'fourth facet.' . . . I am fond of saying that what this College needs is the next good idea akin to that which gave life to our Extended Studies Division, or transforming from a single gender to a coeducational institution; from two to four year degrees." Brouder and Smith stepped up the pace for "contracting with more community colleges in our 2+2 articulation models," leading to agreements with Aurora Community College in Colorado, Metropolitan Community College in Kansas City, and Brevard County Community College in Florida. The college had already concluded programs with the Moberly Area Community College, the Illinois-Elgin Community College, and the McHenry County College.[43]

By the time of Brouder's inauguration, the Extended Studies Division had experienced twenty-two years of development and growth. A study in the fall of 1996 provided a profile of the program, revealing the average student to be thirty-three years old and the student body to be 55 percent female and 24 percent minority students. Some 73 percent of the students received financial aid in the form of veterans' assistance, military tuition assistance, Pell Grants, or Guaranteed Student Loans; 19 percent were military students. The program utilized a staff of 84 full-time and 40 part-time employees at the sites, along with 378 adjunct faculty each session. Faculty longevity averaged five and a half years. In the 1995–1996 academic year, the college awarded 1,012 B.A. degrees and 557 A.A. degrees. Approximately 55 percent of ESD revenue came from military sites and 45 percent from civilian sites. The average grade point average for ESD students was 3.34, compared with 3.20 for Evening Division students and 3.04 for on-campus day program students. By the late 1990s, ESD faculty and staff had demonstrated impressive longevity, indicating significant commitment to the program. Thirty-two faculty members had served between twenty and twenty-five years, and Rene Nichols, director of administration on the Columbia campus, had provided continuity and leadership to the program for eighteen years.[44]

Major reorganization, matched by progressive changes, brought ESD in line with contemporary needs after 1996. An ESD *Faculty Handbook* produced in 1998 not only dealt with procedures, academic regulations, and administrative information, but also stressed teaching responsibilities, professional development, ethics, and demeanor. An ESD student handbook was under way. In addition to semiannual ESD directors' conferences on campus, similar interaction of faculty began. The business administration department conducted an institution-wide faculty conference in March 1998 in which adjunct faculty from seventeen ESD sites and the Evening College joined full-time faculty in discussing departmental issues. A computer information systems adjunct faculty development conference followed in September 1998 with twenty-two adjunct faculty members from eighteen ESD sites and the Evening College joining full-time faculty on campus. A criminal justice faculty development conference in March 1999 continued the ongoing process. In another type of integration, Christine Cotton of the English faculty visited ten sites on behalf of the humanities program, observing classroom teaching, reviewing syllabi and resources, conferring with faculty and site directors, and reporting her findings to Dean Smith.[45]

A significant change for ESD came when sites were connected to the home campus electronically, a move partially precipitated by the surge in enrollments in the 1996–1997 academic year with a 23 percent increase in new students. Communications between the sites and the home campus had been largely a paper process, causing severe procedural difficulties in handling applications for financial aid, transcript evaluations, and cash flow. By 2000, all sites gained "connectivity" with the home mainframe computer, giving instant access to student data and status.[46]

In line with the drive to improve, the college welcomed authoritative site evaluations conducted on a voluntary basis by the American Council of Education (ACE) Center for Adult Learning and Educational Credentials. ACE teams routinely conducted reports, Military Installation Voluntary Education Reviews (MIVER), upon request by the Department of Defense to inform the military whether educational programs on its bases were providing quality opportunities in education. Information from a MIVER report could potentially be used to determine whether a base should end or expand services. Although the reports focused largely on the operations of the base itself, sections for each college functioning on a base provided both constructive recommendations and, where deserved, commendations for exemplary features.

Columbia College ESD sites experienced two MIVER visits in 1999. One produced the report on the naval station Roosevelt Roads, Puerto Rico, resulting in commendations for the college's procedures for monitoring course syllabi, for having home campus faculty and academic administrators visit the Roosevelt Roads site, and for adjunct faculty development conferences and local development initiatives. The MIVER team also commended the college for its meaningful increases in adjunct faculty compensation. The team concluded: "Columbia College's recently established practices for faculty evaluation could well serve as a model for other institutions."[47]

A similar MIVER report on the college's operations at Everett Naval Station in Marysville, Washington, also recognized the college's contributions:

> Students with whom the MIVER team interacted reported that Columbia handles student services well. Admissions decisions are timely, transcripts and degree audits are readily available, and paper is handled expeditiously. Financial aid information is provided in cooperation with Navy Campus. Student files show that Columbia is conscientiously recording every detail. The site director handles the advising of active duty military, civilians, and corporate employees, and the academic adviser handles active duty and retired military.[48]

An outstanding feature of the college's operations at Everett Naval Station was the unusual partnership developed among the college, the base, and Microsoft Corporation when "Naval Station Everett Command and Columbia College administrators agreed to establish a computer laboratory that would serve both Columbia's courses and the naval station community. As a result, Columbia purchased twenty state-of-the-art computers and access to Internet and World Wide Web. The Navy provided network connections, a printer, a furnished classroom, and custodial services. Microsoft Corporation donated software." As a result of this electronic link, ESD students and faculty "will soon be able to search and browse through the college's library holdings in Missouri and can now access the electronic database and search services that Columbia maintains. . . . The Stafford Library Web page also includes links to a variety of helpful tools, e. g., online reference works, business information, government documents, current news, and several search engines." Students reported that they valued these services. The MIVER report for the Everett Naval Station site commended the naval station and the college "for cooperatively establishing and operating a well-equipped laboratory for the benefit of Columbia students and the base community." It further commended the college for "initiating and implementing the MBA program at Naval Station Everett, thereby expanding the educational and career opportunities for local service members and residents."[49]

Capt. Kim Buike, commanding officer at Everett Naval Station, attended the ESD site directors' conference in September 1999 as guest speaker for the culminating luncheon. A strong supporter of the college's educational operations on his base, he praised as well the implementation by the navy of the Navy College Program to enhance the opportunity for personnel to gain college degrees, including graduate degrees, while on active duty. The program, another form of partnership with academic institutions, provided full tuition for selected career officers for appropriate degrees.[50]

By late 2000, ESD expansion was coming about largely through requests from outside the college. Over the years, sites had been culled to continue consolidation of only the most successful centers. The college operated twenty-four campuses—eleven military and thirteen civilian—teaching more than three thousand courses per year and hiring approximately 450 adjunct faculty for each of the five sessions per year. The excitement of operating such a program extended beyond ESD staff, as seen in Smith's description of why he loved to attend ESD commencements: "You know this is the first person in the entire family to graduate from college. You hear the screams. You see the tears. You change lives, in a literal sense." The closer relationship between the home campus and the sites led the college in the summer of 2000 to designate the locations as "Extended Campuses," though retaining the title Extended Studies Division for the whole program. At the same time, what had been the Evening College became the Evening Division with its "Evening Campus."[51]

On campus, the college continued to attract international students, concentrating less on formal relationships but keeping the sister-institution tie to Kinjo College, Japan, and an active program with Kongju, Korea. Brouder brought admission of international students within the regular admissions process and utilized a coordinator of international programs. From 1995 to 1999, students came to the college from forty-six countries, with eighty-two international students enrolled in 1999. Such students continued to enrich the campus culture, especially excelling in the volleyball and soccer programs.[52]

In another area of activity, Columbia College managed to continue to achieve a remarkable sports record in the later 1990s. Bob Burchard's report to the president in August 1998 for the upcoming board meeting counted seventy-five athletes in men's soccer, men's and women's volleyball, women's softball, and men's basketball. Summing up the prior five years, he listed the results: seventeen NAIA All-Americans; ten conference players of the year; ninety-four Academic All-Conference selections; eight NAIA All-American scholar athletes; and ninety-eight All-Conference selections.

The coaches (Susan and Wayne Kreklow, Dan Hogan, Wendy Spratt, and Bob Burchard) had a combined 72.7 winning percentage with a record of 889–333, and the Kreklows had been named 1997–1998 NAIA coaches of the year in volleyball. Susan Kreklow received the Don Faurot Award for outstanding coaching, the first female to be so honored. The Kreklows had compiled a record of 416–86 in nine seasons, winning every American Midwest Conference Championship since the conference's inception in 1993 and the preceding four Midwest Regional Tournaments.[53]

By December 1998, Burchard reported that Columbia College teams had risen to yet greater heights: "I can honestly say that this fall was the best athletic season in our history. Our student-athletes and coaches excelled on the court and playing fields at an unprecedented rate. Our students ranked at the highest level in their coursework placing our institution in an elite category." Even greater successes marked the end of the 1998–1999 academic year: "The athletic department is completing the most successful season in the school's history. Each sport has been ranked nationally in the NAIA, won their conference tournaments, had representation on All-American and Academic All-American teams, All Conference Teams, and All-Region teams." Men's basketball had reached the "Sweet Sixteen" of the NAIA National Tournament, women's softball ranked in the top ten, and men's volleyball—begun on campus only in 1996—was second in a national tournament. Soccer had had the best season in the school's history, winning the American Midwest Conference title.[54]

But the excitement of the year featured the women's volleyball team, national NAIA champions with a 45–0 record, winning 110 consecutive games in the season. The team placed three First-Team All-American and five Academic All-Conference members, and Yang Zhe of Liaoyang Liaoning, China, was named NAIA national player of the year for the second consecutive year. Mariuska Hamilton was the national tournament most valuable player, joining Yang and Deng Yang as First-Team All-Americans. The Kreklows became NAIA coaches of the year in volleyball for the second consecutive year, and the college held a celebration honoring the team at which it was announced that board chairman Tom Atkins would personally have championship rings made for each player. The team received proclamations from the board, Columbia mayor Darwin Hindman, and Missouri governor Mel Carnahan. The first national title by any female team in Columbia, the feat and the Columbia College sports year brought a rave review in the *Columbia Daily Tribune:*

> If you haven't been paying attention to Columbia College athletics maybe you should. The Cougars have put together a year that could fill a pair of scrapbooks. All five Columbia College sports teams . . . won their conference titles. Three of the five teams were also regular-season conference champs. The volleyball teams and softball team were dual winners while basketball and soccer won the American Midwest Conference Tournament. Oh, yeah, every coach on the Columbia College payroll—basketball's Bob Burchard, volleyball's Wayne and Susan Kreklow, softball's Wendy Spratt, and soccer's Dan Hogan—was named Coach of the Year in the AMC.[55]

It could be more than coincidence that one small college would attract and keep such high-caliber athletes in an all-around sports program, with 92 percent of the athletes receiving degrees from the college. Incoming board president Dan Scotten saw the phenomenon as evidence of the whole college's sense of "team play that lifted all accomplishment to its highest potential." Brouder elaborated on that theme: "One of the founding principles of Christian College (now Columbia) was that of building character while at the same time educating . . . the importance of practice, sticking with a well-fashioned plan, alternately being leaders and followers, conflict resolution and techniques of split-second decision-making. One might argue that developing such skills is good preparation for life in general."[56]

Each sport continued to set performance records on the field and in the classroom in the 1999–2000 academic year. The women's volleyball team repeated its national championship and extended its NAIA record match win streak to eighty-five matches, playing the championship game against Fresno, California, on its home court. The softball team, becoming regular season champions and America-Midwest Conference champions, ranked ninth nationally. They also took honors for freshman of the year, pitcher of the year, and player of the year, Tara Gaines of Columbia. Coach Wendy Spratt became back-to-back AMC coach of the year. The men's volleyball team, with a 29–2 overall record, went undefeated in the Midwest Intercollegiate Volleyball Association for the third season in a row and defeated top-ranked California Baptist in Los Angeles in the national invitational men's volleyball tournament. The combined record of the college's four NAIA sports (basketball, softball, soccer, and women's volleyball) stood at 132–29.[57]

Such winning ways invited envy, and it came as no surprise that the 456–86 record of the Kreklows would lead to offers from other institutions. Such an offer finally led the Kreklows to accept positions at the University of Missouri–Columbia. The college then hired Melinda Washington, a former All-American player at Columbia College and a former coach at Westminster College, to lead the women's volleyball program. Despite the coaching change, Washington led the team to an NAIA number-one ranking in the fall of 2000. Dan Hogan, lured to a position at the University of Southern Indiana, was replaced by John Klein, who had served as Hogan's assistant in the 1995 and 1996 seasons. Klein had played professionally for nine years and held a graduate degree from the University of Missouri–Columbia. He continued the team's winning ways, leading the Cougars into the AMC post-season tournament as the number-one seed. The move to reinstate women's basketball went hand in hand with a decision to move men's volleyball from a varsity sport to a club sport, bringing the athletic department into compliance with Title IX requirements on gender equity while conforming to facility plans. Men's volleyball, not recognized by the NAIA as a championship sport, was offered in only 28 institutions in the NAIA, forcing the team to travel to Wisconsin and California to find competition. In contrast, women's basketball was offered in 350 institutions, allowing the college to build almost an entire schedule in Missouri.[58]

In the light of such success, Cougar fans were asked to "put their money where their mouth is" according to a *Columbia Missourian* article announcing the creation of the "Cougar Club" scholarship fund. Funds collected would go largely to athletic scholarships, with portions allocated for family sports passes and season tickets and to the athletic department. By 2000, membership in the Cougar Club had reached two hundred with donations at sixty thousand dollars.[59]

Student leadership took other forms as well during the Brouder years. The Wellness Activity Center began in 1995 to sponsor workshops with guest speakers on leadership qualities and time management with an eye to developing student leaders for clubs. The next year, Smith created a student advisory board to help students "gain a sense of ownership." Also promoting a stronger role for students, Residential Life staff built on the workshop training to create a group of "community consultants." These students learned personal skills through training by the director of Residential Life and director of the Wellness Center and engaged in nonacademic peer advising and conflict resolution. Students not only helped with Summer Connection and fall orientation for new students but also assisted faculty in teaching the Introduction to Columbia College classes. Still greater student responsibility came in 1998 with the introduction of "academic programmers." Unlike resident assistants and community consultants, the new group focused entirely on academically related issues affecting residence hall students both in and outside the classroom. Trained by staff of the Center for Academic Excellence and supervised by an area coordinator and Residential Life staff, academic programmers were serving in all residence halls by the fall of 1998.[60]

As the decade and the century neared their close, Smith addressed the 1999 faculty fall conference. Overriding all else, for Smith, was the progress made in improving the image and culture of the college while retaining its strengths. He cited the hiring of an outstanding faculty, one-third new in four years, which in itself brought change. He also noted the ending of the fashion major: "When we closed fashion, everybody knew at that point that we were serious about quality." Finally came his effort toward raising admissions standards, thus changing the nature of the student body: "The 75 or 100 most important students for the college are the people who are not here because they were denied admission, changing the dynamics in the classroom."[61]

Enhancement of the college's image resulted not only from academic matters but also from Brouder's exceptionally high standing in the community. Active for more than twenty-five years in civic affairs in Columbia, Brouder had built a reputation for fairness, courtesy, and performance that made him much in demand. His more significant contributions to local leadership included: president of the Board of Directors for the Columbia Area United Way; chair of the Public Health Services Review Task Force; chair of the Columbia Chamber of Commerce Health Care Task Force; chair of the Rusk Rehabilitation Center Governance Committee; member of the Board of Directors of the Cancer Research Center; president of the Board of Directors of Regional Economic Development, Inc.; and member of the Board of Directors of the Columbia Regional Hospital. In June 1998, Brouder achieved the city's highest honor when the Chamber of Commerce named him "outstanding citizen of the year." At the state level, Brouder accepted reappointment by Governor Carnahan for a second term (1998–2002) as one of five members of the Midwestern Higher Education Commission.[62]

Yet another enhancement came with the activities of Brouder's wife, Bonnie. When the trustees appointed Brouder to the presidency of the college, he told them that they were getting "two for the price of one," and Bonnie Brouder resigned her position at the University of Missouri Health Sciences Center to devote her full time to the support and welfare of Columbia College. It was she who noticed the absence of historic mementos and artifacts and began a systematic search of the attics of St. Clair and Williams Halls, unearthing a treasure trove of items and records, polishing and repairing where possible. In a real service to the college, she reconnected with the Christian College past, preserving a significant body of history and acquiring space in St. Clair Hall for the establishment of a Columbia College archives. Her salvaging of thousands of photographs provided an impressive array available for special occasions. She especially reconnected with pre-1970 social customs, much to the gratitude of older alumnae, making the traditional high tea a part of reunion celebrations each spring. In addition, she expended time and effort on major beautification of the campus. President Brouder credited her with the idea of outlining all buildings on front campus—Hughes Hall, Launer Auditorium, St. Clair Hall, Dorsey Hall, and Missouri Hall—with thousands of white lights turned on each holiday season as a gift of the college to the college community and to the city of Columbia. She worked with Polly Batterson and Brad Lookingbill, assistant professor of history, on a project to collect and record the history of Williams Hall, resulting in its being dedicated as a historic site by the Boone County Historical Society in September 2000. By that time, she was also immersed in activities in preparation for the college's celebration of its sesquicentennial in 2001.

As the sesquicentennial committee, ably chaired by Barbara Payne, completed its plans for the 2000–2001 academic year, Bonnie Brouder made a special project of overseeing the creation of a program for the Jane Froman Singers that would span the decades of the college's history. She also worked closely with Payne toward publication of a commemorative issue of *Friends*. Other scheduled events included a sixteen-page special section of the *Columbia Daily Tribune* for January 13, 2001, appearance of Ambassador Andrew Young as the main Charter Day speaker on January 18, 2001, and a 150-year jubilee to take place on May 12, 2001.

Just as the college, in looking to the past, must also plan for the future, Brouder's summation of recent accomplishments projected his own view of the future. The endowment had increased by $3 million, massive changes had occurred in technology, and academic areas had produced three graduate programs, new majors and minors, a new mission statement, and new general education requirements. All had been accomplished in a participatory process that brought the college community together in determining its goals. Most of all, however, an emphasis on quality pervaded the administration's initiatives and activities: "We have grown in quality. Our entering day ACT scores are up, retention has improved, our national ranking is up, overall student numbers are up; graduate programs have taken hold and are growing; donations have increased, aesthetics have improved, athletics has had its best year ever; salaries have risen 9% and Columbia College has achieved the stature of being truly admired and respected by the community."[63]

Brouder in large part had accomplished his original goals of seeing the college grow in terms of its reputation and quality while advancing its endowment, determining the right "mix" of degree offerings and bringing progressive changes. These matters would be ongoing, joined by new goals. New goals, however, dealt less with such details than with concepts and less tangible needs of the college as reflected in the president's 1999 State of the College message, calling for academically based entrepreneurial thinking:

> In a book titled *Transforming Higher Education: A Vision for Learning in the 21st Century,* the authors state: "The choice in this closing decade of the 20th century is not between innovation and tradition, but between adaptation and stagnation." Let us use our traditions to full advantage. More importantly, let us use those traditions as a safe harbor from which to launch truly bold new explorations. . . . Where do I envision the College to be 10 years from now? I see it as a model institution: one that has thrived because of its transformative and entrepreneurial strategic thinking. I see it as one of the best colleges in the Midwest at the vanguard of change, having attracted attention because of its diversification, ingenuity, credibility, flexibility and relevancy: all of these characteristics emanating from a core curriculum seasoned with a practical flair and well grounded in the liberal arts and sciences. . . . To quote John August Williams, first president of Christian, now Columbia College: "No education can be regarded as useful or philosophical unless it is adapted to the nature of the individual."

Having begun his remarks with the statement that we "need to plant our feet firmly on a path, one on which we don't just talk about being, but actually become, one of the very best and most creative colleges in the Midwest," Brouder concluded, "I suggest now that we do not follow where that path may lead but that we go instead where there is no path and leave a trail."[64] Christian College had done precisely that 150 years ago, and the spirit remained alive.

Regardless of what issues, policies, programs, or solutions the college had grappled with throughout its first 150 years, one dominant truth held firm: Christian/Columbia College stood first and foremost for outstanding teaching. Faculty had deliberately set teaching and advising at 65 to 80 percent of the total evaluation for promotion or tenure considerations. Smith opened the 1999 faculty fall conference in 1999 in a similar vein:

> I've been thinking about what good teachers you are. . . . Last year student response was the most favorable ever in agreeing to the statement, "This teacher is a good instructor." I am pleased to tell you that the results for spring semester are in, and 2336 student responses give the highest level of student agreement yet. A work entitled *Principles of Erudition* says that a good teacher must have five properties: "a talented mind, good moral conduct, humble knowledge, obligingness, and practical experience of teaching so that his teaching is clear, brief, useful, agreeable, and measured." Some principles stand the test of time. The book I'm quoting from was written in the year 1265.

Reflecting his own love of teaching, Smith regaled faculty with his joy at having had an opportunity to teach a class again: "I am a TEACHER, and it was pure fun to teach again for real. . . . Our goal is for students to write on their evaluations, as did one student I heard about, 'I learned more than I intended in this class.'" Smith closed his remarks by observing, "It is my sincere privilege to teach students at Columbia College. It is also my sincere privilege to stand before you today to thank you for your good work and to wish for you the very best year of your career."[65]

Brouder's own love of teaching was no less: "I believe that teaching is a moral act, and that no electronic intervention can replace that uniquely human moment when teaching and learning coalesce." His inaugural remarks had defined teaching as "a privilege assigned by God or the fates to a few," revealing his own "passion . . . to be called teacher."

Thus, it was at the college—first, last, and always a teaching college. With Brouder and Smith representing values espoused in 1851, the college had come full circle as it approached its sesquicentennial.

Similarities between 2001 and 1851 abounded. Providing for adult education was as empowering in the Extended Studies Division and Evening Division classes as it was for women in 1851. The college held as firmly as ever its belief that education, to be relevant, must change to reflect the needs of society. The essential nature of individual attention stressed by John Augustus Williams in 1851 and quoted by Gerald Brouder in 1999 had not varied. Nor had the belief in the value of education, which Williams called "capital" and the college of 2001 cited in its slogan: "Where learning is a value." The practice of the early college of combining the liberal arts with "domestic science" and other practical studies was reflected as surely in the curriculum 150 years later as was the continued belief in the value of the liberal arts as support for lifelong growth. Emphasis on attracting serious students, undermined in hard times, had returned. The early role of the president's wife as a full-time nurturer of institutional needs had also come full circle. The ethical standards, integrity, and emphasis on "civility and respect" of the Brouder presidency were reminiscent not only of Williams but also of Joseph Kirtley Rogers. Both Rogers and Brouder shared a courtly demeanor and talent for diplomacy that won community as well as collegewide respect.

The much misunderstood college name had changed. The college was no longer single sex, but relevant challenges for women by 2001 came from coexisting and competing with men, rather than from being isolated from them. The curriculum had gone from four-year to junior college and back, then to include graduate courses as trends dictated. Teamwork and collegiality had replaced the vitriol of the Shannon-Williams quarrels, a change to be welcomed, as was the financial stability of 2001, although endowment remained a chronic need.

Continuity and change had worked together to preserve a 150-year-old heritage. Christian/Columbia College had stumbled a time or two, but the persistence with which a courageous little frontier college and its later more complex heir coped with and prevailed over adversity, daring to go where others feared to tread, had not changed.

Appendix

THE HISTORY OF CHRISTIAN COLLEGE as the first women's college in Columbia conflicted with the claim of Stephens College after 1915 that it originated as the Columbia Female Academy in 1833. This claim first appeared in the Stephens College *Annual Catalog* of 1915–1916, even though all previous catalogs since 1857 had used an 1856–1857 founding date. The resulting controversy requires a full examination of that claim.[1]

After the founding of Christian College in 1851, factions that had provided opposition to the Christian Church group in 1849 turned their attention to solidifying or even upgrading the struggling Columbia Female Academy. The academy's best-known teacher and principal, Lucy Wales, had left in 1841 to return to the East to marry, and a series of successors attempted to fill the gap. According to John Crighton, "The Columbia Female Academy, by modern standards, would not be highly rated. It was a combined elementary school and high school. The academy was ungraded, except possibly in the high school level, where junior, middle and senior classes were identified." A legislative act of February 28, 1851, amended the 1837 charter of the Columbia Female Academy to allow trustees "to offer the usual degrees awarded in colleges and seminaries." The legislation specifically stated that it was an amendment to the 1837 charter of the Columbia Female Academy, not the creation of a new institution. However, catalogs gave no indication that any college course was ever taught at the academy. In fact, the academy's catalogs of 1851–1855 list the names of twenty girls who appeared several years later as students or graduates of Christian College.[2]

For a time after 1851, the academy did somewhat better financially but was never able to offer more than its usual courses at the high school level and below. Nor did the amendment in any way change the academy's nonsectarian nature. The academy failed to open in the fall of 1854 after a letter of appointment to Prof. T. J. Sloan of Pennsylvania went astray. Although it did reopen with Sloan as its head in February 1855, Sloan returned to Pennsylvania for the summer, became too ill to resume his duties the next fall, and resigned. The academy failed to reopen in September 1855 and never resumed operation.[3]

Stephens College based its claim to have originated as the Columbia Female Academy of 1833 in part on Switzler's *History of Boone County,* published in 1882. Switzler, a champion of the Baptist group in opposition to the Christian Church plan in 1849, stated: "The nucleus of Stephens College, was the old 'Columbia Female Academy' which originated in 1833." He continued, "While the school [Columbia Female Academy] was thus in operation, some denominational differences sprang up which resulted in changing the Academy from a non-sectarian to a Baptist school, under the name of the 'Baptist Female College.' " Switzler explained: "The same course [denominational differences] gave rise to the establishment of 'Christian College. . . .' The academy passed out of existence in 1853 [actually 1855] and was succeeded by the denominational school above named, which was organized in 1856, and chartered in 1857."

However, Switzler then elaborated:

> It is due the truth of history, however, to say that out of these differences [in 1849] arose, on the part of the members of the Christian Church, a commendable determination to establish a female college under the special patronage of that church, and a like determination on the part of the other churches, to resuscitate and reorganize the old Columbia Female Academy. . . . Out if it grew the Baptist Female College, called afterwards, and now, Stephens College. Out of the other enterprise grew Christian Female College, so that, in truth, the proposition of Hatch and White to establish a "Female Collegiate Institute" finally resulted in the establishment of two female colleges in town.[4]

In other words, the denominational split in 1849 leading to the incorporation of Christian College in 1851 resulted in the founding of both Christian Female College and Baptist Female College. This means that the creation of Baptist Female College was, indeed, an outgrowth of the 1849 disputes and the victory of the Christian Church faction in founding Christian Female College, chartered on January 18, 1851. Amendment of the charter of the Columbia Female Academy to provide for collegiate-level course work came just weeks after Christian College's incorporation. If a women's college had been founded in 1833, as claimed by Stephens College, efforts to upgrade the Columbia Female Academy in 1851 would not have been necessary. The town meetings of 1849, aimed at the founding of a women's college, clearly indicated that no "female college" existed in Columbia at that time.

According to Crighton, "The closing of the [nonsectarian] Columbia Female Academy in the fall of 1855 created a sense of loss and need. Within a few months, a group of Baptists launched a movement for the establishment of a [Baptist] women's college in Columbia." A Baptist history stated that "on the 15th of March 1856, several earnest-hearted brethren met in Columbia, Missouri, and laid plans for the organization of a Baptist female school which should be located in that city."[5] Both of these sources would suggest that organizational efforts toward the creation of Baptist Female College did not take place until after the old academy had failed, and that Baptist Female College, chartered on January 17, 1857, was not a continuation or reorganization of the Columbia Female Academy, which already had authorization to grant collegiate degrees. If it had been a continuation, no new board of trustees would be necessary, as the previous board of the Columbia Female Academy continued to exist for another ten years after the academy closed.

The Baptist group proceeded in 1856–1857 to form what became Columbia Baptist Female College. Proposed articles of incorporation were circulated on March 15, 1856, and an organizational meeting on May 26, 1856, resulted in the election of a board of curators to plan for the opening of the college in September or October. The final act of incorporation, passed by the Missouri General Assembly on January 17, 1857, named twelve major stockholders as the "Curators of Columbia Baptist Female College." The board was authorized to "be capable of receiving, or acquiring, by donation, or purchase, estate, both real and personal." The detailed document, typical of charters establishing new institutions, set forth provisions for hiring, governing, and maintaining the college.[6]

Even before its incorporation, Baptist Female College opened in temporary quarters in the fall of 1856. Curator R. C. Branham "informed the board that he had obtained a statement from the trustees of the Columbia Female Academy, granting the use of the academic building without charge to Professor Rothwell for school purposes." This statement clearly indicated that one group of trustees was acting to allow a wholly separate group use of its property. If Baptist Female College had been an evolution of the earlier academy, the property of the abandoned school would have been transferred to the new college, as was the case in 1870 when Baptist Female College became Stephens College. Baptist Female College did use the academy's building in 1856–1857, occupying the rooms at 920 Cherry Street where Lucy Wales had once taught, a location still intact in Columbia as the Niedermeyer Apartments. An advertisement in the *Missouri Statesman* on June 27, 1856, heralded the opening of the school: "The curators of this Institution hereby announce to the public that the first term of the college will open on the 1st Monday in September next under the management of President Wm. R. Rothwell. . . . For the present the Columbia Female Academy has been secured as a school room."[7]

The words "for the present" reflected the temporary nature of the property arrangement, whereas the phase "has been secured" noted the permission granted for use of the property. Other similar advertisements appeared in local papers throughout the summer of 1856. In some editions of the *Statesman,* adjoining advertisements appeared for Baptist Female College and for Christian Female College, announcing the "Sixth Session" of Christian Female College and the "first term" of Baptist Female College.[8]

Baptist Female College acquired its own quarters when Moss Prewitt purchased eight acres and a two-story brick residence on the eastern edge of Columbia from Mrs. Mary L. Parker, widow of Oliver Parker, for $5,000 The property—purchased on March 4, 1856—was deeded to Baptist Female College curators on April 7, 1857.

The final disposition of the property of the old Columbia Female Academy further illustrated the separate nature of the academy from Baptist Female College. With the Columbia Female Academy no longer in operation, this disposition required another legislative act, occurring on February 15, 1865:

> Whereas, By an act of the General Assembly of this State, approved, 1837, there was incorporated in this State, in the town of Columbia, Boone County, a High School, and institution of learning for the education of females and known by its corporate name, to wit "The Columbia Female Academy." The title to the grounds and buildings erected thereon were vested in the board of trustees therein named and their successors in perpetuity;
>
> And whereas, It appears that the aforesaid property was purchased and the buildings erected thereon by donations made by citizens of said county;
>
> And, whereas, It further appears that said property has not been, for several years past, used for school or any other purposes, and is rapidly going to waste; therefore Be it enacted by the General Assembly of the State of Missouri as follows: That Moss Prewitt . . . is hereby authorized and empowered to sell, either at public or private sale . . . the above described real estate. . . . The proceeds arising from the sale of the property aforesaid . . . shall be distributed *pro rata* among donors or their legal representatives whose funds purchased the property . . . according to the amount subscribed and donated by each person.[9]

The buildings and grounds were sold at public auction on June 20, 1865, to Dr. S. B. Victor for $1,415, and the proceeds were returned to the original subscribers. Turner Gorden later purchased the property and converted it into a hotel. At no point did Baptist Female College, or later Stephens College, claim the property.[10]

A contrasting situation existed when Baptist Female College became Stephens College in 1870. An act of the Missouri General Assembly, passed on March 16, 1870, specifically stated that it was an amendment to the 1857 charter. The Baptist Female College curators completed the transition at their final meeting on November 20, 1873: "Resolved unanimously that John M. Robinson, the President of the Board is hereby authorized and instructed on behalf of this Board, to convey the real estate belonging to the Corporation, known as Columbia Baptist Female College property, by suitable deed to the Corporation known as Stephens College."[11]

When the Missouri Baptist General Association took over Baptist Female College as the State Baptist College in 1870, James L. Stephens of Columbia contributed an endowment of $20,000 and his name to the institution. Stephens later recounted the history of the women's colleges in Columbia: "In 1851 Christian College was organized, and a few years later Baptist College."[12]

Baptist Female College and Stephens College catalogs up through 1914–1915 routinely stated the college's founding date as 1856–1857 with no mention of the Columbia Female Academy. The *Fifty-eighth Annual Catalog* of 1914–1915, the very date and numbering of which indicated an 1856 founding, gave a brief historical sketch: "Stephens College was incorporated as 'Baptist Female College' in 1856. Fourteen years later its properties were surrendered to the General Assembly of the Baptist Church. At that time an endowment fund of $20,000 was created by a gift from the Hon. J. L. Stephens, in recognition of which the name of the institution was changed to 'Stephens Female College.' "[13]

The next catalog, the *Fifty-ninth Annual Catalog* for 1915–1916, for the first time added "Founded as an Academy in 1833" to its title page. The new historic sketch stated: "The nucleus of Stephens College was the Columbia Female Academy, which was organized in 1833. Miss Lucy Wales had charge of the academy after its organization. . . . In 1856 Columbia Female Academy was incorporated as Baptist Female College."[14]

The sudden appearance of this claim after nearly sixty years of institutional statements to the contrary coincided with the coming of President James Madison Wood to Stephens in 1912. President Wood, whose administration continued until 1947, was a highly successful promoter of the college, as well as a progressive educator. Crighton later described the condition of Stephens College at Wood's coming as "a small undistinguished, denominational school with a debt of $65,000–$70,000 which threatened to force it into receivership." By the time of Wood's retirement, the value of the college property "was conservatively estimated at $6 million dollars."[15]

One inspiration for the historical revisionism in the 1915–1916 catalog could have been a newspaper article written by E. W. Stephens in 1869 that Columbia Female Academy "in 1855 was merged into Baptist Female College."[16]

E. W. Stephens, son of James L. Stephens, maintained close ties to Baptist Female College and to Stephens College in a number of ways before his death in 1931. Although only twenty years old in 1869 when he wrote the articles, he later became a well-known local historian. Like his father before him, he served as chairman of the Stephens College Board of Curators and presented the case for the college's financial need to the Baptist General Assembly in 1911, serving as cochairman of an endowment drive to eliminate the college's debt. In 1914–1915, the *Columbia Daily Tribune* reprinted the whole series of Stephens's 1869 articles. The article claiming the "merger" of the Columbia Female Academy into Baptist Female College was reprinted on June 4, 1915, just before the Stephens College *Fifty-ninth Annual Catalog* first claimed the tie to the earlier academy.[17]

Whatever the inspiration for the revision of the founding date, documentary evidence failed to support the claim. The act of incorporation of Baptist Female College on January 17, 1857, made no mention of the Columbia Female Academy or of any "merger." It set forth details typical of an original act of incorporation. In contrast to this, the act to amend the Columbia Female Academy in 1851 had stated explicitly that it was an amendment to the 1837 charter of that academy. In the same way, the 1870 act to reorganize the Baptist Female College stated that it was "An act to amend an act to incorporate Columbia Female College in Boone County, approved January 17, 1857." The incorporation date given as 1856 in the *Fifty-ninth Annual Catalog,* also in error, was actually January 17, 1857.[18]

The ultimate source of evidence concerning the founding date of Stephens College may well be such official college publications as the *First Annual Catalog* of Columbia Baptist Female College for the year ending July 20, 1857, and an advertisement in the *Missouri Statesman* of August 15, 1857, for "the second collegiate year of this Institution." Stephens College bulletins of the early twentieth century routinely stated that "Stephens College was founded in the year 1856 for the education of young women." Finally, until the practice of printing the number of commencements along with the date of the commencement on each year's program was discontinued, commencements coincided with the 1856 date, not with 1833. For example, the "forty-fourth commencement" was held in 1900, the "fifty-ninth" in 1916, and the "seventy-second" in 1929.[19]

The body of evidence supporting 1856–1857 as the founding date for Stephens College would seem to refute the use of 1833 as the actual date, confirming the role of Christian Female College as the first college for women west of the Mississippi River.

Notes

1. Where Others Fear to Tread

1. Barbara Miller Solomon, *In the Company of Educated Women: A History of Women and Higher Education in America,* 56.
2. Thomas Woody, *A History of Women's Education in the United States,* 152–55.
3. Paulina Ann Batterson, *The First Forty Years,* 29, 22, 50.
4. John C. Crighton, "Columbia College Was the Predecessor of the University of Missouri," 70.
5. P. Batterson, *The First Forty Years,* 22; William F. Switzler, *History of Boone County,* 226–27.
6. John C. Crighton, "Columbia's Citizens Provided for the Education of Their Daughters," 58; *Laws of the First Session of the Ninth General Assembly of the State of Missouri, 1826–1837,* 19–20.
7. Crighton, "Predecessor of the University," 71; P. Batterson, *The First Forty Years,* 31.
8. John C. Crighton, "The University of Missouri Was Founded in Columbia in 1839," 72–73; Frank F. Stevens, *A History of the University of Missouri,* 12–16; Jonas Viles, *The University of Missouri: A Centennial History, 1839–1939,* 22.
9. John C. Crighton, "Difficulties Attend Attempts to Start Women's College in Columbia," 76.
10. P. Batterson, *The First Forty Years,* 36.
11. Allean Lemmon Hale, *Petticoat Pioneer: The Story of Christian College,* 9–10.
12. Ibid., 3, 7; T. M. Allen to John Gano, Sept. 29, 1844, Christian College Records, Western Historical Manuscripts Collection. Hereafter cited as CCR-WHMC.
13. Hale, *Petticoat Pioneer,* 3–6; North Todd Gentry, "T. M. Allen: Address Delivered by North Todd Gentry," CCR-WHMC.
14. Hale, *Petticoat Pioneer,* 5–6; *Columbia Herald,* Oct. 12, 1871.
15. Hale, *Petticoat Pioneer,* 8.
16. Ibid., 7–10.
17. Ibid., 284; T. M. Allen to John Allen Gano, June 25, 1839, CCR-WHMC; Hale, *Petticoat Pioneer,* 9–10; Crighton, "Difficulties," 76.

18. *Missouri Statesman,* Nov. 23, 1849, hereafter cited as *Statesman;* Hale, *Petticoat Pioneer,* 11.
19. Crighton, "Difficulties," 76; *Statesman,* Nov. 23, 1849.
20. *Statesman,* Nov. 30, 1849; Crighton, "Difficulties," 77.
21. Crighton, "Difficulties," 77–78; *Statesman,* Dec. 7, 1849.
22. John C. Crighton, "Sectarian Rivalry and Slavery Split Defeated Plan for Women's College," 84.
23. Hale, *Petticoat Pioneer,* 8–12, 284.
24. P. Batterson, *The First Forty Years,* 25.
25. Hale, *Petticoat Pioneer,* 284; Levi T. Smith, D. P. Henderson, and Thomas Grant, Consultation Report, Feb. 18, 1851, Shannon Papers, Archives of the University of Missouri. Hereafter cited as SP-AUM.
26. James Shannon to Col. Switzler, SP-AUM.
27. Hale, *Petticoat Pioneer,* 284.
28. Resolution of the Board of Curators conferring honorary LL.D. on Shannon, Sept. 21, 1856, SP-AUM.
29. Hale, *Petticoat Pioneer,* 13–14; *Laws of the State of Missouri Passed at the Sixteenth General Assembly, 1850–1851,* 310–12; John C. Crighton, "Denominationalism in Religion Gave Birth to Women's Colleges," 85–86.
30. Hale, *Petticoat Pioneer,* 14–17.
31. Keith E. Melder, *Beginnings of Sisterhood: The American Women's Rights Movement, 1800–1850,* 14, 16–17.
32. Woody, *Women's Education,* 113, 325.
33. Ibid., 145–61.
34. E. C. Davis, "Female Education: The Anniversary Address, Commencement, July 2, 1852," CCR-WHMC.

2. Setting the Tone

1. John Augustus Williams, "Inaugural Address of Jno. Aug. Williams," 19–21, CCR-WHMC.
2. Ibid., 8–10.
3. Ibid., 11–16.
4. Hale, *Petticoat Pioneer,* 20–21.
5. Ibid., 29.
6. Christian College, *Circular and Catalogue of the Officers and Students of Christian College for the Year Ending July 4, 1854,* 6.
7. Christian College, *Fourth Annual Register of Christian College,* 3–4; Hale, *Petticoat Pioneer,* 22; Christian College, *1854 Catalogue,* 5.
8. Hale, *Petticoat Pioneer,* 19.
9. Ibid., 19–20; John C. Crighton, "Columbia Early Established Itself as a Medical Center, Second Only to St. Louis," 27; John C. Crighton, "Columbia Was Laid Out in 1821, Incorporated Five Years Later," 101; Crighton, "Predecessor to the University," 71–73; Crighton, "Columbia's Citizens," 58.
10. Hale, *Petticoat Pioneer,* 19–20; Christian College, "Record Book of Female College, 1851–1871," Aug. 13, 1851, 18, CCR-WHMC (hereafter cited as "Record Book").
11. Hale, *Petticoat Pioneer,* 22.

12. Ibid., 22–23.
13. Ibid., 287, 30–31.
14. Ibid., 31–32.
15. Christian College, *1854 Catalogue,* 5; Hale, *Petticoat Pioneer,* 36.
16. Williams, "Inaugural Address," 25–26; "Record Book," May 1, 1852, 30.
17. "Record Book," May 1, 1852, 31–32; Hale, *Petticoat Pioneer,* 286.
18. Hale, *Petticoat Pioneer,* 23–24, 286.
19. Ibid., 27–28; *Missouri Sentinel,* July 8, 1852.
20. *Missouri Sentinel,* July 15, 1852; Hale, *Petticoat Pioneer,* 38.
21. *Statesman,* June 11, 1852; July 15, 1853.
22. Hale, *Petticoat Pioneer,* 32–33, 288.
23. Christian College, *1854 Catalogue,* 11; Hale, *Petticoat Pioneer,* 21.
24. "Record Book," July 3, 1855, 60–61.
25. Christian College, *1854 Catalogue,* 11; Hale, *Petticoat Pioneer,* 20.
26. Hale, *Petticoat Pioneer,* 35–37.
27. Viles, *Centennial History,* 55–56.
28. Stevens, *University of Missouri,* 77–78.
29. Viles, *Centennial History,* 56–58; Stevens, *University of Missouri,* 117–18, 126.
30. Viles, *Centennial History,* 60–63.
31. Ibid., 79–81.
32. Hale, *Petticoat Pioneer,* 25.
33. Viles, *Centennial History,* 76–77; Stevens, *University of Missouri,* 81; *Statesman,* Mar. 28, 1851.
34. *Statesman,* Mar. 28, 1851; Stevens, *University of Missouri,* 84, 123.
35. Hale, *Petticoat Pioneer,* 286.
36. Ibid., 24; "Record Book," Aug. 7, 1851, 18–20.
37. Hale, *Petticoat Pioneer,* 38.
38. Ibid., 39; "Record Book," May 2, 1856, 73–75.
39. "Record Book," May 1, 1852, 73–75.
40. Hale, *Petticoat Pioneer,* 42.
41. Ibid., 40; "Record Book," May 8, 1852, 42; May 1, 1852, 24–28.
42. "Record Book," May 4, 1852, 35–36, 38–40; Hale, *Petticoat Pioneer,* 41, 46–47.
43. "Record Book," July 5, 1853, 51.
44. Ibid., 54–55; *Missouri Sentinel,* Sept. 1, 1853.
45. "Record Book," Feb. 3, 1851, 6.
46. Ibid., Apr. 7, 1851, 10–13; Oct. 20, 1854, 59; May 3, 1856, 72–79.
47. Ibid., May 3, 1856, 79.
48. Ibid., 80–81.
49. Ibid., May 23, 1856, 82–85; June 4, 1856, 86–87.
50. Ibid., July 3, 1856, 92–106, 111.
51. Christian College, *1855 Catalog,* 12.

3. The Crucible

1. *Missouri State Journal,* Mar. 20, 1856.
2. "Record Book," July 3, 1856, 11; Feb. 20, 1857, 123; Hale, *Petticoat Pioneer,* 46.
3. Hale, *Petticoat Pioneer,* 47; *Statesman,* June 13, 1856.

4. Hale, *Petticoat Pioneer,* 47–48, 50–51.
5. "Record Book," Feb. 20, 1857, 124; June 15, 1857, 128, 130.
6. Ibid., June 19, 1857, 131–34; Christian College, *Catalogue of the Officers and Students of Christian College for the Year Ending July 4, 1857,* 13, 21.
7. "Record Book," Jan. 20, 1857, 116; Hale, *Petticoat Pioneer,* 49–50; Christian College, *1857 Catalogue,* 19; "Record Book," Aug. 20, 1858, 16.
8. Hale, *Petticoat Pioneer,* 48–50.
9. "Record Book," Jan. 28, 1858, 162; Feb. 12, 1858, 148.
10. *Statesman,* Nov. 28, 1865; Sept. 4, 1857.
11. "Record Book," Feb. 12, 1857, 150; Feb. 16, 1857, 150–51; Hale, *Petticoat Pioneer,* 53–56; O. A. Carr, *Memorial of J. K. Rogers and Christian College,* 91, 114–16.
13. Hale, *Petticoat Pioneer,* 57–63; Carr, *Memorial,* 111–12.
14. "Record Book," Aug. 6, 1858, 152–60; Aug. 6, 1858, 159; Dec. 10, 1858, 161; Dec. 17, 1858, 163.
15. Ibid., May 21, 1859, 173, 176; Hale, *Petticoat Pioneer,* 60–61.
16. "Record Book," Jan. 14, 1860, 192; Apr. 21, 1860, 199–200; Aug. 4, 1860, 210; Aug. 17, 1860, 210; Hale, *Petticoat Pioneer,* 52.
17. Hale, *Petticoat Pioneer,* 51, 67–68.
18. Ibid., 61–65.
19. Ibid., 65–66.
20. Christian College, *Eighth Annual Announcement of Christian College, Session of 1858–1859,* 5–7.
21. Carr, *Memorial,* 152–53.
22. Christian College, *1858–1859 Catalogue,* 8–10, 13.
23. Ibid., 17–18.
24. Christian College, *Ninth Annual Announcement of Christian College, Session of 1859–1860,* 21.
25. Hale, *Petticoat Pioneer,* 60.
26. "Record Book," Oct. 29, 1859, 186; Hale, *Petticoat Pioneer,* 62.
27. Switzler, *History of Boone County,* 929; John C. Crighton, "Unionists, Secessionists Held Big Public Meetings as Tensions Mounted," 147.
28. *Statesman,* Aug. 9, 1861; Hale, *Petticoat Pioneer,* 79; Carr, *Memorial,* 216.
29. "Record Book," Mar. 9, 1861, 217; Dec. 21, 1861, 218; Feb. 1, 1862, 219; May 10, 1862, 220; June 7, 1862, 220.
30. *Statesman,* Jan. 3, 1862; Mar. 28, 1862; Stevens, *University of Missouri,* 101–4; Hale, *Petticoat Pioneer,* 77; John C. Crighton, "Union Moved Forcefully to Tighten Control Over Missouri," 153–54; Switzler, *History of Boone County,* 419.
31. Switzler, *History of Boone County,* 152–53.
32. Ibid.
33. John C. Crighton, "Confederacy Made Desperate Bid for Attack in Missouri," 176; Switzler, *History of Boone County,* 805.
34. Switzler, *History of Boone County,* 423; *Statesman,* Aug. 15, 1862; North Todd Gentry, "Memoirs," CCR-WHMC; Hale, *Petticoat Pioneer,* 83–84.
35. *Columbia Daily Tribune,* July 12, 1941.
36. Hale, *Petticoat Pioneer,* 80; "Record Book," Feb. 8, 1864, 222; *Laws of the State of Missouri, Adjourned Session of the Twenty-second General Assembly, 1864,* 646.
37. "Record Book," Feb. 18, 1864, 223–24; Apr. 8, 1864, 226; May 7, 1864, 226–27; June 18, 1864, 228–29.

38. Hale, *Petticoat Pioneer,* 73–75.
39. Ibid., 73, 69.
40. Ibid., 77–79.
41. Ibid., 81.
42. Ibid., 84; "Record Book," Apr. 21, 1866, 242; June 30, 1866, 245.
43. "Record Book," July 14, 1869, 257; Sept. 16, 1869, 259; June 23, 1870, 270; Hale, *Petticoat Pioneer,* 87.
44. *Statesman,* Oct. 20, 1871; Christian College, "Minute Records," Oct. 11, 1871, 7, Columbia College Archives (hereafter cited as CC Archives). The "Minute Records" replaced the "Record Book" in July 1871 as the Christian College Board of Trustees minutes.
45. Hale, *Petticoat Pioneer,* 85, 91; *Statesman,* June 7, 1872.
46. Glenn V. Sherwood, *Labor of Love: The Life and Art of Vinnie Ream,* xvii.
47. Ibid., 3–6; Carr, *Memorial,* 241.
48. Sherwood, *Labor of Love,* 6–9; *Statesman,* Dec. 25, 1857; Hale, *Petticoat Pioneer,* 57, 291; Sherwood, *Labor of Love,* 6, 9, 357.
49. Sherwood, *Labor of Love,* 16–19.
50. Ibid., 30–36; Richard L. Hoxie, *Vinnie Ream,* 59.
51. Sherwood, *Labor of Love,* 37–77.
52. Ibid., 77–81, 118.
53. Ibid., 117, 233, 252.
54. Ibid., 119–52.
55. Ibid., 85–99, 301.
56. Hale, *Petticoat Pioneer,* 82, 89.
57. Stevens, *University of Missouri,* 245; Hale, *Petticoat Pioneer,* 75.
58. Hale, *Petticoat Pioneer,* 87.
59. Ibid., 92–93.
60. Ibid., 94–95.
61. Carr, *Memorial,* 130–31.
62. Hale, *Petticoat Pioneer,* 91–92; Christian College, *Twenty-fourth Annual Catalogue of Christian College for the Session Ending June 18, 1875,* 16.
63. Hale, *Petticoat Pioneer,* 90.
64. Ibid., 82.
65. "Minute Records," Feb. 20, 1873, 19; Apr. 1, 1875, 33. Carr, *Memorial,* 158, 165.
66. Carr, *Memorial,* 223–25; "Minute Records," Apr. 17, 1877, 54.
67. Carr, *Memorial,* 221.
68. "Minute Records," May 1, 1877, 57; Christian College, *Thirty-first Annual Catalogue of Christian College for the Session Ending May 31, 1882,* 19–34; Christian College, *Thirty-third Annual Catalogue of Christian College for the Session Ending June 4, 1884,* 27.
69. "Minute Records," Apr. 1, 1875, 36–37; Dec. 10, 1880, 89.
70. Ibid., May 19, 1879, 77; July 10, 1879, 82.
71. Ibid., Apr. 17, 1882, 96–98.
72. Ibid., Feb. 26, 1883, 105.
73. Carr, *Memorial,* 139.
74. Ibid., 169, 189; *Statesman,* Sept. 1, 1882.
75. Carr, *Memorial,* 193.
76. Hale, *Petticoat Pioneer,* 98–99; Carr, *Memorial,* 136.

4. Transition Years

1. "Minute Records," Apr. 30, 1883, 109; *Statesman,* June 1, 1883; Sept. 14, 1883; Hale, *Petticoat Pioneer,* 101, 113.
2. Hale, *Petticoat Pioneer,* 100–101.
3. Ibid.
4. "Minute Records," Oct. 6, 1883, 111–12.
5. George L. Peters, *The Disciples of Christ in Missouri: Celebrating One Hundred Years of Co-operative Work,* 118; Hale, *Petticoat Pioneer,* 293.
6. Christian College, *Thirty-seventh Annual Catalog of Christian College for the Session Ending June 1, 1888,* 53.
7. "Minute Records," Aug. 5, 1887, 136.
8. John C. Crighton, "Columbia's Famed Musician 'Blind' Boone Provided Early Link to Ragtime," 336; Jack A. Batterson, *Blind Boone: Missouri's Ragtime Pioneer,* 95; "Minute Records," Feb. 11, 1890, 156.
9. "Minute Records," May 13, 1890, 160–61; Jan. 16, 1890, 166; Nov. 29, 1890, 178–79.
10. Christian College, *Thirty-eighth Annual Catalog of Christian College for the Session Ending June 5, 1889,* 52–53; Christian College, *1888 Catalog,* 53.
11. Hale, *Petticoat Pioneer,* 103–4.
12. Ibid., 102.
13. Christian College, *Thirty-second Annual Catalog of Christian College for the Session Ending June 6, 1883,* 23; "Minute Records," May 29, 1885, 123.
14. Hale, *Petticoat Pioneer,* 104, 106.
15. Ibid., 108.
16. Christian College, *1883 Catalog,* 23; Hale, *Petticoat Pioneer,* 105–6; Christian College, *1884 Catalog,* 33–34.
17. Christian College, *1888 Catalog,* 22–29.
18. Hale, *Petticoat Pioneer,* 107–10.
19. "Minute Records," Jan. 5, 1893, 202.
20. *Statesman,* June 4, 1890; June 11, 1890.
21. Christian College, *Chronicle* 1:1 (Sept. 1893): 11; *Statesman,* May 25, 1893.
22. "Minute Records," May 23, 1893, 213–14; May 27, 1893, 212–18.
23. Ibid., Nov. 21, 1893, 229.
24. Christian College, *Chronicle* 1:3 (Jan. 1894): 41.
25. "Minute Records," Dec. 4, 1893; Christian College, *Chronicle* 1:3 (Jan. 1894): 41.

5. The Torch Is Passed

1. Maxine Miller Wallace, "Notes Concerning Life of Mrs. St. Clair Moss and Early History of Christian College," 2, CCR-WHMC; Luella St. Clair Moss, "Candidate for President of the Missouri Federation of Women's Clubs," CCR-WHMC.
2. Hale, *Petticoat Pioneer,* 119–20; Christian College, *Thirty-third Annual Catalogue of Christian College for the Session Ending June 4th, 1894,* 5.
3. Luella St. Clair Moss, "The Story of Three Administrations," 1, CCR-WHMC.
4. Christian College, *Chronicle* 1:1 (Sept. 1893): 17; 1:2 (Nov. 1893): 29.

5. Hale, *Petticoat Pioneer,* 116.
6. Ibid.; Christian College, *1894 Catalogue,* 34–38.
7. Christian College, *1894 Catalogue,* 64, 67; Christian College, *Chronicle* 1:9 (June 1894): 123.
8. Christian College, *1894 Catalogue,* 20, 24; Christian College, *Chronicle* 1:3 (Jan. 1894): 38, 39; Christian College, *Forty-fifth Annual Catalogue for Christian College for Young Women Located at Columbia, Missouri, for the Session Ending May 28, 1896,* 29; Hale, *Petticoat Pioneer,* 123.
9. Christian College, *1894 Catalogue,* 10; Christian College, *Forty-Eighth Annual Catalogue, Christian College and School of Music for Young Women Located at Columbia, Missouri for the Session Ending June 1, 1900,* 14.
10. Hale, *Petticoat Pioneer,* 19–21.
11. Ibid., 124; Moss, "Three Administrations," 2.
12. "Minute Records," Mar. 8, 1897, 265–67; Christian College, *Chronicle* 4:5 (Mar. 1897): 86; Christian College, *Forty-sixth Annual Catalogue, Christian College and School of Music for Young Women, Located at Columbia, Missouri, for the Session Ending May 27, 1897,* 15.
13. "Minute Records," Feb. 4, 1895, 247; Oct. 18, 1895, 254; Mar. 18, 1896, 259; June 1, 1897, 279; July 27, 1897, 282; July 6, 1897, 281.
14. Ibid., June 2, 1898, 287–88, 290; Jan. 21, 1899, 293.
15. Moss, "Three Administrations," 2; Hale, *Petticoat Pioneer,* 124; Christian College, *Chronicle* 5:3 (Jan. 1898): 53.
16. "Minute Records," Oct. 8, 1898, 290–91; Christian College, *Chronicle* 6:2 (Nov. 1898): 22.
17. Christian College, *Chronicle* 6:2 (Nov. 1898): 22.
18. Ibid., 7:6 (Mar. 1899): 82; P. Batterson, *The First Forty Years,* 46; Christian College, *Chronicle* 7:4 (Jan. 1899): 53; 7:6 (Mar. 1899): 83.
19. "Minute Records," Apr. 18, 1899, 296–97; May 9, 1899, 299–302.
20. Ibid., June 26, 1900, 306–8.
21. Hale, *Petticoat Pioneer,* 294.
22. Christian College, *Chronicle* 6:9 (June 1899): 138.
23. Moss, "Three Administrations," 2.
24. Christian College, *Chronicle* 7:5 (Feb. 1900): 66; Moss, "Three Administrations," 1, 3.
25. Moss, "Three Administrations," 3.
26. Christian College, *Chronicle* 7:5 (Feb. 1900): 75.
27. Ibid., 7:7 (Apr. 1900): 101; 7:8 (May 1900): 116.
28. Moss, "Three Administrations," 3; Christian College, *Chronicle* 9:1 (Oct. 1901): 2.
29. Christian College, *Christian College Alumnae Bulletin* 70:15 (May–June 1923): 1–2; Christian College, *Chronicle* 7:9 (June 1900): 133.
30. Christian College, *Chronicle* 9:6 (Mar. 1902): 82–83.
31. Ibid., 7:6 (Mar. 1900): 83; 9:6 (Mar. 1902): 89; Viles, *Centennial History,* 411.
32. Hale, *Petticoat Pioneer,* 129.
33. "Minute Records," May 23, 1901, 310–11; May 29, 1901, 312–14.
34. Ibid., Mar. 11, 1902, 315.
35. Ibid., Apr. 10, 1903, 352; Moss, "Three Administrations," 3; Hale, *Petticoat Pioneer,* 132.
36. Christian College, *Chronicle* 9:5 (Feb. 1902): 69; Moss, "Three Administrations," 5.

37. "Minute Records," Apr. 3, 1903, 344.
38. Ibid., Apr. 10, 1903, 346–51.
39. Ibid., May 12, 1903, 353.
40. Ibid., May 25, 1904, 356; Hale, *Petticoat Pioneer,* 137, 138–39; "Minute Records," Mar. 6, 1905, 358.
41. Hale, *Petticoat Pioneer,* 139, 143, 148.
42. "Minute Records," May 21, 1907, 369.
43. Ibid., May 22, 1906, 365.
44. Mrs. Roy J. Curfman (Edith Petty), Mar. 30, 1938, CCR-WHMC; Hale, *Petticoat Pioneer,* 139–40.
45. "Minute Records," May 21, 1907, 369; May 22, 1906, 366–67.
46. Ibid., May 17, 1909, 374; May 21, 1907, 369.
47. Moss, "Three Administrations," 5.
48. Hale, *Petticoat Pioneer,* 141.
49. "Minute Records," Oct. 22, 1909, 456; Hale, *Petticoat Pioneer,* 295; "Minute Records," Mar. 9, 1910, 462; May 29, 1911, 471.
50. "Minute Records," Apr. 5, 1910, 464; Apr. 9, 1910, 465.
51. Christian College, *Bulletin* 95:5 (Mar. 1946): 8; Hale, *Petticoat Pioneer,* 217, 140, 295.
52. "Minute Records," Apr. 5, 1910, 464–65; May 23, 1910, 469; Hale, *Petticoat Pioneer,* 142–43.
53. Hale, *Petticoat Pioneer,* 143–44; "Minute Records," May 29, 1911, 475.
54. *Columbia Daily Tribune,* May 25, 1911; Hale, *Petticoat Pioneer,* 144.
55. "Minute Records," May 29, 1911, 471, 473; Hale, *Petticoat Pioneer,* 145; Moss, "Three Administrations," 5.
56. "Minute Records," May 26, 1913, 487; Moss, "Three Administrations," 5; Hale, *Petticoat Pioneer,* 145.
57. Hale, *Petticoat Pioneer,* 133–35.
58. Christian College, "Honor Roll Pledge," CCR-WHMC.
59. Mrs. G. R. Clark to Allean Hale, CCR-WHMC; Hale, *Petticoat Pioneer,* 146.
60. Hale, *Petticoat Pioneer,* 295.
61. Ibid., 145–46; Luella Wilcox St. Clair Moss to Martha T. Banker, Apr. 8, 1916, CCR-WHMC; Hale, *Petticoat Pioneer,* 146; Christian College, *Bulletin* 2:4 (June 1916): 3.
62. Christian College, *Bulletin* 2:4 (June 1916): 8; Hale, *Petticoat Pioneer,* 146–47.
63. John Crighton, "Boone County Home Front during World War I Was a Hive of Activity," 359–60; Christian College, *Bulletin* 69:1 (Nov. 1918): 6.
64. Hale, *Petticoat Pioneer,* 141–42; Christian College, *Chronicle* 6:2 (Nov. 1898): 22–23.
65. "Minute Records," May 29, 1911, 474; May 26, 1913, 488; Christian College, *Sixty-eighth Annual Catalog of Christian College, 1919–1920,* 25; Hale, *Petticoat Pioneer,* 149.
66. Hale, *Petticoat Pioneer,* 148–49; Christian College, *Bulletin* 2:4 (June 1916): 1.
67. "Minute Records," Oct. 14, 1915, 501; Christian College, *Bulletin* 68:1 (Nov. 1918): 1.
68. Moss, "Three Administrations," 6.
69. Ibid.; "Minute Records," May 26, 1913, 488; *Columbia Missourian,* Sept. 26, 1919; Nov. 16, 1920; Hale, *Petticoat Pioneer,* 150.

70. Hale, *Petticoat Pioneer,* 148–50; "Minute Records," May 31, 1920; *Columbia Daily Tribune,* Oct. 5, 1920.
71. Hale, *Petticoat Pioneer,* 148.
72. St. Clair Moss, "Candidate," CCR-WHMC; Hale, *Petticoat Pioneer,* 151.
73. Christian College, *Bulletin* 70:12 (Nov.–Dec. 1912): 7.
74. Hale, *Petticoat Pioneer,* 151.
75. Christian College, *Bulletin* 97:2 (Dec. 1947): 1, 7.

6. Heritage Revisited

1. Hale, *Petticoat Pioneer,* 153–55; Christian College, *Seventieth Annual Catalog of Christian College,* 5; "Minute Records," May 31, 1920; Edgar Lee, "Speech upon Becoming President," CCR-WHMC.
2. Hale, *Petticoat Pioneer,* 162–63.
3. Christian College, *Seventy-fifth Annual Catalog of Christian College,* 5.
4. Christian College, *Bulletin* 74:3 (Dec. 1923): 3–4; Hale, *Petticoat Pioneer,* 160; Lee, "Speech upon Becoming President."
5. Hale, *Petticoat Pioneer,* 165–66; Christian College, *Bulletin* 70:14 (Mar.–Apr. 1923): 2; 74:3 (Dec. 1923): 3; 75:1 (Oct. 1925): 6; "Minute Records," May 25, 1925.
6. Hale, *Petticoat Pioneer,* 156; Christian College, *Seventy-first Annual Catalog of Christian College,* 21–23; Christian College, *Bulletin* 74:3 (Dec. 1923): 2; Christian College, *Student Handbook, 1925,* CCR-WHMC.
7. Christian College, *Student Handbook, 1935,* CCR-WHMC; Hale, *Petticoat Pioneer,* 160–61.
8. Desmond Lee, telephone interview by author, St. Louis, Aug. 21, 1998.
9. Edgar Lee, "Speech upon Becoming President"; Christian College, *Seventy-first Catalog,* 70–71.
10. Christian College, *Bulletin* 84:4 (Feb. 1936): 2; 119:2 (Feb. 1972): 1; Hale, *Petticoat Pioneer,* 164.
11. Christian College, *Bulletin* 78:8 (May 1929): 1; Hale, *Petticoat Pioneer,* 163–65.
12. *Columbia Missourian,* Dec. 8, 1986; Paula L. McNeill, "Mary Paxton Keeley," 147.
13. Hale, *Petticoat Pioneer,* 190–92, 194.
14. Ibid., 194–96, 217; Christian College, *Bulletin* 96:3 (Mar. 1947): 5.
15. Hale, *Petticoat Pioneer,* 164; Christian College, *Bulletin* 70:7 (Apr. 1922): 1–2; 75:5 (Mar. 1924): 1.
16. Hale, *Petticoat Pioneer,* 164–65; Louise Yeager Wightman, interview by author, Columbia, Sept. 21, 1998.
17. Edgar Lee, "President's Annual Report," May 29, 1922, 2; May 30, 1923, 1; May 28, 1924, 1; May 25, 1925, 3; May 31, 1926, 1, 4, CC Archives.
18. Hale, *Petticoat Pioneer,* 167–68; Christian College, *Bulletin* 70:11 (Sept.–Oct. 1922): 2.
19. "Minute Records," May 30, 1921; July 7, 1923.
20. *Columbia Daily Tribune,* Mar. 23, 1926.
21. "Minute Records," Mar. 22, 1926.
22. *Columbia Missourian,* Mar. 23, 1926.
23. Ibid., Mar. 29, 1926; "Minute Records," Mar. 29, 1926.
24. Christian College, "Minute Records," May 10, 1926; Hale, *Petticoat Pioneer,* 168.

25. *Columbia Missourian,* May 11, 1926.
26. Ibid., Dec. 2, 1926; Lee, interview.
27. "Minute Records," May 18, 1926; Christian College, *Bulletin* 76:1 (Oct. 1926): 2; 77:1 (Oct. 1927): 2–3; Hale, *Petticoat Pioneer,* 171–72.
28. Christian College, *Bulletin* 77:4 (Jan. 1928): 1; Hale, *Petticoat Pioneer,* 166.
29. Floyd W. Reeves, "Report of a Survey of Christian College, 1925–26, Prepared for the Department of Endowments, Board of Education, Disciples of Christ," 38, CC Archives.
30. Ibid., 44–45, 114.
31. Ibid., 39, 41–42, 56, 121.
32. Christian College, *Bulletin* 77:4 (Jan. 1928): 1; Christian College, *Eightieth Annual Catalog of Christian College,* 5.
33. Hale, *Petticoat Pioneer,* 154–55; Lee, "President's Annual Report," May 25, 1925, 4.
34. Lee, "President's Annual Report," May 25, 1925, 4; Hale, *Petticoat Pioneer,* 169–70.
35. George F. Zook to Edgar D. Lee, "Report of the Survey Committee on Christian Junior College, February 4, 1927," CC Archives.
36. Ibid.; Hale, *Petticoat Pioneer,* 172, 174.
37. Hale, *Petticoat Pioneer,* 175.
38. George R. Moon, "Report of Inspection of Christian Junior College," 1928, 2–3, CC Archives.
39. Ibid., 4–6.
40. James C. Miller, "Dear Fellow Teacher," Sept. 21, 1933, CC Archives.
41. "Minute Records," May 28, 1928.
42. Ibid., May 27, 1929; Christian College, *Bulletin* 79:1 (Oct. 1929): 6; Hale, *Petticoat Pioneer,* 176–81; "Minute Records," May 28, 1928.
43. Christian College, *Eightieth Catalog,* 3; Hale, *Petticoat Pioneer,* 177–80.
44. Christian College, *Eighty-third Annual Catalog of Christian College, Jan. 1934,* 43–44; Hale, *Petticoat Pioneer,* 179–80, 184.
45. "Minute Records," Oct. 24, 1929; May 30, 1930; Jan. 17, 1930; Dec. 9, 1930; Mar. 10, 1931.
46. Ibid., Jan. 11, 1928; Sept. 19, 1930.
47. Ibid., Mar. 16, 1931; Mar. 28, 1931; May 5, 1931.
48. Ibid., May 25, 1931; July 14, 1931; Lee, "President's Annual Report," May 30, 1932; "Minute Records," Oct. 4, 1932; Sept. 1, 1932.
49. Hale, *Petticoat Pioneer,* 183–85.
50. "Minute Records," May 28, 1934; June 12, 1934; Oct. 2, 1934.
51. Ibid., Dec. 18, 1934.
52. Ibid., Dec. 19, 1934.
53. Hale, *Petticoat Pioneer,* 186–87.
54. "Minute Records," Jan. 28, 1935; Feb. 5, 1935; May 30, 1935; Mar. 29, 1935; Mar. 30, 1935.
55. Ibid., Feb. 12, 1935; James C. Miller, letter to field representatives, Mar. 16, 1935, CC Archives; James C. Miller, "President's Annual Report," May 27, 1935.
56. "Minute Records," Jan. 8, 1935.
57. Ibid.
58. Ibid., Apr. 9, 1935; May 11, 1935; Hale, *Petticoat Pioneer,* 189.
59. Christian College, *Bulletin* 84:1 (Oct. 1935): 2; *Columbia Daily Tribune,* Aug. 8, 1935; Hale, *Petticoat Pioneer,* 198.

60. "Minute Records," Oct. 8, 1935.
61. Ibid., May 25, 1936.
62. Ibid., May 31, 1937; Nov. 9, 1936.
63. Hale, *Petticoat Pioneer,* 199; "Minute Records," May 31, 1937.
64. Hale, *Petticoat Pioneer,* 197–98; Christian College, *Eighty-fourth Annual Catalog of Christian College, 1935,* 57–68; Christian College, *Bulletin* 85:1 (Oct. 1936): 3.
65. *Columbia Daily Tribune,* Jan. 6, 1938.
66. Ibid., Jan. 28, 1938.
67. "Minute Records," Feb. 7, 1955; *Columbia Missourian,* Jan. 29, 1955.
68. Lee, interview; *St. Louis Commerce,* Aug. 1966, 10–18.
69. *St. Louis Commerce,* Aug. 1966, 10–18; *St. Louis Post-Dispatch,* Dec. 29, 1996.

7. One Life to Give

1. Hale, *Petticoat Pioneer,* 201; Miller, "President's Report," May 30, 1938; "Minutes," May 30, 1939; Sept. 14, 1943, CC Archives. The "Minutes" replaced the "Minute Records" in 1938 as the Christian College Board of Trustees minutes.
2. Miller, "President's Report," Sept. 17, 1940.
3. *Christian College Microphone,* Mar. 24, 1942. Hereafter cited as *Microphone.*
4. Miller, "President's Report," May 30, 1938.
5. Christian College, *Bulletin* 88:1 (Oct. 1938): 1; 90:5 (Feb. 1941): 2; Miller, "President's Report," May 29, 1940; Hale, *Petticoat Pioneer,* 210–11.
6. Hale, *Petticoat Pioneer,* 211.
7. Sue Gerard, interview by author, Columbia, Nov. 29, 1998.
8. Miller, "President's Report," June 5, 1944.
9. Ibid., June 8, 1952.
10. Christian College, "Profiles for Parents," 3–4, CC Archives; Sidney Larson, interview by author, Columbia, Nov. 6, 1998.
11. Miller, "President's Report," Sept. 14, 1943.
12. *Columbia Missourian,* Mar. 4, 1941; Jan. 18, 1944; *Microphone,* Apr. 16, 1946.
13. Hale, *Petticoat Pioneer,* 202–3; Miller, "President's Report," Sept. 26, 1939; Miller, "Newsletter," May 22, 1941, CCR-WHMC.
14. Miller, "President's Report," Sept. 27, 1938; May 30, 1939; June 2, 1941.
15. Hale, *Petticoat Pioneer,* 202–3; Miller, "Newsletter," Dec. 4, 1941; Christian College, "Minutes," Dec. 2, 1941.
16. Miller, "President's Report," Sept. 27, 1938; May 30, 1939; "Minutes," May 30, 1939.
17. Christian College, *Bulletin* 87:3 (Dec. 1937): 8; "Minutes," Mar. 7, 1939; May 30, 1939.
18. "Minutes," May 30, 1939; Hale, *Petticoat Pioneer,* 203–4.
19. Christian College, *Bulletin* 90:6 (Mar. 1941): 2; "Minutes," May 30, 1938.
20. Miller, "President's Report," Sept. 26, 1939; Hale, *Petticoat Pioneer,* 204–5, 216.
21. *Columbia Daily Tribune,* July 30, 1941; *Columbia Missourian,* July 31, 1941; Hale, *Petticoat Pioneer,* 212–13.
22. Miller, "Newsletter," Dec. 12, 1941.
23. Ibid., Jan. 14, 1942; Miller, "President's Report," May 27, 1942; *Columbia Missourian,* Dec. 22, 1941.

24. Miller, "Newsletter," Aug. 20, 1942; Hale, *Petticoat Pioneer,* 212–14.
25. *Microphone,* Sept. 30, 1941; May 5, 1942; Jan. 20, 1942; Dec. 7, 1943; "Minutes," Jan. 20, 1942; Oct. 13, 1942; May 27, 1942.
26. Miller, "Newsletter," Nov. 24, 1942; Feb. 9, 1944; Feb. 16, 1944.
27. Christian College, *Bulletin* 90:6 (May 1941): 2; 96:2 (Dec. 1946): 2.
28. Miller, "President's Report," June 7, 1943; Wightman, interview.
29. Miller, "Newsletter," Mar. 26, 1942.
30. Ibid., Aug. 26, 1943; Mar. 11, 1943; Miller, "President's Report," June 5, 1944; June 3, 1946; Mar. 11, 1947.
31. "Minutes," June 5, 1944; Feb. 13, 1945; Sept. 12, 1944; Hale, *Petticoat Pioneer,* 216; Miller, "Annual Report," June 8, 1953, CC Archives.
32. "Minutes," June 4, 1945.
33. Ibid., June 3, 1946.
34. Ibid., May 31, 1948; June 6, 1949; June 5, 1950.
35. Christian College, "Report of Study of 1949–50 Graduating Class," CCR-WHMC.
36. "Minutes," Feb. 13, 1945; June 4, 1945.
37. Miller, "President's Report," Sept. 24, 1946; June 9, 1948; Sept. 16, 1948; June 6, 1949.
38. Ibid., Sept. 15, 1949; Sept. 14, 1950; Feb. 3, 1951.
39. Ibid., June 5, 1950.
40. "Minutes," July 14, 1947; June 3, 1946; May 31, 1948; *Microphone,* June 10, 1947.
41. Christian College, *Bulletin* 95:6 (June 1946): 4; "Minutes," July 14, 1947; Hale, *Petticoat Pioneer,* 264.
42. "Minutes," June 5, 1950.
43. Christian College, *Bulletin* 96:2 (Dec. 1946): 2; 105:6 (Dec. 1956): 5; "Minutes," July 22, 1948; Sept. 16, 1948; June 6, 1949; June 8, 1953.
44. Christian College, *Bulletin* 100:11 (June 1951): 1–59; Hale, *Petticoat Pioneer,* 222; "Minutes," June 4, 1951.
45. "Minutes," Feb. 14, 1950; Christian College, *Bulletin* 99:5 (Mar. 1950): 3.
46. Miller, "President's Report," June 4, 1951.
47. Hale, *Petticoat Pioneer,* 224.
48. Ibid., 225–27, 229.
49. "Minutes," Feb. 13, 1951; June 4, 1951; Christian College, *Bulletin* 100:9 (Apr. 1951): 2.
50. Allean Lemmon Hale to Polly Batterson, Aug. 12, 1998; "Minutes," May 10, 1952.
51. Christian College, *Bulletin* 100:11 (June 1951): 4–6; 100:9 (Apr. 1951): 3; Hale, *Petticoat Pioneer,* 232–36.
52. "Minutes," June 2, 1952; Christian College, *Bulletin* 101:1 (Oct. 1951): 2.
53. Kyle Chrichton, "Singing Girl," *Collier's* 29 (Feb. 1936): 15–16; Ilene Stone and Suzanna Grenz, *One Little Candle: Remembering Jane Froman,* 17.
54. Stone and Grenz, *One Little Candle,* 17; *Microphone,* Dec. 7, 1943.
55. Stone and Grenz, *One Little Candle,* 19–21, 52; *Microphone,* May 5, 1942; *Columbia Daily Tribune,* Aug. 8, 1945.
56. Stone and Grenz, *One Little Candle,* 52.
57. Ibid., 21, 27; *Microphone,* Oct. 5, 1948.
58. *Columbia Daily Tribune,* Apr. 12, 1952.
59. Stone and Grenz, *One Little Candle,* 27–30.
60. Ibid., 35–36, 61.

61. Ibid., 50–52, 70–71.
62. Ibid., 41–45, 47.
63. *Columbia Daily Tribune,* Apr. 23, 1980; Stone and Grenz, *One Little Candle,* 74.
64. "Minutes," June 2, 1952; June 8, 1953.
65. *Columbia Missourian,* May 20, 1952; *Columbia Daily Tribune,* May 20, 1952.
66. *Columbia Missourian,* May 23, 1952; Miller, "President's Report," June 2, 1952.
67. Miller, "President's Report," June 2, 1952.
68. Ibid., July 13, 1955.
69. Ibid., Aug. 19, 1956; Christian College, *Bulletin* 105:6 (Dec. 1956): 5; Christian College, "Minute Record," Aug. 9, 1956, CC Archives. The "Minute Record" replaced the "Minutes" in 1954 as the Christian College Board of Trustees minutes.
70. Christian College, *Bulletin* 105:5 (Oct. 1956): 8; *Columbia Missourian,* Oct. 1, 1956.
71. "Minute Record," Nov. 14, 1956; C. E. Lemmon, "Memorial Services for James C. Miller, Nov. 19, 1956," CCR-WHMC.
72. *Columbia Missourian,* Nov. 20, 1956; Lemmon, "Memorial Services"; "Minute Record," Dec. 17, 1956.

8. Small, Select, Serious in Purpose

1. Christian College, *Alumnae Magazine* 108:6 (Dec. 1959): 3.
2. Hale, *Petticoat Pioneer,* 247; Christian College, *109th Catalog,* 11–12.
3. Christian College, *Bulletin* 106:3 (Mar. 1957): 4–5; *Microphone,* Mar. 25, 1957; "Minute Record," July 17, 1957; Nov. 20, 1957; Kenneth Freeman, "President's Report," June 2, 1958, CC Archives.
4. Christian College, *Bulletin* 107:4 (June 1928): 2; "Minute Record," Freeman, "President's Report," June 2, 1958; Hale, *Petticoat Pioneer,* 245; Christian College, *Alumnae Magazine* 108:6 (Dec. 1959): 3; "Minute Record," Nov. 5, 1963. C. E. Lemmon arranged for the portrait by Frank Bensing of Grand Central Art Galleries in New York, raising fifteen hundred dollars from Miller's friends.
5. Hale, *Petticoat Pioneer,* 243; "Minute Record," Jan. 19, 1961; June 2, 1964; Hale, *Petticoat Pioneer,* 246.
6. "Minute Record," Freeman, "President's Report," June 3, 1957, 5; Sept. 19, 1962; Hale, *Petticoat Pioneer,* 246.
7. "Minute Record, Apr. 16, 1958; July 16, 1958; "Admissions Report," June 22, 1962, CCR-WHMC.
8. Christian College, *Bulletin* 106:5 (Oct. 1957): 9; "Minute Record," Sept. 21, 1960; Sept. 19, 1962.
9. "Minute Record," Freeman, "President's Report," June 3, 1957; June 2, 1958; Hale, *Petticoat Pioneer,* 241–42.
10. "Minute Record," Feb. 19, 1958; July 16, 1958; Christian College, *Bulletin* 107:5 (Oct. 1958): 1–2; *Microphone,* Oct. 27, 1958.
11. "Minute Record," Jan. 21, 1959; Nov. 19, 1958; Christian College, *Bulletin* 108:3 (Apr. 1959): 4.
12. "Minute Record," Jan. 20, 1960; Nov. 18, 1959; Feb. 17, 1960.
13. Ibid., Feb. 17, 1960.

14. Christian College, *Bulletin* 108:3 (Apr. 1959): 3–5; "Minute Record," Jan. 17, 1962; *Microphone,* May 14, 1962.
15. "Minute Record," Sept. 16, 1959; Apr. 20, 1960; Sept. 20, 1961.
16. Ibid., July 20, 1960; July 19, 1961; Sept. 20, 1961; Mar. 16, 1960; Freeman, "President's Report," Sept. 19, 1962.
17. Hale, *Petticoat Pioneer,* 240.
18. *Columbia College Columbian,* Dec. 13, 1985. Hereafter cited as *Columbian.*
19. Ibid., May 3, 1996; Columbia College, "Profiles for Parents," fall 1995, 21, CC Archives.
20. Hale, *Petticoat Pioneer,* 244; Columbia College, "Profiles for Parents," 20.
21. Columbia College, "Profiles for Parents," 27; *Columbian,* May 3, 1996; Dennis Grev, interview by author, Columbia, Dec. 29, 1998.
22. Penelope Carroll Braun, interview by author, Columbia, Dec. 30, 1998.
23. William D. Brown, telephone interview by author, Wichita Falls, Texas, Dec. 30, 1998.
24. Freeman, "From the Desk of the President," Apr. 1, 1963, CC Archives; "Minute Record," Apr. 19, 1961.
25. Christian College, "Profiles and Purpose," CC Archives.
26. Ibid.; "Minute Record," Mar. 20, 1963.
27. Jack L. Batterson, "The Present Curriculum: A Revision in Need of Revising," Sept. 10, 1963, CC Archives; "Minute Record," June 2, 1964.
28. "Minute Record," June 2, 1964.
29. Ibid., July 19, 1961.
30. Ibid., Jan. 15, 1964; Christian College, *Alumnae Magazine* 113:1 (Jan. 1963): 9.
31. Jack Batterson, "And Gladly Learn: Faculty Summer Workshops," *Alumnae Magazine* 111:4 (Oct. 1962): 5–7; "Minute Record," Mar. 20, 1963; Oct. 5, 1963; June 2, 1964.
32. "Minute Record," Sept. 20, 1960; Oct. 26, 1960; May 23, 1962; June 2, 1964; June 1, 1965.
33. Christian College, "Parents Handbook, 1963–64," 7–9, CCR-WHMC.
34. Christian College, "Administrative Committee," May 22, 1961, CCR-WHMC.
35. Christian College, "Parents Handbook, 1963–64," 6.
36. Christian College, *106th Catalog,* 47–63.
37. Christian College, *Christian College Catalog, 1964–1965,* 44–50.
38. "Minute Record," Freeman, "President's Report," May 25, 1959.
39. Christian College, *109th Catalog,* 33; "Minute Record," Freeman, "President's Report," July 19, 1961; Christian College, "Parents Handbook, 1963–64," 10.
40. Hale, *Petticoat Pioneer,* 250; Christian College, *106th Catalog,* 26–32.
41. "Minute Record," Feb. 17, 1960.
42. Ibid., July 20, 1961; Christian College, "Trusteeship at Christian College," CC Archives.
43. "Minute Record," Jan. 15, 1964.
44. Ibid., Jan. 18, 1961; May 23, 1962; Christian College, *Alumnae Magazine* 111:1 (July 1962): 7.
45. "Minute Record," July 19, 1961.
46. Ibid., July 19, 1961; Feb. 20, 1963; May 25, 1962; Freeman, "President's Report," Sept. 19, 1962.

47. Freeman, "President's Report," May 23, 1962; Oct. 17, 1962; Nov. 9, 1962; Nov. 28, 1962.
48. Hale, *Petticoat Pioneer,* 255; "Minute Record," Freeman, "President's Report," Oct. 5, 1963; June 26, 1963.
49. "Minute Record," Freeman, "President's Report," Oct. 5, 1963; Nov. 5, 1963.
50. Freeman, "President's Report," Oct. 5, 1963.
51. Ibid.; Nov. 5, 1963.
52. Ibid., Nov. 20, 1963; Christian College, *Alumnae Magazine* 112:6 (Apr. 1964): 5; "Minute Record, Finance Committee Report," Apr. 14 and 29, 1964, CC Archives.
53. "Minute Record," June 2, 1964; Christian College, "News Release," June 1964, CC Archives; "Minute Record," Howard Kelley, "Admissions Report," Apr. 20, 1965, CC Archives; Hale, *Petticoat Pioneer,* 246.
54. "Minute Record," Oct. 17, 1964; Oct. 16, 1964; Christian College, *Alumnae Magazine* 113:2 (Apr. 1965): 2; Jessie Ellis to Polly Batterson, Feb. 12, 1998.
55. "Minute Record," Kelley, "Admissions Report," July 1965.
56. B. D. Simon, interview by author, Columbia, May 3, 1998.
57. Don Landers, interview by author, Columbia, Nov. 27, 1997; "Minute Record," Apr. 20, 1965; Freeman, "President's Report," Oct. 5, 1963.
58. "Minute Record," May 15, 1963.
59. W. Merle Hill, "Annual Report of the Dean of Faculty, July 1, 1964–June 30, 1965," CC Archives.
60. "Minute Record," Mar. 16, 1965; Apr. 20, 1965; Nancy Freeman Paul to Polly Batterson, Dec. 23, 1998.
61. Christian College, *Alumnae Magazine* 111:2 (Apr. 1962): 2; "Minute Record," Mar. 25, 1964; Hale, *Petticoat Pioneer,* 247.
62. J. Batterson to Allean Hale, Feb. 17, 1967, CC Archives.

9. Change and Continuity

1. Hale, *Petticoat Pioneer,* 260.
2. Ibid., 257–58; Christian College, Inaugural Program, Oct. 19, 1965, CC Archives.
3. Hale, *Petticoat Pioneer,* 258–60.
4. Landers, interview; "Minute Record," Oct. 22–23, 1965, 4.
5. "Minute Record," Oct. 22–23, 1965, app. 7, 2–6, 21.
6. Ibid., 3–6; J. Batterson to Hill, Feb. 5, 1996, CC Archives; Hill to J. Batterson, May 4, 1966, CC Archives.
7. "Minute Record," Oct. 20, 1967, 3; Oct. 11–12, 1968, 5; Oct. 22–23, 1965, 5; Oct. 18, 1966, 2–3; Oct. 20, 1967, 4–5.
8. Hale, *Petticoat Pioneer,* 268.
9. Ibid.; "Minute Record," Oct. 20, 1967, 2; Christian College, *Alumnae Magazine* 114:1 (Jan. 1965): 6.
10. Christian College, *Alumnae Magazine* 114:1 (Jan. 1965): 6; Hale, *Petticoat Pioneer,* 269.
11. Columbia College, "Profiles," 23, 25, CC Archives; Elaine Grev, interview by author, Columbia, Mar. 3, 1999; David O'Hagan, interview by author, Columbia, Mar. 3, 1999.

12. Diane Berry O'Hagan, interview by author, Columbia, Mar. 3, 1999; Columbia College, "Board of Trustees Minutes and Permanent Records," Oct. 15, 1976, 9, CC Archives.
13. Columbia College, "Profiles," 9–10; Joann Scrogin Wayman, interview by author, Columbia, Mar. 4, 1999.
14. Columbia College, "Profiles," 22; Christine Cotton, interview by author, Columbia, Mar. 4, 1999.
15. Columbia College, "Profiles," 16; Novelle Dunathan, interview by author, Columbia, Mar. 30, 1999.
16. William Houston, interview by author, Columbia, Mar. 1, 1999.
17. Columbia College, "Profiles," 3–4.
18. Hale, *Petticoat Pioneer,* 262, 271; "Minute Record," Merle Hill, "President's Report," Oct. 18, 1966, 9, CC Archives.
19. "Minute Record," Finance Committee Minutes, Dec. 21, 1965, 1–2; June 7, 1966, 4; Oct. 18, 1966, 9; "Minute Record," Hill to Trustees, Jan. 30, 1967; Oct. 27, 1967; Christian College, *Bulletin* 117:5 (May 1970): 11–12.
20. "Minute Record," June 4, 1968, 2; Oct. 11–12, 1968, 4.
21. Ibid., Hill to Trustees, July 19, 1968; July 22, 1968; Columbia College, *Bulletin* 119:2 (Feb. 1972): 3.
22. "Minute Record," Hill to Trustees, Mar. 22, 1968; Hill to Elizabeth Kirkman, Mar. 28, 1967; May 21, 1969, 2, CC Archives.
23. Hill, "Letter to Parents," Mar. 27, 1967, CC Archives; "Minute Record," Hill, "President's Report," Oct. 1968, 8; "Minute Record," Hill to Trustees, Dec. 1, 1969.
24. "Minute Record," Finance Committee Minutes, Feb. 3, 1967, 3–4; *Microphone,* Sept. 2, 1970.
25. "Minute Record," Hill to Trustees, Mar. 22, 1968; Hill, "Letter to Parents," Mar. 27, 1967.
26. Hale, *Petticoat Pioneer,* 277; *Microphone,* Oct. 29, 1965; Oct. 21, 1966; Christian College, "Press Release," Apr. 8, 1966, CC Archives.
27. "Minute Record," Oct. 23, 1965, app. 6; Oct. 20, 1967, 6; *Microphone,* Oct. 21, 1966.
28. "Minute Record," June 7, 1966, 3; Oct. 18, 1966, 4; Oct. 20, 1967, 6; "Minute Record," Hill to Trustees, Mar. 22, 1968; Hill, "A College of Consequence," Oct. 1968, 2, CC Archives; Hale, *Petticoat Pioneer,* 262.
29. "Minute Record," Oct. 22–23, 1965, 9; Oct. 18, 1966, 6; Hill, "President's Report," May 27, 1968, 3.
30. "Minute Record," Hill to Trustees, May 31, 1967; Mar. 22, 1968; June 4, 1968, 7.
31. Kelley to Hill, May 23, 1968, CC Archives.
32. J. Batterson to Hill, June 12, 1968, CC Archives.
33. "Minute Record," Hill, "Christian College: 1968–69??? 1969–70!!!" CC Archives.
34. J. Batterson to Hill, Sept. 2, 1968, CC Archives.
35. Houston, interview. Houston was president of the Christian College Chapter of the American Association of University Professors when the response was written by chapter members.
36. "Minute Record," Hill, "A Different College: Reflections and Recommendations by the President for the Board of Trustees and Faculty of Christian College," Dec. 17, 1968.

37. Ibid., Christian College Chapter, "Response from the Christian College Chapter of the American Association of University Professors to Reflections and Recommendations of the President," Feb. 7, 1969. Parsons College in Fairfield, Iowa, became infamous in the 1960s for hyperbole in sales techniques, poor academic standards, and resultant low retention rate.
38. Ibid.; Arden K. Smith, "Christian College: A Question of Survival: A Report to the Board of Trustees of Christian College," Jan. 1969, CC Archives.
39. Christian College, *Bulletin* 116:1 (July 1968): 86–88.
40. Hill to J. Batterson, Feb. 1, 1969, CC Archives.
41. J. Batterson to Hill, Feb. 8, 1969, CC Archives.
42. "Minute Record," Hill to Trustees, Feb. 20, 1969.
43. Ibid., "A Case for Survival," Mar. 12, 1969.
44. Ibid., May 21, 1969, 3.
45. Ibid., "A Case for Survival," Mar. 12, 1969, 1, 3; Christian College, "Press Release," June 4, 1969, CC Archives; Hill to Polly Batterson, Feb. 2, 2000.
46. "Minute Record," app. A-1, July 8, 1969; Christian College, "Press Release," May 27, 1969, CC Archives.
47. J. Batterson, "Rough Draft from Dean Batterson for North Central Meeting," July 7, 1969, CC Archives.
48. "Minute Record," Laurance Barrett, "Report of a Review Visit to Christian College, Columbia, Missouri on April 28–29, 1969, for the Commission on Colleges and Universities, North Central Association of Colleges and Secondary Schools," July 10, 1969.
49. J. Batterson to Hill, July 29, 1969, CC Archives.
50. Merle Hill, telephone interview by author, Mar. 7, 1999.
51. "Minute Record," July 8, 1968, 8; Oct. 25, 1969, 8.
52. Christian College, "Faculty Meeting Minutes," Oct. 9, 1969, CC Archives.
53. Christian College, *Bulletin* 117:1 (July 1969): 1; "Minute Record," Hill, "Transition I: A Report to the Board of Trustees," Sept. 1970; Columbia College, "Board of Trustees Minutes and Permanent Records," Hill, "A Decade in Review: A Preliminary to Long-Term Planning," Oct. 22, 1974, 3, CC Archives. Minutes began to use the name Columbia College in the fall of 1971. Minutes after this time took the name "Board of Trustees Minutes and Permanent Records." Hereafter cited as "Minutes and Records."
54. "Minutes and Records," Hill, "Transition I," Sept. 1970, 2.
55. Ibid., 4.
56. "Minutes and Records," Hill, "Transition III: A Report to the Board of Trustees," Sept. 1972, 8.
57. Ibid., June 13, 1970, 4.
58. Ibid., Sept. 1972, 5–6; Feb. 6, 1971, 7–8; June 18, 1971, 2–3; Columbia College, *Bulletin* 118:2 (Nov. 1970): 5–6.
59. "Minute Record," June 18, 1971, 7–8; "Minutes and Records," Nov. 19–20, 1971, 4.
60. "Minutes and Records," Oct. 27, 1972, 9–10.
61. Columbia College, *Self-Study for Preliminary Accreditation of Columbia College*, Nov. 15, 1972, 9, CC Archives.
62. Ibid., 1.
63. Ibid., 95–96; "Minutes and Records," Hill, "Transition II: A Report to the Board of Trustees," Sept. 1971, 5.

64. *Microphone,* Sept. 24, 1971; "Faculty Meeting Minutes," Aug. 26, 1972, 4; "Minutes and Records," Feb. 5–6, 1971, 1–2.
65. Columbia College, *Self-Study,* Nov. 15, 1972, 13.
66. Ibid., Nov. 16, 1973, app. 4, 1–2; "Minutes and Records," Apr. 26, 1974, 6.
67. *Microphone,* Oct. 6, 1970; Sept. 11, 1976.
68. Ibid., Sept. 2, 1970; Sept. 11, 1971; Columbia College, *Bulletin* 118:5 (Aug. 1971): 3.
69. "Minutes and Records," Oct. 27, 1972, 11–12; Dec. 7, 1973; *Microphone,* Oct. 19, 1973; Columbia College, *Bulletin* 120:6 (Nov. 1973): 10–11.
70. "Faculty Meeting Minutes," Oct. 9, 1969; American Association of University Professors, *Bulletin* (spring 1973): 34, 40; *Columbia Daily Tribune,* May 8, 1971; Bill Wickersham, "Recollections of May 1970: The Vietnam War, Non-Violent Protest, and the University of Missouri," Wickersham private papers, Columbia.
71. *Columbia Daily Tribune,* Jan. 27, 1972; *Columbia Missourian,* Mar. 28, 1973.
72. "Minute Record," Hill, "Transition I," Sept. 1970, 3; Oct. 25, 1969, 8; *Microphone,* Sept. 11, 1971.
73. "Minutes and Records," Hill to Trustees, May 5, 1972; Columbia College, *Self-Study, 1972,* 17.
74. "Minutes and Records," Hill, "Transition III," 3; Hill, "Base for Discussion," Jan. 12, 1972, 14, CC Archives; Columbia College, *Self-Study, 1972,* 129.
75. "Minutes and Records," Hill to Trustees, Dec. 17, 1971.
76. Ibid., John Bare, "Report of a Visit to Columbia College, Columbia, Missouri, May 2–4, 1973, for the Commission on Institutions of Higher Education of the North Central Association of Colleges and Secondary Schools," 15.
77. "Minutes and Records," Hill to Trustees, Aug. 1, 1973; Hill to Students, July 20, 1973, CC Archives.
78. *Columbia Missourian,* Sept. 13, 1973; *Columbia Daily Tribune,* Jan. 27, 1974.

10. A Living Endowment

1. Columbia College, *Self-Study Report of Columbia College: Submitted as an Affirmation of Accreditation to the North Central Association of Colleges and Schools,* Nov. 20, 1975, 94–97, CC Archives; "Minutes and Records," Hill to Trustees, Feb. 15, 1973.
2. "Minutes and Records," Hill to Trustees, June 15, 1973; "Faculty Meeting Minutes," Aug. 30, 1973.
3. "Minutes and Records," Hill, "Trustee Newsletter," Aug. 1, 1973; Sept. 15, 1973; *Microphone,* Dec. 7, 1973.
4. "Minutes and Records," Apr. 26, 1974, 1–2; Columbia College, *Self-Study,* 1975, 29–30.
5. Hill, "The Extended Studies Program of Columbia College, Columbia, Missouri," June 27, 1975, 4–6, CC Archives; "Minutes and Records," Nov. 1, 1974, 10; Hill, Memorandum, June 27, 1974, CC Archives.
6. "Minutes and Records," Finance Committee Minutes, Oct. 24, 1974.
7. Hill to "B. D., George, Sid, Andy," Oct. 28, 1974, CC Archives.
8. Donald Foster, interview by author, Columbia, Mar. 31, 1999; "Minutes and Records," Apr. 25, 1975, 6; Hill to Trustees, Oct. 14, 1975, 4.

9. Hill, “Extended Studies Program,” 7, CC Archives; “Minutes and Records,” Apr. 25, 1975, 6; Apr. 23, 1976, 2; Hill to Trustees, Oct. 14, 1975.
10. Foster, interview.
11. “Minutes and Records,” Hill to Trustees, Apr. 10, 1975; Hill, “Columbia College, Columbia, Missouri, and the Extended Studies Division,” Aug. 17, 1976, CC Archives.
12. George N. Rainsford, “Report of a Consultant Visit to Columbia College, Columbia, Missouri for the Commission on Institutions of Higher Education of the North Central Association of Colleges and Schools, December 9–11, 1974,” 1–3, CC Archives.
13. Ibid., 7–13; “Minutes and Records,” Hill to Trustees, Mar. 25, 1974; Apr. 15, 1974.
14. Rainsford, “Report of a Consultant Visit, 1974,” 4.
15. Ibid., 6, 14, 16.
16. Robert F. Ray, “Report of a Consultant Visit to Columbia College, Columbia, Missouri, October 13–15, 1975, for the Commission on Institutions of Higher Education of the North Central Association of Colleges and Schools,” 11, 13, CC Archives.
17. Ibid., 4–6, 13.
18. George N. Rainsford, “Report of a Consultant Visit to Columbia College, Columbia, Missouri, for the Commission on Institutions of Higher Education of the North Central Association of Colleges and Schools, January 6, 1976,” 2, CC Archives.
19. Columbia College, *Self-Study,* 1975, 98–105.
20. William R. Hazard, “Report of an Evaluation of Columbia College Focused on the Extended Studies Division including Visits to Eleven Program Locations, July 1976–February 1977 for the Commission on Institutions of Higher Education of the North Central Association of Colleges and Schools,” 11–15, CC Archives.
21. Ibid., 5–6, 16.
22. Ibid., 10–11.
23. Ibid., 16–17.
24. Ibid., 17–18.
25. Hill to Faculty and Staff, Mar. 29, 1976, CC Archives; “Minutes and Records,” Hill to Trustees, Apr. 6, 1976.
26. “Minutes and Records,” app. 5, Hill to Trustees, Apr. 23, 1976, 3–4.
27. Hill, “Extended Studies,” Aug. 17, 1976, CC Archives.
28. “Minutes and Records,” Hill to Trustees, Apr. 16, 1976.
29. Ibid., Apr. 23, 1976, 6.
30. Ibid., 8; Oct. 15, 1976, 7.
31. Ibid., Oct. 15, 1976, 2, 6.
32. “Faculty Meeting Minutes,” Nov. 2, 1976; “Minutes and Records,” Oct. 31, 1975, 4; Mar. 24, 1976, 2; Apr. 23, 1976, 2; Oct. 15, 1976, 16; *Microphone,* Oct. 24, 1975.
33. Columbia College, *Bulletin* 123:5 (Nov. 1976): 5; Hill to J. Batterson, Apr. 14, 1976, CC Archives.
34. J. Batterson to Hill, Apr. 16, 1976, CC Archives; J. Batterson to All Faculty, Apr. 14, 1976, CC Archives.
35. Brown to Hill, Apr. 19, 1976, CC Archives.
36. Hazard, “Report of an Evaluation,” 1–2, 10–13, 18–21.
37. Ibid., 10–11, 18–23; Thurston E. Manning to Hill, Apr. 18, 1977, CC Archives.
38. Columbia College, *Bulletin* 118:1 (May 1970): 1; 118:5 (Aug. 1971): 1; 121:5 (Sept. 1974): 3; B. D. Simon, interview by author, Columbia, May 22, 1998.

39. Columbia College, *Bulletin* 118:1 (May 1970): 1.
40. "Minutes and Records," Apr. 15, 1977, 1–3, 5, 17; Hill to Executive Committee, Mar. 23, 1977, CC Archives.
41. "Minutes and Records," Oct. 15, 1976, 12; Apr. 15, 1977, 29; "Faculty Meeting Minutes," Oct. 5, 1976; Apr. 13, 1977; Dennis Grev, "An Evaluation of the Columbia College Bio-Nutrition Program," Feb. 5, 1977, CC Archives.
42. "Minutes and Records," Hill to Trustees, Mar. 1, 1977; Apr. 15, 1977, 27.
43. Simon, interview, May 22, 1998; Hill, interview, Mar. 15, 1999; "Minutes and Records," Hill to Trustees and Administrative Staff, June 2, 1977.
44. Columbia College, *Bulletin* 124:5 (Nov. 1977): 1.
45. Hill, interview, Mar. 7, 1999.
46. Foster, interview, June 4, 1999; Landers, interview.

11. Guarding the Heritage

1. Don Schubert, interview by author, Columbia, Nov. 24, 1997; David Rogers, interview by author, Columbia, May 6, 1998; Simon, interview; Columbia College, *Friends* 125:3 (June 1978): 1.
2. "Minutes and Records," Bruce Kelly to Executive Committee of the Board of Trustees, July 18, 1977.
3. Foster, interview, Dec. 15, 1997.
4. "Minutes and Records," Executive Committee, Aug. 12, 1977; Wilson Thiede, "Report of a Visit to Columbia College, Columbia, Missouri, April 3–7, 1978, June 1–2, 1978, Including Visits to ESD Sites during April and May, 1978, for the Commission on Institutions of Higher Education of the North Central Association of Colleges and Schools," 45, CC Archives.
5. "Faculty Meeting Minutes," Sept. 13, 1977; Sept. 23, 1977, 7; Oct. 20, 1978, 6; Foster to All Faculty, Sept. 5, 1978, CC Archives.
6. *Microphone,* Nov. 18, 1977; "Faculty Meeting Minutes," Dec. 13, 1977; Columbia College, *Friends* 125:3 (June 1978): 2; *Columbia Daily Tribune,* quoted in *Friends* 125:1 (Jan. 1978): 1.
7. "Minutes and Records," Apr. 21, 1978; Eldon Drennan, "Report," CC Archives.
8. "Minutes and Records," Oct. 20, 1978, 11–12; Sept. 23, 1977, 16.
9. Patricia Thrash to Kelly, "Notes of Meeting of Jan. 12, 1978," Feb. 7, 1978, CC Archives; "Minutes and Records," Foster, "Report," Apr. 21, 1978.
10. Thiede, "Report of a Visit, 1978," 32–33.
11. Ibid., 47–48, 15, 25, 30, 43, 47–48.
12. Ibid., 40–49.
13. Ibid., 40–47.
14. *Microphone,* Apr. 14, 1978; Foster, interview, Dec. 15, 1997; "Minutes and Records," Apr. 12, 1978, 12; Thiede, "Report of a Visit, 1978," 50–52.
15. Thiede, "Report of a Visit, 1978," 52–53; "Minutes and Records," Oct. 20, 1978, 13.
16. "Minutes and Records," Oct. 20, 1978, 13; "Minutes," Jan. 19, 1979, 3, CC Archives. Columbia College minutes in 1979 began to use the title, "Minutes."
17. "Minutes," Jan. 19, 1979, 3.
18. Ibid., Oct. 20, 1978, 5; "Faculty Meeting Minutes," Dec. 12, 1978.

19. "Faculty Meeting Minutes," Feb. 7, 1979; "Minutes," May 11, 1979, 5.
20. "Faculty Meeting Minutes," Apr. 10, 1979.
21. "Minutes," Apr. 21, 1978, 14; May 11, 1979, 9, 4.
22. *Columbia Daily Tribune,* Apr. 20, 1979; *Columbian,* Apr. 27, 1979.
23. Bernard Adams, "Report of a Visit to Columbia College, Columbia, Missouri, May 7–9, 1979, for the Commission on Institutions of Higher Education of the North Central Association of Colleges and Schools," 2–3, CC Archives.
24. Ibid., 20.
25. Ibid., 9, 11–12, 16.
26. Ibid., 22.
27. Ibid., 15, 5, 8.
28. Ibid., 13–18.
29. Ibid., 23–26; Thurston E. Manning to Kelly, July 31, 1979, CC Archives.
30. Simon to Virginia Singletary, June 29, 1977; Singletary to Kelly, May 8, 1980, CC Archives; *Friends* 127:2 (June 1980): 8–9.
31. "Faculty Meeting Minutes," May 14, 1980.
32. Tom Atkins, interview by author, Columbia, May 5, 1998; Don Schubert, interview by author, Columbia, Nov. 24, 1997.
33. Marty Toler, interview by author, Columbia, Dec. 2, 1997.
34. "Minutes," Foster, "Facilities Report," May 9, 1980, 6–7.
35. Ibid., "Finance Committee Minutes," July 19, 1977; Dec. 27, 1976; Sept. 26, 1980, 21; *Microphone,* Oct. 28, 1977.
36. *Columbian,* Sept. 21, 1979; "Minutes," Foster, "Facilities Report," Apr. 29, 1980.
37. Genie Rogers to Polly Batterson, May 1, 1999, CC Archives; Schubert, interview.
38. Toler, interview; Columbia College, *Friends* 129:5 (Mar. 1983): 2.
39. "Minutes," Sept. 26, 1980, 2, 39.
40. Elmer Jagow, "Report of a Focused Visit to Columbia College, Columbia, Missouri, November 20–21, 1980, for the Commission on Institutions of Higher Education of the North Central Association of Colleges and Schools," 4–10, 16, CC Archives.
41. "Faculty Meeting Minutes," May 5, 1980; Jan. 27, 1981.
42. Novelle Dunathan and J. Batterson, "RE Board of Trustees Meeting," Jan. 9, 1981; "Faculty Meeting Minutes," Apr. 16, 1981.
43. Ibid., Sept. 22, 1981; Mar. 30, 1982.
44. Ibid., Apr. 21, 1982.
45. "Minutes," May 14, 1982, 2; "Faculty Meeting Minutes," May 12, 1982; May 19, 1982.
46. "Minutes," Sept. 18, 1981, 2; Kelly to Trustees, EMS, and Department Chairmen, July 14, 1981, 2, CC Archives; "Faculty Meeting Minutes," Oct. 21, 1981.
47. Roger Fritz to EMS, June 19, 1981, CC Archives.
48. "Minutes," Jerry L. Harris to Kelly, Dec. 4, 1981, 1, 4.
49. Ibid., 4–5, 8, 10.
50. Ibid., 10, app., 1–8.
51. Harris, "Confidential Working Paper," n.d., CC Archives.
52. "Minutes," Feb. 23, 1982, 4–5.
53. Ibid., Kelly to Trustees, Feb. 24, 1982.
54. J. Batterson to Harris, Apr. 19, 1982, CC Archives; *Columbian,* May 5, 1982.
55. Burton Augst, Joe Davis, and Dorothy King to Harris, Apr. 9, 1982, 1–6, CC Archives.

56. J. Batterson to Harris, "Realistic Response," Apr. 12, 1982, 1–6, CC Archives.
57. Ibid., 1.
58. Kenneth Rothman to Kelly, Apr. 13, 1982, CC Archives.
59. Harris to Jack Batterson, Sid Larson, Penny Braun, Burt Augst, Dottie King, and Joe Davis, Apr. 13, 1982, CC Archives.
60. "Faculty Meeting Minutes," Apr. 12, 1982; Apr. 21, 1982.
61. Faculty Representatives in LRPC to Faculty, Administration, and Trustees, May 12, 1982, CC Archives.
62. Kelly to Rogers, Apr. 22, 1982, CC Archives.
63. "Faculty Meeting Minutes," May 12, 1982; "Minutes," May 14, 1982, 12–13.
64. "Faculty Meeting Minutes," May 26, 1982.
65. Kelly, Harris, Foster, Kay E. Kanger, and Dunathan to Rogers, June 4, 1982, CC Archives; Marty Toler, interview by author, Columbia, June 16, 1999; Don Schubert, interview by author, Columbia, June 6, 1999; Atkins, interview; Foster, interview, June 4, 1999.
66. "Minutes," Executive Committee, July 2, 1982, 1–2; Schubert, interview, June 6, 1999.
67. "Minutes," Executive Committee, Aug. 11, 1982, 1; Harris to All Faculty and Administrative Staff, July 14, 1982, CC Archives; "Faculty Meeting Minutes," Aug. 20, 1982.
68. "Minutes," Sept. 17, 1982, 13; *Columbia Daily Tribune,* Sept. 19, 1982.
69. Ray Troutt, "Report of a Visit to Columbia College, Columbia, Missouri, November 29–December 2, 1982, for the Commission on Institutions of Higher Education of the North Central Association of Colleges and Schools," 10–11, 27, CC Archives.
70. Ibid., 17.
71. Ibid., 19, 12–13, 23.
72. Ibid., 27.
73. "Minutes," John Henricks to Trustees, Apr. 27, 1983; Dunathan to Trustees, May 6, 1983, CC Archives; Columbia College, *Friends* 129:4 (Dec. 1982): 6; 129:2 (Sept. 1982): 3.
74. Columbia College, *Friends* 129:6 (June 1983): 9; "Minutes," Sept. 9, 1983, 2; *Columbian,* Oct. 28, 1983.
75. Columbia College, *Friends* 129:5 (Mar. 1983): 5, 8; Schubert, interview, June 6, 1999.
76. Mary Miller to Robert Evans, "Task Force on Teaching Effectiveness," Jan. 26, 1984, 1–6, CC Archives.
77. Ibid.
78. Miller, telephone interview by author, Hamilton, N.J., May 26, 1999.
79. Columbia College, "Profiles," 20, 23, 10; Anthony Alioto, interview by author, Columbia, July 22, 1999; Carolyn Dickinson, interview by author, Columbia, July 22, 1999; Sally Wells, interview by author, Columbia, July 22, 1999.
80. "Minutes," Sept. 9, 1983, 10; Columbia College, *Friends* 130:4 (Sept. 1983): 3; "Minutes," Henricks to Trustees, Apr. 23, 1984, 3.
81. "Minutes," Foster to Atkins, "Periodic Report," Mar. 13, 1984; June 13, 1984.
82. Atkins, interview; Toler, interview, June 16, 1999.
83. Columbia College, *Friends* 131:2 (June 1984): 1; Atkins, interview; *Columbian,* May 15, 1984.

84. Schubert, interview, June 6, 1999.
85. Charles Koelling, interview by author, Columbia, Apr. 26, 1999.

12. Securing the Heritage, Part 1

1. Donald B. Ruthenberg to Marvin Owens, May 4, 1984, CC Archives; "Minutes," May 18, 1984, 2.
2. Ruthenberg to Patricia Thrash, June 28, 1984, CC Archives; Ruthenberg, interview by author, Ozark, Mo., Sept. 7, 1999.
3. Robert Burchard, interview by author, Columbia, Sept. 2, 1999; *Columbia Daily Tribune,* June 2, 1984.
4. Columbia College, *Friends* 131:3 (Sept. 1984): 1.
5. Ibid., 1–2; 131:4 (Dec. 1984): 1–2.
6. "Minutes," Jan. 18, 1985, 10; Columbia College, *Friends* 133:1 (Mar. 1986): 5.
7. Columbia College, *Friends* 131:3 (Sept. 1984): 2; "Minutes," Jan. 17, 1986, 2.
8. Ruthenberg, interview.
9. "Minutes," Sept. 21, 1984, 5.
10. Ibid., 5–6.
11. Ibid., 2–11; Ruthenberg, "President's Report," Jan. 18, 1985, 2–3.
12. Ruthenberg, "President's Report," May 17, 1985, 1; *Columbia Missourian,* Sept. 8, 1985; Feb. 5, 1986.
13. "Minutes," Sept. 19, 1986, 21–22; *Columbia Missourian,* Aug. 14, 1985; *Columbia Daily Tribune,* Aug. 14, 1985; Columbia College, *Friends* 132:3 (Sept. 1985): 1.
14. *Kansas City Times,* Oct. 31, 1986; Columbia College, *Friends* 133:4 (Dec. 1986): 1; *Columbia Daily Tribune,* Oct. 30, 1986.
15. Columbia College, *1986 Self-Study,* 84, 101–2, CC Archives; "Minutes," Sept. 19, 1986, 11–12.
16. Columbia College, *1986 Self-Study,* 1.
17. Ibid., 7, 15.
18. Ibid.; Glenn A. Niemeyer, "Report of a Visit to Columbia College, Columbia, Missouri, October 27–29, 1986, for the Commission on Institutions of Higher Education of the North Central Association of Colleges and Schools," 36, 29, 20–21, CC Archives.
19. Ibid., 37, 8–9.
20. Ibid., 39; J. Batterson to Ruthenberg, Oct. 30, 1986, CC Archives.
21. "Minutes," Henricks, "Report to the President," Sept. 10, 1984; Columbia College, *Friends* 131:3 (Sept. 1984): 2.
22. *Columbian,* May 4, 1990; Columbia College, *Friends* 133:1 (Mar. 1986): 8; Ruthenberg to All Faculty and Staff, Nov. 12, 1985, CC Archives.
23. Larson, interview; "Minutes," Sept. 18, 1987.
24. Columbia College, "Profiles," 9; Anthony Marshall, interview by author, Columbia, Sept. 2, 1999.
25. Columbia College, "Profiles," 6, 8; Timothy Ireland, interview by author, Columbia, Aug. 20, 1999.
26. Columbia College, "Profiles," 7; Hoyt Hayes, interview by author, Columbia, Sept. 17, 1999.

27. Columbia College, "Profiles," 18; Ronald Taylor, interview by author, Columbia, Aug. 23, 1999.
28. Columbia College, "Profiles," 17; Cheryl-Ann Hardy, interview by author, Columbia, Sept. 15, 1999.
29. Columbia College, "Profiles," 14; Michael Lyman, interview by author, Columbia, Aug. 23, 1999.
30. Columbia College, "Profiles," 42; Michael Polley, interview by author, Columbia, Aug. 26, 1999.
31. Columbia College, "Profiles," 24; Terry Lass, interview by author, Columbia, Aug. 24, 1999.
32. Columbia College, "Profiles," 28; Ken Torke, interview by author, Columbia, Sept. 27, 1999.
33. Columbia College, "Profiles," 28–29; Peter Meserve, interview by author, Columbia, Aug. 23, 1999; Soumitra Chattopadhyay, interview by author, Aug. 23, 1999.
34. Columbia College, "Profiles," 4; Michael Sleadd, interview by author, Columbia, Sept. 26, 1999.
35. "Minutes," Jan. 17, 1986; Mary Miller, "Report to the President," Aug. 27, 1990, CC Archives; Columbia College, *Friends* 139:3 (fall 1992): 3; "Faculty Meeting Minutes," Mar. 29, 1990.
36. *Columbian,* Mar. 9, 1990.
37. "Faculty Meeting Minutes," Mar. 30, 1989; "Minutes," May 12, 1989; Sept. 22, 1989; *Columbian,* Oct. 20, 1989; Cotton, interview.
38. *Columbian,* Feb. 9, 1990; Columbia College, *Friends* 136:4 (Dec. 1989): 1; *Columbia Daily Tribune,* Jan. 30, 1990; Owen Jackson, interview by author, Columbia, Aug. 23, 1999.
39. Columbia College, "Profiles," 30; "Faculty Meeting Minutes," Nov. 8, 1994; "Minutes," May 15, 1992, 3; Jan. 13, 1995; Dec. 11, 1992; Michael Polley, "Report to the President," Apr. 12, 1995, CC Archives.
40. *Columbia Daily Tribune,* Nov. 23, 1990; *Columbian,* Dec. 14, 1990; Columbia College, *Friends* 137:1 (Mar. 1990): 1.
41. "Minutes," Miller, "Report to the President," Sept. 18, 1987.
42. Miller, interview.
43. "Faculty Meeting Minutes," Aug. 20, 1987; Aug. 27, 1987; "Minutes," Sept. 18, 1987.
44. "Minutes," Sept. 30, 1988, 11; "Faculty Meeting Minutes," Oct. 27, 1988.
45. "Notes on Faculty Discussion of December 5, 1988," CC Archives; Columbia College, *1989 Faculty Handbook,* CC Archives.
46. "Faculty Meeting Minutes," Apr. 23, 1987; "Minutes," Miller, "Report to the President," Apr. 19, 1991, 2; Columbia College, *1992 Self-Study,* 9–11.
47. Columbia College, *1992 Self-Study,* 6–7; "Faculty Meeting Minutes," Feb. 25, 1998.
48. Columbia College, *1992 Self-Study,* 9–11.
49. Ibid., 11–14.
50. Ibid., 6–9.
51. James Ballowe, "Report of a Visit to Columbia College, November 12, 16–19, 1992, for the Commission on Institutions of Higher Education of the North Central Association of Colleges and Schools," 2, CC Archives.
52. "Faculty Meeting Minutes," Nov. 19, 1992.
53. Ballowe, "Report of a Visit, 1992," 9–10, 16.

54. Ibid., 11–13.
55. Ibid., 20.
56. Ibid., 33–34.
57. Ibid., 37–38; Patricia Thrash to Ruthenberg, Apr. 8, 1993, CC Archives.
58. Marty Toler, interview by author, Sept. 27, 1999; Columbia College, *Friends* 140:2 (summer 1993): 5.
59. *Columbian,* May 1, 1992; Oct. 2, 1992.
60. Frank Vivelo to Academic Council and Academic Affairs Committee, Oct. 7, 1992, CC Archives. Faculty views of Vivelo's management style throughout this section come from interviews with faculty, including Ronald Taylor, Novelle Dunathan, Anthony Marshall, Peter Meserve, Michael Lyman, Michael Polley, and Christine Cotton.
61. Vivelo to Academic Council and Academic Affairs Committee, Oct. 6, 1992.
62. "Faculty Meeting Minutes," Apr. 15, 1993; Sept. 9, 1993; Nov. 8, 1993; Columbia College, *1993 Faculty Handbook,* 4–5, CC Archives.
63. "Faculty Meeting Minutes," Sept. 27, 1994; Dec. 8, 1994.
64. "Minutes," Apr. 20, 1993; Vivelo to Academic Council and All Department Heads, Nov. 13, 1992, CC Archives.
65. "Minutes," Vivelo, "Report to the President," Sept. 14, 1993; Columbia College, *1993 Faculty Handbook;* "Faculty Meeting Minutes," Feb. 17, 1994; Terry Obermoeller, interview by author, Columbia, Sept. 27, 1999.
66. Columbia College, "Academic Affairs Regulations; Policies and Procedures of the Office of Academic Affairs, Dean of Faculty Office," CC Archives; Polley, interview.
67. Polley, interview; "Faculty Meeting Minutes," May 5, 1994.
68. *Columbia Daily Tribune,* Aug. 20, 1994; "Faculty Meeting Minutes," Aug. 19, 1994; Polley, interview.
69. "Faculty Meeting Minutes," Sept. 27, 1994; Oct. 6, 1994.

13. Securing the Heritage, Part 2

1. "Minutes," Jan. 18, 1985, 5; Columbia College, *Friends* 132:3 (Sept. 1985): 2; 132:4 (Dec. 1985): 2.
2. "Minutes," Sept. 19, 1986, 2; May 15, 1987, 12–13; Sept. 18, 1987, 11; May 13, 1988, 6.
3. Columbia College, *Friends* 137:1 (Mar. 1990): 1; 138:3 (Sept. 1991): 3; "Minutes," May 1990, 9–10.
4. "Minutes," Jan. 17, 1989, 8–9; May 12, 1989, 9; Columbia College, *Friends* 136:4 (Dec. 1989): 1; Columbia College, *1986 Self-Study,* 45–46; "Stafford Library Annual Report, 1993–1994," CC Archives.
5. Columbia College, "Profiles," 39; Carol Jones, interview by author, Columbia, Sept. 3, 1999; "Stafford Library Annual Report, 1998–1999," CC Archives.
6. *Columbia Daily Tribune,* Sept. 5, 1995; "Minutes," Sept. 24, 1993, 3, 5; Sept. 23, 1994, 3; Dona Sue Cool, "Report to the President," Apr. 21, 1994; May 13, 1994, 2, CC Archives.
7. Columbia College, *Friends* 138:4 (Dec. 1991): 3–4; 137:4 (Dec. 1990): 1, 3; "Minutes," Sept. 27, 1991, 4.

8. "Minutes," Sept. 25, 1992, 7; Sept. 20, 1991; Columbia College, *Friends* 139:3 (fall 1992): 1; 140:1 (spring 1993): 1–3; "Minute Record," Feb. 7, 1955.
9. Columbia College, *1986 Self-Study,* 99–100; *Columbian,* Mar. 6, 1992; "Minutes," May 13, 1994, 8.
10. *Columbia Daily Tribune,* Dec. 15, 1992.
11. Ibid., June 15, 1986; Columbia College, *Friends* 133:3 (Sept. 1986): 5; "Minutes," Sept. 18, 1987, 21; Patrick Overton, "Report to the President," Apr. 25, 1988, CC Archives.
12. *Columbian,* Sept. 24, 1987; "Minutes," Overton, "Report to the President," Apr. 23, 1990.
13. Columbia College, *Friends* 140:2 (summer 1993): 3.
14. "Minutes," Sept. 19, 1986, 8; Columbia College, *Friends* 137:2 (July 1990): 3.
15. Columbia College, *Friends* 137:2 (July 1990): 3; "Minutes," Steve Chao, "Report to the President," Aug. 23, 1990, CC Archives; Columbia College, *Friends* 137:3 (Nov. 1990): 1.
16. Atkins, interview.
17. "Minutes," Sept. 19, 1986, 8–9; Cathie Muschany, "Report to the President," Sept. 22, 1989, CC Archives; Miller, "Report to the President," Aug. 28, 1991; Steve Chao, "Report to the President," Apr. 18, 1991.
18. Columbia College, *1992 Self-Study,* 32; "Minutes," Sept. 30, 1988, 13–15.
19. Miller, interview.
20. "Minutes," Miller, "Report to the President," Sept. 6, 1988, 1.
21. Miller, interview.
22. Susan T. Rydell, "Report of a Focused Visit to Columbia College, Columbia, Missouri, January 30–31 and March 12–14, 1989, for the Commission on Institutions of Higher Education of the North Central Association of Colleges and Schools," 1–7, CC Archives.
23. Ibid., 10, 1.
24. Ruthenberg to Kan Terada, May 5, 1989, CC Archives; "Minutes," May 12, 1989, 4; Sept. 25, 1992, 7.
25. Columbia College, *1986 Self-Study,* 29–38.
26. "Minutes," Henricks, "Report to the President," Sept. 10, 1984; Jan. 17, 1989, 5; Jan. 18, 1985, 3; Columbia College, *Friends* 141:3 (fall 1994): 1.
27. Columbia College, *Friends* 141:2 (summer 1994): 3.
28. Ibid., 137:3 (Nov. 1990): 3; "Minutes," Sept. 14, 1990, 4–5; Sept. 25, 1992, 8–9; Ballowe, "Report of a Visit, 1992," 32.
29. "Minutes," Sept. 14, 1990, 2, 4–5; Moon, "Report to the President," Aug. 27, 1990, CC Archives.
30. "Minutes," Jan. 14, 1993, 6–7.
31. Columbia College, *Friends* 131:4 (Dec. 1984): 9; 135:4 (Dec. 1988): 3; "Minutes," Miller, "Report to the President," May 1, 1989, 3; Apr. 20, 1990, 5–6; *Columbian,* Mar. 9, 1990.
32. Columbia College, *1986 Self-Study,* 55; *Columbian,* Feb. 5, 1987; Mar. 5, 1987.
33. Columbia College, "Profiles," 33; *Columbian,* May 4, 1990.
34. *Columbian,* Nov. 20, 1992; Burchard, interview.
35. "Minutes," Jan. 17, 1989, 9.
36. Burchard, interview; *Columbian,* Feb. 17, 1995.
37. Columbia College, *1999 Cougar Softball,* 25–27, CC Archives.

38. *Columbian,* Feb. 9, 1990; Wendy Mertz Slifka, telephone interview by author, Knoxville, Tenn., Oct. 15, 1999; Columbia College, *Friends* 141:2 (summer 1994): 7.
39. *Columbian,* Dec. 13, 1991; May 1, 1992.
40. "Minutes," May 12, 1989, 1.
41. Columbia College, "Profiles," 33; Columbia College, *Cougars 1999 Women's Volleyball Schedule,* CC Archives.
42. Columbia College, *1999 Men's Soccer Schedule,* 8, CC Archives.
43. Columbia College, *Friends* 140:3 (fall 1993): 16; 138:4 (Dec. 1991): 6; Burchard, interview.
44. Columbia College, *1986 Self-Study,* 54.
45. Faye Burchard, interview by author, Columbia, Sept. 2, 1999.
46. "Minutes," Ron Cronacker, "Report to the President," Apr. 20, 1994, CC Archives; Miller, "Report to the President," Sept. 6, 1988; *Columbian,* Apr. 28, 1995.
47. *Columbian,* May 3, 1991; Apr. 14, 1987; Feb. 26, 1986; Apr. 28, 1995.
48. "Minutes," Jane Crow, "Report to the President," Apr. 25, 1988, CC Archives; Diane O'Hagan, "Report to the President," Apr. 25, 1988; Sept. 30, 1988, 16; Sept. 23, 1994, 10, CC Archives.
49. Ibid., Cool, "Report to the President," Apr. 12, 1995.
50. Columbia College, *Friends* 141:2 (summer 1994): 3.
51. Ibid., 133:4 (Dec. 1986): 1; 135:3 (Sept. 1988): 3; 139:4 (fall 1992): 4; *Columbia Daily Tribune,* Dec. 15, 1986.
52. "Minutes," Sept. 20, 1991, 5; Miller, "Report to the President," Apr. 22, 1992; Sept. 24, 1993, 6; May 12, 1994, 1; Cool, "Report to the President," Sept. 1, 1994; Apr. 12, 1995.
53. Ibid., Ruthenberg, "President's Report," May 17, 1985; Sept. 13, 1985, 17; Columbia College, *Friends* 135:1 (Mar. 1988): 1; Daniel L. Scotten, interview by author, Columbia, Sept. 21, 1999.
54. "Minutes," Ruthenberg, "Positioning Columbia College for the Future: Strategic and Long Range Planning," May 11, 1990, 5–10.
55. Ibid., May 14, 1993, 11.
56. Ibid., Jan. 13, 1995, 6–8.
57. Columbia College, *Friends* 141:4 (winter 1994): 1, 2, 6; "Minutes," May 12, 1995, 5–6.
58. "Minutes," Jan. 21, 1994, 5; Sept. 23, 1994, 10–12; *Columbian,* Feb. 17, 1995.
59. Columbia College, *Friends* 142:1 (spring 1995): 4; *Columbian,* Feb. 17, 1995.
60. Atkins, "An Ode to Dr. Donald B. Ruthenberg," CC Archives.
61. *Columbia Daily Tribune,* May 17, 1995; *Columbian,* Feb. 17, 1995.
62. Ruthenberg, interview.
63. *Columbia Daily Tribune,* Jan. 16, 1995; Columbia College, *Friends* 142:1 (spring 1995): 1; *Columbian,* Feb. 17, 1995.
64. *Columbian,* Feb. 17, 1995.

14. Full Circle

1. Gerald Brouder, "Inaugural Address," Sept. 15, 1995, CC Archives.
2. *Columbia Daily Tribune,* Jan. 16, 1995; *Columbian,* Sept. 22, 1995.

3. "Minutes," Jan. 12, 1996, 5; May 17, 1996, 1, 10.
4. Ibid., May 12, 2000; Sept. 30, 1998, 1.
5. Ibid., Jan. 15, 1999, 3–4; May 7, 1999, 1.
6. Bob Hutton, interview by author, Columbia, Nov. 15, 1999; Mike Randerson, interview by author, Columbia, Nov. 17, 1999; Terry Smith, interview by author, Columbia, Nov. 19, 1999.
7. Columbia College, *Friends* 143:1 (spring 1996): 1.
8. *Columbian,* May 3, 1996; "Minutes," Jan. 12, 1996, 6–7; May 1, 1998, 4.
9. *Columbian,* Feb. 23, 1996; Oct. 10, 1997; "Minutes," Jan. 16, 1998, 3; May 7, 1999, 2.
10. Smith, interview; *Columbian,* Sept. 27, 1996.
11. "Minutes," Jan. 12, 1996, 5, 8; Smith, interview; Gerald T. Brouder, interview by author, Columbia, Nov. 30, 1999.
12. Columbia College, *Friends* 142:3 (fall 1995): 5; 143:1 (spring 1996): 1, 4.
13. Ibid., 3; "Minutes," May 17, 1996, 3.
14. "Minutes," May 17, 1996, 3.
15. Ibid., May 1, 1998; May 16, 1997, 10; Columbia College, *Friends* 146:3 (fall 1999): 7; "Faculty Meeting Minutes," Mar. 20, 1998; Apr. 9, 1998; Mar. 18, 1999.
16. Columbia College, *1999–2000 Undergraduate Catalog,* 52.
17. "Minutes," May 16, 1997, 10–12; Jan. 17, 1997, 4; *Columbia Daily Tribune,* Apr. 5, 1997; *Columbia Missourian,* Oct. 10, 1997.
18. *Columbia Missourian,* May 7, 1999, 6; Smith, interview; "Faculty Meeting Minutes," Dec. 8, 1998.
19. *Columbian,* Nov. 10, 1995; "Minutes," Jan. 12, 1996, 4, 7–8; May 17, 1996, 8; Smith to Brouder, Nov. 24, 1997, CC Archives.
20. "Minutes," Sept. 20, 1996, 9; Jan. 17, 1997, 3; Columbia College, *Friends* 145:3 (fall 1998): 6; Smith to Brouder, Mar. 20, 1998, CC Archives.
21. "Minutes," Jan. 16, 1998, 5; Columbia College, *Faculty Handbook 1998,* 70, 17–19, CC Archives.
22. "Minutes," May 17, 1996, 9.
23. "Faculty Meeting Minutes," Feb. 17, 2000.
24. Ibid., Oct. 5, 1995; "Welfare and Personnel Policies Committee Report on Use of Non-Tenure Track Appointments," Mar. 6, 1996, CC Archives; Brouder to Atkins, Oct. 9, 1996, CC Archives; "Faculty Meeting Minutes," Mar. 5, 1996; "Minutes," May 17, 1996, 15; Brouder, interview.
25. "Minutes," Jan. 17, 1997, 3; May 16, 1997, 2; Stafford Library, "Annual Report, 1995–96"; "Annual Report, 1996–97," CC Archives.
26. Stafford Library, "Annual Report, 1998–99," CC Archives; "Long Range Plan, 1999," CC Archives.
27. Columbia College, *Friends* 143:2 (summer 1996): 4; 144:1 (spring 1997): 13; "Minutes," May 17, 1997, 13.
28. "Minutes," May 1, 1998, 5; *Columbian,* Apr. 17, 1998.
29. "Faculty Meeting Minutes," Jan. 20, 2000; "Minutes," May 12, 2000.
30. Columbia College, *Friends* 144:3 (fall 1997): 3; Brouder, "Memorial Service," Oct. 1, 1997, CC Archives.
31. "Minutes," May 16, 1997, 9; Sept. 30, 1998, 3.
32. Columbia College, *Friends* 143:2 (summer 1996): 8–9; *Columbian,* Dec. 12, 1997; "Minutes," Jan. 12, 1996, 4.

33. *Columbian,* Sept. 22, 1995; "Minutes," Sept. 26, 1997, 11; May 1, 1998, 4.
34. Brouder, interview; Hutton, interview.
35. "Minutes," Sept. 26, 1997, 9–13; Jan. 16, 1998, 11; Bob Hutton, "Columbia College Master Plan, May 1998," 9–10, CC Archives.
36. *Columbia Missourian,* July 7, 2000.
37. Brouder, "State of the College," Sept. 4, 1997; "State of the College," Sept. 16, 1999, CC Archives; "Faculty Meeting Minutes," Apr. 13, 2000.
38. "Minutes," Jan. 12, 1996, 7; May 7, 1999, 2.
39. Ibid., Sept. 30, 1998, 6; Jan. 15, 1999, 1–2.
40. Ibid., Sept. 15, 1995, 4; Sept. 20, 1996, 9; Sept. 26, 1997, 4; Sheila Brynjulfson to Polly Batterson, Sept. 13, 1999.
41. "Minutes," Jan. 17, 1997; Sept. 9, 1999; Jan. 16, 1998; Sept. 30, 1998; "Faculty Meeting Minutes," Mar. 27, 1997; Columbia College, *1999–2000 Undergraduate Catalog,* 57–60; Smith, "Report to the President," Apr. 16, 1999.
42. Columbia College, *Friends* 144:3 (fall 1997): 1.
43. Brouder, "Address to University of Missouri School of Nursing," Apr. 18, 1997, CC Archives; Brouder, "An Impending Revolution in Higher Education," Aug. 27, 1998, CC Archives; Brouder, "State of the College," Sept. 16, 1999, CC Archives; "Minutes," Apr. 17, 1998, 2.
44. "Minutes," May 16, 1997, 4–5; Rene Nichols, interview by author, Sept. 20, 1999.
45. "Minutes," Mike Randerson, "Report to President Brouder," Dec. 21, 1998; "Minutes," Mar. 30, 1998.
46. Randerson, interview.
47. Ibid.; American Council on Education, Center for Adult Learning and Educational Credentials, *Military Installation Voluntary Education Review Final Report, MIVER Revisit, Naval Station Roosevelt Roads, Puerto Rico, 21–23 February 1999,* 44, CC Archives.
48. American Council on Education, Center for Adult Learning and Educational Credentials, *Military Installation Voluntary Education Review Final Report, Everett Naval Station, Marysville, Washington, 16–19 May 1999,* 43, CC Archives.
49. Ibid., 41–44.
50. Kim Buike, interview by author, Columbia, Sept. 16, 1999.
51. Randerson, interview; Smith, interview.
52. Britta Wright, interview by author, Columbia, Sept. 16, 1999.
53. "Minutes," Bob Burchard, "Report to President Brouder," Aug. 14, 1998; May 1, 1998; Columbia College, *Friends* 145:4 (winter 1998): 8.
54. Columbia College, *Friends* 145:4 (winter 1998): 8; "Minutes," Burchard, "Report to President Brouder," Dec. 21, 1998; "Minutes," Apr. 12, 1999.
55. Columbia College, *Friends* 146:1 (spring 1999): 6; "Minutes," Jan. 15, 1999, 5–6; May 7, 1999, 1; *Columbia Daily Tribune,* May 10, 1999.
56. Dan Scotten, interview by author, Columbia, Sept. 21, 1999; Columbia College, *Friends* 144:2 (summer 1998): 5.
57. *Columbia Daily Tribune,* May 6, 2000; *Columbia Missourian,* Apr. 30, 2000.
58. *Columbia Daily Tribune,* Mar. 7, 2000; Feb. 12, 2000; "Minutes," May 13, 2000.
59. *Columbia Missourian,* Sept. 9, 1998.
60. *Columbian,* Dec. 6, 1996; Oct. 18, 1996; Oct. 10, 1997; Apr. 17, 1998; F. Burchard, interview; Columbia College, *Friends* 143:2 (fall 1996): 3; 146:3 (fall 1999): 18.
61. Smith, "Speech to Fall Conference," Aug. 20, 1999, CC Archives; Smith, interview.

62. Brouder, *Vitae,* CC Archives; *Columbian,* Dec. 4, 1998.
63. Brouder, interview; Brouder, "State of the College," 1999.
64. Brouder, "State of the College," 1999.
65. Smith, "Speech to Faculty," Aug. 21, 1998; Aug. 20, 1999, CC Archives.

Appendix

1. Much of the history of the Columbia Female Academy, and of its relationship to the Baptist Female College and thus to Stephens College, comes from the late John Crighton. A member of the Stephens College social science faculty for thirty-five years before his retirement in 1970, Crighton was the author of *Stephens College: A Story of Educational Innovation* and subsequently published a series of articles in the *Columbia Daily Tribune* from June 25, 1972, to Nov. 30, 1975. Crighton and the *Tribune* in 1975 received the American Association for State and Local History Award of Merit. In 1987, the collected articles, along with some new ones, were combined into *A History of Columbia and Boone County* and published by the Boone County Historical Society.
2. Crighton, "Columbia's Citizens," 62; *Statesman,* Mar. 7, 1851; *Laws of the State of Missouri Passed at the Sixteenth General Assembly, 1850–1851,* 409; Hale, *Petticoat Pioneer,* 289.
3. *Statesman,* Jan. 5, 1855; Aug. 3, 1855; Sept. 21, 1855.
4. Switzler, *Boone County,* 806–7, 810–11.
5. John C. Crighton, "Closing of Academy Prompted Establishment of Baptist Female College," 88; Hale, *Petticoat Pioneer,* 291.
6. Crighton, "Closing of Academy," 88–89; *Laws of the State of Missouri Passed at the Nineteenth General Assembly, 1856–1857,* 227–28; Crighton, "Closing of Academy," 88–89.
7. *Statesman,* June 27, 1856. Later advertisements replaced the first Monday in September starting date with the third Monday in September.
8. Ibid., Sept. 5, 1856.
9. Crighton, "Closing of Academy," 88; *Laws of the State of Missouri Passed at the Regular Session of the Twenty-third General Assembly, 1864–1865,* 388–89.
10. Hale, *Petticoat Pioneer,* 289.
11. *Laws of the State of Missouri Passed at the Adjourned Session of the Twenty-fifth General Assembly, 1870,* 174–75; John C. Crighton, "Columbia Baptist Female College Was the Forerunner of Stephens College," 131.
12. Hale, *Petticoat Pioneer,* 289; *Columbia Herald,* 25th Anniversary Edition, 1895, 12.
13. Stephens College, *Fifty-eighth Annual Catalog,* 13.
14. Stephens College, *Fifty-ninth Annual Catalog,* 16.
15. John C. Crighton, "Wood's Early Task Was Building Financial Foundation of Stephens College," 266.
16. E. W. Stephens, "Article Number 99," *Statesman,* 1869. Reprinted in *Columbia Daily Tribune,* June 4, 1915.
17. John C. Crighton, "Taylor Brought Business Efficiency to Stephens College Operations," 207; John C. Crighton, "Wood's First Problem Was Reduction of Stephens College Debt," 232.
18. *Laws, 1856–1857,* 227–28.

19. Stephens College, *First Annual Catalogue of the Columbia Baptist Female College, Boone County, Mo, for the Year Ending July 2D, 1857; Statesman,* Aug. 15, 1857; Stephens College, *Bulletin of Stephens College and School of Music, 1906–1907;* Stephens College, *The Forty-Fourth Annual Commencement, May 21–31, 1900,* 1; *Official Programme of the Fifty-ninth Commencement, May 26–30, 1916,* 1; *Program of the Seventy-second Commencement, May 23–28, 1929,* 1.

Bibliography

COLLECTIONS

Columbia College Archives, Columbia, Mo. Although many of the earliest records of the college have been deposited on permanent loan in the Western Historical Manuscript Collection, a large portion of the college's history remains on campus, especially items coming after the mid-nineteenth century. An effort to collect materials moved into storage resulted in the "rediscovery" of hundreds of boxes of college papers in the attics of St. Clair Hall and Williams Hall. Through the efforts of Bonnie Brouder, relevant material is now stored in a special archives room on the third floor of St. Clair Hall. The papers, though mostly sorted, are yet to be cataloged. These materials consist of publications, yearbooks, correspondence, speeches, self-studies, reports, catalogs, and internal papers such as faculty minutes and campus correspondence. The college's photographs also reside in the archives. Minute records, often including administrative reports in more recent administrations, remain in the offices of the president of the college, although the earliest volume (1851–1871) is in the Western Historical Manuscript Collection. Faculty meeting minutes and reports reside in the offices of the academic dean, and college alumni journals are located in the alumni office.

Western Historical Manuscript Collection. Ellis Library, University of Missouri, Columbia. The Columbia College Records of the Western Historical Manuscripts Collection consist of 1,352 folders of materials including administrative records, account books, financial records, student records, and publications from the earliest days of the college. Smaller items include memoirs, correspondence, programs, mementos, newsletters, faculty information, student handbooks, club records, and photographs. Little is included after the 1960s.

MAJOR MANUSCRIPT SOURCES

Columbia College catalogs, 1851–2000.
Columbia College journals and college newspapers in the Columbia College Archives:
Alumnae Bulletin, 1914–1951.
Bulletin, 1969–1977.
Christian College Chronicle, 1893–1907.
Christian College Magazine, 1959–1965.
Christian College Microphone, 1929–1971.
Columbia College Columbian, 1979–present.
Friends, 1978–present.
Minutes of the Board of Trustees of Columbia College:
"Record Book of Female College," 1851–1871.
"Minute Records," 1871–1938.
"Minutes," 1938–1954.
"Minute Record," 1954–1970.
"Minutes and Records," 1971–1978.
"Minutes," 1979–present.

PUBLISHED MATERIALS

Batterson, Jack A. *Blind Boone: Missouri's Ragtime Pioneer.* Columbia: University of Missouri Press, 1998.
Batterson, Paulina Ann. *The First Forty Years.* Columbia: Columbia Chamber of Commerce, 1965.
Carr, O. A. *Memorial of J. K. Rogers and Christian College.* St. Louis: John Burns Publishing, 1885.
Crighton, John C. "Boone County Home Front during World War I Was a Hive of Activity." In *A History of Columbia and Boone County,* no. 119. Columbia: Boone County Historical Society, 1987.
———. "Closing of Academy Prompted Establishment of Baptist Female Academy." In *A History of Columbia and Boone County,* no. 31. Columbia: Boone County Historical Society, 1987.
———. "Columbia Baptist Female College Was the Forerunner of Stephens

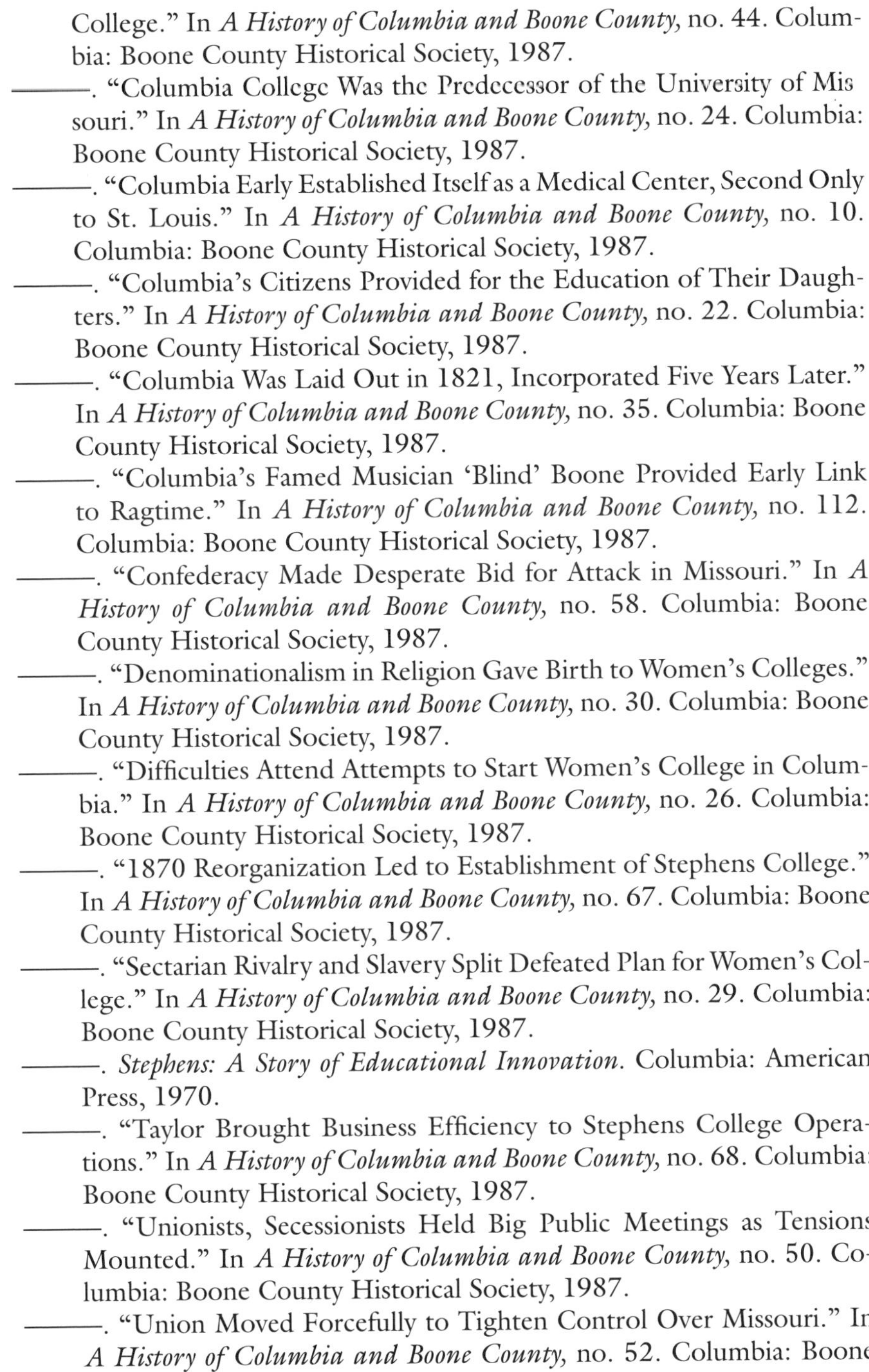

College." In *A History of Columbia and Boone County,* no. 44. Columbia: Boone County Historical Society, 1987.

———. "Columbia College Was the Predecessor of the University of Missouri." In *A History of Columbia and Boone County,* no. 24. Columbia: Boone County Historical Society, 1987.

———. "Columbia Early Established Itself as a Medical Center, Second Only to St. Louis." In *A History of Columbia and Boone County,* no. 10. Columbia: Boone County Historical Society, 1987.

———. "Columbia's Citizens Provided for the Education of Their Daughters." In *A History of Columbia and Boone County,* no. 22. Columbia: Boone County Historical Society, 1987.

———. "Columbia Was Laid Out in 1821, Incorporated Five Years Later." In *A History of Columbia and Boone County,* no. 35. Columbia: Boone County Historical Society, 1987.

———. "Columbia's Famed Musician 'Blind' Boone Provided Early Link to Ragtime." In *A History of Columbia and Boone County,* no. 112. Columbia: Boone County Historical Society, 1987.

———. "Confederacy Made Desperate Bid for Attack in Missouri." In *A History of Columbia and Boone County,* no. 58. Columbia: Boone County Historical Society, 1987.

———. "Denominationalism in Religion Gave Birth to Women's Colleges." In *A History of Columbia and Boone County,* no. 30. Columbia: Boone County Historical Society, 1987.

———. "Difficulties Attend Attempts to Start Women's College in Columbia." In *A History of Columbia and Boone County,* no. 26. Columbia: Boone County Historical Society, 1987.

———. "1870 Reorganization Led to Establishment of Stephens College." In *A History of Columbia and Boone County,* no. 67. Columbia: Boone County Historical Society, 1987.

———. "Sectarian Rivalry and Slavery Split Defeated Plan for Women's College." In *A History of Columbia and Boone County,* no. 29. Columbia: Boone County Historical Society, 1987.

———. *Stephens: A Story of Educational Innovation.* Columbia: American Press, 1970.

———. "Taylor Brought Business Efficiency to Stephens College Operations." In *A History of Columbia and Boone County,* no. 68. Columbia: Boone County Historical Society, 1987.

———. "Unionists, Secessionists Held Big Public Meetings as Tensions Mounted." In *A History of Columbia and Boone County,* no. 50. Columbia: Boone County Historical Society, 1987.

———. "Union Moved Forcefully to Tighten Control Over Missouri." In *A History of Columbia and Boone County,* no. 52. Columbia: Boone County Historical Society, 1987.

———. "The University of Missouri Was Founded in Columbia in 1839." In *A History of Columbia and Boone County,* no. 25. Columbia: Boone County Historical Society, 1987.

———. "Wood's Early Task Was Building Financial Foundation of Stephens College." In *A History of Columbia and Boone County,* no. 90. Columbia: Boone County Historical Society, 1987.

———. Wood's First Problem Was Reduction of Stephens College Debt." In *A History of Columbia and Boone County,* no. 78. Columbia: Boone County Historical Society, 1987.

Duncan, R. S. *History of the Baptists in Missouri.* St. Louis: Scammell, 1882.

Hale, Allean Lemmon. *Petticoat Pioneer: The Story of Christian College.* St. Paul, Minn.: North Central Publishing, 1956, 1968.

Hoxie, Richard L. *Vinnie Ream.* Washington, D.C.: Gibson Brothers, 1908. Printed for private distribution only.

Laws of the First Session of the Ninth General Assembly of the State of Missouri, 1826–1837. Jefferson City: Calvin Gunn, 1837.

Laws of the State of Missouri, Adjourned Session of the Twenty-second General Assembly, 1864. Jefferson City: W. A. Curry, 1864.

Laws of the State of Missouri, Ninth General Assembly, 1836–1837. St. Louis: Chambers and Knapp, 1841.

Laws of the State of Missouri, Passed at the First Session of the Ninth General Assembly, Begun at Jefferson City, November 21, 1836. St. Louis: Chambers and Knapp, 1841.

Laws of the State of Missouri Passed at the Adjourned Session of the Twenty-fifth General Assembly. Jefferson City: Horace Wilcox, 1870.

Laws of the State of Missouri Passed at the Nineteenth General Assembly, 1856–1857. Jefferson City: James Lusk, 1857.

Laws of the State of Missouri Passed at the Regular Session of the Twenty-third General Assembly, 1864–1865. Jefferson City: W. A. Curry, 1865.

Laws of the State of Missouri Passed at the Sixteenth General Assembly, 1850–1851. Jefferson City: James Lusk, 1851.

McNeill, Paula L. "Mary Paxton Keeley." In *Show Me Missouri Women: Selected Biographies,* ed. Mary K. Dains. Kirksville, Mo.: Thomas Jefferson University Press, 1989.

Melder, Keith E. *Beginnings of Sisterhood: The American Women's Rights Movement, 1800–1850.* New York: Schocken Press, 1977.

Peters, George L. *The Disciples of Christ in Missouri: Celebrating One Hundred Years of Co-operative Work.* Columbia: Centennial Commission, 1937.

Sherwood, Glenn V. *Labor of Love: The Life and Art of Vinnie Ream.* Hygiene, Colo.: Sunshine Press, 1997.

Solomon, Barbara Miller. *In the Company of Educated Women: A History of*

Women and Higher Education in America. New Haven: Yale University Press, 1985.

Stephens, E. W. "History of Boone County." Reprinted in the *Columbia Daily Tribune*, June 4, 1915.

Stevens, Frank F. *A History of the University of Missouri*. Columbia: University of Missouri Press, 1962.

Stone, Ilene, and Suzanna Grenz. *One Little Candle: Remembering Jane Froman*. San Diego: Petunia Publishing, 1997.

Switzler, William F. *History of Boone County*. St. Louis: Western Historical, 1882.

Viles, Jonas. *The University of Missouri: A Centennial History, 1839–1939*. Columbia, Mo.: E. W. Stephens, 1939.

Woody, Thomas. *A History of Women's Education in the United States*. Vol. 2. New York: Science Press, 1929.

Index